Collaboration Among Professionals, Students, Families, and Communities

Collaboration Among Professionals, Students, Families, and Communities provides a foundation for understanding concepts of collaborative learning along with strategies for the application of collaborative skills in teaching. The book moves logically from issues of macro-collaboration (district and school) to micro-collaboration (individual student focus and co-teaching) in K–12 environments before concluding with strategies for family and community collaboration. Significant emphasis is placed on knowledge, skills, and teaching models for pre-service and in-service teachers in general education, special education, and of diverse students including English Learners.

Each chapter includes meaningful pedagogical features such as:

- Learning objectives
- A case study illustrating the implementation of information presented
- A case study challenging the reader to apply the information learned in the chapter
- Study questions for readers in Comprehension Checks at key points in the chapter
- Highlights of major points in a chapter summary for aid in studying content
- University, school, and community-based application activities

A companion website features additional resources, including PowerPoint presentations, practice tests, suggested video and Internet resources, and advanced application activities.

Stephen B. Richards is Associate Professor and Coordinator of Intervention Specialist Programs, School of Education and Health Sciences, University of Dayton, USA.

Catherine Lawless Frank is Visiting Professor of Special Education and Early Childhood Education, School of Education and Health Sciences, University of Dayton, USA.

Mary-Kate Sableski is Assistant Professor of Literacy and Special Needs and Director of the Dyslexia Certificate Program, School of Education and Health Sciences, University of Dayton, USA.

Jackie M. Arnold is Assistant Professor of Reading and Early and Middle Childhood Education, School of Education and Health Sciences, University of Dayton, USA.

COLLABORATION AMONG PROFESSIONALS, STUDENTS, FAMILIES, AND COMMUNITIES

Effective Teaming for Student Learning

Stephen B. Richards
Catherine Lawless Frank
Mary-Kate Sableski
Jackie M. Arnold

Routledge
Taylor & Francis Group

NEW YORK AND LONDON

First published 2016
by Routledge
711 Third Avenue, New York, NY 10017

and by Routledge
2 Park Square, Milton Park, Abingdon, Oxon OX14 4RN

Routledge is an imprint of the Taylor & Francis Group, an informa business

© 2016 Taylor & Francis

The right of Stephen B. Richards, Catherine Lawless Frank, Mary-Kate Sableski, and Jackie M. Arnold to be identified as the authors of this work has been asserted by them in accordance with sections 77 and 78 of the Copyright, Designs and Patents Act 1988.

Library of Congress Cataloging-in-Publication Data
Names: Richards, Steve, 1954– author.
Title: Collaboration among professionals, students, families, and communities : effective teaming for student
     learning / Stephen B. Richards, Catherine Lawless Frank, Mary-Kate Sableski, and Jacqualine M. Arnold.
Description: New York, NY : Routledge, 2016. | Includes bibliographical references and index.
Identifiers: LCCN 2015044120 | ISBN 9781138886490 (hardback) | ISBN 9781138886506 (pbk.) |
     ISBN 9781315714783 (ebook)
Subjects: LCSH: Teachers—Professional relationships. | Teacher-student relationships. |
     Parent-teacher relationships. | Communication in education. | Group work in education. |
     Teaching teams. | Education—Parent participation. | Community and school.
Classification: LCC LB1775 .R496 2016 | DDC 371.1—dc23
LC record available at http://lccn.loc.gov/2015044120

ISBN: 978-1-138-88649-0 (hbk)
ISBN: 978-1-138-88650-6 (pbk)
ISBN: 978-1-315-71478-3 (ebk)

Typeset in Minion
by Apex CoVantage, LLC

We would like to dedicate this text to:
Ron Taylor, friend and mentor;
Geoff, Christopher, and Jaidyn with much love;
Matt, for the love and support;
Greg Arnold, always my supporter;
Steve Richards, friend and wonderful mentor.

CONTENTS

PREFACE

In this new text, you will find 17 chapters that logically progress from macro-collaboration at the district and school levels to micro-collaboration among educators for working with individual students and co-teaching. The text concludes with strategies for working with families, including those from diverse cultural/linguistic populations. We also address collaborating with community members.

Additionally, what we believe is exciting about this text is it is designed for use in courses with general and special educators. The text includes the information general educators need to know about special education law and the various disability categories. This also serves as an excellent introduction or review for special educators. The overall content in other chapters is relevant to general and special educators.

The knowledge and strategies presented are user-friendly, well-referenced, and accessible reading for undergraduate or graduate teachers in training. While U.S. schools are referenced, you will find references to research from other countries as well. The knowledge and strategies are applicable in schools outside the U.S.

The companion website supports instructors and students alike with presentations for each chapter, quizzes, chapter outlines, and additional resources. Each chapter in the text includes chapter objectives, a detailed chapter summary, an illustrative case study, and an application case study. Comprehension Checks that include study questions are at key points in the chapters. Each chapter concludes with application activities applicable in university classrooms as well as in schools or communities. References are at the end of each chapter, making it easy to locate specific resources for interested readers.

We believe you will find this new text to be comprehensive and practical in its content and presentation.

1

COLLABORATION PRINCIPLES AND PRACTICES

Stephen B. Richards

Chapter Objectives

Following reading the chapter, students should:

1. Identify similarities and differences in collaboration, teaming, and consultation
2. Explain the principles and practices for collaboration
3. Cite examples of positive and negative collaboration
4. Identify pragmatic issues that present barriers to collaboration

COLLABORATION, TEAMING, AND CONSULTATION

Collaboration is not new to K–12 schools. For years, teachers, students, families, and community members have worked together to improve the learning environment and learning outcomes of students. However, in our experience, individuals use different terms to refer to collaborative processes that may be quite different. Three terms used in reference to collaborative processes are collaboration, teaming, and consultation. Collaboration is a process concerning, and an approach to, human interactions and the goals of those interactions. Teaming is also an approach but often occurs in more specific groups in schools, such as committees. Consultation is a process and approach but is less collaborative than teaming. Ultimately, collaboration is an orientation toward working with others to generate improvements in education for an individual or group of individuals (students, families, community members, and/or professionals). Each of these terms will be used in this text as appropriate, but it is important for the reader to understand the distinction between such terms may be blurred in any particular scholarly work or works.

Collaboration

Hord (1981) made distinctions between cooperation and collaboration. This author suggested that collaboration involves joint planning, implementation, and evaluation among collaborators. Hord (1981) also stressed that mutual goals are critical to collaboration. Individuals or organizations may cooperate, but if there is not shared planning, implementation, and evaluation toward one or more common goals, then collaboration will not occur (Hord, 1981). Also, definitions of and concepts about collaboration may differ among general and special educators (Robinson & Buly, 2007). Wood and Gray (1991) identified at least six definitions of collaboration appearing in applied behavioral science literature. These authors stated that "Collaboration occurs when a group of autonomous stakeholders of a problem domain engage in an interactive process, using shared rules, norms, and structure, to act or decide on issues related to that domain" (p. 146). For our purposes, each of these earlier authors contributes to an understanding of collaboration as differentiated from teaming and consultation. We define collaboration as follows:

> **Collaboration** is a goal-oriented, mutually beneficial process used to address problems, promote strengths, resolve differences, and educate involved individuals through shared responsibility for the outcomes of the collaborative process.

Our definition draws upon earlier concepts provided by other authors as well (Friend & Cook, 2000; Welch, 2000). Perhaps most important in any definition of collaboration is an emphasis on shared goals and shared responsibility for meeting those goals. Collaboration frequently occurs through teaming.

Teaming

Teams in individual schools and school districts are usually formed as ongoing entities or on an as-needed basis. Teams may, in fact, be collaborative; typically, teams have a specific agenda. For example, Buck, Polloway, Smith-Thomas, and Cook (2003) stated that **teaming** is:

- A preventive process that aims at anticipating and resolving issues (explore a problem or present a solution)
- Determining steps that must be taken to resolve a problem (complete a specified task)

An example of a team that might explore a problem would be a high school team considering block scheduling. An example of a team presenting a solution would be a school-based team focused on establishing positive school-wide supports to prevent or lessen discipline problems. An example of a team completing a specified task would be an Individualized Education Program (IEP) team. In each of these examples, the members would likely be different individuals, including students, family members, community members, and professionals.

Buck et al. (2003) also stated that teams can be focused on action research methods such as evaluating effectiveness of policies or on evaluating interventions aimed at student or professional success. Examples of these types of teams are a team focused on whether new teacher evaluation policies were resulting in increased student achievement or a team working in a Response to Intervention program, respectively.

Teams may have a particular philosophy to which they subscribe. In the example of the positive school-wide behavioral supports team, members may need to agree on a largely behavior analytic approach to their endeavors. A team focused on Response to Intervention may be concerned with developmental theories that explain how young learners respond to their environment and the activities in that environment. A team focused on writing an IEP may need to have a holistic approach to human development such that goals are social, communicative, behavioral, and academic for the learner. Certainly, team members may subscribe to different or even competing philosophies or approaches so long as they engage in the collaborative process as fully vested and responsible team members.

Historically, educational teams, particularly those concerned with Individualized Education Programs for students with disabilities have been distinguished as multi-, inter-, or transdisciplinary. Multidisciplinary teams come together to share information, but much of the work of individual team members is done with little or no collaboration or consultation with other team members. Interdisciplinary teams ensure members are better informed about the practices and activities of other team members. They may seek ways in which they can reinforce one another's efforts. For example, a general education teacher may use strategies suggested by the speech and language pathologist to encourage language development in a child. A special education teacher might use adaptive equipment in her classroom provided by an occupational therapist for a child with physical disabilities. Transdisciplinary teams work to ensure each member is informed of the others' efforts, but team members also share expertise, train other team members in using strategies to assist students, and often work together in the same setting to provide services (e.g., general and special education teachers in a co-teaching setting). For our purposes, we will discuss teams in a transdisciplinary model, as this is the preferred option for many if not most professionals.

Consultation

Worrell (2007) pointed out that some authors and researchers use the terms consultation and collaboration interchangeably. Indeed, consultation is a collaborative process. Consultation typically involves a consultant and a person who is receiving the consultation. An example of this would be a mentor teacher consulting with a newer teacher on how to improve her lesson plans. Sometimes, consultation may focus on a third party, such as a speech and language pathologist consulting with a special educator as to how to improve the articulation issues of a student with a speech disorder. In either example, a key is that the consultant possesses knowledge and/or skills that benefit the consultee directly or someone who the consultee is charged with assisting. **Consultation** is clearly a collaborative process but may have a hierarchical element because of the consultant's expertise and role, which reduces the equality of the relationship among those involved.

Meyers, Meyers, Graybill, Proctor, and Huddleston (2012) described three types of consultation. First, there is consultation that is focused on a teacher in a direct effort to change variables in the classroom that affect children and their learning. Second, there is consultation focused on a student to identify and implement interventions to improve the educational, behavioral, social, communication, etc., outcomes for a student. Third, there is organizational consultation aimed at educational systems changes that affect many individuals in educational programs and settings.

Consultation is a collaborative process but may be less so in certain respects than is teaming. In teaming and consultation, there are certain principles and practices that are associated with successful outcomes.

Comprehension Check

1. What is a definition of collaboration? Can you put this in your own words?
2. What is a definition of consultation? Can you put this in your own words?
3. Are you able to distinguish between collaboration and consultation?

COLLABORATION PRINCIPLES AND PRACTICES

From our definition of collaboration, we identify two early sources that are useful today. Friend and Cook (2000), Welch (2000), and Taylor, Smiley, and Richards (2015) identified several principles and practices that impact collaborative processes. Collaboration involves:

- Two or more parties working together.
- Considers the collaborating individuals as equal partners.
- A choice of those involved and is voluntary.
- Sharing responsibility among those involved for outcomes, positive or negative.
- Identifying and working toward a common goal.
- The influence of factors (such as school climate, resources) other than the individuals involved.
- A planned, formal process or a more spontaneous and more informal process.
- Sharing of resources, knowledge, and skills.
- Developing a community.
- At times, uneven amounts and levels of work among those involved.
- At times, a process where the parties working together change.

In the following paragraphs, we offer examples and explanations of each of these principles and practices. These examples are not the only possibilities but serve as illustrations for the reader. We also include non-examples to further illustrate the principles and practices.

Working Together

As noted earlier, teaming and consultation should be collaborative processes. Each involves individuals working together. While this may seem an obvious principle, it may be violated rather easily. For example, two individuals on a team could work at cross-purposes. They disagree on what is the role of the team. They may also disagree as to the goals of the team. They may, in fact, work against one another trying to win allies for their individual purposes. In consultation, a related services individual (e.g., a speech and language pathologist) could make suggestions to a teacher on how to work with a student in addressing speech problems. The teacher may resent the consultant and decide she will ignore or modify some of the suggestions without informing the related services staff member.

Equal Partners

On a team, it is possible for a single member or small group of individuals to dominate the process. For example, when working at a high school, one of our authors was involved with a team that was investigating the lunch schedules to make recommendations for changes. When the team was deep into its work, the principal announced he did not like the decisions he perceived that the team was moving toward and summarily decided what the new lunch schedule would be. In a consultation, the consultant may dictate to a teacher what she must or must not do without concern for the teacher's classroom, curriculum, learning activities, etc.

On another team, all members agree that they must work as a unit, sharing their thoughts, feelings, concerns, strengths, and weaknesses in order to achieve their goals. They elect their own facilitator, recorder, and timekeeper. They form a cohesive group sharing their knowledge and skills for the common good. Similarly, in consultation, a speech and language pathologist spends time in the classroom of a student she serves. The pathologist observes the classroom routines, activities, curriculum, and the teaching and learning styles in the classroom. After her observations, the pathologist works with the teacher to make suggestions as to how the teacher might help the student during the typical daily learning activities of the class. The pathologist asks the teacher about her concerns and if the teacher has any suggestions that she feels would be of benefit to the student. In this example, the pathologist possesses special knowledge and skills but is working together with the teacher to ensure better outcomes for the student.

A Choice

On some teams or in some consultations, one or more members may be "ordered" to participate. This, in turn, can lead to resentment and a failure to work together or as equal partners. For a non-example, a teacher who feels she has success in managing her classroom routines and students' behaviors is nevertheless ordered by the principal to serve on a team to develop new short-cycle assessment strategies. Because the teacher has not chosen to participate, she may be less committed and involved. She may also be unconcerned with the team's goals or the outcomes of the team. In a consultation non-example, a related services individual is ordered to work with a large number of students in an itinerary role (i.e., traveling from school to school and providing consulting services for a larger number of students). She prefers working with students individually or in small groups. Because she has been ordered to provide services only through consultation, she may lack the enthusiasm (and possibly time and knowledge of students' issues) to truly provide quality consultant input.

A positive example would be a teacher who is interested in the results of statewide achievement tests administered to her students. She volunteers to serve on a school-wide committee to analyze the results and make recommendations for curriculum and instructional improvements. An example in consultation services would be a first grade teacher who approaches an occupational therapist (OT). The teacher has a student who has difficulty with his handwriting. Although the student has not been identified for occupational therapy services, the therapist observes the student and makes recommendations to the teacher on how to provide a pencil with a built up handle to make handwriting easier. The teacher follows through and later reports to the OT that her suggestion worked. They touch base occasionally on other issues related to the same student and others.

Sharing Responsibility

For successful collaboration, members of the team (at least two or more persons) must share responsibility for the outcomes of the process. The outcomes may be positive or negative but regardless, team members accept that collectively and independently they are answerable for whatever is derived from the collaboration. A negative example might be a team of several teachers who are charged with planning school-wide activities for the first day of school. However, for various reasons, the first day goes poorly due to what appears to be inadequate planning. Team members begin "finger-pointing" and blaming each other for any activity that is not working on the first day, while claiming credit for those that do succeed. In a consultation, a speech and language pathologist could outline some procedures for a general education teacher to assist a child with a stuttering disorder. After several weeks, the child's parents take note that their child's stuttering actually seems to be getting worse. The speech and language pathologist blames the teacher for not following through on the provided guidelines, while the teacher blames the pathologist for not explaining the guidelines and not spending more time in the actual classroom with the child. In each of these examples, it is quite possible team or consultation members will harbor hard feelings toward one another and find that future collaboration or consultation is strained at best.

In a more positive example, team members could have planned the first day of school and the activities still could have not gone well. The team members report to their principal and peers the next day why they think things did not go as well as hoped and make suggestions for how the first day activities could be improved the next year. If given the opportunity, all team members pledge to make the first day of school the following year the best one ever. No team members engage in finger-pointing or blaming. In a positive consultation, the speech and language pathologist could provide guidelines as mentioned in the non-example, and the child's parents could complain their child's dysfluency is not improving. The speech and language pathologist pledges to increase her time in the child's classroom to model her guidelines and to analyze why they are not working in consultation with the general education teacher.

The general education teacher pledges to increase her attention to the child and ensure he is receiving all the support she can provide to reduce his fluency problems.

Identifying a Common Goal

For collaboration to be successful, those involved must agree on one or more common goals. These goals could be ones that are temporary and quickly resolved or ones that are longer term or even continuous. A poor example could involve four team members who are collaborating to analyze the outcomes of school-wide achievement testing. Three team members are committed to analyzing the data as objectively as possible, identifying in what areas students are performing well and those where improvement is needed. However, one team member is vested in presenting her area of teaching and her classes (and friends' classes) as outstanding and the achievement of students in other areas and with particular teachers she does not like as less than desired. She is using the process to promote her own agenda for the school and to work against those who do not agree with her. Over time, she thwarts much of the efforts of the team by focusing on data with a slanted viewpoint. In a consultation, a special education teacher is working with her general education partner in identifying how to alter the presentation of materials/content to make them more accessible to students with specific learning disabilities. The general education teacher follows through faithfully on the special educator's suggestions for changes. Yet when achievement results are received and the class's performance is lacking, the special educator blames the general education teacher for not implementing her suggestions as agreed to in their consultation. It appears that while the general education teacher thought they were working toward improving student learning, the special education teacher was actually more concerned with her own reputation than the students' achievement.

A more positive example would be a team that is formed to study student achievement from the first semester. The team has different ideas about what they are actually to do. One member thinks they are identifying teachers whose students are doing well or not so well. Another thinks they are charged with identifying ways to improve the testing itself. Another member believes they are to identify which achievement tests are useful and which ones do not reflect the curriculum being taught. After meeting, the team agrees that their goal is to organize the data, create tables and graphs illustrating trends, and then report the results to the entire school faculty, while avoiding identifying any particular teachers as doing better or worse than others. In a consultation model, a school psychologist is asked to observe a student during a general education second grade class. The psychologist believes his observations are aimed at gathering evidence for the need for referral for an evaluation to identify the student as having a disability. The general education teacher is concerned with gaining ideas on how to reduce the students' outbursts and to keep the student more engaged. After their initial meeting, the two decide to work toward the teacher's goal and to monitor whether the student is making improvements or might benefit from an evaluation at a later date.

The Influence of Other Factors

At times, even when other principles and practices of good collaboration are present, other factors may influence the success or lack thereof of the work. A negative example that is quite common involves planning time. In either a teaming or consultation model, the parties must have time for meeting to identify and accomplish their goals. In many schools, teachers and other professionals have different planning periods. If this is the case, collaborative team members or those involved in a consultation might meet after or before students arrive. However, one or more of the teachers expresses that she has her own children whom she must be with before and after school. These teachers insist they cannot meet with any regularity outside the regular school hours. If the administration is unable to alter their planning period times, then the collaboration or consultation process may break down.

However, in another school, the administration and the teachers are committed to collaborative grade-level teams to engage in various goals including in-service, planning, instructional design, assessment, managing student behavior, and analyzing student performance data. Each grade-level team at this elementary school has the same planning period and is able to meet regularly during typical school hours. Professionals who are consultants (e.g., school psychologist) are also allowed to adjust their schedules to meet with grade-level teams on an as-needed basis.

A Planned, Formal Process or an Informal, Spontaneous Process

Generally, a planned process is desirable as it demonstrates organizational commitment to the collaborative or consultative processes. However, this is not always possible and at times may not be necessary. One example would be similar to the one discussed in the previous section on other factors affecting collaboration. If the grade-level team of teachers cannot have specific planning time, they may be able to exchange ideas and concerns informally during lunch, passing periods in the halls, or other random times. This may be sufficient for some goals and concerns such as alerting one another that a particular student is having a "bad day", or to let each other know what portion of the curriculum they are currently teaching. Similarly, a teacher might consult with parents during arrival or dismissal times when the parent is dropping off or picking up her child. Again, this may be sufficient for relatively minor matters. However, a planned, formal process (e.g., an Individualized Education Program team meeting) is likely to demonstrate commitment to the process and to provide ample time for all team members to be engaged. The overall team plans ways in which their guidelines can be modified and how to implement those modifications.

Sharing of Resources, Knowledge, and Skills

In a transdisciplinary model of collaboration and consultation, professionals and parents as well share their resources, knowledge, and skills to the betterment of other team members or consultants as well as the students being taught. A negative example of this would be a team that is working to develop an IEP for a student. Prior to and during the meeting, the various team members, including the parents, are sharing their ideas, knowledge of the student and curriculum, and skills at instruction and assessment. However, the speech and language pathologist insists she will need to work with the student in a quiet environment outside of the classroom (which could be for a very legitimate reason). However, she writes her own goal and identifies her own progress monitoring methods, and makes no plan to share her expertise with other team members or make arrangements to consult with others. She simply has "too large" a caseload.

A more positive example could involve the same situation. However, in this example, the speech and language pathologist consults with the parents and teachers to gain knowledge of and insight into the student's speech issues in school and at home. During the IEP meeting, the speech and language pathologist takes the lead in developing communication goals, but works with the others to ensure the goal is meaningful to the student, parents, and teachers. She also includes on the IEP that she will consult with teachers and parents on a regular basis to check on student progress and provide in-service on how best to help the student in school, at home, and in the community. While the pathologist will still need a quiet area outside of the classroom to work on her specific goal, she includes collaboration and consultation in the process of improving communication outcomes.

Developing a Community

When people collaborate or consult regularly, they must by necessity get to know each other better. This includes sharing professional knowledge and skills but often also results in knowledge about individual team members' lives outside the professional realm. People often come to understand and respect colleagues and team members even when there may be disagreements about the goals and outcomes of the process. In essence, school becomes more than just a place to work. Team members develop a sense of community and are supportive of one another to their own and their students' benefits. A negative example of this principle could involve a grade-level team of teachers working together to analyze their students' achievement, how they might best deliver the instructional content, what resources and materials work well, and how best to monitor student progress. One teacher on the team insists everything is fine in her classroom and with her students, and she simply doesn't have the time to work with anyone else. This teacher might be completely sincere about her own situation, but her attitude toward collaboration and consultation is likely to leave her at least appearing as an "outsider" and possibly demoralize the efforts of the other teachers to form a learning community.

A more positive example would be the same team meeting to achieve the goals mentioned in the previous paragraph. In addition, this team of teachers begins to celebrate their collective and individual achievements at school. They also occasionally go to conferences and in-services together as well as have social events outside of school. These team members feel a comradeship that yields a strong support system for their professional lives and to some extent, their private lives as well.

Uneven Amounts and Levels of Work

Perhaps there are few variables that can derail collaboration and consultation efforts more than perceptions by one or more team members that he/she/they are bearing the brunt of the work evolving from the collaboration process. Again, consider the example of a grade-level team of teachers working together. One teacher, who possesses excellent background knowledge and skills in teaching phonics is asked by the other team members to provide them with in-service on selecting materials, delivering instruction, and assessing student performance. This teacher perceives she is spending a good deal of her daily planning period helping others and decides to abandon the team, as she feels there is no benefit to her.

On a more positive note, this same team could meet at the outset of the year and decide on areas where they collectively need better knowledge and skills. Each team member is assigned one of the areas to lead the team's efforts and to obtain special knowledge and skills in the assigned area to share with other team members. Each team member will, at some point, do more work and put forth more effort than other team members. However, each is aware that this is not permanent and is necessary for the benefit of all.

A Process Where the Parties Change

In any collaborative or consultative effort, it may become apparent that new members need to be involved and/or perhaps one or more current members need not remain on the team. This can be an adaptive, healthy process or one that is likely to harm the process. In a negative example, a collaborative team finds that there are "personality" conflicts among several members, and the principal of the school steps in to take over the team and more directly guide the team's efforts. In this case, one or more team members may feel less commitment, feel it is no longer a voluntary process, and not be responsive to his goals.

More positively, a team could be working toward a common goal such as providing school-wide positive supports and realize they need to bring in an expert to help them toward their goal. They also invite a teacher from another school who has been involved in the process before. Finally, they enlist the assistance of a math teacher in helping them organize how they are going to collect and analyze data to evaluate the success of the program. In this example, inviting new team members is a healthy and adaptive practice.

Comprehension Check
1. Can you identify each of the principles and practices of collaboration and consultation?
2. Are you able to cite a positive example of each principle and practice?
3. Are you able to cite a negative example of each principle and practice?

In Case Study 1.1, you will read an illustrative case study. As you read, identify the various positive examples of principles and practices of collaboration and consultation.

1.1 ILLUSTRATIVE CASE STUDY

At the end of her first quarter as the new principal of a high school, Ms. Hodges noticed that her assistant principal, Mr. Getty, is spending nearly all his time handling discipline referrals to the office. Ms. Hodges consults with Mr. Getty and understands that he is unable to perform other duties and that the referrals are coming from a wide variety of teachers from different grade levels and content subject areas. It appears the issue is a school-wide one.

Ms. Hodges and Mr. Getty decide they need a team to discover why there are so many referrals and what might be done to reduce this trend. They ask the teachers who have sent many students to the office with referrals for three volunteers and a group of teachers who have made no or very few referrals for three volunteers. After getting their six volunteers, they realize they have no teachers responsible for teaching mathematics, so they ask for another volunteer from that group. Finally, they ask the school counselors for a volunteer from among that group. Mr. Getty agrees to serve as the initial facilitator for the team, but he agrees with Ms. Hodges that at the initial team meeting, the members should elect a facilitator, timekeeper, recorder, and spokesperson. The team members are given time after school to meet, and they elect members to different roles.

The team identifies goals including: (a) analyzing the data from referrals, including what days and times of the day they occur; (b) whether students being referred are repeat offenders and how many are new or one-time referrals; (c) what are typical reasons (infractions) for referrals and the outcomes of the referrals. Team members form subcommittees to study each goal area and to report back to the entire team in two weeks. Following the subcommittee reports, the whole team is able to identify that the primary problem seems to be there are not sufficiently articulated behavior management guidelines for teachers or students and that because each teacher is using her or his own classroom management plan, students are often unclear about behavioral expectations, resulting in referrals.

The team proposes a set of guidelines for teachers and students and plans for a day of training for teachers and a morning of training for students where they act out examples and non-examples of appropriate behavior. The team also identifies clear consequences for infractions. They also form a subcommittee to continuously study data from referrals and the impact on the changes made.

After a few weeks, the subcommittee reports to the entire team that the new procedures are resulting in fewer referrals. The team surveys all teachers and students about the new procedures and how they help and what, if any, questions or concerns they have. The overall team plans ways in which their guidelines can be modified and how to implement those modifications. Finally, the team continues to monitor outcomes and report to the faculty the results of their data collection. All the team members accept their responsibilities and collectively respond to the positive and negative outcomes of their efforts. The team continues to function for the remainder of the year, and many team members volunteer to continue the next year.

BARRIERS TO SUCCESSFUL COLLABORATION AND CONSULTATION

In the discussion in the previous section, we presented a number of situations that are detrimental to the collaborative or consultative processes. Therefore, we will limit further discussion of examples in this chapter section, except for those barriers that may not have been illustrated already. Barriers to collaboration and consultation may be factors associated with the individuals involved or factors present in the environment. Also, these barriers are discussed in Chapter Seven and strategies for how they might be overcome are included in Chapter Seven and throughout the text. Welch (2000) and Taylor et al. (2015) identified several barriers to collaboration.

Conceptual Barriers

Schools and individuals develop their own concepts about the way schools and teachers operate and the roles of teachers, professionals, families, and students (Welch, 2000). For example, teachers may be used to students with IEPs spending considerable time in resource rooms. A new effort to move to more direct collaboration such as co-teaching could disturb both general and special education teachers, as this would change their roles in teaching and include greater collaboration and consultation. It is worth noting that the development of new collaborative and consultative skills often takes time, and substantial changes in people's roles and how the school operates need time to develop and improve (Niles & Marcellino, 2004).

Pragmatic Barriers

Pragmatic barriers are often logistical in nature and significantly impact formal, planned collaboration and consultation processes. Scheduling time for planning is typically a challenge and competes with responsibilities of those involved (Welch, 2000; Taylor et al., 2015). We cited an example earlier of one teacher who had no time before or after school, as she had to be available for her own children. Pragmatic barriers may be addressed by the school administration whose support for formal, planned collaboration is essential. DiPaola and Walther-Thomas (2003) discussed building-level support from the principal and general education colleagues as very important in collaboration among general and special education teachers. A school culture of support and rewarding creative solutions to problems through consensus team building is critical in change and adaptation (DiPaola & Walther-Thomas, 2003).

Attitudinal Barriers

Being involved in collaborative teaming may very well require those involved to change attitudes about their roles and the school culture. Change often breeds anxiety, particularly when the change requires development of new knowledge and skill sets. Again, administrators and colleagues need to support one another and encourage a more ecological or holistic perspective on the school and its role in educating students. That is, rather than viewing themselves as essentially autonomous professionals in their own classrooms, teachers can develop teams and consultative relationships that focus on improving school systems and student achievement in all grades and content areas (Welch, 2000).

Professional Barriers

Another barrier to collaboration and consultation can be professionals themselves. Most schools have teachers from different age groups who were educated in different philosophies and skills in teaching or providing other services. Because beliefs and values, as well as knowledge and skills, may differ significantly, it may be difficult for teams to identify and achieve common goals. However, Welch (2000) pointed out that collaboration does not necessarily require team members to be congenial. Respect is necessary but friendship is not. Therefore, collaborative team members can possess differing beliefs and values and still have success, so long as they also possess a willingness to listen to others, compromise, and focus on the overall well-being of the school culture and the students. Because future and current teachers may have varying experiences, have been trained differently, and have been introduced to different philosophies, it is natural that there may be disproportionate skills in, and experience with, collaboration. It is important that educators share and be willing to accept the expertise of one another. It is also critical that each participant understands that collaboration does not necessarily equate to congeniality, but should equate to trust and respect (Welch, 2000).

Principles, practices, and barriers influence collaboration such that it may occur in different forms in different schools. In some schools, more informal, spontaneous collaboration may be valued, while in others, formal, planned collaboration is the only successful model (Taylor et al., 2015). In some instances (e.g., IEP teams), collaboration is required by law, and this is when respect is required if congeniality is not achievable. So long as teams can focus on the more positive examples of the principles and practices of collaboration, the barriers will be diminished. Case Study 1.2 includes an application case study where readers may explore factors that affect collaboration and consultation.

Comprehension Check

1. What are the barriers to collaboration and consultation?
2. Can you articulate positive examples of how barriers might be overcome?

1.2 APPLICATION CASE STUDY

Assume you (a third grade general education teacher) and a colleague (a third grade special education teacher) are charged with forming a collaborative team to analyze student achievement test data and make recommendations for improving student outcomes. The principal asked for volunteers to steer the committee at the outset, and you and your colleague volunteered. Your school is a K–5 building with 9% of students on IEPs. There are six grade-level teams consisting of four teachers on each team (three general education teachers and one special education teacher). In addition, the school has the principal, one assistant principal, one school counselor, and one speech and language pathologist.

Divide your own classroom (college/university classroom) into pairs or small groups and consider and discuss each of the following:

1. What would be the ideal number of team members to address student achievement testing?
2. Who would be ideal as members?
3. How would you select members if you have an abundance of volunteers, or would you include everyone who volunteered?
4. Would you have an election once the committee was formed for various roles (facilitator, timekeeper, recorder, spokesperson)?
5. What might be your global goals (e.g., compile all achievement testing data)?
6. What might you consider to be the most likely barriers?
7. What principles and practices did you apply on your own college/university team?

   a. Were there any disagreements and if so, which principles, practices, or barriers were illustrated in your own group?

Return to a large group and compare your pair/small group responses. Were different approaches to collaboration present in different groups? Were different principles, practices, and barriers identified in different pairs/small groups?

CHAPTER SUMMARY

The terms collaboration, teaming, and consultation are often used interchangeably. While many areas of these three overlap, each is its own separate process.

- ✓ **Collaboration** involves joint planning, implementation, and evaluation by everyone in the collaboration process. Collaboration is defined as a goal-oriented, mutually beneficial process used to address problems, promote strengths, resolve differences, and educate involved individuals through shared responsibility for the outcomes of the collaborative process.
- ✓ **Teaming** involves behaving collaboratively, but it is designed around a specific agenda (e.g., a team working toward the goal of lessening behavioral referrals in a school setting). In schools, teams can be formed as ongoing entities or on a need-to-need basis. Teaming is also seen as a preventive process that aims to anticipate and resolve issues before they happen, as well as determine what steps need to be taken to solve the perceived problem. Teams may be multidisciplinary, interdisciplinary, or transdisciplinary.

✓ **Consultation** is also a collaborative process but involves a hierarchical relationship. The consultant's expertise and role reduces the equality of the relationship when compared to teaming or pure collaboration. Three types of consultation are outlined:

1. Consultation that focuses on a teacher in a direct effort to change variables in the classroom that affect children and their learning.
2. Consultation focused on a student that is to identify and implement interventions to improve the educational, behavioral, social, communication, etc., outcomes for a student.
3. Organizational consultation aimed at educational systems changes that affect many individuals in educational programs and settings.

Collaboration Principles and Practices

✓ The first key to collaboration success is working together.
✓ The next key to success is working as equal partners.
✓ Team members should share responsibility for outcomes.
✓ Collaboration should be voluntary.
✓ Identifying a common goal is one of the first steps to a successful outcome.
✓ Allocating an appropriate time to meet and share information and ideas for a positive collaboration process.
✓ Avoid uneven amounts or levels of work.
✓ Team members will change as a result of collaboration; this change can be positive or negative.
✓ Collaboration can occur in a structured and formal process, or spontaneous and fluid progression.
✓ Factors, outside of individuals collaborating, will affect the process. These can be items such as resources or professional climate.
✓ Collaboration, if done correctly, results in a sense of community and sharing of resources, knowledge, and skills.

Barriers to Successful Collaboration and Consultation

✓ Conceptually, teachers may already have their own ideas and thoughts of how a school system should operate; direct collaboration could disturb these ideas.
✓ Pragmatically, a logical time or schedule for collaboration to occur may be difficult to ascertain.
✓ Attitudinally, change of roles, practices, or schedule can breed anxiety without collegial support.
✓ Professionally, educators may be at different levels of professional development themselves. Different philosophies and skills among professionals can lead to a break down in collaboration.
✓ Collaboration requires respect, not friendship, and can succeed despite different beliefs and values, as long as each member possesses a willingness to listen to others and work together.

APPLICATION ACTIVITIES

1. Form teams in your college/university class to make a brief presentation on one of the principles or practices or barriers to collaboration. Cite positive and negative examples not included in your text. Identify and discuss what principles and practices you used or did not use in your own team and what, if any, barriers you experienced.

2. Obtain permission to observe an IEP meeting. Identify the principles and practices and any barriers you witness the team attempting to address.

3. Invite one or more K–12 educators who are participants in collaborative teams. Construct a series of questions to explore with the speaker the principles and practices and barriers to collaboration.

REFERENCES

Buck, G. H., Polloway, E. A., Smith-Thomas, A., & Cook, K. W. (2003). Prereferral intervention processes: A survey of state practices. *Exceptional Children*, 69(3), 349–360.

DiPaola, M. F., & Walther-Thomas, C. (2003). *Principals and special education: The critical role of school leaders.* ERIC Document Reproduction Service No. ED 477 115.

Friend, M., & Cook, L. (2000). *Interactions: Collaboration skills for school professionals* (3rd ed.). New York, NY: Longman, Inc.

Hord, S. M. (1981). *Working together: Cooperation or collaboration?* ERIC Document Reproduction Service No. ED 226 450.

Meyers, A. B., Meyers, J., Graybill, E. C., Proctor, S. L., & Huddleston, L. (2012). Ecological approaches to organizational consultation and systems change in educational settings. *Journal of Educational and Psychological Consultation*, 22, 106–124. doi: 10.1080/10474412.2011.649649

Niles, W. J., & Marcellino, P. A. (2004). Needs-based negotiation: A promising practice in school collaboration. *Teacher Education and Special Education*, 27, 419–432.

Robinson, L., & Buly, R. (2007). Breaking the language barrier: Promoting collaboration between general and special educators. *Teacher Education Quarterly*, 34(3), 83–94.

Taylor, R. L., Smiley, L. R., & Richards, S. B. (2015). *Exceptional students: Preparing teachers for the 21st century* (2nd ed.). New York, NY: McGraw-Hill Education.

Welch, M. (2000). Collaboration a tool for inclusion. In S.E. Wade (Ed.), *Inclusive education: A casebook and readings for prospective and practicing teachers* (pp. 71–96). Mahwah, NJ: Erlbaum.

Wood, D. J., & Gray, B. (1991). Toward a comprehensive theory of collaboration. *The Journal of Applied Behavioral Science*, 27(2), 139–162.

Worrell, F. C. (2007). Consultation in the gifted-education arena: Old wine in a new skin [special issue]. *Journal of Educational and Psychological Consultation*, 17(4), 375–386.

2

EFFECTIVE COLLABORATION AT THE SCHOOL AND DISTRICT LEVELS

Stephen B. Richards

Chapter Objectives

Following reading the chapter, students should:

1. Identify similarities and differences in continuing teams and ad hoc teams at the school and district levels
2. Explain how to organize effective meetings
3. Explain how to facilitate effective meetings

PURPOSES OF SCHOOL AND DISTRICT COLLABORATIVE TEAMS

Jennings (2007) identified two types of teams one is likely to find at both school and district levels. The first are **continuing teams** that are focused on ongoing tasks that schools and districts must contend with yearly. Examples of these types of teams would be ones that oversee achievement testing in a school or district, teams that make decisions on textbook and curriculum adoptions, teams that address disciplinary and behavioral issues, and IEP teams. The second type Jennings (2007) referred to as task forces, but we will refer to them as **ad hoc teams.** These teams are organized when a need arises and are focused on a particular issue that is not typically ongoing. Examples of these types of teams might be one that is providing in-service and training to teachers on a new math curriculum, a team exploring the closure of one or more schools, and a team that is reviewing bids for construction of new playground equipment. Each type of team is important and typically, they include administrators, teachers, and often parent representatives and sometimes support staff representatives as members. Most schools and districts will have an organizational chart that includes continuing teams, their purposes, the administrator (or other individual) who facilitates the team's meetings, reports, and actions, and who are the members of the teams. In essence, these two types of teams are examples of teams discussed in Chapter One. We will use the term "teams" as a substitute in this chapter for the term "committee", which is frequently used by other authors, as committees are, by their very nature, teams.

Jennings (2007) outlined five advantages to teams, including:

- Allowing for broader perspectives from various members and input from diverse parties.
- Helping all members learn more about how decisions are made at the school and district levels.
- Making better informed decisions.
- Creating a culture of collaboration and commitment to the betterment of the school and district.
- Increasing morale as greater participation in decision making tends to mediate at least some disagreement with decisions.

Jennings also identified at least four disadvantages to school- and district-level teams, including:

- They are time consuming and sometimes difficult to schedule.
- Encourage "group think", where members go along with decisions to get along with other members.
- Possibly being more prone to riskier interventions or solutions to problems, as no one must assume personal responsibility for outcomes.
- Group polarization, where either team members or groups affected by the team's decisions perceive there is some unfairness in the representation on the team or in the decisions.
- Our addition to the list is difficulty with logistics of organizing an ad hoc team in particular.

High-performing teams avoid the pitfalls associated with these disadvantages. These high-performing teams are able to identify their purpose and goals (Jackson & Madsen, 2004). Jackson and Madsen (2004) stressed that high-performing teams are effective because they recruit their best talent while simultaneously helping those who are affected by decisions understand decisions and perspectives. Team members' talents, skills, and knowledge often complement one another, "making the whole greater than the parts". Effective teams have incentives (intrinsic as well as potentially extrinsic) for members. These incentives help to build morale, recognition, and motivation (Jackson & Madsen, 2004). Effective leadership is critical. Laine, Behrstock-Sherratt, and Lasagna (2011) pointed out that good school administrators promote a school culture that encourages collaboration, provides adequate time for planning, and helps teachers to feel respected and useful. High-performing teams typically have high-performing leaders, whether the leaders are administrators or other personnel. Managing conflict and communication are essential elements of high-performing teams. These teams tend to have established value systems, high levels of trust and

respect among members, and open discussion around areas of conflict that leads to new perspectives and paradigms that enhance the teams' movement toward accomplishing their goals. High-performing teams typically have each member empowered so as to increase ownership of outcomes, provide opportunities for all team members to learn new skills from one another, increase interest in the outcomes, and facilitate team decision making. Empowerment can also lead to a greater appreciation of how decisions are made and how one's work affects the work of others. Finally, high-performing teams have norms of behavior and performance standards that govern their communication and conflict and are used to assess the success of their efforts, respectively (Jackson & Madsen, 2004).

A recent example in our own experiences in higher education is that of a team formed to create a dual-licensure, pre-service teacher program. The overall purpose and goal of the team was clear in terms of final outcome, the timeline for completion, and the requirements to meet state approval. On the dual-licensure team, representatives from each licensure program were included, as well as members from other affected bodies, such as advisors and instructors of courses that might have to alter their course content and delivery. While the team began with hierarchical leadership (i.e., the responsible administrator served as the facilitator and leader) (Jackson & Madsen, 2004), over time, the team selected different members to serve as facilitators and leaders for different tasks. This empowered all team members, as each had an area of responsibility. All team members recognized the decisions made would affect them and, more importantly, pre-service teacher candidates matriculating through the program. The norms for communication included respecting the opinions of others, allowing everyone to raise concerns and to discuss openly those concerns rather than among one or two members. These norms were effective to the extent that at one critical point, there appeared to be a complete impasse concerning the distribution and nature of field experience requirements. The team was able to achieve a compromise satisfactory to all parties by maintaining those norms and engaging in civil, if sometimes heated, debate. The team understood the requirements for state approval and used these requirements as the best measure of team outcomes, at least initially. The team recognized that when the program was implemented, other measures concerning candidate performance and effectiveness would also be needed. The administrator in charge ensured there were incentives for the team members. While this team was an ad hoc team for development of the dual-licensure program, it will need to exist in one form or another once the program is implemented to provide leadership and monitoring of success. Therefore, this serves as an example of an ad hoc team that becomes a continuing team.

Comprehension Check

1. What is a continuing team? Give an example of an area a continuing team might address.
2. What is an ad hoc team? Give an example of an area an ad hoc team might address.

3. What are some advantages to using teams to address school and district issues?
4. What might be some disadvantages to using teams to address school and district issues?
5. What are some characteristics of high-performance teams?

ORGANIZING AND FACILITATING EFFECTIVE TEAM MEETINGS

Once the need for a team is identified, the team must be organized. Once organized, a team must begin its work with someone facilitating the process. This facilitation process can be hierarchical in nature (i.e., a school or district leader automatically assumes the role of facilitator) or can be more empowering with team members identifying the role of each team member without regard to hierarchical standing in the organizational structure (Jackson & Madsen, 2004). Empowered teams do offer some advantages, and empowered teams will be our focus in this chapter. Such teams tend to encourage a sense of team efficacy. Team members see their roles and the team tasks as meaningful. Empowered teams tend to believe in their control over outcomes. Finally, empowered teams derive a sense of accomplishment from their collaboration (Kirkman & Rosen, 2000; Jackson & Madsen, 2004).

There are some initial considerations prior to actual team formation (Jennings, 2007). These are included in Table 2.1.

Organizing Teams

Teams can be organized initially beginning with a hierarchical approach (e.g., the district superintendent identifies that the teachers in her district need increased in-service in working with English Learners in their classes) and revert to being an empowered team (e.g., the superintendent identifies and invites initial team members but then allows them to organize and facilitate the collaborative process) (Jackson & Madsen, 2004). Regardless of whether a team is hierarchical, fully empowered, or some combination, there are some identifiable considerations for organizing a team including:

- Identifying the team members.
- Identifying the roles of team members.
- Identifying the specific task(s) to be addressed (in some cases where a team is formed to explore a problem, this step may be part of an ongoing process).
- Identifying outcomes for the team to deliver.
- Identifying methods for evaluating the success of the collaboration for achieving the outcomes.

Each of these considerations can be examined more closely, and by necessity there will be some overlap here with the following section on facilitating team meetings, as these two processes are interrelated.

Table 2.1 Initial Considerations Prior to Organizing a Team

Making the Team's Task Clear:

Determine the task to be accomplished. Is it to be an ongoing task or a specific, temporary task or possibly both?

Be specific as possible. Using the same criteria as for a learning objective is a good model. The task should be specific, measurable, ambitious, realistic, and be time-oriented.

Establishing Authority:

If a hierarchical approach is used and an administrator is the leader, then that authority and responsibility should be clearly delineated to all team members at the outset prior to members' agreeing to serve on the team.

If the team is to be empowered with distributed leadership, this should also be clearly established. Additionally, it should also be specified that any recommendations or outcomes will be considered seriously by the administration if the team is primarily led by and populated with teachers and other nonadministrative personnel.

Consider the Size of the Group:

Large groups increase input from various stakeholders but may result in low-quality or protracted outcomes. Achieving consensus may be difficult.

Small groups may increase likelihood of consensus but limit input from stakeholders.

Adapted from Jennings (2007).

Identifying the Team Members

Farris-Berg, Dirkswager, and Junge (2013) emphasized that one way to address many of the issues in K–12 schools today is to trust teachers. These authors point out that over the years, teachers have sought to influence decisions affecting schools through various avenues (e.g., unions, legislative action) and are willing to accept responsibility for their decisions. Therefore, including teachers on virtually all school-oriented teams is important both for their input and to ensure that these important stakeholders are heard. Taylor, Smiley, and Richards (2015) emphasized the importance of selecting family members, perhaps students themselves, and representatives from many constituencies. Administrators may have important roles as leaders, team members, or facilitators of the process (Taylor et al., 2015). However, as pointed out in Table 2.1, the size of any team must be balanced such that all the voices affected are heard, but the team is not so large that it is unlikely to accomplish its task(s) through lack of consensus. Jennings (2007) suggested that:

- Team members are motivated and engaged by the team tasks.
- Teams include newcomers as well as veterans of the teaming process to build capacity and institutional memory.
- Teams include members with varied skills and talents.
- Try to ensure team members will see the final product, even if their charge is not completing the entire product.
- Emphasize team decisions affect others to ensure members know their decisions matter.

- Allow team autonomy; this often makes members feel their decisions are more meaningful, as opposed to making only recommendations to an administrator.
- Ensure those affected by team decisions have the opportunity to provide feedback to the team.
- Ensure there is a process for assessing team outcomes related to the appointed task(s).

Identify Team Members Who Are Skilled at Collaboration

It is important in forming teams that at least some members are selected because they are skilled at collaboration. This is critical to the process. Including such individuals increases the likelihood of having a sufficient number of members who know how to overcome obstacles, barriers, and disagreements (Jennings, 2007). Of course, individuals on the team should also include those who are affected by the team's outcomes and are motivated to be involved. Teams sometimes look to a facilitator who has little "skin in the game" in a direct way as far as the team outcomes, but the facilitator is committed to the process and to completion of the team tasks. As noted previously, some teams are also hierarchical in nature, and this may be necessary in some respects (e.g., when legal issues are involved). However, Krovetz and Arriaza (2006) suggested that relying on a charismatic individual to lead the group may not create the overall capacity and "buy-in" needed by all constituents to make the overall organization flexible and responsive to ongoing and immediate issues. Instead, Krovetz and Arriaza suggested teams use distributed leadership, which fits nicely with Jennings's (2007) call to include those skilled in collaboration. Including team members who are excellent at collaborative processes, regardless of whether a team is hierarchical or empowered (Jackson & Madsen, 2004), is likely to help the team to keep making progress toward achievement of their tasks.

Identify the Specific Task(s) for the Team

Using the SMART (specific, measurable, ambitious, realistic, and time-oriented) objective approach to identifying specific tasks for a team helps the team to understand their mission, what the outcomes should be, and the timeline for accomplishing their tasks. Tasks should be specific enough so that everyone understands the team's charge. For example, a specific task would be to poll students, families, community members, and faculty/staff as to their attitudes and opinions about changing the mascot for the school district from a Native American mascot to one less offensive to community members. The team could also be charged with polling respondents for suggested mascot names and symbols. A poor example would be to "explore whether the mascot of the district should be changed". The prior example offers direction toward a specific task, while the latter provides only some vague direction. Another good example might be to "rearrange the school schedule such that a free breakfast period can be accommodated without sacrificing instructional time". Another poor example would be to "figure out how and where students can get their free breakfasts".

Identify the Outcomes of the Team Process

This task is imminently more achievable if the task(s) given to the team are specific. In the aforementioned school mascot example, an outcome for the first example could be to develop a questionnaire, distribute the questionnaire to a representative sample of the affected constituencies, collate the findings, and present those findings in a document of no longer than ten type-written pages with data charts summarizing the results across all constituencies and for each group as well. A poor example, such as the second one for the school mascot issue, might result in an outcome that is equally vague, such as "report back what people think about the possible change". Specificity in task identification supports specificity in outcome identification.

Identify Methods for Assessing the Collaborative Process and the Identified Outcomes

More specific tasks and outcomes also tend to be more measurable. Of importance here is that the evaluation of the team's work is really twofold. One, the team should assess whether they were able to collaborate successfully as a team, what barriers were met, what strengths assisted the team, whether the process allowed for all members to participate meaningfully, and so on. It is critical to determine if the team process itself is such that all team members support the team's decisions and accept responsibility for the outcomes (Jennings, 2007). If it should be found through assessments (e.g., survey of team members, interviews with team members, focus groups) that the process itself is perceived by at least some team members as flawed, then it is less likely that the outcomes will be successfully implemented. There is almost certain to be discord and lack of support among some of those affected. One example from my own experience was serving on a committee whose charge was to "determine faculty opinions on a single or two lunch periods and how the preferred choice would be implemented". After some effort to achieve the task, the principal eventually stated that it didn't really matter what anyone else thought, he was implementing a single lunch period. Needless to say, there was considerable discord among team members and those affected by the team's decisions.

In a second level of assessment, assuming the first assessment indicates the team was collaborative and the process successful and equitable, the team should then evaluate the actual outcomes identified. This may take several forms, including surveys, observations, data analysis, and so on. The important aspect of this task is to initially and henceforth ensure that the outcomes are successful in meeting the team's mission and that whatever procedures might be needed to implement those outcomes are with fidelity (i.e., in accordance with the team's decisions and recommendations).

Comprehension Check

1. What are some important considerations in selecting team members?
2. What constitutes a good description of a team task?
3. What are important considerations in identifying team outcomes and assessing those outcomes?

Facilitating Effective Teams

Clearly, the previous section on organizing effective teams overlaps in both time and implementation with actually facilitating teams. For convenience, we are discussing them in this order. Facilitating teams may begin with an identified facilitator (often an administrator) or begin the initial meeting with selecting a facilitator. In either case, these principles of how to effectively facilitate team meetings are helpful.

First, Meyer and Watson (2004) provided one tip that intersects with the prior section on "Organizing Teams." As a facilitator, you must know who to invite to the meeting. These authors suggest that facilitators invite individuals who:

- Are responsible for any final decisions or actions taken by the team.
- Are involved in the implementation (or advising those implementing) a plan.
- May react strongly if their input is not considered.
- Will be affected by the team's decisions and planned outcomes.

(Meyer & Watson, 2004)

Second, good facilitators develop an agenda for the meeting. The agenda might include four major components for each item:

- Decide how much time to spend on each agenda item.
- Determine what is the topic, activity, or task associated with each item.
- Explain why the agenda item is important to the team and its constituents.
- Describe how the agenda items will be addressed and by whom.

(Aguilar, 2014)

Another excellent suggestion is to provide premeeting information, activities, or instructions so that participants may be better prepared to address the agenda items. Finally, make sure that team members stay on topic and that the facilitator gauges the team's progress to help keep the process moving toward outcomes, to table agenda items, or prioritize items to be addressed when time is limited (jessicabell.org, 2013).

Third, make sure everyone knows the location and times of the meeting and begin and end on time (Meyer & Watson, 2004). As needed, provide opening and ending activities and assign roles of team members. These roles may be dynamic or static.

Fourth, establish the rules for the team process, particularly decision making. Voting rules may be particularly important and come in various forms (jessicabell.org, 2013). One method can be by consensus where everyone must agree or not agree for a decision to be made. A second method is decision making by a supermajority of members (e.g., 75% of the members). A third method can be having a simple majority (51%) of the members voting in the same direction to make a decision. In hierarchical teams, one or two members may make final decisions after receiving input from others (jessicabell.org, 2013).

Fifth, the facilitator should be authentic (Aguilar, 2014). That is, this person should bring interest, seriousness, and vitality to the process. If the facilitator is uninspired or appears uncaring, the other team members are quite likely to take their cues from the facilitator as to the importance of the team processes and outcomes.

Sixth, during the meeting, the facilitator may deal with difficult people who are members of the team or interested observers. One strategy is to simply talk with any-one in advance of the meeting who might be anticipated to be difficult. The talk can involve setting the rules, establishing where in the agenda the individual has a vested interest, and ensuring voices of interested parties are heard. A second strategy to be used during the meeting is to use the power of the group. In this strategy, the facilita-tor uses the group to make decisions about the importance of agenda items and how much time to spend on each if there are attempts to focus the process on a single or particular item. Use the ground rules for respecting others, waiting for your turn to speak, etc., as established by the team to maintain order. Finally, do verify to those who are disruptive that legitimate concerns will be addressed (jessicabell.org, 2013).

Finally, after a meeting, the facilitator should follow up to make sure that decisions are being implemented, actions are being taken, information is being distributed, and the team process/meeting is evaluated as to its effectiveness and how it might be improved. Make sure minutes are maintained and accurate for future reference. Celebrate team successes (Meyer & Watson, 2004). In Case Study 2.1, you will find an application case study with which to use your knowledge and skills.

2.1 ILLUSTRATIVE CASE STUDY

It is August of the new school year and Ms. Higgins, the principal of Richards Middle School, is anxious to implement a new program. The faculty is at the school days ahead of the students to receive in-service and practice in imple-mentation of a new writing program across the curriculum program. While all teachers are not directly responsible for teaching English Language Arts, the school is implementing this program to strengthen their students' writing skills in each academic content area.

Initially, in the previous school year, Ms. Higgins and her continuing team of faculty who examine achievement test scores noted that their students' writing scores had been edging downward for two years, with more students scoring lower than proficient and fewer scoring at advanced levels. Ms. Higgins initi-ated an ad hoc committee to determine what programs might be implemented to reverse this trend. Specifically, she identified team members and asked them to address a specific task: Identify and recommend one or more writing pro-grams that could possibly be implemented school-wide to increase writing test achievement test scores. The ad hoc team, having been formed from a combina-tion of volunteers and some specific people identified by Ms. Higgins, identified their outcomes: (a) identify at least two writing programs that would be feasible to be implemented; (b) present these programs to the faculty and administra-tion; (c) outline costs, advantages, disadvantages, and implementation issues for each program presented; and (d) poll the faculty and administration as to which program was preferred.

The same ad hoc team worked throughout the summer, learning all the "in's and out's" of implementing the preferred program and preparing for the in-service. Ms. Higgins was available for consultation and support, but she let the team make decisions and plan, as she wanted this to be a faculty-led initiative. Finally, the team provided the in-service to the faculty and the new school year began.

Ms. Higgins realized the ad hoc committee should become a continuing committee so that fidelity of implementation of the writing program, ongoing in-service, and assessment of student learning outcomes could occur during the school year (not just in terms of achievement test scores). Some of the ad hoc committee members chose to remain on the new continuing team, while some were replaced with new volunteers and selected individuals. In this way, the continuing team had new members to provide new insights and ideas. The continuing team identified its tasks, outcomes, and assessment procedures for measuring the outcomes and presented these to faculty and the administration to obtain approval from all constituencies prior to implementation of their plan.

Organizing and facilitating effective team meetings are sometimes thankless tasks. Yet these processes are vital to successful collaboration among team members and to ensure satisfied constituents. Nierengarten (2013) stressed that team members need professional development, time for reflection, and vision. It may be the facilitator who establishes belief in the team members and their combined abilities to make things happen for the general good.

Comprehension Check
1. What is the importance of the agenda for a meeting, and how might it be organized?
2. What strategies should a facilitator use during a team meeting to ensure the process is moving forward?
3. What are some strategies for interacting with difficult people in a team meeting?
4. What should the facilitator do as a follow up to the team meeting?

CHAPTER SUMMARY

The creation of teams that focus on solutions to issues that may arise in a school or school district are common. The two types of teams likely to be found in a school setting are continuing teams and "task forces" or ad hoc teams.

- ✓ Continuing teams are focused on ongoing issues in a school setting or in an entire district
- ✓ Ad hoc teams are formed when a special issue arises in a school setting or district. These issues are typically not ongoing

✓ Each one of these teams is likely to contain the same team members: administrators, teachers, and community representatives

✓ Schools should remain organized with a chart that includes continuing teams, their purposes, the team coordinator, team facilitator, and all members

✓ Five advantages to school- and district-level teams include:

- Allowing for broader perspectives from various members and input from diverse parties
- Helping all members learn more about how decisions are made at the school and district levels
- Helping the team to make better informed decisions
- Creating a culture of collaboration and commitment to the betterment of the school and district
- Increasing morale, as greater participation in decision making tends to mediate at least some disagreement with decisions

✓ Five disadvantages to school- and district-level teams include:

- They are time consuming and sometimes difficult to schedule
- Encouraging "group think" where members go along with decisions to get along with other members
- Possibly being more prone to riskier interventions or solutions to problems, as no one must assume personal responsibility for outcomes
- Group polarization where either team members or groups affected by the team's decisions perceive there is some unfairness in the representation of the team or in the decisions
- Difficulty with the logistics of organizing an ad hoc team in particular may be an issue

✓ High-performing teams avoid pitfalls and have several things in common.

- High-performing teams are able to identify their purpose and their goals
- High-performing teams recruit the best talent, while helping those who are affected by decisions understand the outcomes and perspectives of others
- High-performing teams have incentives for its members that help build morale, recognition, and motivation
- High-performing teams typically have empowered members, as to increase ownership of outcomes, provide opportunities for all to learn skills, increase interest in the outcomes, and facilitate team decision making

Organizing and Facilitating Effective Team Meetings

✓ The organization and facilitation of a team may be hierarchical in nature, or it may be more empowered.

✓ An empowered team has members that identify individual roles without regard to a hierarchical standing in the organizational structure.

✓ Empowered teams tend to believe they have more control over the outcomes, in turn deriving a sense of accomplishment from their collaboration.
✓ Teams may begin with a hierarchical approach and evolve to a more empowered team as time goes on.
✓ Important steps for organizing a team include:

- Identifying the team members
- Identifying the roles of team members
- Identifying the specific task(s) to be addressed (in some cases where a team is formed to explore a problem, this step may be part of an ongoing process)
- Identifying outcomes for the team to deliver
- Identifying methods for evaluating the success of the collaboration for achieving the outcomes

✓ Team members consist of a variety of people and can include, but are not limited to, teachers, family members, students, and administrators.
✓ It is important to balance all team members so that all voices may be heard.
✓ It is important to recruit members who are skilled or have previous experience in collaboration—this will increase the likelihood of overcoming obstacles, barriers, and disagreements.
✓ The SMART objective approach should be used so that teams understand their mission, what outcomes should be, and the timeline for completing tasks.
✓ It is important that the missions, outcomes, and timelines of the team are specific. This will allow for a much more effective collaborative process.

The facilitator of a team is tasked with many important responsibilities. It is important that any facilitator take the appropriate steps in order to create a successful and collaborative experience.

✓ First the facilitator should invite anyone who is responsible for any final decisions, is involved in the implementation, may react strongly if his or her opinion is not considered, or will be affected by the team's decisions and planned outcomes.
✓ Second, facilitators should develop an agenda for meetings that should include four components for each item:

- How much time to spend on each item
- Determine the topic, activity, or task associated with each item
- Note why the agenda item is important to the team and its constituents
- Describe how the agenda items will be addressed and by whom

✓ Third, make sure everyone knows the location and times of the meeting.
✓ Fourth, establish the rules for the team process, particularly decision-making rules. There are a variety of voting rules, but the three common rules are:

- Unanimous (everyone agrees, no one is in disagreement with the group)
- Supermajority (at least 75% of members vote a certain way)
- Simple majority (at least 51% of members vote the same direction)

✓ Fifth, the facilitator should remain authentic in order to bring interest, seriousness, and vitality to the process.

✓ Sixth, the facilitator needs to deal with difficult people who are members of the team or interested observers.

✓ Finally, the facilitator should follow up on decisions to ensure that actions are being taken or decisions are being implemented.

Assessment of the collaborative process is a key factor to identify if outcomes were successful, as well as for successful collaboration in the future.

✓ First, teams should assess whether they were able to collaborate successfully as a team. This may include discussing what barriers were met, what strengths assisted the team, whether the process allowed for all members to participate, etc.

✓ Second, teams should assess the actual outcomes that were produced. This may be assessed in a variety of ways, including surveys, observations, data analysis, etc.

APPLICATION ACTIVITIES

1. Form teams in your college/university class. Make visits and/or interview local school district teachers and/or officials. Describe various continuous and ad hoc teams found in the district and their purposes. Present your findings in class and compare among districts.

2. Observe a meeting of one of your college campus organizations. Evaluate how the meeting is organized and facilitated. Report what you found were best practices and perhaps what were not. Describe how the use (or lack of use) of best practices appeared to impact the meeting.

3. Invite one or more K–12 educators who are participants in collaborative teams. Construct a series of questions to explore with the speaker the principles and practices teams use that involve best practices in organizing and facilitating team meetings.

REFERENCES

Aguilar, E. (2014, February 13). Five tips for facilitating a meeting. Retrieved on September 14, 2015, from http://blogs.edweek.org/teachers/coaching_teachers/2014/02/five_tips_for_facilitatingam.html

Farris-Berg, K., Dirkswager, E., & Junge, A. (2013). *Trusting teachers with school success.* Lanham, MD: Rowan & Littlefield Education.

Jackson, B., & Madsen, S. R. (2004). *Common factors of high performance teams.* Online submission to ERIC: ED 492231.

Jennings, M. (2007). *Leading effective meetings, teams, and work groups in districts and schools.* Alexandria, VA: Association for Supervision and Curriculum Development.

jessicabell.org (2013, August 8). Seven tips to help you facilitate an effective meeting. Retrieved on September 14, 2015, from http://www.jessicabell.org/seven-tips-to-help-you-facilitate-an-effective-meeting

Kirkman, B. L., & Rosen, B. (2000). Powering up teams. *Organizational Dynamics, 23*(3), 48–66.

Krovetz, M. L., & Arriaza, G. (2006). *Collaborative teacher leadership: How teachers can foster equitable schools.* Thousand Oaks, CA: Corwin Press.

Laine, S., Behrstock-Sherratt, E., & Lasagna, M. (2011). *Improving teacher quality: A guide for education leaders*. San Francisco, CA: Jossey-Bass.

Meyer, T., & Watson, S. (2004, June 1). Tips for effective meeting structure and facilitation. Retrieved on September 14, 2015, from http://fngovernance.org/resources_docs/Tips_for_Effective_Meetings.pdf

Nierengarten, G. (2013). Supporting co-teaching teams in high schools: Twenty research-based Practices. *American Secondary Education*, 42(1), 73–83.

Taylor, R. L., Smiley, L. R., & Richards, S. B. (2015). *Exceptional students: Preparing teachers for the 21st century* (2nd ed.). New York, NY: McGraw-Hill.

3

PRE-REFERRAL ASSESSMENT AND INTERVENTION
RTI Tiers One and Two

Catherine Lawless Frank

Chapter Objectives

Following reading the chapter, students should:

1. Identify roles of the special education teacher in Response to Intervention and/or the pre-referral process
2. Determine main components of Tiers One and Two
3. Understand purpose and types of assessments used in Tier Two
4. Realize purpose of the team in RTI and the pre-referral process

Approximately twenty percent of students struggle in Language Arts and Reading, and only a small percentage will eventually qualify for special education services. The remainder will rely on services and supports provided in the general education classroom to meet their diverse academic and behavioral needs. The growth of the English as a Second Language population (also known as English Language Learners and simply English Learners) in U.S. schools as well as the continuing struggles of the students who are at risk for school failure makes meeting the needs of all students a difficult task that requires a team effort. The days when a teacher could close his or her classroom door and be the solo instructor responsible for the academic and behavioral success of the students have passed. The door is now open, and with that open door, the potential for and accountability for student academic and behavioral growth has increased. If it takes a village to raise a child, it takes the entire school and community to educate that child, especially a child with diverse learning needs. No one person can know all the right answers or teaching techniques to meet the range of needs found in a typical classroom. Teams must use a collaborative process with shared goals, dedication, and the commitment of professionals and parents to working together with a shared responsibility for the success of all students.

Teaching and instruction are evolving to meet the needs of all students, including those with disabilities. The role of the special education teacher has also evolved to meet this change and to provide supports for all struggling students with or without disabilities. This change has led to shared responsibility among general and special education teachers. It has also highlighted the need for greater collaboration between special education, general education, and related services personnel, while mandating the need for special education teachers to reevaluate their roles and responsibility within the school (Lamar-Dukes & Dukes, 2005).

In Chapter Three, we will look at a common continuing team-based process used by schools to meet the needs of all students, Response to Intervention (RTI). RTI is typically implemented as a three-tier process. We will focus on how RTI has redefined the role of the special education teacher, as well as the essential components of Tiers One and Two and the pre-referral process. We will begin with an overview of RTI to ensure understanding of the process.

PRE-REFERRAL INTERVENTIONS AND TEAMWORK

The Education for All Handicapped Children Act became U.S. Public Law (PL) 94–142 when it was signed by President Gerald Ford in 1975. While the implementation of the law brought about great strides for students with disabilities, the education of all who struggled academically and behaviorally continued to be a concern. During the 1970s and early 1980s, reform efforts began to focus on improving instruction for all struggling students, not just those with disabilities, and to prevent the inappropriate identification and referral of students, especially minority students, into special education. Special education and general education teachers began working together; and the results were team-based, pre-referral procedures and interventions. This team-based approach continues to be a central component in today's schools. As discussed in Chapters One and Two, team based means that the procedures and interventions are determined by a group of professionals, including general and special education teachers, school administrators, and parents or guardians and possibly counselors, psychologists, related services personnel, and even the students themselves. Pre-referral means that the services and interventions are provided before a student is referred for evaluation for special education. RTI has the intention of remediating students' areas of need and preventing inappropriate referrals for special education. While the general education teacher typically initiates the pre-referral process, which is often implemented in the general education classroom, it also includes support services from other professionals, including special education and related services personnel. The interventions are developed and implemented to help provide needed supports, improve instruction, and help all teachers meet the curriculum, instructional, and behavioral needs of students (Nellis, 2012).

The pre-referral process exists as a vital part of educating students and is often incorporated into a team-based multi-tiered system of support. While not federally mandated, most states implement multi-tiered systems of support that share common features emphasizing data-driven, evidence-based instruction, progress monitoring, and increasing levels of instructional support (Berkeley, Bender,

Peaster, & Saunders, 2009). A variety of multi-tiered systems exist, with the most common being a three-tiered system called Response to Intervention (RTI). In this chapter, we will focus on Tiers One and Two of RTI (Tier Three will be discussed in Chapter Four), but the concepts and framework are similar to other systems of support and to the pre-referral process in general.

An Overview of Response to Intervention

RTI or any multi-tiered system of support is not a special education initiative or a general education initiative. According to the *Response to Intervention Blueprints for Implementation* (2008), RTI is "the practice of (1) providing high quality instruction/intervention matched to students' needs and (2) using learning rate over time and levels of performance to (3) make important educational decisions (p. 3)." RTI is a team-based, problem-solving initiative with the goal to better meet the needs of all students by collecting student data, identifying potential problems, brainstorming interventions, implementing the interventions, progress monitoring, and revising the process as needed (NJCLD, 2005). For RTI to be successful, there must be collaboration and shared responsibility among special educators, general educators, related services personnel, administrators, and parents. As discussed in Chapter Two, this type of collaborative teaming may require school personnel to adjust their views on their traditional job roles and forge new job descriptions that better facilitate the RTI collaborative practices (Ehren, Laster, & Watts-Taffe, 2009).

Each tier in RTI provides more intensive interventions for students. The process begins with all students in the general education classroom and increasing levels of intervention and support are provided to students who fail to make adequate achievement in the general education curriculum. All tiers are designed by the team to provide effective instruction, using ongoing curriculum-based assessment and progress monitoring of student achievement to inform instruction, thus ensuring that students receive high-quality instruction in every tier. High-quality instruction is the foundation for an effective educational program and frequent assessment and progress monitoring ensures students who are experiencing learning difficulties are identified early. If students do not make adequate progress in Tier One, they are referred to more intensive interventions in Tier Two. If students do not make adequate progress in Tier Two, they may be referred to Tier Three or assessed for special education eligibility. RTI's three-tiered, team-based process is designed to eliminate inappropriate referrals to special education and provide interventions as early as possible. Table 3.1 summarizes RTI and illustrates the primary components and collaborators of each tier.

RTI is also one possible pathway to determining eligibility of students for special education with a specific learning disability. When the U.S. Individuals with Disabilities Act was reauthorized in 2004, it made the use of a failure to respond to intervention approach, such as RTI, an option for identifying students for the first time (IDEA, 2005 300.614). In some schools and districts, it has replaced the traditional Ability-Achievement Severe Discrepancy model for identifying students with a specific learning disability. This model often resulted in a "wait to fail" approach to identification for special education, as evaluation teams had to ensure the discrepancy was significant between ability (often measured by IQ) and achievement (often measured

Table 3.1 Tier Components of RTI

Tier	Components	Primary Responsibility
Tier 1	• Universal screening • Effective evidence-based instruction • Ongoing curriculum-based assessments • Progress monitoring used to guide instruction	General Education Teacher
Tier 2	• Effective evidence-based instruction • Ongoing curriculum-based assessments • Progress monitoring used to guide instruction • Referral to pre-referral intervention team • Pre-referral assessments • Pre-referral interventions • Fidelity assessment	General Education Teacher, Special Education Teacher, Pre-referral Team
Tier 3	• Effective evidence-based instruction • Ongoing curriculum-based assessments • Progress monitoring used to guide instruction • Referral for special education services • Multi-factored evaluation for special education services • Determination of eligibility for special education services • Individualized Education Program • Fidelity assessment	General Education Teacher, Special Education Teacher, Multi-factored Evaluation Team, Individualized Education Program Team

by classroom performance and norm-referenced standardized tests). Therefore, many students did not receive the educational interventions they needed early in their schooling, although professionals may have been aware that concerns existed. The RTI model gives teams the option to use effective data-driven instruction and interventions in the general education classroom to meet the needs of the student before referral for evaluation for eligibility for special education. RTI can also be used in conjunction with the Ability-Achievement Severe Discrepancy model to ensure appropriate instruction and to verify that an adverse effect on educational performance exists through assessments that compares the student's performance with her or his normative groups.

The Four Main Roles of the Special Education Teacher in RTI

In RTI, the role of the special education teacher has evolved to include collecting and interpreting student growth data, providing academic and behavioral instruction and support, collaborating with parents and school personnel, and ensuring the proper use of scientifically valid interventions and instruction (Simonsen, Shaw, Faggella-Luby,

Sugai, Coyne, Rhein, Madaus, & Alfano, 2010). These new roles require special education teachers to perform the duties of a manager, a diagnostician, an interventionist, and/or a collaborator. The four roles play a vital part in the successful implementation of any student support process.

The first role of a special education teacher is that of a manager. The special education teacher is responsible for monitoring the students on his or her caseload or grade level(s). This management role includes collaborating with others to develop and complete the necessary paper work, such as intervention plans, progress reports, and in Tier Three, multi-factored evaluations and Individualized Education Programs (IEPs). In Tiers One, Two, and Three, as a manager, the special education teacher is responsible for conducting meetings and participating in administrative duties. She/he may also work with students, parents, teachers, and other professionals in a non-academic role, such as managing student behaviors and developing behavior intervention plans. This position often requires the special education teacher to assume a leadership or managerial role and is often the most time consuming of the roles (Mitchell, Deshler, & Ben-Hanania Lenz, 2012; Gates, Fischetti, & Moody, 2013).

The second role of the special education teacher is that of diagnostician. The special education teacher assesses students' strengths and areas of need. This role includes researching different assessments, administering them (short-cycle, standardized, norm-referenced, basic academics, and functional skills), interpreting results, and assisting in and/or conducting progress monitoring. The special education teacher may attend professional development on different types of assessments and assessment techniques, as well as evaluate students using a variety of methods, including traditional assessments, observations of students' classroom performance and behavior, and functional behavioral analysis. This role also involves interpreting and analyzing assessment results, as well as explaining the results to other team members, including parents and caregivers. The special education teacher also conducts or assists in progress monitoring student growth, communicating those results to other team members, and using that data to determine appropriate interventions and accommodations. As a diagnostician, the special education teacher may also be responsible for providing professional development on various tests, assessment techniques, and interpreting results (Mitchell et al., 2012; Gates et al., 2013).

The third role is that of an interventionist. In this role, the special education teacher spends her/his time providing interventions and instruction to students with or without disabilities (Mitchell et al., 2012). The special education teacher may be responsible for directly providing the intervention and instruction in a resource room or through co-teaching in a general education classroom (co-teaching models are discussed in detail in Chapter Eight) and work with other team members, such as general education teachers, reading specialists, paraprofessionals, or related services providers. The interventions in Tier One are typically provided by the general education teacher, but in Tier Two, the interventions may be provided by the general education teacher, special education teacher, reading specialist, and/or related services personnel. As an interventionist, special educators may also be responsible for providing professional development or training as to implementation of interventions and ensuring the interventions are conducted with fidelity (Gates et al., 2013).

Collaborator is the fourth and perhaps most important role of the special education teacher. To be a successful manager, diagnostician, and interventionist, the special education teacher must be an effective collaborator (Mitchell et al., 2012; Gates et al., 2013). Collaboration is needed every day and typically throughout the day. On any given day, as a manager, she/he may be responsible for scheduling and managing paraprofessionals. The same day she/he may act as a diagnostician and consultant on assessments, observations, and interpreting data. The special educator may then spend part of that day as an interventionist, co-teaching and participating in grade-level team meetings. The day could also include providing support and consultation (discussed in Chapter One) to general education teachers and related services personnel in terms of accommodations and student issues, assessments, interventions, pedagogy, and planning. She/he may consult and collaborate with parents and guardians. All of these activities require collaboration in order to be carried out effectively (Mitchell et al., 2012; Gates et al., 2013). As discussed in Chapter One, collaboration can be informal, such as a discussion in the hallway or lunch room, or formal, as in a structured meeting with school personnel or parents. All four roles are necessary to effectively support student growth, but collaboration is the most essential and fundamental to being a manager, diagnostician, and interventionist.

3.1 ILLUSTRATIVE CASE STUDY

Mrs. Jones is a special education teacher at Millford Heights Elementary School. She begins her workday before school starts, attending a meeting with the school administrator and other teachers on the third grade level team to discuss the results of a district-wide reading assessment. Mrs. Jones assists in interpreting the data and looking at the overall strengths and weaknesses of the curriculum currently being implemented (diagnostician role). The team decides that while overall the curriculum is meeting their students' needs, more support is needed comprehending figurative language. At the conclusion of the meeting, the reading specialist agrees to look into supplemental curriculum materials for teaching figurative language. The general education teachers and Mrs. Jones agree to contact the parents of seven students the team has identified who are not making adequate progress and work together to develop additional interventions and supports.

During the first two periods, Mrs. Jones co-teaches in Mrs. Roth's third grade classroom (interventionist role). In this class, there are two students on IEPs, as well as three who require Tier Two interventions in math and/or language arts. During math, Mrs. Jones supports Mrs. Roth's instruction and then provides more intensive and guided support to a small group of students. During the second period, Mrs. Jones and Mrs. Roth divide the class into two heterogeneous groups and parallel teach a lesson they co-planned. They decide to discuss the effectiveness of the lesson at lunch and analyze which students need additional support.

Third period is Mrs. Jones planning period. During this time, she calls the parents of one of her students to discuss his progress and address any concerns the parents may have (manager role). A fourth grade teacher, Mr. Parnell, stops in to ask Mrs. Jones for suggestions on how to support a student's classroom behavior. Mrs. Jones agrees to observe the student after lunch and meet with Mr. Parnell and the parents before school the next day. Mrs. Jones spends the rest of the period completing progress reports for parents.

During lunch, Mrs. Jones meets with Mrs. Roth to discuss the language arts lesson they co-taught, makes adjustments to tomorrow's lesson plan, and then performs recess duty where she informally observes two of her students' social skills (diagnostician role). She makes a mental note to meet with their classroom teacher to develop a plan to address social skills, mainly turn taking, with these two, as well as four other students in the class.

After lunch, Mrs. Jones conducts small group interventions in four half-hour intervals in the resource room for students in grades three and four. The first three groups involve language arts interventions in fluency and comprehension. The last group is math intervention for fourth graders involving reteaching and building on the concepts their classroom teacher taught earlier that day. This last group requires a great deal of communication with the fourth grade teacher to ensure that the lessons are providing the proper curriculum and the needed supports to ensure optimal student progress.

During the last period of the day, Mrs. Jones conducts the observation on Mr. Parnell's fourth grade student and develops a list of suggestions and ideas to discuss with Mr. Parnell and the student's parents in the morning (diagnostician role).

After school, Mrs. Jones completes all the needed documentation for the day. She grades her students' math and language arts work, reflects on her day, and makes sure she has planned and prepared for her lessons and meeting tomorrow.

Throughout the day, Mrs. Jones is collaborating with various professionals and parents to fulfill the four roles often required in the RTI process.

Comprehension Check

1. What is the pre-referral process?
2. Why is the pre-referral process team based?
3. What are the four roles of the special education teacher in the RTI process? Give an example of a duty that would be performed in each role.

Typically RTI begins with a universal screening and consists of three tiers of increasing levels of student support. Tier One consists of effective instruction using evidence-based methods and curriculum to all students in the general education classroom. Tier Two is provided to students who did not make adequate progress in Tier One and consists of frequent short-cycle targeted assessments based on individual student's needs (e.g., alphabetic principles, reading fluency, math computations, on-task behavior), with more intensive instruction and interventions to address those needs. Tier Three may be provided to students who continue to struggle after the more intensive interventions of Tier Two and usually consists of a referral and evaluation for special education services. Some versions of RTI may contain more tiers, but those additional tiers tend to be an expansion of the three tiers found in the more traditional model. In the following sections, we will look at Tiers One and Two and the role of the special education teacher in each tier. In Chapter Four, we will discuss Tier Three and the eligibility and IEP process.

TIER ONE

RTI begins with a universal screening or assessment in core content areas. This universal screening is initially done at the beginning of the school year. This screening provides a means of identifying struggling students early and before they have a history of academic or behavioral failures. The results of these assessments are used as a baseline for individual student academic growth and to identify students who may be in need of additional support. Typically the determination of which students need additional support is not strictly made based on this one assessment. This initial assessment, though, does provide the baseline, and with continued progress monitoring, allows issues to be identified and addressed before they become a larger concern.

A fundamental aspect of Tier One is that all students receive high-quality, evidence-based instruction in the general education classroom. This high-quality, evidence-based instruction means that the methods used have been "demonstrated through scientific research and practice to produce high learning rates for most students (Blueprint, p. 3)" and include both instruction and curriculum. Students receive ongoing curriculum-based assessments that progress monitor their growth; the results of which are used to guide instruction. For example, a typical student in the fall of first grade should be reading at a beginning first grade level. The universal screening is administered to determine which students are at, above, or below grade level and the academic strengths and weaknesses of the class. The general education teacher then teaches the first grade curriculum using evidence-based practices and frequently monitors her/his students' progress.

The teacher uses the progress monitoring data to determine which students are not making expected growth toward developmental and/or academic benchmarks or milestones. The general education teacher then provides additional supports to help address these areas of concern. These supports could be provided to the entire class, such as providing more remediation or instruction on basic skills (e.g., daily basic math fact drills), the use of more visual supports (e.g., graphic organizers, guided notes, or writing the lesson objective or/and daily schedule on the board), or incorporating more cooperative learning projects. These supports could also be provided individually or in small groups, such as differentiated reading groups, small group intervention before school, or greater proximity to specific students during lessons to provide immediate feedback and support. The general education teacher continues to assess and progress monitor the students to determine the effectiveness of the additional instruction and intervention.

While Tier One is primarily conducted by the general education teacher in the general education classroom, teachers often begin collaborating with each other about student concerns or progress before officially referring a student to Tier Two (NJCLD, 2005). This collaboration may be informal (e.g., talking with another teacher at lunch about strategies for working with a particular student) but should also involve formal collaboration. Formal collaboration is needed if the additional instructional interventions and supports provided by the general education teacher do not result in adequate student growth or indicates academic or behavioral decline. This formal support is provided by a school-based team, such as the RTI, problem solving, or Intervention Assistance Team. At this point, the team may recommend additional supports for the general education teacher (e.g., more hands-on activities, a self-progress monitoring program for the student, or changes in classroom seating or structure) or refer the student to Tier Two for more intensive interventions. It is important to remember, however, that different districts and schools modify the activities in the three tiers to suit the needs of their students, faculty, staff, and school.

Role of the Special Education Teacher in Tier One

While RTI is a joint effort between special and general education, the Council for Exceptional Children's (2007) position states that in Tier One, general education teachers provide the primary instruction and intervention while special education teachers provide support mainly through collaborative membership on a problem-solving team. This support is designed to provide early intervention on behavior and academic issues and prevent inappropriate referrals to Tier Two or Three.

Comprehension Check

1. What are the main components of Tier One?
2. How does Tier One ensure that the needs of all students are being addressed?
3. What duties do you expect to assume as a special education teacher in Tier One?

TIER TWO—THE PRE-REFERRAL PROCESS

After options in Tier One are exhausted and an individual student does not make adequate academic progress, the student may then be referred to Tier Two's more intensive interventions. Tier Two typically begins when a general education teacher's observations and data shows that a student is continuing to struggle even after scientifically validated data-driven instruction has been provided. Tier Two incorporates the components of what has traditionally been referred to as the team-based, pre-referral process and is designed to provide additional support and interventions beyond what is provided for the typical general education student. Tier Two incorporates the same components of an effective classroom found in Tier One, including high-quality effective teaching, ongoing curriculum-based assessments, monitoring student progress, using that data to inform instruction, and it also incorporates fidelity checks to verify interventions and instruction are implemented appropriately. The instruction in Tier Two is more intensive and focused on the specific needs of a student in an attempt to remediate academic concerns before special education becomes necessary. The interventions used continue to be scientific and research-based and are geared more specifically to individual students' strengths and areas of need. Progress continues to be monitored to determine if the instruction provided is effective or needs to be adjusted or intensified. In Tier Two, fidelity checks are implemented to ensure that the instruction and interventions are being used to ensure validity (NJCLD, 2005). Tier Two is not designed to provide whole-class interventions but is a more specialized approach that aligns proven intervention with specific student needs.

Because of its more intensive nature, Tier Two involves more collaboration and team-based support. The team is responsible for engaging in a problem-solving process by reviewing student data and determining needed interventions to increase academic progress. The team supports implementation of those interventions and the collection of student progress data to evaluate its effectiveness and determine any necessary future action (Nellis, 2012). Since the pre-referral process existed before the 2004 revisions of IDEA and the RTI movement, these teams traditionally have a variety of names, such as the Teacher Assistance Teams, Child Study Teams, Pre-referral Intervention Teams, Mainstream Assistance Teams, Problem-Solving Teams, Intervention Assistance Teams, or even RTI teams. While the teams' names vary, their general collaborative process and purpose of improving learning outcomes for all students remains the same.

Parents and guardians play a key role in Tier Two and should be notified, included, and seen as vital team members in the planning and monitoring of their child's progress. Strong parent-school connections are essential in the academic and behavioral growth of students and enhance the RTI process (Martinez & Young, 2011).

Role of the Special Education Teacher in Tier Two

In Tier Two, the special education teacher assumes four roles as a manager, diagnostician, interventionist, and collaborator but typically is not the primary provider of instruction (Mitchell et al., 2012; Gates et al., 2013). As a manager, the special education teacher may have Tier Two students on their caseload for which they manage interventions and report progress. As a diagnostician, the special education teacher may assess and progress monitor students, use the data to make instructional decisions, and conduct fidelity checks to ensure interventions are conducted correctly. As an interventionist, the special education teacher may provide small group or individualized instruction or co-teaching in a general education classroom. As these three roles expand and become more focused, the role as a collaborator becomes even more essential. In Tier Two, the special education teacher plays a larger role as the services and instruction become more targeted and specialized. This requires the special education teacher to work more closely with general education teachers, paraprofessionals, parents and guardians, related service personnel, and school administrators, which increase the necessity to be an effective collaborator (Simonsen et al., 2010).

The role of the special education teacher and other team members in Tier Two can be that of a consultant or collaborator (see Chapter One for more information on collaboration and consultation). Team members share their experience and expertise on interventions and accommodations that are then implemented by the general education teacher (IRIS, 2008). The special education teacher may offer suggestions on specific teaching methods or interventions. The school counselor may offer suggestions on behavioral management ideas. A speech and language pathologist may provide information on specific articulation strategies. A school administrator may provide resources for professional development. But while all team members share their knowledge and resources, they do not provide direct assistance in the classroom or with the students.

In the collaborative approach, team members provide their expertise and direct assistance. Team members share their experience and knowledge to develop and implement interventions (IRIS, 2008). The special education teacher may co-teach with the general education teacher or provide small group, specially designed interventions in a resource room. The school counselor may conduct classes on social skills to the entire class or a small group of students. The speech and language pathologist may work directly in the classroom to provide articulation interventions or outside the classroom with a small group of students. Often times the result is a blended program where both the consultant and collaborative approaches are used. All team members assist in the brainstorming and development of assessment techniques and interventions, while some members also assist in implementation.

Tier Two—Pre-Referral Assessments and Interventions

Tier Two can be divided into two broad areas: pre-referral assessment and pre-referral interventions. Pre-referral assessment is gathering data to determine a clear picture of a student's specific strengths and areas of need. Pre-referral intervention analyzes and applies the information learned in the pre-referral assessment to determine the curriculum, supports, and strategies needed to address the areas of concern. While a similar approach of gathering assessment data and using it to guide instruction is used in Tier One, in Tier Two, it is more specific and focused on an individual student rather than a whole class. These two pre-referral areas may have different teams or team members based on the strengths and needs of the student and team members. For instance, a teacher who is especially strong in assessments but not so strong in determining interventions may be on the pre-referral assessment team but not on the pre-referral intervention team. A student who struggles in language arts may have a reading specialist teacher on the team who would not necessary be included for a student who struggles in math. Sometimes a student's former teacher may be on the team.

Table 3.2 Elements of Developing a Common Language

- Mindfulness – be mindful that people may have different interpretations of the same words or language or may be unfamiliar with specific terms or concepts
- Openness – be open to the views and definitions of others
- Willingness – be willing to discuss areas of confusion or start a dialog about developing a common language
- Establish – establish a working definition of terms that are known and agreed upon by all team members

---

Adapted from Ehren et al. (2009).

It is important for every team member to have a general understanding of the components and process of pre-referral, as well as a shared understanding of the common language used. Parents, teachers, and students may have differing degrees of awareness or understanding of specific terms such as intervention, progress monitoring, and fidelity that are commonly used in RTI but not necessarily clearly defined. A parent may view an intervention as a separate process from what happens in the general education classroom, while a teacher may see it as a form of differentiation or providing extra assistance or accommodations. Team members may also question or disagree about what is meant by progress monitoring or fidelity. Is progress monitoring the same as benchmarking or running records? Does progress monitoring need to be tied to an academic content standard or formal assessment? What constitutes a fidelity check? How often should fidelity checks occur? Having common understandings is critical for active participation by all team members. It is also important to remember that the meaning of terms may change and evolve and that common language should be an open ongoing discussion among team members (Ehren et al., 2009). See Table 3.2 on elements of developing a common language.

Pre-Referral Assessment

Gathering assessment data in the pre-referral process tends to be a more informal process than gathering assessment data for determining eligibility for special education; but although it is more informal, it is no less critical. The first step in the process is identifying the problem behavior (Taylor, 2009). There are often three components to this step, identifying the target behavior in general terms; defining the target behavior in specific, observable, and measureable terms; and analyzing the target behavior to determine the cause. It is important to be as specific as possible in identifying the target behavior. Specific target behaviors allow for valid objective progress monitoring and determining appropriate interventions.

The general education teacher typically identifies a student's lack of adequate progress through observations or test scores. This begins the process of identifying the problem behavior. This first determination tends to be more general in nature and based off of summative assessment results, such as a failed math test. Pre-referral assessment data, though, should be both summative and formative in nature. The summative data, such as the failed math test or standardized achievement test results, provide an overall picture of the student's performance, especially in comparison to their same grade peers. It provides the big picture of how a student is performing and helps identify problem areas in general terms. Summative data alone, though, typically is not enough. It does not provide sufficient detail to determine specific areas of strengths and weaknesses needed to guide instruction (Lamar-Dukes & Dukes, 2005).

Formative data derived from short-cycle, curriculum-based assessments and progress monitoring done on an ongoing basis provides more specific data on students' areas of need and growth. Formative data has greater potential to more accurately determine the specific skill needs in observable and measureable terms. Both formative and summative data are needed to develop a clear, well-rounded picture of the student (Lamar-Dukes & Dukes, 2005).

While summative data can show that a student failed his or her math test or that he or she is functioning two to three grade levels behind his or her peers in reading comprehension, it does not provide information as to why the student failed math or with which parts of reading comprehension he or she is struggling. Formative data based on progress monitoring or short-cycle assessment can provide a clearer picture as to the specific skill deficits that need to be addressed to potentially abate the issue. This data is used to guide the pre-referral process in much the same way as it was used to guide instruction in Tier One.

While assessment is often thought of as testing, tests are just one part of the assessment process. Assessment information should be gathered through multiple means, including observations, evaluation of student work, such as error analysis or task analysis, developmental checklists, interviews, and behavioral rating scales (Polloway, Patton, & Serna, 2008). There is greater emphasis on multiple means of assessment in Tier Three and in Chapter Four of this text, but it is important to remember that multiple types to assessment should also be used in Tier Two.

The cause of the target behavior or academic area of concern is also often assessed and analyzed with the help of the team to determine why a student is struggling or to specifically define the problem. The cause may be failure to comprehend the information, deficits in basic skills, lack of background knowledge, or a mismatch in teaching and learning styles. For academic issues, the cause is often determined with an error analysis to look for patterns in mistakes made to determine why the error occurs. For example, if the area of concern is mathematics, then an error analysis may point to a lack of knowledge of basic math facts (e.g., multiplication of numbers greater than six). If the concern is comprehension, an error analysis could point to troubles with fluency or reading for detail or determining what, how, or why questions. The error analysis helps pinpoint the specific area of concern, which then makes it possible to define the behavior in observable and measureable terms and to determine the appropriate intervention and instructional changes.

For a behavioral issue, a functional behavioral analysis may need to be conducted. The functional behavioral analysis will determine the antecedents and consequences of the behavior, as well as when, where, and with whom the behavior occurs. This information is then used to determine why a behavior exists and helps pinpoint its reinforcers. Conducting a functional behavioral analysis often requires an observation and is typically a collaborative process with general or special education teachers, a consultant or other school personal, and the student's parents or caregivers.

Once a target behavior is identified and defined, the next step is to establish a baseline or a clear picture of where the student is currently functioning. This helps determine the degree of effectiveness of the instructional changes. Determining a baseline can be done in a variety of ways, depending on the behavior. If the target behavior is academic, then often a curriculum-based assessment is used. If the target behavior is behavioral, then often an observation is conducted to determine the frequency or duration of the behavior. While an observation could be done by the student's classroom teacher, it is often much more effective and accurate if it is conducted by a special education teacher or other school personnel. The baseline results are typically graphed to provide a visual in which to compare a student's progress or lack of progress once the instructional changes have been made.

Once the target behavior is identified and a baseline recoded, the team then determines the pre-referral interventions and makes the necessary instructional changes (Taylor, 2009).

Pre-referral Interventions

For pre-referral interventions, the team examines the target behavior, its cause and baseline, and then identifies appropriate interventions and makes the instructional changes necessary to implement the interventions. Proper identification and implementation of interventions is crucial for the success of the pre-referral process in remediating the target behavior and preventing inappropriate referrals to special education (Daly, Martens, Barnett, Witt, & Olson, 2007). Pre-referral interventions may include providing more instruction (e.g., longer reading classes or extra time in a resource room), different types of instruction (e.g., more hands-on or collaborative activities), more individualized attention (e.g., small group or one-on-one tutoring), or a different curriculum that addresses the student's area of need. The team also determines who will administer the intervention, typically the general education teacher, special education teacher, or reading specialist. Pre-referral interventions should continue to be data driven. The student's progress is assessed on a more intensive basis and possibly weekly or biweekly (Simonsen et al., 2010). The progress monitoring results are graphed and compared with the baseline to determine if the interventions are successful and the student is making adequate progress.

3.2 APPLICATION CASE STUDY

Charlie is a student in Mrs. Murray's third grade class. Charlie's universal screening at the beginning of the year indicated that he was substantially behind his peers in reading fluency and comprehension. Mrs. Murray reported the assessment results to Charlie's mother and implemented scientifically valid teaching practices using curriculum-based, short-cycle assessments to guide her instruction in the general education classroom. Mrs. Murray continued to monitor all of her students, including Charlie, and made adjustments to her teaching to meet the students' needs.

Mrs. Murray noticed that Charlie's assessment results indicated that he was continuing to struggle. She then began to provide Charlie with more supports, working with him one-on-one or in small groups, teaching specific skills and providing additional supports to assist him. She made adjustments to lessons, provided more choral reading, rereading of passages, and oral as well as written instruction. Mrs. Murray continued to monitor Charlie and noticed that that the changes were having limited impact on Charlie's performance.

Mrs. Murray spoke with Charlie's mother about her concerns, and together they decided to refer Charlie to the school's Tier Two pre-referral support team.

You are a member of the team charged with determining Tier Two supports and interventions for Charlie. In small groups, answer the following questions to help guide your discussion and decision.

1. What do you currently know about Charlie and his academic concerns?
2. What additional information would you like to know about Charlie? What assessments would you recommend? What other types of information would be beneficial?
3. What interventions have already been tried?
4. Who are the team members who should be involved in determining Tier Two supports and services for Charlie?
5. Brainstorm possible interventions for Charlie.
6. What interventions and supports does your group recommend for Charlie in Tier Two? Who is responsible for providing those services or supports? How will they be progress monitored?

Return to a large group and compare your small group responses. What challenges or difficulties did each group face in determining Tier Two supports and interventions? Were the interventions and supports the same in every group? Was each team member's input valued? Discuss as a large group how a team must compromise and collaborate in this process.

Tier Two functions vary from state to state and school district to school district, but there are two general approaches to determining interventions: the standard protocol and the problem-solving approach. Both of these approaches share similar characteristics but differ in how targeted interventions are chosen.

Standard Protocol versus Problem Solving

In the standard protocol, there is a set procedure or standard protocol for which interventions are chosen. These evidence-based interventions are predetermined and meet students' needs in a general way. Students are grouped by the nature of their problems and then matched to the predetermined protocol (Sharpiro, 2009). For example, all third and fourth grade students in Tier Two reading intervention at Jaidyn Lisset

Elementary School may receive small group instruction using the WILSON Reading System. The WILSON Reading System is the standard protocol. It is an evidence-based intervention that has been proven to increase student learning but may not necessarily be geared toward a specific student's needs.

While standard protocol requires a team approach, the core team members in this model tend to remain stable, since the protocol is standardized and not subject to change based on the individual needs of the students. The core members typically include general and special education teachers and may include school administrators, related service personal, and students' parents or guardians. While parental or guardian roles may be diminished in the standard protocol as opposed to other approaches, their input is still critical and fosters greater collaboration. The team members are responsible for analyzing the student's needs and determining which predetermined intervention most closely addresses those needs.

Advantages of the standard protocol in Tier Two include time and resources. Standard protocol tends to require less time from faculty and staff for meetings, brainstorming, and identifying interventions. Standard protocol may also reduce the amount of time between the identification of a student in need and addressing that need, since the interventions are predetermined and usually readily available. Often fewer faculty and staff resources are required for conducting interventions. Group sizes for these interventions can typically be larger (up to ten) since the interventions are more general and systematic. Fidelity checks for the standard protocol require someone on the faculty to be knowledgeable about a limited number of interventions. Since the same interventions are used throughout the building, the person conducting the fidelity check needs to be knowledgeable on those few specific interventions and often only needs to complete a simple step-by-step checklist showing each step or procedure is done properly (Sharpiro, 2009).

A disadvantage of the standard protocol is that it meets the general needs of students rather than the specific needs (Sharpiro, 2009). Addressing students' general needs rather than specific needs can prevent them from getting the interventions and instruction needed to maximize growth. Some students may be bored receiving interventions they do not need. Other students may continue to struggle and fall even further behind. This may lead to greater frustration, a longer history of failure, and more behavioral issues. Standard protocol may also lead to more students being referred to Tier Three or special education (Sharpiro, 2009).

Problem-Solving Approach

The problem solving is the second approach used to determine interventions. This approach tends to be more collaborative in nature and places more emphasis on identify the factors that are contributing to the problem and determining the interventions to address the problem. Rather than looking at the general needs of the student and using a predetermined set of interventions, the team looks at the specific needs of each student before determining individualized interventions.

The team plays a larger role in the problem-solving approach in determining each individual student's process. Since the team focuses on individual students' needs, membership tends to fluctuate based on the students, teachers, grade, age, disability, or need. The members of the team should include the student's current classroom teacher, the student's parents or guardian, a special education teacher, and possibly other grade-level teachers, the student's previous teachers, a school administrator, counselors, and even the student him or herself. Former teachers can provide input on the student's past successes and struggles, while grade-level teachers can share additional expertise on possible strategies and interventions. The team brainstorms possible interventions before determining which one, or ones, best meets the needs of the student. Since this approach is more collaborative, team members may feel more vested, because they have greater say in the process.

An advantage of the problem-solving approach is that it is designed to meet the specific needs of an individual student. The interventions identified are geared toward each individual student, thus ensuring that the students' academic and behavioral needs are directly addressed. Since needs and interventions are more closely aligned, fewer students are then referred to Tier Three or special education (Sharpiro, 2009).

A disadvantage of the problem-solving approach is that it requires more time and resources than the standards protocol. The problem-solving team collaborates on each individual student, identifies the problem, determines its cause, and identifies appropriate interventions. This requires the team to meet more often and for a greater amount of time. Since the interventions are geared toward specific individual needs, group sizes often need to be smaller and thereby requiring more teacher resources. Fidelity is also harder to assess. With a variety of different interventions in place, it is more difficult to have faculty and staff who are experts in the interventions and trained to effectively conduct fidelity checks (Sharpiro, 2009).

There are advantages and disadvantages to both the standard protocol and problem-solving approaches. The advantages of one tend to be the disadvantages of the other and vice versa. While time is an advantage in the standard protocol, it is a disadvantage in problem solving; and while individualization is an advantage in problem solving, it is a disadvantage in the standard protocol.

A third option is for schools to adopt a hybrid approach where the standard protocol is the norm for Tier Two targeted interventions and the problem-solving approach is the norm for Tier Three intensive interventions. The students referred to Tier Three have already shown a lack of adequate progress to the standard protocol in Tier Two, increasing the need to have a more focused problem-solving intervention in Tier Three. Tier Two interventions should result in fewer students referred to Tier Three, making the problem-solving approach more manageable (Sharpiro, 2009).

No matter which approach is used, student progress is monitoring after instructional changes have been made to determine the effectiveness of the changes and to guide instruction (Taylor, 2009). If the data shows a student is making overall academic improvement but struggles with a specific concept, then the instruction of that concept is revisited until adequate growth is achieved. For example, suppose a student's progress monitoring indicates that she has made adequate progress on learning her multiplication facts but still struggles with her seven facts. The overall intervention is successful, but the student needs further instruction on the sevens multiplication facts. The teacher then provides that instruction until the student has made adequate progress or mastered the sevens multiplication facts.

The data from the progress monitoring is graphed and compared with the baseline. If the graph shows adequate and continued improvement, then the instructional changes are working. If the changes are working, then they should continue to be used and progress monitored until the results indicate and the team decides they are no longer needed or they are no longer successful. If the data does not show adequate improvement or show a decline when compared with the baseline, then the instructional changes are not working. If the interventions are not working, then the team needs to make a decision. The team can decide to make adjustments (e.g., smaller group size or increased dosage), try a different intervention, or refer the student to Tier Three. There is no set amount of time that a student spends in Tier Two, and it is dependent on the student and the team to make that determination.

For RTI to be successful, there needs to be true collaboration, not just cooperation. This collaboration does not just happen after school or during meetings but needs to be ongoing, intentional, and goal focused. It means working together as a school and sharing resources, knowledge, and time in an intentional way to achieve those goals and meet the needs of all students (Ehren et al., 2009).

The pre-referral process can benefit all its members. It provides a forum for discussion and problem solving that can lead to greater collaboration and communication among all team members. The pre-referral process provides the supports and services to meet the needs of students and helps prevent inappropriate referrals and identification into special education.

One of the main barriers to RTI or any multidisciplinary team approach is time. In Chapter One, we discussed the logistical barriers to effective collaboration with a key one being time. Having adequate time is essential for effective collaboration among multidisciplinary teams to develop effective problem-solving approaches, conduct fidelity checks, and for needed professional development.

Even with the strongest pre-referral process, some students will need more support and specialized education. In those cases, a referral to special education is warranted. The work of the pre-referral team will provide needed information on interventions, assessment results, and progress monitoring documentation that will be used to determine a student's eligibility for special education and help in planning his or her Individualized Education Program.

The Role of the Building Leadership Team

As with many decisions within the RTI process, a multidisciplinary team should make decisions about its implementation. This team is typically a building leadership team that is responsible for coordinating and communicating the RTI efforts within the school. RTI is a framework rather than a prescriptive measure, allowing for many decisions to be made throughout the process (Metcalf, 2015). This team has a problem-solving focus at the school level (NJCLD, 2005). This multidisciplinary team assesses the effectiveness of instruction on students at a school-wide level rather than individual or class level. On the school level, the team may determine whether or not the core curriculum is effective for student learning outcomes by analyzing and monitoring school-wide data through an ongoing process to determine the effectiveness of the overall instructional process. This analysis of school-wide data allows for early identification of school-wide problems and may help determine solutions to the problem (e.g., curriculum or scheduling changes, professional development needs). It focuses on balancing the needs of all students with the resources available. These decisions rely on accurate and timely data for all critical aspects of the RTI process (screening, curriculum, interventions, progress monitoring, and evaluation) (Metcalf, 2015).

Comprehension Check

1. Why is Tier Two typically more collaborative than Tier One?
2. What are the roles of the special education teacher in Tier Two?
3. What are the teams' responsibilities in pre-referral assessments and pre-referral interventions?
4. How is the pre-referral process designed to meet the needs of struggling students?

CHAPTER SUMMARY

Many children struggling in the classroom will receive support through the general education classroom, not through special education. These supports and services will be provided in Tier One and Tier Two of the RTI model. These two tiers of the RTI model provide the pre-referral data of services and interventions tried before special education services are investigated.

✓ The RTI model aims to produce three things:

- High-quality instruction and interventions matched to students' individual needs
- The utilization of learning rate and levels of academic performance
- Developing important academic decisions based on data from learning rate and levels of academic performance

✓ Each tier of the RTI model provides more intensive interventions for students, beginning at Tier One.
✓ The RTI model has replaced the discrepancy model in some schools and districts.
✓ In the RTI model, a special education teacher plays four main roles:

- Manager
- Diagnostician
- Interventionist
- Collaborator

✓ As a manager, the special education teacher is responsible for managing his/her caseload or grade levels. This may include completing paper work for intervention plans, progress reports, or IEPs.

✓ As a diagnostician, the special education teacher diagnoses students' strengths and weaknesses. This may be done through administering assessments, observations, interviews, or record reviews.

✓ As an interventionist, the special education teacher is responsible for providing his/her time to either provide interventions or instruct others on how to provide interventions. In some schools, special education teachers may provide interventions through a resource room or co-teaching models.

✓ In order to be successful at each of the three aforementioned roles, a special education teacher must be an excellent collaborator. The previous mentioned roles cannot be successfully performed without assistance and information from other education professionals.

Tier One of the RTI model consists of effective instruction using evidence-based methods in the general education classroom. This tier begins with a universal screening or assessment in core content areas.

✓ Ongoing curriculum-based measurements monitor progress in this tier.

✓ Services, mainly differentiation of instruction, are completed by the general education teacher in this tier.

✓ Special education teachers provide support and collaborative relationships in Tier One, but do not provide the primary instruction or intervention.

Tier Two of the RTI model consists of more intensive interventions and services. The beginning of this tier usually starts when the general education teacher's observations and data show that the student is continuing to struggle despite the evidence-based practices at Tier One.

✓ Tier Two incorporates the same interventions and services found at Tier One.

✓ Tier Two incorporates fidelity checks to verify that interventions and instructions are implemented appropriately.

✓ Tier Two involves more collaboration and team-based support.

✓ Parents play a key role in Tier Two services and interventions and should be involved in the process.

✓ In Tier Two, the special education teacher plays a larger role in terms of services and instruction. This requires more collaboration with other professionals.

✓ Tier Two can be divided into two broad areas:

- Pre-referral assessments
- Pre-referral intervention

✓ There are three steps to pre-referral assessment:

- Identifying the target behavior in general terms
- Defining the target behavior in observable and measurable terms
- Analyzing the target behavior to determine cause

✓ Pre-referral intervention may include providing more instruction, different types of instruction, more individualized attention, or a different curriculum that addresses the student's area of need.

The way Tier Two operates and functions will depend on the school and district. Two generally accepted forms of Tier Two models are *standard protocol* and *problem solving.*

✓ The standard protocol approach allows for evidence-based interventions that are predetermined to be implemented quickly to meet a student's needs.
✓ The standard protocol approach may save a district time and resources, but it meets only the general needs of a student instead of the specific and individual needs.
✓ The problem-solving approach tends to be more collaborative, as there is more of an emphasis to choose the specific intervention that will work best for a specific child.
✓ The problem-solving approach is designed to meet the specific needs of an individual child; however, it requires much more time and resources.
✓ Schools may also implement a hybrid approach, combining both standard protocol and problem solving, depending on the child.

APPLICATION ACTIVITIES

1. Have candidates develop a step-by-step flowchart on the main components of Tiers One and Two of RTI. Make sure the candidates include decision-making points. Have candidates reflect on how their role will impact each of these decisions.
2. Have candidates interview a special education teacher about his or her role in the RTI process. Be sure to have the candidates include questions about each of the four roles.
3. Have candidates develop a Venn diagram about how the roles of the special education teacher and general education teacher are alike and different in Tiers One and Two of the RTI process.

REFERENCES

Berkeley, S., Bender, W., Peaster, L. G., & Saunders, L. (2009). Implementation of response to intervention: A snapshot of progress. *Journal of Learning Disabilities,* 42(1), 85–95.

Council for Exceptional Children. (2007). *Position on response to intervention (RTI): The unique role of special education and special educators.* Washington, DC: Author.

Daly, E. J. III, Martens, B. K., Barnett, D., Witt, J. C., & Olson, S. C. (2007). Varying intervention delivery in response-to-intervention: Confronting and resolving challenges with measurement, instruction, and intensity. *School Psychology Review,* 36, 562–581.

Ehren, B., Laster, B., & Watts-Taffe, S. (2009). *Creating shared language for collaboration in JAASEP WINTER, 2013 37 RTI.* National Center for Learning Disabilities, Inc. Retrieved from www.rtinetwork.org

Florida Problem-Solving & Response to Intervention Project. (2007). Perception of RTI skills survey. Retrieved from http://www.floridarti.usf.edu

Gates, L. K., Fischetti, J. C., & Moody, A. (2013). Implementing and monitoring the response to intervention process: The special educator perspective. *Journal of the American Academy of Special Education Professionals*, Winter, 20–47.

Individuals with Disabilities Education Act of 2004. (2005). Public Law 101–476, 104 Stat. 328.

IRIS Center for Training Enhancement. (2008). The pre-referral process: Procedures for supporting students with academic and behavioral concerns. Retrieved on November 17, 2014, from http://iris.peabody.vanderbilt.edu/module/preref/

Lamar-Dukes, P., & Dukes, C. (2005). Consider the roles and responsibilities of the inclusion support teacher. *Intervention in School and Clinic*, 41(1), 55–61.

Martinez, R., & Young, A. (2011). Response to interventions: How is it practiced and perceived? *International Journal of Special Education*, 26(1), 44–52.

Metcalf, T. (2015). What's your plan? Accurate decision making within a multi-tier system of supports: Critical areas in tier 1. Retrieved on June 2015, from http://rtinetwork.org/essential/tieredinstruction/tier1/accurate-decision-making-within-a-multi-tier-system-of-supports-critical-areas-in-tier-1

Mitchell, B. B., Deshler, D. D., & Ben-Hanania Lenz, B. (2012). Examining the role of the special educator in a response to intervention model. *Learning Disabilities—A Contemporary Journal*, 10(2), 53–74.

National Association of State Directors of Special Education, Inc. (2008). *Response to intervention: Blueprints for implementation*. Alexandria, VA: National Association of State Directors of Special Education, Inc.

National Joint Committee on Learning Disabilities (NJCLD). (2005). *Responsiveness to intervention and learning disabilities*. Retrieved on September 2015, from http://www.ldonline.org/about/partners/njcld

Nellis, L. (2012). Maximizing the effectiveness of building teams in response to intervention implementation. *Psychology in the Schools*, 49(3), 245–256. doi: 10.1002/pits.2159

Sharpiro, E. S. (2009). The two models of RTI: Standard protocol and problem solving. Bethlehem, PA. Retrieved on September 2015, from http://www.doe.virginia.gov/instruction/virginia_tiered_system_supports/response_intervention/two_models.pdf

Simonsen, B., Shaw, S. T., Faggella-Luby, M., Sugai, G., Coyne, M. D., Rhein, B., Madaus, J. W., & Alfano, M. (2010). A schoolwide model for service delivery: Redefining special educators as interventionists. *Remedial and Special Education*, 31(1), 17–23.

Polloway, E. A., Patton, J. R., & Serna, L. (2008). *Strategies for teaching learners with special needs* (9th ed.). Columbus: Pearson.

Taylor, R. (2009). *Assessment of exceptional students: Educational and psychological procedures* (8th ed.). Boston, MA: Allyn & Bacon.

4

REFERRAL AND IDENTIFICATION FOR SPECIAL EDUCATION
RTI Tier Three

Catherine Lawless Frank

Chapter Objectives

Following reading the chapter, students should be able to:

1. Summarize the laws that guide special education and protect the rights of people with disabilities
2. Explain the team-based procedures used to determine eligibility for special education
3. Identify the types of formal and informal assessments used in the eligibility process
4. Cite the importance of the team in the IEP process
5. Determine the role of team members in the eligibility and IEP process

REFERRAL PROCEDURES

Chapter Three examined Tiers One and Two of Response to Intervention and the pre-referral process for special education. In this chapter, we will discuss the next steps in the referral and identification process by looking at what happens if a student does not adequately respond to the interventions administered in Tier Two. In Tier Three, teams determine eligibility and develop Individualized Education Programs (IEPs).

In Chapter One, we learned that collaborative teams must have a common goal and shared vision for planning, implementing, and evaluating that goal (Hord, 1981). This is especially true in determining eligibility and the needed special education supports and services. In the eligibility process, the team's goal is to determine if a student qualifies for special education services. If a student does qualify, the team's goal is to develop an appropriate IEP. If the student does not qualify, the team's goal is to develop a plan for how to best meet the student's needs in general education with Tier

Two supports. While the goal for these teams may be largely predetermined, the planning, implementing, and evaluating involved in effectively reaching the goal requires considerable collaborative teamwork.

Legal Provisions

Laws designed to protect the rights of people with disabilities and ensure they receive an appropriate education guide the eligibility determination and implementation of the special education process. It is the team's responsibility to make sure all members are knowledgeable about the legal provisions that guide special education, especially parents/caregivers.

There are over one billion people (about 15% of the world's population) with a disability and an estimated 93 to 150 million of those are children between the ages of birth and 14 years. Throughout the world, people with disabilities often face discrimination and other challenges, such as accessibility, employment, health care, and education. According to the World Health Organization, many of these barriers can be overcome with governmental supports (WHO, n.d.). In the U.S., there are three laws that provide those supports, protect people with disabilities against discrimination, and promote an inclusive society: the Americans with Disabilities Act (ADA), Section 504 of the Rehabilitation Act (Section 504), and the Individuals with Disabilities Education Improvement Act (IDEA).

Americans with Disabilities Act

The Americans with Disabilities Act (ADA) defines a disability as a physical or mental impairment that impacts one or more major life activities. It is a civil rights law designed to protect people with disabilities from discrimination by promoting accessibility in places of employment and in any entity that provides services. For example, businesses must be accessible to all people, even though they are private enterprises. This law guarantees a person with a disability "reasonable accommodations". It does not guarantee a person a job or service but protects them from being denied the job or service based on their disability alone (DREDF, n.d.).

ADA has the least impact in schools for students with disabilities of the three laws. ADA has a broader definition of a disability than does IDEA, but ADA does not provide as much protection to students with disabilities in school settings. This law may impact a child with a disability in extracurricular activities that do not receive federal funds, such as camps or clubs, and requires them to provide reasonable accommodations. The definition of reasonable accommodation varies depending on the situation. Providing reasonable accommodations may mean extended time to complete an activity or an additional snack time for a child with diabetes. Reasonable accommodations are not expected to disrupt others. For example, providing reasonable accommodations does not necessarily mean changing the schedule of an extracurricular activity or prohibiting all sugar snacks for all children to accommodate one child (Lee, 2014).

Section 504 of the Rehabilitation Act

Section 504 of the Rehabilitation Act is also a civil rights law and has the same definition of a disability as ADA (i.e., a physical or mental impairment that impacts one or more major life activities, such as walking, talking, working, or learning). It protects a person with disabilities from discrimination in any place, program, and/or organization that receives federal financial assistance by requiring that they provide reasonable accommodations to people with disabilities.

Section 504 impacts all schools that receive federal funding (which is the vast majority of schools in the U.S.). This law is not designed to provide special education but to prevent discrimination by providing access and accommodations for students with disabilities in regard to their education (Wright & Wright, 2015). For example, a student who qualifies under Section 504 as having a disability could receive accommodations in the general education curriculum and classroom.

Section 504 is not as closely regulated as IDEA, nor does it provide as much protection. However, Section 504 does allow some students to qualify for accommodations that might not otherwise be made available to them. All students who qualify for IDEA also qualify for Section 504, but not all students who qualify for Section 504 qualify for IDEA. Students qualify for services under Section 504 through a similar multidisciplinary team process as in IDEA (This process will be discussed later in the chapter.). Students who fail to qualify under IDEA may qualify under Section 504 if they have a disability that impacts their learning and/or participation in school. Section 504 provides students with disabilities the same opportunities to learn and participate as general education students by providing reasonable accommodations and services that mitigate the impact of the disability. Determining reasonable accommodations and services should be a multidisciplinary team decision (DREDF, n.d.; Skalski, 2010). For example, the team may decide that reasonable accommodations for a student with attention deficit disorder (ADD) are extended time on tests, preferential seating, and possibly assistive technology to aid in writing. There should be written documentation in place for the services and accommodations provided, which is typically referred to as a 504 Plan (it may sometimes be referred to as an Individualized Accommodations Plan). The components of the 504 Plan are not federally mandated as in the case of an IEP, but the plan should outline students' needs and the reasonable accommodations and services provided to meet those needs (DREDF, n.d.; Skalski, 2010; Stanberry, 2014).

Individuals with Disabilities Education Act

The Individuals with Disabilities Act (IDEA—most recently reauthorized as the Individuals with Disabilities Education Improvement Act) identifies 13 specific disabilities, each with a qualifying definition, that have the potential to impact a student's education and learning (For a list of the specific categories, see Table 4.1. For more details on the qualifying definitions, see Chapter Five.). IDEA is an educational law that provides more protection for students with disabilities, age birth to 21 years, than the reasonable accommodations provided by either ADA or Section 504. IDEA guarantees students with disabilities the right to zero rejection, nondiscriminatory testing, a free and appropriate public education, least restrictive environment, due process, and parental participation.

Zero Rejection

Zero rejection means that a child with a disability, age birth to 21 years, cannot be denied a publicly funded, appropriate education regardless of the severity of her or

Table 4.1 IDEA Disability Categories

Autism

Deaf-Blind

Deafness

Emotional Disturbance

Hearing Impairment

Intellectual Disability

Multiple Disabilities

Orthopedic Impairment

Other Health Impaired

Specific Learning Disability

Speech and Language Impairment

Traumatic Brain Injury

Visual Impairment

his disability. A student with a severe intellectual disability or emotional disturbance is afforded the guaranteed right to a public education as is a student with a mild learning disability or hearing impairment. No child with a disability can be denied an education (Taylor, Smiley, & Richards, 2015).

Since IDEA's protections begin at birth and not when a child enters school, states are required to have in place "child find" systems. Child find systems allow schools to locate and identify young children with disabilities in order to provide early intervention services. The child find system requires collaboration and commitment from the community at large to be successful. Child find agencies must work with doctors, nurses, child-care workers, and anyone involved with young people to help identify children with disabilities and refer them to the appropriate child find agency (Taylor et al., 2015).

Nondiscriminatory Testing

Nondiscriminatory testing means that eligibility for special education is determined through a multi-factored evaluation using unbiased assessments. A multi-factored evaluation consists of the use of RTI data and multiple assessments administered by a variety of team members (which may include general and special education teachers, parents, related service providers, and school psychologists) to determine if a student is eligible for special education. To ensure that the testing is nondiscriminatory, the provision requires eligibility be determined by a team of people (rather than just one person), using multiple measures (rather than just one test) that are culturally and linguistically unbiased and administered in the student's primary language. This means that if a student's primary language is Spanish (Spanish is the language spoken in the student's home), then the student must be assessed in Spanish. Students who speak Turkish, Navajo, Mandarin Chinese, Swahili, or any other language must be assessed in their primary language when determining eligibility for special education.

Nondiscriminatory testing is designed to prevent inappropriate referrals to special education and will be discussed further later in the chapter (Taylor et al., 2015).

Free and Appropriate Public Education

All students with disabilities are guaranteed the right to a free and appropriate public education (FAPE). This means that students with disabilities must be provided an appropriate public education at no additional cost to the student or parents. This appropriate education includes curriculum and instruction and any related services, transportation, equipment, supplementary aids, or materials that a student with disabilities may need to support her or his education. The services and supports that a student needs for an appropriate education are detailed in the IEP (Taylor et al., 2015). Determining FAPE and writing a student's IEP is a team process that will be discussed in more detail later in the chapter.

Least Restrictive Environment

Least restricted environment (LRE) ensures that a student with disabilities is educated alongside his or her general education peers to the "maximum extent appropriate". This does not mean all students with special needs spend all day in the general education classroom, nor does it mean the same placement is used for every student with the same disability. It is an individualized process that requires a collaborative discussion about how, and where, a student would be most appropriately served based on her or his educational needs. However, it is important to remember that the focus should be on including the student with general education peers to the maximum extent appropriate (Taylor et al., 2015).

Due Process

Due process guarantees that the process and procedures are in place to determine eligibility, develop an IEP, and provide services in a timely and nondiscriminatory manner. Due process also establishes a procedure to resolve disputes that may arise, safeguards the rights of all team members, and ensures confidentiality of student records (Taylor et al., 2008).

Parental Participation

Parental participation provisions of IDEA ensure that parents have a right to participate in the design and implementation of their child's education program. Parents have the right to fully participate as team members and must be provided with the information they need (e.g., assessment results) to fully participate in the process. Parents must also provide informed consent to the process, design, and implementation of the IEP and have the right to disagree with any part of it through the due process provisions. Parent participation and due process procedures ensure that special education is not a process implemented by school personnel alone but a joint endeavor where all parties work together in the best interest of the student (Taylor et al., 2015).

The provisions of IDEA outline the rights of students and parents regarding special education and ensure that procedures remain a collaborative process. The provisions guide the process by making sure that a student is receiving an appropriate education through a team-based system of checks and balances. Zero rejection checks to make certain that all children age birth to 21 years with disabilities are identified, located, and served. Nondiscriminatory assessment provides checks through ensuring an unbiased process that determines a student's eligibility for special education. FAPE and LRE check to ensure that a student is receiving an appropriate education alongside her or his peers to the maximum extent appropriate. Due process checks that the process and procedures are followed correctly and disagreements are resolved. Parental participation checks to make sure families have rights, input, and decision-making power in the process. The "checks" are the IDEA provisions. The team provides the "balance." The multidisciplinary (or transdisciplinary) team supports a collaborative approach necessary to most effectively meet the needs of each identified student.

Comprehension Check

1. Why is it important for team members to be knowledgeable about the laws designed to protect people with disabilities?
2. How do IDEA and Section 504 differ? How are they alike?
3. Which provisions of IDEA affirm the team's role in the special education process?
4. How does IDEA support a check and balance system approach?

ELIGIBILITY TEAM-BASED PRACTICES

In U.S. schools, eligibility for special education begins with a referral. The referral is most commonly initiated by the general education teacher and the pre-referral team after a student fails to make adequate progress in the pre-referral process (see Chapter Three for more detail on Tiers One and Two and the pre-referral process), but it can be initiated by parents or guardians, doctors, therapists, or anyone who provides care or education to the student. The referral begins the process but does not automatically qualify a student for special education. Eligibility for special education is determined through a team-based multi-factored evaluation provided at no cost to the parents or guardians (Project IDEAL, 2013).

It is important to note that not all students with special needs go through a school team-based pre-referral, referral, and eligibility process. Special education services under IDEA can begin at birth and can be initiated at any time up until a student graduates from high school. Children who participate in special education services before beginning traditional schooling will typically be automatically referred for school-age special education services and be assessed using a multi-factored evaluation to determine if services are still warranted. This multi-factored evaluation is repeated every three years for all eligible students to ensure proper identification and prevent inappropriate referral into special education. The process for identifying a child age birth to three years will be discussed later in the chapter.

Once a referral is made, the team contacts the parents or guardians to explain the process, establish a collaborative working relationship, and obtain parental consent. It is important that parents are fully aware of the eligibility process and procedures, as well as their rights of parental participation. Parents play a significant role establishing eligibility, and it is important to ensure that they feel like equal members of the team. Written parental consent must be given before any testing can occur. Once parental consent is given, the team has 60 days to complete the eligibility assessments and develop an Evaluation Team Report. These 60 days include weekends, holidays, teacher in-service days, and any unexpected day off from school. The team must be aware of this and set an appropriate schedule to complete the assessments and determine eligibility in a timely fashion. While this timeline may seem strict, it is used to ensure that the student is being provided the supports and services he or she needs within a reasonable time frame. IDEA does allow states to develop their own timelines between parental consent and an eligibility determination, but in most states it is 60 days (Project IDEAL, 2013).

Multi-Factored Evaluation

After consent is given, then the next step is a multi-factored evaluation. A multi-factored evaluation (MFE) is a team-based information gathering process to determine if a student is eligible for special education. This evaluation falls under the nondiscriminatory testing provision of IDEA. This means that the evaluation must be conducted by multiple people and include information from multiple sources. Eligibility for special education cannot be based solely on one person giving one assessment (e.g., based on an IQ test). A clear, unbiased determination of the student's strengths and areas of need, using a variety of formal and informal assessment results, is needed for an accurate determination of eligibility. Imagine if a teacher suspected a student has a disability and asked the school psychologist to conduct an assessment. The school psychologist conducts the assessment using an IQ test and the student scores in the intellectual-disability range (typically an IQ of 70–75 and below). Under IDEA, that IQ test alone cannot qualify the student as having an intellectual disability. While the test score may show that the student meets a major requirement for an intellectual disabilities diagnosis, it does provide a clear overall multi-factored evaluation. There could be a multitude of reasons for the student's assessment results that are only partially due to the student's actual IQ. The student could have previously undiagnosed mild hearing loss and therefore could not clearly hear or correctly distinguish the assessor's words. The student's primary language may not have been English, causing language to be a barrier in comprehending and completing the assessment. The student may not have received an appropriate education. The assessor may not have established rapport, making the student feel uncomfortable and inhibiting her or his performance. There are multiple reasons why a student's single assessment result may be skewed, making multiple assessments conducted by multiple assessors essential in developing an objective, unbiased, and complete evaluation of a student from which to determine eligibility for special education.

Formal and Assessment Instruments

The MFE is a comprehensive evaluation of the student's abilities and includes a variety of formal and informal assessments depending on the suspected disability. The pre-referral intervention team typically provides the MFE team with data and with a suspected disability. The suspected disability designation provides guidance to the MFE team as to what assessments might be more appropriate. The types of formal assessments used in an MFE may include developmental assessment, screenings, individualized intelligence tests, individualized academic achievement tests, adaptive behavior scales, behavior rating scales, and specific related services assessments (e.g., speech and language assessment). Informal assessments often include background information, observations, curriculum-based assessments, and a review of the student's academic history and current levels of academic performance. The pre-referral team typically provides this information, at least in part.

Formal Assessments

Developmental assessments are a type of rating scale typically used with children from birth to five years. They are designed to compare a child's development to that of typically developing children to identify strengths and areas of concern. Developmental assessments may evaluate communication and language, fine and gross motor, social, cognitive, and self-help skills. These assessments often consist of a questionnaire completed by someone familiar with the child, typically a parent or caregiver, and a direct observation of the child by a qualified assessor (Rosenburg, Westling, & McLeskey, 2010).

A **screening** is a short assessment designed to identify potential problems. The most common of these are hearing and vision screenings. These are quick checks to determine if a student has any possible sensory problems that may be contributing to the student's difficulties. If the screener detects a potential problem, then the student is referred to a doctor for further assessment (Rosenburg et al., 2010). If a screening is administered to all students and is not strictly part of the eligibility process, then parental consent is not needed. For example, many schools conduct routine vision and hearing screenings.

Individual intelligence tests measure a student's cognitive ability or intelligence quotient (IQ) in comparison to others. Average intelligence tends to correlate with a standard score of 85–115 depending on the assessment used. A score above 115 is considered above average (or above 130 to be considered significantly above average) and a score below 85 is considered below average (or below 70 to be considered significantly below average). Intelligence tests are used because the results tend to correlate with a student's academic potential and predict academic achievement. Intelligence tests often provide results on subtests such as verbal skills, visual reasoning, spatial skills, and motor performance, as well as provide an overall or full scale IQ. A qualified scorer, typically a school psychologist or diagnostician trained and certified in administering the test, administers the IQ tests individually. The outcome of this assessment will help determine if the student's academic problems or difficulties in school are related to their IQ (as with an intellectual disability) or not (as with a specific learning disability or an emotional disorder) (Rosenburg et al., 2010).

A qualifying disability must affect a student's ability to learn and/or participate in school; therefore, an **individual academic achievement test** is often administered if there is an academic content area of concern (e.g., reading). These assessments are given individually in specific content areas (e.g., math, reading, language arts, writing) but typically do not require a special certification to administer, as in the case of intelligence tests. Individual achievement test results may be compared with those of the individual intelligence test to help diagnosis disabilities (e.g., learning disability) and pinpoint areas of concern. Achievement test results can also be used as a basis for goals on an individual education plan and as a means to progress monitor a student's growth over an extended period of time (Rosenburg et al., 2010).

Adaptive behavior scales assess strengths and areas of need in general areas, such as daily living skills and community participation, and more specific areas, such as social skills, motor skills, communication, and generalizing basic academic skills. Adaptive behavior scales are typically a rating scale completed by a teacher and/or parent to determine a student's ability to perform tasks and skills integral to everyday living (Rosenburg et al., 2010).

When a student exhibits inappropriate classroom behaviors that interfere with her or his learning or the learning of others, then a **behavior rating scale** may be administered. A behavior rating scale is completed by a teacher, parent, or someone familiar with the student to assess the intensity or frequency of the behavior(s) to help determine its impact on the student's learning (Rosenburg et al., 2010).

If the team determines there is a potential need for related services, then specific assessments in those areas may be administered. The most common areas for related services are speech and language, physical therapy and occupational therapy. Speech and language assessments may include developmental checklists, language sample analysis, observations, and assessments of speech and sound production, voice, fluency, and oral communication to determine potential receptive and express language needs (Freiburg & Wicklund, 2003). A physical therapy evaluation may be conducted if a student has problems with physical movement that impede the student's daily activities. In this case, tests and observations will be used to measure the student's gross motor skills and her or his range of motion, balance, gait, muscle tone, and strength. An occupational therapy evaluation will assess a student's fine motor skills and integration using standardized assessments, parent interviews, and observations to determine deficits in a student's ability to physically care for him or herself, play, and complete school work (Advocates for Children of New York, 2009).

All the assessments used in the MFE process must be culturally and racially unbiased and administered in the student's primary language. If a student's primary language is not English, or the language spoken in the student's home is not English, then assessments must be administered in that other language. The assessments must also be culturally and racially unbiased so as not to skew or bias the results. The disability must be present in the student's primary language and not be a result of a language barrier. A student cannot have a disability when assessed in English and not have a disability when assessed in her or his primary language and still qualify for special education services.

Informal Assessments

There is more to a student than what can be determined by tests, and therefore formal assessments alone cannot provide a complete picture of a student and her or his strengths and areas of need. Informal assessment information should also be obtained to provide a clearer picture and ensure proper identification. Informal assessments can include background information, observations, curriculum-based assessments, or progress monitoring results and academic history.

A team member should request background information and a medical history of the student from her or his parent or primary caregiver. This is often done through a questionnaire or an interview. An interview may garner more information and should be conducted by the team member with the strongest rapport with the parents or guardian. It is important that the questionnaire or interview be conducted in an open, nonjudgmental way that ensures the parents feel comfortable and valued. The questions should be predetermined but allow for follow-up or clarification. The information gathered may include academics, student's interests, family and home life, medical history and language, behavior and adaptive skills. For a list of potential questions, see Table 4.2. Parents should be aware that this information will be shared with others on the team and may become part of the student's school records.

Table 4.2 Possible Parent Interview Questions

Academic and Student Interests Information
- How do you feel your child is doing in school?
- What do you feel are your child's strengths?
- What do you feel are your child's areas of need?
- What does your child like about school? What is his or her favorite subject?
- What does your child dislike about school? What is his or her least favorite subject?
- What does your child like to do after school?
- What are your child's favorite activities or sports? Is he or she involved in any clubs or teams?
- Do you have any academic or behavioral concerns about your child? If so, what and when did you first begin to notice them?
- What do you do at home to help support your child in these areas of need? Have you tried any interventions? If so, what worked and what did not work?
- Is there any other information about your child's schooling that you think the school should be aware of?

Family and Home life
- With whom does your child live (e.g., mother, father, both mother and father, grandparents . . .) ?
- Does your child have any brothers or sisters? If so, do siblings live with the child? What are the genders and ages of the siblings? How well does this child get along with his or her siblings? Have any of the siblings been diagnosed with a disability? Have you noticed any developmental differences between this child and his or her siblings?
- What is the primary language spoken in your home?
- How long has your child lived in this country?
- Are there any cultural concerns that you feel the school should be aware of?
- Is there any additional information about the family or home life that you would like to share?

Table 4.2 (Continued)

Medical Background Information

- Was your child born prematurely? If so, how many weeks?
- Have you noticed any problems with your child's vision or hearing? Does your child wear glasses or have a hearing aid?
- Does your child have a history of ear infections?
- Has your child been checked for exposure to lead or diagnosed as having lead poisoning?
- Has your child ever been diagnosed with a medical condition (e.g., asthma, ADHD)? If so, what has been done to treat this condition?
- Has your child ever been hospitalized? If so, for what?
- Is your child on any medication? If so, what medication and why?
- Does your child have any known allergies? If so, to what?
- Is there any other medical information that you think the school should know about?

Language, Behavior, and Adaptive Skills Information

- Do you or have you noticed anyone having difficulty understanding your child's speech?
- Does your child have a history of stuttering?
- Does your child exhibit any behaviors that concern you (e.g., unusual fears, difficulty sleeping, school avoidance, disobeying parents, fighting . . .) ?
- How does your child do socially? Does he or she have friends? Get along with others?
- Does your child need assistance with daily living tasks (e.g., tying shoes, dressing, bathing . . .) ?
- How is your child's gross motor skills? Do you have any concerns about your child's balance or physical abilities?
- Do you have any concerns about your child's fine motor abilities (e.g., using scissors, handwriting . . .) ?
- Do you have any other language, behavioral, or adaptive concerns that the school should be aware of?

Final questions

- Is there any other information that you can provide that will help the school better understand your child?

Another common type of student assessment found in an MFE is an observation. Teachers routinely monitor and observe students but rarely do so in a systematic manner or for documentation used in making important decisions. It is difficult for the general education teacher to conduct such an observation while teaching a class of 20 or more students, and therefore it is helpful if another team member who is not directly involved in the lesson or class conduct the observation (Allen & Graden, 2002). Observations are most often done for students who exhibit emotional or behavioral concerns but often provide beneficial information for any student suspected of a disability. Observation can contribute to a more comprehensive view of the student's academic and behavioral performance in the classroom setting that is not captured in a formal assessment. Observations can show a student's general behavior or demeanor in a classroom and can provide more specific information, such as patterns or frequency of behavior. For a student with a behavioral or emotional concern, multiple observations should occur, typically at least three, conducted by different assessors, at different locations and/or times, and on different days (Ohio Coalition for the Education of Children with Disabilities, 2001).

The student's progress monitoring or curriculum-based assessments results from the RTI or the pre-referral process provide details about the student's present levels of performance. Curriculum-based assessments, such as those used in RTI (see Chapter Three), can be used to determine how a student responds to intervention over time and under IDEA (2004) can be used to determine a learning disability. The results from curriculum-based assessments provide a more detailed look at the student's strengths and areas of need. Formal academic assessments provide the big picture but typically lack the specifics provided by ongoing curriculum-based measurements. These assessments provide insight into success or lack of success of previous interventions and can also be used to determine a student's goals and objectives.

A student's academic history such as end-of-year or end-of-course grades and the results of other school-wide assessments are also considered in an MFE. This information helps provide a historical perspective of the student's area of concern and may help pinpoint or determine potential important information. For example, if the team knows a third grade student has an academic history of struggles with language arts since first grade or that an eighth grade student's academic concerns began to arise in sixth grade, it may impact the assessments used, information gathered, and, ultimately, the eligibility decision made.

Formal and informal assessments provide information about a student in regard to her or his development, hearing and vision, IQ, academic achievement, adaptive and overall behavior, and related service's needs, as well as background information, observations, curriculum-based assessments, or progress monitoring and academic history. The assessments used in an MFE vary based on the student's strengths, areas of need, and suspected disability. Which assessments are used is a team decision, and not all students will receive all the same assessments.

The MFE is a comprehensive battery of assessments administered by a team of evaluators. The team members should include the student's general education teacher, a special education teacher, a school principal or administrator, the parents or guardians, and may include the student, related service personnel, school psychologist or diagnostician, medical personnel such as a school nurse, and other professionals. Each team member may be assigned a particular assessment or task to complete. The school nurse may perform a vision and hearing screening. The school psychologist may administer the individual intelligence test, while a special education teacher may conduct the individual academic achievement test. A general education teacher may collaborate with a parent or guardian to complete an adaptive rating scale or a behavioral rating scale and gather background information. An administrator may be responsible for compiling the academic history, including end-of-year grades and previous assessment results. Special education teachers, administrators, school psychologists, and other professionals may conduct observations. It is important to develop an agenda for who is responsible for each assessment and a timeline for administering them. Each team member has a specific and vital role in developing a detailed picture of the student in this collaborative information gathering process.

Once all the assessments are completed, the information is compiled into an Evaluation Team Report (ETR). This report summarizes all of the formal and informal assessment results and is used by the team to determine eligibility. The team will meet to discuss the ETR, identify the student's strengths and areas of need, and then determine if the student meets the eligibility requirements for special education in one of the 13 disability categories (see Table 4.1 for the disability categories and Chapter Five for eligibility requirements). Eligibility is determined by a team decision, and parents or guardians play a critical role. Before a student is officially identified as having a disability, the parents or guardian must agree to have their child identified with the disability and provide their consent in writing.

4.1 ILLUSTRATIVE CASE STUDY

Samantha is a student in Mrs. Washington's third grade class with a history of reading difficulties. Samantha has attended the same school since kindergarten, and her teachers first reported concerns about her reading fluency in first grade. Samantha has been provided effective Tier One instruction and was referred to Tier Two intervention in the middle of second grade. While in third grade, Samantha has continued to receive Tier Two interventions, but Mrs. Washington is concerned that Samantha is not making adequate progress and is falling further behind her peers. Mrs. Washington expresses her concerns to Samantha's parents, and together they decide to refer Samantha to determine if she is eligible for special education.

The eligibility team consists of a special education teacher, the school psychologist, the school principal, Mrs. Washington, and Samantha's parents. During the team's first meeting, the eligibility process and their parental rights are conveyed to Samantha's parents. Her parents gave written consent to the process. The team decided that as part of the multi-factored evaluation, Samantha should receive an individualized intelligence test, an individualized reading achievement test (since reading is her academic area of concern), a hearing and vision screen, and be formally observed. They decided against conducting an adaptive behavior scale and a behavioral rating scale because Samantha was not experiencing difficulties in either of those areas. The team also decided that they did not foresee a need for Samantha to receive any related services and determined that assessment for those services were not needed at that point. The team did decide that background information, a medical history, and academic history, as well as progress monitoring or curriculum-based measurement results should be included in the MFE. The team then assigned tasks to each member and developed a timeline and assessment schedule to ensure that the MFE was completed and the ETR written within 60 days.

The school psychologist trained to administer an individualized intelligence test will assess Samantha using the Woodcock-Johnson III Tests of Cognitive Abilities to determine her general intelligence ability and specific cognitive abilities.

The individualized reading achievement test will be administered by the special education teacher using the Wechsler Individual Achievement Test—Third Edition (WIAT-III). This assessment will be used to determine Samantha's oral language, total reading, basic reading, reading comprehension and fluency, and written expression achievement scores. The team decided not to administer the mathematics or math fluency portions of the WIAT-III because mathematics is not an area of concern for Samantha.

The school nurse agreed to conduct hearing and vision screenings on Samantha and report her findings to the team.

Mrs. Washington stated that Samantha appears to have a harder time focusing as the school day progresses, so the team decided to conduct two observations, one in the morning and one in the afternoon. The school psychologist will observe Samantha in the morning, while the special education teacher will observe her in the afternoon.

Mrs. Washington and Samantha's parents will meet to gather Samantha's background information and medical history. The team discussed the type of information they felt would be most beneficial.

The school administrator will gather Samantha's school recorders, including school and district-wide assessment results, as well as previous report cards. The administrator also plans on meeting with Samantha's previous teachers to get their input.

Mrs. Washington will also provide her progress monitoring data and current grades and assessment records for Samantha.

Once all the assessments are complete and the need information gathered, the results will be complied into an ETR. The team will then reconvene to determine if Samantha is eligible for special education and if so, under which disability category.

If a student is determined to be eligible for special education and written parental consent is obtained, then the team, with most of the same team members, begins developing the students Individualized Education Program (IEP). If the student is not eligible for special education under IDEA, he or she may qualify for a 504 Plan under Section 504 of the Rehabilitation Act. As you may recall, this Act has a broader definition of a disability than IDEA and enables a student "reasonable accommodations" in school. If the student does not qualify under IDEA or Section 504 or parents do not give consent, then the student may still receive interventions through Tier Two of RTI or the pre-referral process.

Determining Eligibility for Early Intervention
Service—Children Birth to Three

Under IDEA, special education services begin at birth, and therefore community-based early intervention programs are in place for children age birth to three years. Early intervention services are provided for parents of children with significant delays in self-help, physical, social, emotional, and/or cognitive development. This is a community-based service rather than a school-based service but follows a similar referral and eligibility process. The process begins with a referral through the child find provisions of IDEA from a parent, caregiver, physician, or any individual with knowledge of developmental concerns in a child. Once a referral has been made to the community agency, then a service coordinator is assigned to help guide the parents through the process. If a child has been diagnosed by a physician with a physical or mental condition that is typically associated with developmental delays, then he or she is automatically eligible for early intervention services (e.g., Down syndrome), but the evaluation should still be conducted to determine the child's strengths and areas of need (NICHCY, 2014a).

The team, led by the service coordinator, explains the process to the parents and obtains their written consent before any assessments are conducted. The multi-factored evaluation team consists of the parents, the service coordinator, and a team of professionals who assess the child through an MFE. This assessment is conducted by the community's early intervention program personnel and consists of observations, evaluations, and screenings to determine the child's strengths and areas of need and whether he or she is eligible for services under IDEA and state guidelines. If the team decides that services are warranted and the parents agree, then the team begins writing an Individualized Family Services Plan (IFSP). An IFSP is similar to the IEP used in school, but an IFSP is based not only on the child's strengths and needs but also on the strengths, needs, and priorities of the family (NICHCY, 2014a).

Comprehension Check

1. Why is it important to have a team-based approach for determining eligibility for special education?
2. What determines which assessments are used in a student's MFE?
3. How is determining eligibility for early intervention services different from determining eligibility for school-based services? How are they alike?

INDIVIDUALIZED EDUCATION PROGRAM

Once the team is in agreement that a student is eligible for special education, and the parents have given written permission, the team begins the process of writing the student's IEP. The IEP is an annual legal written contract that details an individual student's FAPE and LRE. It documents the services and supports that a school will provide for a student to help meet her or his academic, behavioral, functional, and other needs. Most of the team members from the assessment and eligibility process will typically become a part of the IEP team, but some members may change. The school psychologist may no longer be on the team, and a parent advocate or others may join, but for the most part, the team remains the same.

Writing an IEP

Writing an IEP is an annual collaborative team process. IEPs may look different across U.S. states, but all must contain the student's present levels of performance, annual goals and short-term objectives, and the needed special education and related services. In the following section, we will discuss these common areas and what the team must consider in writing each section.

Present Levels of Performance (PLOP)

The PLOP, also known as Present Levels of Academic Achievement and Functional Performance (PLAAFP), serves as a baseline on which to measure a student's growth and justifies the student's need for a particular goal. It is a summary statement that objectively details the student's current levels of performance (e.g., summative and formative assessment results or frequency of a behavior) in an area of need. The PLOP is used as the basis for the student's annual goal and compares the student's current levels of performance with that of their general education peers. The PLOP also includes how this area of need impacts the student's progress in the general education curriculum. A different PLOP is written and aligned with each individual goal. See Table 4.3 for a sample PLOP. In writing the PLOP, the team should consider:

- Which academic, functional, or behavioral challenge does the student face that most affects her or his participation in school or learning?
- What is the student's current level of performance in regard to this challenge?
- What strategies, assistive technology, and/or accommodations have previously been used to address this challenge and to what degree of success?
- How does the student's performance compare with that of his or her general education peers? How does the student's performance compare with the grade-level standards (if appropriate)?
- How does this challenge affect the student's progress in the general education curriculum?
- What other information is needed to develop a clear picture of the student's current levels?

The PLOP should be a clear, concise, and objective portrayal of a student's specific need based on which the team writes goals to measure future growth (Pacer Center, 2011).

Goals

IEP goals state a student's expected degree of growth in one year in a particular area of need. They are observable, measureable statements aligned with a PLOP and detail a learning target the student will work toward during the course of a year. Each goal is then broken down into smaller steps called short-term objectives or benchmarks.

Table 4.3 Sample IEP

Background Information

Theodore is a third grade student with a learning disability.

Present Level of Performance

Based on the results of curriculum-based measurements, Theodore is able to solve single-digit addition and subtraction problems with 95% accuracy and double-digit problems with 85% accuracy. Theodore struggles with word problems, especially determining the needed information in the problem and solving it using the correct operation. Theodore averages 20% on curriculum-based measurements involving addition and subtraction word problems, while the class average is 85%. Being able to determine needed information from a word problem and solve it correctly is a skill that is necessary for Theodore to be successful in the general education mathematic curriculum.

Goal

When given grade-level word problems, Theodore will be able to identify the relevant information and operations needed to correctly solve the problem with a minimum accuracy rate of 80% or eight out of ten correct in at least three consecutive trials.

Objectives

1. When given a grade-level word problem involving addition or subtraction, Theodore will identify (highlight, underline, or circle) the needed information to solve the problem.

2. When given a grade-level word problem involving addition or subtraction, Theodore will identify the key words necessary in determining the correct operations and steps involved in solving the problem.

3. When given a grade-level word problem involving addition or subtraction, Theodore will independently solve the problem.

These smaller steps are observable learning targets to mark student progress toward the goal. Academic goals should be aligned with the student's grade-level academic content standards, but goals can also be functional or behavioral in nature. See Table 4.3 for a sample goal and objective. In determining and writing a goal, the team should examine the following questions:

- What does the student need to learn or accomplish to make academic, functional, or behavioral progress in school?
- How much progress is an appropriate expectation for one year?
- What specifically does the student have to do to meet this goal? Does he or she need to increase, decrease, or learn a specific skill or behavior?
- Is the goal aligned with a grade-level standard (if appropriate)?
- What observable and measureable steps are needed to accomplish this goal? What are the short-term objectives or benchmarks?
- Is the goal aligned with the PLOP?
- How will the goal and objectives be measured? How often will progress be reported to parents?

Goals provide an annual target for student learning, while short-term objectives and benchmarks are the steps that measure the student's progress toward the goal. These steps are monitored through data collection on student performance, and the progress is reported to the parents or guardian periodically (at least as often as grades or report cards are provided to students without disabilities). This ensures that parents are aware of their child's progress and can help determine if any adjustments to the curriculum or instruction are needed (Pacer Center, 2011). Goals and objectives guide a student's education, and determining appropriate ones is arguably one of the most important decisions facing the team.

Special Education and Related Services

The IEP also documents the specific special education and related services that a student needs to participate and make progress in school. The IEP team considers the individual student and her/his goals to determine the appropriate academic supports and instructional procedures necessary to achieve annual goals.

Related services are the typically nonacademic supports a student needs to make appropriate academic or behavioral progress. These supports can include, but are not limited to, transportation, speech and language, audiology, occupational therapy, physical therapy, counseling, interpreting services, mental health services, and any other service required to assist a student with disabilities (IDEA, §300.34).

In determining special education and related services, the team needs to consider:

- Does the general education instructional content need to be adjusted to meet this student's needs? If so, how?
- What instructional methods are most appropriate for the student to make progress?
- How will the instruction be delivered? Where? How frequently? By whom?
- What is the student's LRE? To what extend will he or she be educated in the general education environment?
- Are there any transportation concerns or needs to be considered?
- Are there any related service needs? If so, what? How frequently? By whom?

The special education and related services provided to a student include how a school adapts instruction and offers accommodations, modifications, and any other needed supports to ensure a student an appropriate education. In considering special education and related services, the team looks at the student's areas of concern and her/his annual IEP goals to design a program in the student's LRE to help reach those goals (IDEA, 2004; NICHCY, 2010; Wisconsin Department of Public Instruction, 2010).

Other Team Decisions

Some other important decisions the IEP team must make regard assessments and transitions. The team must decide if the student will participate in state- and district-wide assessments or alternate assessments and what accommodations are necessary, if any, to adequately measure a student's academic or functional achievement. The IEP must also address transition goals and services once the student is 16 years old. The team, with appropriate student input, must determine postsecondary goals related to training, education, employment, and independent living skills, along with the services needed to reach those goals (Wisconsin Department of Public Instruction, 2010).

4.2 APPLICATION CASE STUDY

You are a team member charged with writing an IEP for Jeremy. For this activity you are charged with writing two IEP goals, one academic and one behavioral or functional, based on the following case study:

You are in an IEP meeting for Jeremy, a fourth grade student with a learning disability. According to the progress monitoring and assessment results, Jeremy is able to add single- and two-digit numbers under 20 without carrying consistently (nine out of ten problems correct on average), but he is not able to subtract either single- or double-digit numbers with any consistency (two out of ten problems correct on average).

Jeremy is able to work cooperatively in groups but does not appear to have any friends. Jeremy, at times, acts out when he is frustrated, especially in math class (on average four times per week). When frustrated, Jeremy typically balls his paper up, throws it on the floor, puts his head down, and yells out "math is stupid".

Jeremy is also missing approximately 50% of all independent in-class assignments and 40% of homework assignments in all of his classes (language arts, math, science, and social studies). His teachers have reported that if they stand next to Jeremy and help him with his work, he is more likely to complete the assignment. Jeremy has expressed the he "does not do homework" and thinks it is "stupid".

Divide your class into groups of three and assign each member a role of a parent, general education teacher, or special education teacher. Role-play an IEP meeting, and as a team, determine the following:

1. Which academic challenge does Jeremy face that most affects his participation in school or learning?
2. What is Jeremy's current level of performance in regard to this academic challenge?
3. What other information, if any, is needed to develop a clear picture of Jeremy's current levels?
4. Write an academic IEP goal for Jeremy.
5. Which functional or behavioral challenge does Jeremy face that most affects his participation in school or learning?
6. What is Jeremy's current level of performance in regard to this functional or behavioral challenge?
7. What other information, if any, is needed to develop a clear picture of Jeremy's current levels?
8. Write a behavioral or functional IEP goal for Jeremy.
9. What special education and related services are needed to support Jeremy in achieving these goals?

Return to a large group and compare your small group responses. What challenges or difficulties did each group face in determining their goals? Were the goals the same? Was each team members' input valued? Discuss as a large group how a team must compromise and collaborate in the IEP process.

Individualized Family Service Plan

As discussed earlier, an IFSP is used for children age birth to three years who are found eligible for early intervention services. The IFSP is similar to an IEP but has a family focus and is designed to build upon the strengths of the family in order to meet the needs of the child. Each state has its own regulations and guidelines for an IFSP, but its development follows a similar process as the IEP. Writing an IFSP involves a multidisciplinary team with the parents as the main contributors and the service coordinator as facilitator. The other team members involved depend upon the strengths and needs of the child, as well as the priorities of the parents or guardian to assist in writing the IFSP.

The IFSP is a written document that includes the child's PLOP in terms of the child's physical, cognitive, communication, social and emotional, and adaptive developmental needs. The PLOP is used to determine what supports will be provided and may include nutritional, medical, nursing, speech and language, audiology services, physical or occupational therapy, and counseling or training for the parents or caregivers. The IFSP states the expected outcome or goal of the services, as well as the funding source, frequency, duration, and location of the service. The services should be provided, if at all possible, in the child's natural environment and if not, then the IFSP team must justify why. The IFSP may also contain any family information that the parents are willing to provide that would be beneficial to the team in working with the family and child (NICHCY, 2014b).

Team Members Roles

Determining eligibility and writing an IEP are both team-based processes. While other team members may vary, the key team members for both eligibility and IEP are the parents or guardians, general education teacher, special education teacher, school administrator (known as the Local Education Agency representative) and if at all possible, the student her or himself.

Parents are the experts on their child and the only consistent team members throughout their child's educational career. Their right to participate in the eligibility and IEP processes is guaranteed by law, and their consent is mandated throughout the process. They have a history with their child and a large investment in the child's future. As team members, parents can provide information on the student's strengths and areas of need, social relationships, and behavior outside of school to provide a clearer picture of the student. They can also help gather pertinent background information, share plans for the child's future, and provide input into the goals and services they want for their child (Pacer Center, 2011).

There should be at least one general education teacher as a team member if the student is, or possibly will be, included in a general education classroom. This should be the student's current teacher or a future teacher who will be responsible for implementing portions of the IEP but preferably both. The student's current teacher can provide information about the student's academic strengths and weaknesses, as well as her or his classroom behavior and relationships with peers. The current teacher knows the day in and day out aspects of the classroom (structure, schedule, management plans) and how that impacts the student. Future teachers will be able to answer questions and provide input as to the academic and behavioral expectations that the student will face during the next grade or over the course of the IEP. Being part of the team will also give the future teacher a chance to ask questions and begin planning how to integrate the student into her or his classroom (Pacer Center, 2011).

The team should include at least one special education teacher. The special education teacher will continue to have the same four roles held in Tiers One and Two (see Chapter Three for more information) and include being a manager, a diagnostician, an interventionist, and a collaborator. The special education teacher may be responsible for managing the student's paper work and conducting meetings, as well as diagnosing the student's strengths and areas of need. He or she may be responsible for administering assessments, interpreting assessment results, and assisting in progress monitoring to help determine eligibility, establish PLOP, and determine appropriate goals and objectives. As an interventionist, the special education teacher works with the team to determine appropriate interventions, services, and supports and often provides instruction. Collaboration continues to be the most important role of the special education teacher. To be an effective manager, diagnostician, and interventionist, the special education teacher must be an effective collaborator (Mitchell, Deshler, & Ben-Hanania Lenz, 2012; Gates, Fischetti, & Moody, 2013).

A school administrator, licensed to supervise or provide special education services, must also be part of the team. This team member is knowledgeable about special education services, instruction, and must know the resources available to meet the individual needs of a student. This person provides knowledge of both special and general education and has the authority to commit the resources necessary for the implementation of the IEP (Pacer Center, 2011).

The students themselves are often overlooked but should be key team members, if at all appropriate. Students should be involved in determining their goals, supports, and services. The more involved a student is in the eligibility and IEP process, the more likely he or she is to be vested in that process. Too often students are not consulted or even aware of the goals stated on their IEP, making it difficult for them to know what they are working toward or feel vested in the process. It is their IEP and their future, and the more involved they are, the better (Goepel, 2009).

The team may consist of other members, depending on the needs of a student and the request of the parents. For example, students who have an articulation disorder may qualify for speech therapy and have a speech and language pathologist on both the eligibility and IEP teams. A student who is visually impaired may have a mobility specialist on their teams. A parent can request an advocate or other individual who has knowledge of the student to be a member.

While each team may look different, the key component that all teams and team members mutually share is collaboration. Navigating the eligibility and IEP process can be tricky, but if team members share a common goal and a shared vision on how to plan, implement, and evaluate that goal, then a stronger team and a better educational process is the result.

Comprehension Check
1. What are some of the important decisions that the team must make in the IEP process?
2. What is the purpose of establishing a PLOP?
3. How is the IFSP different from the IEP?
4. What is the role of each of the key team members in the eligibility and IEP process?

CHAPTER SUMMARY

If a student does not adequately respond to Tier One or Tier Two instruction, she or he may be evaluated for Tier Three services. In this tier, educators determine eligibility for special education and work toward an Individualized Education Program if necessary. While the goals for these Tier Three evaluation teams may be largely predetermined, the planning, implementing, and evaluating involved requires collaboration and will look different for each individual child and team.

✓ In the U.S. there are three specific laws that provide support and protect people with disabilities.
✓ Americans with Disabilities Act (ADA)

- ADA defines a disability as a physical or mental impairment that impacts one or more major life activities.
- This law guarantees a person with a disability "reasonable accommodations".
- "Reasonable accommodations" does not necessarily mean changing schedules, curriculums, or rules due to one child.

✓ Section 504 of the Rehabilitation Act (Section 504)

- Section 504 holds the same definition of a disability as ADA.
- This section protects a person with disabilities from discrimination in any place, program, and/or organization that receives federal funding.
- Preventing discrimination can include providing access or removing obstacles for students with disabilities.
- Some students who fail to qualify under IDEA may qualify under Section 504.

✓ Individuals with Disabilities Education Improvement Act (IDEA)

- Identifies 13 specific disability categories that can impact a student's education.
- Guarantees students with disabilities the right to zero rejection, nondiscriminatory testing, a free appropriate public education, least restrictive environment, due process, and parental participation.

In the U.S., it is common for the special education process to begin with a referral. Many times this is done by a general education teacher, but it may also be done by a parent or guardian, a doctor/therapist, or any other provider of care for the student.

- ✓ Once parental consent for a special education evaluation has been signed, an evaluation team has 60 days (including weekends and holidays) to determine eligibility.
- ✓ A multi-factored evaluation (MFE) is completed so the team can gather information to determine eligibility for special education services.
- ✓ Formal assessments and informal assessments are included in an MFE. These may include IQ tests, individualized academic achievement tests, screenings, curriculum-based measurements, observations, etc. All assessments should be unbiased, nondiscriminatory, and culturally/language appropriate.
- ✓ When all assessments are complete, the information is compiled into an Evaluation Team Report or ETR. This form is used as a tool to determine eligibility; however, parental consent to have a child officially identified with a disability is needed.

Once a child has been identified as having a disability and deemed eligible for special education services, the team then begins writing an Individualized Education Program or IEP. The IEP is a legal document that details the students free and appropriate public education, as well as his/her least restrictive environment.

- ✓ In the IEP documentation, the students Present Levels of Performance (PLOP) are utilized to create and monitor educational goals.
- ✓ Goals are written to state the expected growth of the student in one academic year. These goals should be both measureable and observable.
- ✓ Each goal can be broken down into smaller steps called objectives or benchmarks.
- ✓ IEPs will also document the specific special educational and related services that a student will need to participate and make progress in school (e.g., PT, OT, or speech services).

Children who are not yet in school are also eligible for special services. However, at this age the services are community based as opposed to educationally based.

- ✓ Child find services are for children from birth to age three.
- ✓ Services are considered early intervention services and are designed to help parents of children with significant delays in self-help skills, physical, social, emotional, and/or cognitive development.
- ✓ Once a referral is made, an evaluation team completes an MFE, similar to evaluation teams determining eligibility for special education services.
- ✓ If a child is deemed eligible for services, an Individualized Family Service Plan (IFSP) is constructed. This plan is similar to an IEP; however, goals and supports for the entire family, not just the child, can be written into the plan.

APPLICATION ACTIVITIES

1. Have candidates research court cases that led up to the passage of the Education of All Handicap Children Act (currently known as IDEA). Candidates should include cases such as *Brown v. Board of Education of Topeka, Kansas, Diana v. State Board of Education, Guadalupe v. Tempe Elementary School, Mills v. Board of Education of the District of Columbia,* and *PARC v. Commonwealth of Pennsylvania.*
2. Have candidates develop a flowchart of the steps leading from referral to determining eligibility and writing the IEP. Be sure to include the steps where parental consent is needed.
3. Have the candidates observe an eligibility and/or IEP meeting. Candidates should pay special attention to the role of each team member. If attending a meeting is not possible, have the students participate in a mock IEP meeting and assume different roles (e.g., general education teacher, special education teacher, parent, and student).
4. Have candidates develop a chart identifying the roles of each of the team members in the eligibility and IEP process.

REFERENCES

Advocates for Children of New York. (2009). Special education evaluations. Retrieved on September 2015, from http://www.advocatesforchildren.org/sites/default/files/library/sp_ed_evaluations.pdf?pt=1

Allen, Sarah J., & Graden, Janet L. (2002). Best practices in collaborative problem solving for intervention design. In A. Thomas & J. Grimes (Eds.), *Best practices in school psychology IV* (Vol. 1, Vol. 2) (565–582). Washington, DC: National Association of School Psychologists.

Disability Rights Education & Defense Fund (DREDF) (n.d.). A comparison of ADA, IDEA, and section 504. Retrieved on September 2015, from http://dredf.org/advocacy/comparison.html

Freiburg, C., & Wicklund, A. (2003). Speech and language impairments assessment and decision making: Technical assistance guide. Retrieved on September 2015, from http://sped.dpi.wi.gov/sites/default/files/imce/sped/pdf/slguide.pdf

Gates, L. K., Fischetti, J. C., & Moody, A. (2013). Implementing and monitoring the response to intervention process: The special educator perspective. *Journal of the American Academy of Special Education Professionals*, Winter, 20–47.

Goepel, J. (2009). Constructing the individual education plan: Confusion or collaboration? *Support for Learning*, 24(3), 126–132.

Hord, S. M. (1981). Working together: Cooperation or collaboration? Retrieved on September 2015, from http://files.eric.ed.gov/fulltext/ED226450.pdf

Individuals with Disabilities Education Act, 20 U.S.C. § 1400 (2004).

Mitchell, B. B., Deshler, D. D., & Ben-Hanania Lenz, B. (2012). Examining the role of the special educator in a response to intervention model. *Learning Disabilities—A Contemporary Journal*, 10(2), 53–74.

NICHCY. (2010). Supports, modifications, and accommodations for students. Retrieved on September 2015, from http://www.parentcenterhub.org/repository/accommodations/

NICHCY. (2014a). Overview of early intervention. Retrieved on September 2015, from http://www.parentcenterhub.org/repository/ei-overview/

NICHCY. (2014b). Writing the IFSP for your child. Retrieved on September 2015, from http://www.parentcenterhub.org/repository/ifsp/

Ohio Coalition for the Education of Children with Disabilities. (2001). A guide to the multifactored evaluation (MFE). Retrieved on September 2015, from http://www.gpo.gov/fdsys/pkg/ERIC-ED466923/pdf/ERIC-ED466923.pdf

Pacer Center. (2011). A place to start: Understanding the present level of academic achievement and functional performance statement. Retrieved on September 2015, from http://www.pacer.org/parent/php/php-c186.pdf

Project IDEAL. (2013). The special education referral process. Retrieved on September 2015, from http://www.projectidealonline.org/v/special-education-referral-process/

Rosenburg, M. S., Westling, D. L., & McLeskey, J. (2010). Types of tests used in special education. Retrieved on September 2015, from http://www.education.com/reference/article/types-tests-used-special-education/

Skalski, A. K. (2010). Section 504: A guide for parents and educators. *National Association of School Psychologists*. Retrieved on September 2015, from http://www.nasponline.org/families/documents/35-1_S8-35_section_504.pdf

Stanberry, K. (2014). Understanding 504 plans. *Understood*. Retrieved on September 2015, from https://www.understood.org/en/school-learning/special-services/504-plan/understanding-504-plans

Taylor, R.L., Smiley, L.R., & Richards, S.B. (2008). *Exceptional students: Preparing teachers for the 21st century*. Boston, MA: McGraw-Hill.

Taylor, R. L., Smiley, L. R., & Richards, S. B. (2015). *Exceptional students: Preparing teachers for the 21st century* (2nd ed.). Boston, MA: McGraw-Hill.

Wisconsin Department of Public Instruction. (2010). A guide for writing IEP's. Retrieved on September 2015, from http://sped.dpi.wi.gov/sites/default/files/imce/sped/pdf/iepguide.pdf

World Health Organization (WHO). (n.d.). World report on disability. Retrieved September 2015 from http://www.who.int/disabilities/world_report/2011/factsheet.pdf?ua=1

Wright, P., & Wright, P. (2015). My child with a 504 plan is failing, school won't help: Your eligibility game plan. Retrieved on September 2015, from http://www.wrightslaw.com/info/sec504.idea.eligibility.htm

5

STUDENTS WITH DISABILITIES

Catherine Lawless Frank

Chapter Objectives

Following reading the chapter, students should:

1. Identify the role of the team in determining the existence of disabilities, especially learning disabilities, intellectual disabilities, and emotional disturbances
2. Understand the primary characteristics of the disabilities under IDEA
3. Recognize the importance in considering the individual person rather than the characteristics of the disability in determining an educational plan
4. Recognize the types of instructional considerations needed to determine the appropriate education for a student with disabilities

In Chapter Four, we looked at the laws designed to protect people with disabilities and focused mainly on the Individuals with Disabilities Education Improvement Act (IDEA). We then examined the team-based approach for determining eligibility for special education and writing Individualized Education Programs (IEPs). In Chapter Five, we will examine the categories of disabilities that fall under IDEA, as well as considerations for the school-based team in determining eligibility and developing an IEP.

The IDEA disability categories are often grouped as either high-incidence or low-incidence disabilities. High-incidence disabilities make up 80% of the students serviced under IDEA and include learning disabilities, intellectual disabilities, emotional disturbances, and communication disorders (Google, n.d.). Low-incidence disabilities are those that are included in the remaining 20% of the total number of students served and include autism, deaf-blindness, deafness, hearing impairment, multiple disabilities, orthopedic impairment, other health impairment, traumatic brain injury, and visual impairment.

Some categories of disabilities, typically low-incidence disabilities, are related to medical diagnoses. In these cases, it is not the team's responsibility to diagnosis the disorder (only a medical professional can do that), but it is the team's responsibility to determine if the diagnosed disorder affects the student's ability to learn and/or participate in school. For example, a student will typically not be determined eligible for services under the autism category without a medical diagnosis of an autism spectrum disorder. If a student is diagnosed with an autism spectrum disorder, it is the team's responsibility to determine if the disorder adversely affects a student's ability to learn or participate in school. Notice that the requirement is that the condition adversely affects a student's ability to learn *or* participate in school. A student is not required to have a condition that affects only his or her ability to learn to qualify for special education. For example, a physician may diagnose a student as having Osteogenesis imperfecta (brittle bone disease), which affects a person physically but not intellectually. Osteogenesis imperfecta may not affect a student's ability to learn but may affect his or her ability to participate in school. The student may use a wheelchair and require special seating, use of an elevator, extended time to change classes, or services from a school nurse but not require any specialized instruction. These disabilities tend to be low-incidence disabilities.

For some disabilities, the team is typically involved in the diagnosis. Disabilities such as learning disabilities, intellectual disabilities, and emotional disturbances primarily affect a student's ability to learn. In these cases, the team determines the existence of the disabilities and the student's eligibility for special education based on specific assessment criteria determined by IDEA. The team also determines if and how the disability affects the student's ability to learn and/or participate in school and the appropriate educational plan. These disabilities tend to be the high-incidence disabilities.

The team must also remember that a disability cannot be due to the fact that a student's primary language isn't English nor may it be the result of a lack of appropriate education. Students must be assessed in their native or primary language when determining eligibility for a diagnosis. For example, Miguel is a third grader recently enrolled in your school. Miguel's family members are migrant farmers who recently immigrated to the U.S. from Honduras. The family primarily speaks Spanish, and Miguel has not attended school regularly due to the family's migrant employment. His teacher's assessments and observations show that he is having difficulties in reading fluency and comprehension, even after Tier One and Tier Two interventions were used. Miguel was subsequently referred for an evaluation for special education. In evaluating Miguel, the team assessed him in his primary language, Spanish, and ruled out a lack of regular school attendance and a language barrier in determining his eligibility for special education. Miguel may be deemed eligible for special education, however his disability must be evident in his primary language and not be the result of inappropriate or lack of education.

Every student is unique and disabilities affect each student differently. In this chapter, we will discuss the defining characteristics of each category, beginning with the high-incidence disabilities, keeping in mind that what is described are general characteristics and may present differently for the individual. It is important for the team to remember to focus on the individual needs of a student rather than the general characteristics of a category.

STUDENTS WITH HIGH-INCIDENCE DISABILITIES

High-incidence disabilities are the ones that teams will work with most often. In these disabilities, especially learning disabilities, intellectual disabilities, and emotional disturbances, the team will typically play a larger role in determining the existence of the disability and eligibility for special education. Since the team will play a greater role in these three disability categories, we will look at them in more depth than the remaining disability groups.

Learning Disabilities

The term "learning disabilities" as it is used in this chapter and defined under IDEA is not a universal term and may have different meanings in different fields and in different countries. In the legal profession and in countries such as the United Kingdom, the term learning disabilities may be more closely associated with the definition of an intellectual disability under IDEA. Under IDEA, a learning disability affects the way a person learns and processes information. It accounts for the largest category of students under IDEA and affects approximately five percent of the total U.S. public school population (2.4 million students) and over half of the students in special education (Cortiella & Horowitz, 2014). IDEA defines a specific learning disability as a:

> disorder in 1 or more of the basic psychological processes involved in understanding or in using language, spoken or written, which disorder may manifest itself in the imperfect ability to listen, think, speak, read, write, spell, or do mathematical calculations.
>
> (B) DISORDERS INCLUDED- Such term includes such conditions as perceptual disabilities, brain injury, minimal brain dysfunction, dyslexia, and developmental aphasia.
>
> (C) DISORDERS NOT INCLUDED- Such term does not include a learning problem that is primarily the result of visual, hearing, or motor disabilities, of mental retardation, of emotional disturbance, or of environmental, cultural, or economic disadvantage.
>
> (20 U.S.C. § 1401 (30))

Considerations for the Team

Learning disabilities (LD) are often seen as a category of exclusion. The student has difficulties processing, understanding, and/or using language, but typically the cause of this difficulty is unknown. Through the eligibility process, the team will exclude vision, hearing, physical or motor impairments, an intellectual disability, emotional disturbances, or any environmental, cultural, or economic factors as the cause for the learning difficulties. These exclusions leave a learning disability as the most likely cause. While some conditions are stated under the definition (perceptual disabilities, brain injury, minimal brain dysfunction, dyslexia, and developmental aphasia), determining the specific type of learning condition a student has can be tricky and is not required for eligibility purposes (see Table 5.1 for the most common types of LD).

Table 5.1 Common Types of Learning Disabilities

Dyslexia	Associated with a specific learning disability in reading. Common characteristics include difficulty with phonemic awareness and phonological processing, and difficulties with word decoding, fluency, rate of reading, rhyming, spelling, vocabulary, comprehension, and written expression.
Dyscalculia	Associated with specific learning disability in math. Common characteristics include difficulty with counting, learning number facts, and doing math calculations; difficulty with measurement, telling time, counting money, and estimating number quantities; and trouble with mental math and problem-solving strategies.
Dysgraphia	Associated with a specific learning disability in writing. The term is used to capture both the physical act of writing and the quality of written expression. Often this is seen in individuals who struggle with dyslexia and dyscalculia. Common characteristics include tight and awkward pencil grip and body position, tiring quickly while writing, trouble forming letter shapes as well as inconsistent spacing between letters or words, difficulty writing or drawing on a line or within margins, difficulty with syntax structure and grammar, and a large gap between written ideas and understanding demonstrated through speech.
Auditory Processing Deficit	Term used to describe a weakness in the ability to understand and use auditory information. Individuals with these types of difficulties often have trouble with auditory discrimination, auditory figure-ground discrimination, auditory memory, auditory sequencing, and difficulties in spelling, reading, and written expression.
Visual Processing Deficit	Term used to describe a weakness in the ability to understand and use visual information. Individuals with these types of difficulties often have trouble with visual discrimination, visual figure-ground discrimination, visual sequencing, visual motor processing, visual memory, visual closure, and spatial relationships.
Nonverbal Learning Disability	Term used to describe the characteristics of individuals who have unique learning and behavioral profiles that may overlap with dyslexia, dyscalculia, and dysgraphia but differ in significant ways. These individuals have strengths in the areas of verbal expression, vocabulary, reading, comprehension, auditory memory, and attention to detail. However, they have trouble with math computation and problem-solving, visual-spatial tasks and motor coordination, and reading body language and social cues are difficult for these students, as well as seeing the "big picture" in social and academic contexts.
Executive Functioning Deficits	Term used to describe weaknesses in the ability to plan, organize, strategize, remember details, and manage time and space efficiently.
Attention Deficit/Hyperactivity Disorder (ADHD)	Brain-based disorder that results in significant inattention, hyperactivity, distractibility, or a combination of any of these characteristics. Like a learning disability, this disorder is linked both to heredity as well as to brain structure and function.

Source: Cortiella, C., & Horowitz, S. H. (2014) *The state of learning disabilities* (3rd ed.). New York, NY: National Center of Learning Disabilities.

Determining eligibility for an LD requires the team to determine if the student processes language in a manner that affects the way he or she learns. There are two ways the team can do this. The first is the traditional method, the Ability-Achievement Severe Discrepancy model, which compares a student's intellectual ability to that of his or her academic achievement. As part of a multi-factored evaluation, a student is assessed using an individualized intelligence test (IQ test) and an individualized academic achievement test. If the results show that the student's intellectual level is average or above average (a standard score of 85 or above on most intelligence tests), then that score is compared with the results of the student's academic achievement test. If a significant discrepancy exists between these two assessment scores (the student has an average or above average IQ but a significantly lower academic achievement score), then the student could be considered to have a learning disability once all other possible factors are ruled out (e.g., hearing, vision, and appropriate education). What is considered a significant discrepancy depends on the district, school, or team. In some schools or districts, a discrepancy of two standard deviations may be needed to determine eligibility (the standard score of the intelligence test is at least two standard deviations or typically 30 points higher than the score on the academic achievement test), while in others a lower threshold may be needed (e.g., one standard deviation or a 15 point discrepancy). After eliminating all other possible causes, these two assessments are designed to show that a student's academic achievement is significantly lower than one would expect based on the student's IQ, resulting in the diagnosis of a learning disability.

The second way a team can determine eligibility for LD under IDEA is by documenting a student's lack of response to appropriate intervention. This is often done through a multi-tiered system of support, such as RTI. Through this approach, the student is provided effective data-driven instruction with increasing levels of evidence-based intensive interventions designed to address individual student needs. If a student fails to respond to the interventions or make appropriate progress, then the team can determine the student has a learning disability and is eligible for special education services. In many cases, a combination of both approaches are used. The student is provided effective data-driven instruction and increasingly intensive interventions in conjunction with the Ability-Achievement Severe Discrepancy model to ensure appropriate instruction. In any case, there must be evidence that appropriate education has been provided and that the student has not responded to this high-quality instruction and interventions, resulting in a diagnosis of a learning disability. See Chapters Three and Four for more information on RTI and the pre-referral process.

Even though it is the largest category, the symptoms of LD are not always easy to recognize. Some students develop ways to compensate for their learning differences, while others have behaviors that interfere with identification, thus causing the symptoms to go unrecognized until the child starts school (Lambros & Leslie, 2005). For many students, the general education teacher is the first person to suspect a problem and will ultimately provide the majority of the student's instruction (66% of students with LD spend at least 80% of their school day in general education classrooms) (National Center of Learning Disabilities, 2014).

Approximately 80% of students with LD experience difficulties in reading but may also have difficulties with oral processing, writing, mathematics, speaking, and other language or nonacademic issues, such as perceptual impairments and maladaptive behaviors including impulsivity, distractibility, low frustration tolerance, and difficulty interacting socially with peers or adults (Lambros & Leslie, 2005).

It is important for the team to remember that a high-quality pre-referral process and a team approach are essential in determining LD eligibility and to support the parents, students, and teachers and to prevent inappropriate referral. Students with LD disproportionately live in poverty and are twice as likely to be in foster care or experience homelessness. Blacks and Hispanics tend to be overrepresented in this category, while whites and Asians are underrepresented. Two-thirds of the students with LD are male, even though males and females are equally as likely to experience difficulties with reading, the most common characteristic of LD (National Center of Learning Disabilities, 2014). Young adults with LD enroll in some type of postsecondary education within eight years of leaving high school at the same rate (67%) as the general population but are half as likely to attend a four-year college. Students with LD report that they are less likely to be supported in how to prepare for college by teachers and guidance counselors (Harris Interactive, 2011).

Intellectual Disability

Intelligence refers to a person's general mental capability and involves the ability to reason, plan, solve problems, think abstractly, comprehend complex ideas, learn quickly, and learn from experience (Intellectual Disability, 2015). IDEA defines an intellectual disability as a:

> significantly sub average general intellectual functioning, existing concurrently [at the same time] with deficits in adaptive behavior and manifested during the developmental period, that adversely affects a child's educational performance.

Considerations for the Team

IDEA's definition of an intellectual disability (ID) has four main eligibility components: cognitive ability, adaptive behavior, age of onset, and effect on education. The team needs to consider all four in determining eligibility for special education and related services. The first component relates to a "significant sub average general intellectual functioning." A qualified team member, typically a school psychologist, will assess the student's intellectual functioning using an individual intelligence test or IQ test. To qualify as significantly subaverage, the results of the individual intelligence test must indicate that the student's IQ is at or below a standard score of 70–75 or the equivalent of two standard deviations below average (average IQ is 100). For more information on individual intelligence tests, see Chapter Four.

The team, especially the parents and classroom teacher, will also observe and assess the student to determine strengths and areas of need in his or her adaptive behavior skills. Adaptive behaviors are learned conceptual (time, money, language, literacy), social (interpersonal skills, gullibility, social responsibility and problem solving, self-esteem), and practical (daily living, health care, transportation, financial aware-ness) skills that are used in everyday life. Adaptive behaviors are typically assessed using a rating scale to determine if there are any developmental deficits in the skills used in everyday life (Definition of Intellectual Disability, 2013).

The third criterion that must be examined is the age of onset. ID must manifest itself during a person's developmental years, birth to age 18. Since these are the years a student is typically in school, it becomes less of an issue for a school-based team.

The final criterion is the impact the disability has on a student's educational per-formance and if it negatively affects the student's ability to learn and participate in school. The subaverage IQ of at or below 70–75 and deficits in adaptive behavior skills should correlate to an academic performance in school that is significantly behind typically developing peers. This final criterion ensures that the assessment results are compared with school performance before a student is eligible for services under ID.

Since ID adversely affects a person's cognitive functioning and causes a person to develop and learn more slowly, parents may suspect or have concerns about their child's development before they reach school age (NICHCY, 2015b). In some cases, there may be co-occurring health issues (e.g., whooping cough, measles, or meningitis), syndromes (e.g., autism, Down syndrome, fragile X syndrome, and fetal alcohol spectrum disorder), genetic disorders (e.g., Down syndrome and fragile X syndrome), or problems during pregnancy or birth that lead to early identification of ID, while in other cases, the dis-ability may not be noticeable until a child begins school (Intellectual Disability, 2015).

It is important for the team to remember that one to three percent of the world's population, or two hundred million people, are thought to have an intellectual dis-ability (World Health Organization, 2001). People with ID are thought to be some of the most discriminated against and marginalized groups of people throughout the world due to the attitudes and biases of others. People with ID are less likely to have access to education, be included in schools or classrooms, or be employed and are more likely to be institutionalized (Special Olympics, 2009).

The impact and range of abilities among people with ID varies considerably. Some children with ID may take longer to learn to walk, speak, perform daily care tasks, or learn in school. Some adults may be fully employed and live independent lives, while others may need specialized care their entire lives. Early intervention and an appropri-ate supportive education and related services can make a tremendous impact in the lives of students with ID and their families (Intellectual Disability, 2015).

Emotional Disturbance

Emotional disturbance (ED) means that a student's mental health or behaviors inter-feres with their learning and/or participation in school. It is defined by IDEA as:

> a condition exhibiting one or more of the following characteristics over a long period of time and to a marked degree that adversely affects a child's educational performance:
>
> A. An inability to learn that cannot be explained by intellectual, sensory, or health factors;

B. An inability to build or maintain satisfactory interpersonal relationships with peers and teachers;

C. Inappropriate types of behavior or feelings under normal circumstances;

D. A general pervasive mood of unhappiness or depression; or

E. A tendency to develop physical symptoms or fears associated with personal or school problems. The term includes schizophrenia.

The term does not apply to children who are socially maladjusted, unless it is determined that they have an emotional disturbance (ED).

Considerations for the Team

IDEA provides a list of qualifying conditions that a student must exhibit to be eligible for special education services under ED. The student may have an unexplained inability to learn that is not the result of a cognitive deficit (low IQ), a sensory problem (hearing or vision), or a health problem. The student may appear to have no friends or close relationships and/or have difficulties developing relationships with either peers or adults. The student may exhibit behaviors that are deemed improper for the situation or respond in emotionally inappropriate ways (e.g., laugh at a tragic event). The student may be withdrawn, show symptoms of depression, or have unexplained fears or illnesses related to school or personal problems. Any one or combination of these behaviors must be present and exhibited for a long period of time and to a significant degree with a negative impact on a student's learning and/or participation in school to qualify a student as having ED. See Table 5.2 for common types of disorders served under ED.

It is important for the team to remember that the range of behaviors and lack of specific defining characteristics can make determining ED eligibility more subjective than for other disabilities that rely on more specific characteristics or assessment scores. This possible subjectivity makes team collaboration all the more essential. The team needs to consider what determines a "long period of time" and "to a marked degree." The team must also determine if the effect of the behavior on learning and/or participation in school is significant enough to deem a student eligible for special education. The team must have an open dialog to consider these defining characteristics, as well as the qualifying behaviors to ensure proper services are provided and inappropriate referrals are prevented.

Suppose you are on a team collaborating to determine ED eligibility for three students, Leroy, Jeremey, and Sally, who have behavioral issues that meet one or more of the conditions. Leroy has average intelligence but appears to be withdrawn (a general pervasive mood of unhappiness or depression), does not appear to have any friends (an inability to build or maintain satisfactory interpersonal relationships), and is failing his classes, mainly due to missing and incomplete assignments. Jeremey is very popular in class but acts in inappropriate ways (yelling out, throwing paper wads, teasing peers) during class, laughs when reprimanded (inappropriate types of behavior or feelings under normal circumstances), and appears to be more concerned about being the "class clown" than passing his classes. Sally has an average IQ but struggles academically (an inability to learn that cannot be explained by intellectual, sensory, or health factors) and often complains of stomachaches and fears going to the restroom

Table 5.2 Common Types of Disorders Served under ED

Disorder	Description
Anxiety Disorders	Anxiety disorder is characterized by anxiety that is "excessive, persistent, seemingly uncontrollable, and overwhelming." The term "anxiety disorder" encapsulates several disabilities that share the common core characteristic of an irrational fear: generalized anxiety disorder (GAD), obsessive-compulsive disorder (OCD), panic disorder, post-traumatic stress disorder (PTSD), social anxiety disorder, and specific phobias. These disorders are the most common psychiatric illnesses affecting both children and adults.
Bipolar Disorder	Also known as manic-depressive illness, bipolar disorder is a serious mental illness that causes extreme and dramatic mood swings, ranging from extreme "highs" to extreme "lows," characterized by hopelessness and sadness. Severe changes in energy and behavior are common with the mood changes.
Conduct Disorder	Conduct disorder refers to a cluster of behavioral and emotional problems in young children and adolescents. Those with this disorder often have difficulty following rules and behaving in a socially acceptable way. Behaviors that may be seen in children with conduct disorder include aggression to people and animals, destruction of property, deceitfulness, lying or stealing, and truancy or other serious violations of rules.
Eating Disorders	These disorders are characterized by extremes in eating behavior—whether that is eating too much or too little—or feelings of extreme distress or concern about body weight or shape. Two types of eating disorders are more prominent than the rest: Anorexia nervosa (self-starvation and dramatic weight loss) and bulimia nervosa (cyclic binge eating, followed by self-induced vomiting or purging).
Obsessive-Compulsive Disorder	Commonly referred to as OCD, obsessive-compulsive disorder is an anxiety disorder characterized by recurrent and unwanted thoughts and/or repetitive behaviors that are performed with the hope of preventing obsessive thoughts or making the thoughts go away. Performing these "rituals" provides temporary relief, and not performing the behaviors significantly increases anxiety.
Psychotic Disorders	An umbrella term that is used to refer to severe mental disorders that cause abnormal thinking and perceptions. Two main symptoms of psychotic disorders are delusions and hallucinations.

Adapted from "Emotional Disturbance" (2010, June 1). Retrieved June 22, 2015, from http://www.parentcenterhub.org/wp-content/uploads/repo_items/fs5.pdf.

at school (tendency to develop physical symptoms or fears associated with personal or school problems). Leroy, Jeremey, and Sally all exhibit qualifying behavioral characteristics of ED; but determining which, if any, of these students is eligible for special education requires a multi-factored evaluation, shared definitions, and collaboration and input from the entire team.

Once the team determines that the behavior has been exhibited for a long period of time, to a significant degree, and adversely effects school performance, the team must then look at why the behavior is occurring and if it is the result of a social maladjustment. If so, the student cannot qualify for eligibility under ED unless the social maladjustment is comorbid with the ED. This can be a difficult and controversial question to answer. IDEA does not specifically define socially maladjusted, which leaves the interpretation of its meaning open to subjectivity. Team members, districts, parents, and therapists may have differing views of the meaning of socially maladjusted (Kehle, Bray, Theodore, Zhou, & McCoach, 2004).

Speech and Language Impairment

A speech and language impairment (SLI) affects a student's ability to communicate. It is defined under IDEA as

> a communication disorder, such as stuttering, impaired articulation, a language impairment, or a voice impairment, that adversely affects a child's educational performance.

Considerations for the Team

A speech and language impairment is an abnormal development of speech or language and is typically diagnosed by a speech and language pathologist (see Chapter Ten for information on the role of a speech and language pathologist). This abnormal development can be found in the student's articulation (difficulty making particular sounds), fluency (flow or rhythm of speech and includes stuttering), voice (pitch, volume, tone, or quality of sound), and/or language (expressing and/or understanding ideas). It is important for the team to remember that an SLI differs from a language delay. A language delay is common in many young children and means that a child's language is developing in the proper sequence but does so at a slower rate. SLI is an abnormal development in speech or language, meaning that it is not developing properly or in the typical sequence (NICHCY, 2014).

Since speech and language begin developing before age three, parents, doctors, and caregivers are often the first to realize a concern, and the child may be provided early intervention services. No matter when a person is referred for speech and language services, it is important to include a hearing screening as part of the multi-factored evaluation. Hearing problems can cause speech and language issues. People having difficulties hearing sounds may not realize they are pronouncing or interpreting sounds incorrectly. Speech and language disorders often co-occur with other disabilities, such as intellectual disabilities, learning disabilities, and emotional disturbance, and it is important to consider a speech and language screening as part of the multi-factored evaluation.

Comprehension Check

1. What does the team need to know when determining eligibility for an LD?
2. What are the eligibility criteria for ID?
3. What makes collaboration essential for determining ED?
4. Why does the team need know the difference between a speech and language delay and a speech and language impairment?

LOW-INCIDENCE DISABILITIES

Nine disabilities (autism, deaf-blindness, deafness, hearing impairment, multiple disabilities, orthopedic impairments, other health impairments, traumatic brain injury, and visual impairments) are considered to be low-incidence disabilities because combined they encompass only about twenty percent of students served under IDEA. Low-incidence disabilities include a wide range of students with differing degrees of cognitive, physical, behavioral, and functional abilities and medical needs. These students may have above average or significantly below average cognitive abilities. They may be gifted athletes or quadriplegic. They may be medically fragile or on the football team. They may or may not have behavioral needs or difficulties with daily living skills. While the numbers of low-incidence disability students may be small, the variety and uniqueness of these students is quite large. It should be noted that as the number of students diagnosed with autism increases, this category may be considered a high-incidence disability.

Low-incidence disabilities often involve a diagnosis by a medical professional of a specific condition, disease, or impairment. Medical professionals may become an integral part of the team by working with the school and providing input on accommodations and needed supports and services. While it is the team's responsibility to determine eligibility for services, a physician may provide input on the type of desk or setting accommodations that would benefit a student with an orthopedic impairment or how to best work with a student who has osteogenesis imperfecta (brittle bone disease) or is medically fragile. Team members may provide physicians with input as to how specific medication appears to be affecting a student, or they may be asked by a medical professional to conduct certain assessments (e.g., a behavioral rating scale for an other health impaired student who has ADHD).

While a team will typically not be responsible for diagnosing these disabilities, they will determine its educational impact and the student's eligibility for special education. All team members need to have an understanding of these disability categories and their potential effect on students.

Autism

Autism is a neurological disorder that affects three million people in the U.S. and tens of millions of people around the world. It is the fastest growing developmental disability in the U.S. and is five times more likely to affect males than females (1 in 42 males vs. 1 in 189 females) ("What Is Autism", 2015). It is defined by IDEA as:

> a developmental disability significantly affecting verbal and nonverbal communication and social interaction, generally evident before age three, that adversely affects a child's educational performance.
>
> Other characteristics often associated with autism are engaging in repetitive activities and stereotyped movements, resistance to environmental change or change in daily routines, and unusual responses to sensory experiences. The term autism does not apply if the child's educational performance is adversely affected primarily because the child has an emotional disturbance.

Considerations for the Team

Autism affects a person's behavior (repetitive or fixated patterns of behavior), socialization (play and developing relationships), and communication (use and understanding pragmatics, expressive and receptive language). Autism is diagnosed by a medical professional through the *Diagnostic and Statistical Manual of Mental Disorders*, Fifth Edition, (DSM-5) as an autism spectrum disorder (ASD). Autism was previously diagnosis in the fourth edition of the DSM as a pervasive developmental disorder (PDD) with five subcategories (autism, Asperger's disorder, childhood disintegrative disorder, Rett's disorder, and pervasive developmental disorder not otherwise specified). Currently, ASD contains no diagnostic subcategories and people who were previously diagnosed with an autistic disorder, Asperger's, or pervasive developmental disorder not otherwise specified are now considered to have ASD. Rett's disorder or childhood disintegrative disorder are not included in the ASD diagnosis. See Table 5.3 for the DSM-5 definition of autism spectrum disorder.

Students may or may not have been diagnosed with ASD before beginning school, since some of the symptoms may not be apparent until the child is two to three years

Table 5.3 Autism Spectrum Disorder 299.00 (F84.0)

Diagnostic Criteria

A. Persistent deficits in social communication and social interaction across multiple contexts, as manifested by all three of the following, currently or by history:

1. Deficits in social-emotional reciprocity, ranging, for example, from abnormal social approach and failure of normal back-and-forth conversation; to reduced sharing of interests, emotions, or affect; to failure to initiate or respond to social interactions.

2. Deficits in nonverbal communicative behaviors used for social interaction, ranging, for example, from poorly integrated verbal and nonverbal communication; to abnormalities in eye contact and body language or deficits in understanding and use of gestures; to a total lack of facial expressions and nonverbal communication.

3. Deficits in developing, maintaining, and understanding relationships, ranging, for example, from difficulties adjusting behavior to suit various social contexts; to difficulties in sharing imaginative play or in making friends; to absence of interest in peers.

B. Restricted, repetitive patterns of behavior, interests, or activities, as manifested by at least two of the following, currently or by history:

1. Stereotyped or repetitive motor movements, use of objects, or speech (e.g., simple motor stereotypies, lining up toys or flipping objects, echolalia, idiosyncratic phrases).

2. Insistence on sameness, inflexible adherence to routines, or ritualized patterns or verbal nonverbal behavior (e.g., extreme distress at small changes, difficulties with transitions, rigid thinking patterns, greeting rituals, need to take same route or eat food every day).

3. Highly restricted, fixated interests that are abnormal in intensity or focus (e.g., strong attachment to or preoccupation with unusual objects, excessively circumscribed or perseverative interest).

4. Hyper- or hyporeactivity to sensory input or unusual interests in sensory aspects of the environment (e.g., apparent indifference to pain/temperature, adverse response to specific sounds or textures, excessive smelling or touching of objects, visual fascination with lights or movement).

C. Symptoms must be present in the early developmental period (but may not become fully manifest until social demands exceed limited capacities, or may be masked by learned strategies in later life).

(Continued)

Table 5.3 (Continued)

D. Symptoms cause clinically significant impairment in social, occupational, or other important areas of current functioning.

E. These disturbances are not better explained by intellectual disability (intellectual developmental disorder) or global developmental delay. Intellectual disability and autism spectrum disorder frequently co-occur; to make comorbid diagnoses of autism spectrum disorder and intellectual disability, social communication should be below that expected for general developmental level.

Source: American Psychiatric Association (2013). *Diagnostic and Statistical Manual of Mental Disorders* (5th ed.). Arlington, VA: American Psychiatric Publishing.

old. If the team suspects a student has ASD, they may request that a parent see a doctor for a formal medical evaluation.

It is important for the team to remember that autism is a spectrum disorder and does not affect all student's the same. Forty percent of students with ASD have average or above average intelligence, twenty-five percent are nonverbal, others may have an intellectual disability or strong visual, math, artistic, or musical abilities. The team needs to consider each individual student's specific strengths and needs in determining the appropriate supports and services ("What Is Autism", 2015).

Deaf-Blindness

Deaf-blindness affects about 40,000–50,000 people and 10,000 children in the U.S. It is defined by IDEA as:

concomitant [simultaneous] hearing and visual impairments, the combination of which causes such severe communication and other developmental and educational needs that they cannot be accommodated in special education programs solely for children with deafness or children with blindness.

Considerations for the Team

Deaf-blindness does not mean that a student has no vision and no hearing, but they do have a significant degree of both vision and hearing loss that causes such educational issues that the student cannot be accommodated in a special education program for students who are only deaf, only blind, or have multiple disabilities. Deaf-blindness co-occurs with other physical, medical, or cognitive disabilities up to 90% of the time. The team must remember that learning to communicate and being able to communicate with others is often the greatest challenge facing students who are deaf and blind (National Consortium on Deaf-Blindness, 2007; NICHCY, 2012a).

Deafness

Less than one percent of students who are served under IDEA are deaf. It is defined by IDEA as

a hearing impairment so severe that a child is impaired in processing linguistic information through hearing, with or without amplification, that it adversely affects a child's educational performance.

Considerations for the Team

A person who is deaf cannot hear most, if any, sound, including spoken language. Deafness does not affect a student's cognitive ability, but students who are deaf often need specialized instruction to help with speech, communicating, and participating in school. The team must provide opportunities for the student to communicate with peers and adults through the student's primary mode of communication (e.g., American Sign Language, lip reading) (NICHCY, 2015a).

Hearing Impairment

In the U.S, about 12,000 babies are born each year with some degree of hearing loss. IDEA defines a hearing impairment as

> an impairment in hearing, whether permanent or fluctuating, that adversely affects a child's educational performance but is not included under the definition of "deafness."

Considerations for the Team

As opposed to deafness, students who are hard of hearing do have some degree of hearing. The hearing impairments may be slight, mild, moderate, severe, or profound and may make it difficult for the student to hear, decipher, and use spoken language. Hearing impairments do not affect a student's cognitive ability but do affect how they learn and participate in school. Students who are hearing impaired need to have a way to communicate with adults and peers as well as be provided with appropriate means of instruction (e.g., FM or infrared system, audio, or hearing loops) (NICHCY, 2015a).

Multiple Disabilities

Multiple disabilities (MD) account for approximately two percent of students served under IDEA. MD means that a student has more than one severe disability and is defined by IDEA as

> concomitant [simultaneous] impairments (such as intellectual disability blindness, intellectual disability orthopedic impairment), the combination of which causes such severe educational needs that they cannot be accommodated in special education programs solely for one of the impairments. The term does not include deaf-blindness.

Considerations for the Team

The team needs to remember that IDEA does not define how many, how severe, or what types of disabilities are included under the law and that many possible combinations exist. A student may have an orthopedic impairment and an ID, or autism and deafness, or ID and autism, or any of multiple combinations that vary in needs and severity. MD typically affects more than a student's cognitive ability, therefore functional, behavioral, and daily living skills should be considered when developing an educational plan (NICHCY, 2015c).

Orthopedic Impairment

Approximately one percent of students have an orthopedic impairment or a physical disability that negatively impacts a student's ability to learn or participate in school. Orthopedic impairment is defined by IDEA as

> a severe orthopedic impairment that adversely affects a child's educational performance. The term includes impairments caused by a congenital anomaly, impairments caused by disease (e.g., poliomyelitis, bone tuberculosis), and impairments from other causes (e.g., cerebral palsy, amputations, and fractures or burns that cause contractures).

Considerations for the Team

It is important for the team to know that there are three main types of orthopedic impairments: neuromotor impairments, degenerative diseases, and musculoskeletal disorders. Neuromotor impairments (e.g., spina bifida and cerebral palsy) are an abnormality of, or damage to, the brain, spinal cord, or nervous system that sends impulses to the muscles. Degenerative diseases (e.g., muscular dystrophy) affect how muscles develop and musculoskeletal disorders (e.g., rheumatoid arthritis and limb deficiency) are disorders that result in physical limitations. Most orthopedic impairments do not affect a student's cognitive ability. Many students with orthopedic impairments can do most things typically developing students can do but often need more time and complete the task in a different way. They may have greater difficulty navigating crowded hallways, need preferential seating, and take more time to write or come to the board to do a math problem. While it may take longer and be more difficult, these obstacles are surmountable. Students with neuromotor impairments do have a greater risk of cognitive deficits, especially if there is an abnormality or damage to the brain (Texas Council for Developmental Disabilities, 2013).

Other Health Impairment

Other health impairment (OHI) is an umbrella category that includes disabilities that adversely affect a student's ability to learn and/or participate in school but do not meet the criteria for any other IDEA disability category. OHI is defined by IDEA as

> having limited strength, vitality, or alertness, including a heightened alertness to environmental stimuli, that results in limited alertness with respect to the educational environment, that—
>
> (a) is due to chronic or acute health problems such as asthma, attention deficit disorder or attention deficit hyperactivity disorder, diabetes, epilepsy, a heart condition, hemophilia, lead poisoning, leukemia, nephritis, rheumatic fever, sickle cell anemia, and Tourette syndrome; and
> (b) adversely affects a child's educational performance

Considerations for the Team

While the law includes examples of multiple types of neurological and medical disabilities, the team needs to remember that those are not the only disabilities covered under OHI. Disabilities such as dysphagia (swallowing difficulties), fetal alcohol syndrome, and other medical or neurological disorders may also be eligible for OHI if the disorder affects a student's strength, vitality, or alertness and adversely affects a student's ability to learn and/or participate in school. The team needs to consider not only the student's academics but also the amount of his or her strength, energy level, and/or attentiveness when determining appropriate interventions, services, and supports (NICHCY, 2012b).

Traumatic Brain Injury

Although approximately 1.7 million people receive a traumatic brain injury every year resulting in over 600,000 trips to the emergency room for children age 0–19, students with traumatic brain injury account for less than one-half of a percent of students with disabilities served under IDEA (NICHCY, 2014). Traumatic brain injury is defined as

> an acquired injury to the brain caused by an external physical force, resulting in total or partial functional disability or psychosocial impairment, or both, that adversely affects a child's educational performance. The term applies to open or closed head injuries resulting in impairments in one or more areas, such as cognition; language; memory; attention; reasoning; abstract thinking; judgment; problem solving; sensory, perceptual, and motor abilities; psychosocial behavior; physical functions; information processing; and speech.
>
> The term does not apply to brain injuries that are congenital or degenerative, or to brain injuries induced by birth trauma.

Considerations for the Team

A person is not born with a traumatic brain injury (TBI), nor is it a disease; but it is brain damage that occurs after birth and is typically caused by an accident or injury (e.g., car accident or football injury) that changes how the brain functions. The effects of the injury depend on the person, the type of injury, and location on the brain where the trauma occurred. Traumatic brain injuries can affect how a person moves, acts, thinks, and learns, leading to physical disabilities (e.g., problems speaking, seeing, hearing, experiencing headaches), social and/or emotional problems (e.g., mood swings, anxiety, depression, troubles relating to others), cognitive issues (e.g., trouble with short- and long-term memory, concentration), and behavioral problems (e.g., problems with motivation or controlling emotions). The team needs to remember that the student and/or parents may remember what the student was like before the TBI, which may cause emotional issues and difficulties with acceptance for both the parents and student (NICHCY, 2014).

Visual Impairment Including Blindness

Visual impairments are defined under IDEA as:

> an impairment in vision that, even with correction, adversely affects a child's educational performance. The term includes both partial sight and blindness.

Considerations for the Team

It is important for the team to remember that visual impairment does not necessarily mean blindness; in fact, amblyopia (lazy eye) is the most common type of visual impairment. Visual impairments can range from mild to severe but do not affect a student's cognitive abilities. Many students who are blind or have low vision can do most tasks that sighted students can, but it may take them longer and it may be done in a different way. Students with visual impairments rely on their other senses, especially touch, smell and hearing, to compensate for the loss of vision (NICHCY, 2012c).

Developmental Delay

Some states use the term developmental delay as an additional disability category for students age three to nine, or a subset of that (e.g., three to five years old), which is defined under IDEA as

delays in one or more of the following areas:

- physical development;
- cognitive development;
- communication development;
- social or emotional development; or
- adaptive development; and

who, because of the developmental delays, need special education and related services.

Considerations for the Team

Teams need to remember that developmental delay is not a mandatory category under IDEA for students three to nine years old, and while some states use it, others do not. Students with developmental delays have deficits in at least two areas of physical, cognitive, communication, social or emotional, or adaptive development. This delay may be temporary in that the student overcomes the deficit with the appropriate interventions, or the student may eventually become eligible for services under another disability category. For example, after an MFE, a four-year-old boy was found to have delays in his communication and social development that require special education and related services. The team could provide those services and interventions as a developmental delay in an effort to remediate the delays before the student is nine years old. The student would be reassessed through an MFE every three years, and if the delays were remediated, then the student would no longer need special education services. If the delays were not remediated, remained consistent, or got worse, then the team could evaluate the student for eligibility under one of the other 13 IDEA categories.

Comprehension Check

1. What are the low-incidence disabilities?
2. Why are disabilities considered low incidence?
3. Why does the team need to remember to consider the student first when developing an individualized plan rather than relying on the characteristics of the disability?

OTHER EDUCATIONAL CONSIDERATIONS FOR THE TEAM

While each student is different, there are some general teaching practices that all team members should keep in mind when working with students with disabilities, including a student's LRE, accommodations, modification, and direct instruction.

IDEA mandates that students with disabilities be educated in their least restrictive environment or alongside their general education peers in the same classroom using the same curriculum to the greatest extent appropriate. A student with a disability can be educated in a general education classroom and receive services and supports in that environment that are not provided to the remaining students. Students cannot be removed from the general education classroom just because they need an accommodation or modification and should only be removed if it benefits the student's education. Students can be educated in a more restrictive environment (e.g., a resource room or a self-contained classroom) if that environment is needed for the student to make academic or behavioral progress. If a student responds better to instruction in a resource room or in a self-contained classroom, then instruction should be provided in that environment. If the student's educational needs do not require services be provided outside of the general education classroom, then the supports and services should be provided in the general education classroom.

Accommodations

Students with special needs should be provided the least intrusive intervention necessary. This means students should be provided as close to the same education, with the fewest and the least interventions possible, to that of their general education peers. Accommodations are less intrusive than modifications and should be *considered* first. Accommodations are supports provided or changes made to how information is presented, but they do not change the expectations set for typically developing peers. Accommodations are designed to allow students to learn or show their knowledge without the interference of their disability or lowering expectations. Modifications lower expectations by typically making a student accountable for less knowledge. An accommodation for a student capable of completing the same assignment or test as their general education peers but who does so at a slower rate could be providing him or her with an additional ten minutes to complete a test. A modification for that same student would be shortening or modifying the test, making it possible for the student to complete it in the same amount of time as her or his peers but diminishing the amount of information that the student is expected to know. Accommodations are less intrusive to a student's education and set higher standards than modifications (Ohio Department of Education, 2011).

The four main types of accommodations that the team should consider when determining a student's education plan are setting, time, presentation, and response.

Setting accommodations are those that somehow change the student's environment. A setting accommodation may mean a completely different location, such as taking a test in a resource room where there are fewer distractions. It can also mean changing the classroom environment in some way, like providing preferential seating by the door, special lighting, or adaptive furniture for a student with an orthopedic impairment.

Timing accommodations affect when, where, or how long a lesson, assessment, or assignment takes place. If a student tends to be more focused in the morning than in the afternoon, a timing accommodation could be administering assessments in the morning when the student is more focused rather than the afternoon when he or she is less so. Timing accommodations can include providing the student with short breaks between assignments or lessons or providing more time to complete assignments.

Presentation accommodations change how the information is presented to a student. This does not necessarily mean that the teacher needs to change the way they teach or present the information but that supports are provided to enhance a student's comprehension of the lesson. This may mean providing audio books for students with fluency issues or visual impairments. It could be allowing a student to record a lesson in order to replay it later to address any missing notes or confusion. Presentation accommodations can also include graphic organizers, guided notes, directions read aloud, or other supports that allow the student greater clarity of the lesson.

A final main type of accommodation is how the student responds or demonstrates his or her knowledge. For some students, their disability interferes with demonstrating what they know. A student could be a gifted storyteller but have problems with writing or spelling, which interferes with her or his ability to write a story in class. Allowing that student to use a computer and/or spell checker, audio record the story, or use a scribe does not reduce the expectation of developing a story with all the main elements (characters, setting, plot, conflict, and resolution) but does accommodate for problems such as spelling or fine motor coordination, which otherwise would have inhibited the student from successfully completing the assignment. For additional examples of the types of accommodations, see Table 5.4. Case Study 5.1 includes an illustration of the information presented in the chapter to this point.

Table 5.4 Examples of Accommodations

Setting

      Different location

      Preferential seating

      Lighting

      Adaptive furniture

      Fidgets

Timing

      Extended time

      Breaks

      Time of day

Presentation

      Recording lessons

      Audio books

      Graphic organizers

      Guided notes

      Large print

      Magnification device

      Visual or auditory cues

      Clarifying directions or instruction

      FM system or amplification devise

      Manipulatives

Response

      Scriber

      Braille

      Keyboard, computer

      Speech to word processor

      Thicker pencil or use of pencil grips

      Spell checker

      Assisted communication devise

      Calculator

      Dictionary or thesaurus

      Different paper—wider lines, graph paper

      Manipulative

Source: Ohio Department of Education (2011) http://education.ohio.gov/getattachment/Topics/Testing/Special-Testing-Accomodations/Accommodations-on-State-Assessments/Accommodations-Manual-February-2011.pdf.aspx

5.1 ILLUSTRATIVE CASE STUDY

Connie is a second grader at C. J. Frank Elementary school and has been referred to the team for a suspected learning disability in reading. She is eight years old and has normal vision and hearing. Her teacher, Mr. Joel, describes her as cooperative and likable with no behavioral problems.

Since kindergarten, Connie has been taught using an evidence-based curriculum and instructional approach but has had difficulty with reading, including learning the letters of the alphabet, decoding initial sounds, and memorizing sight words. Connie enjoys being read to, but when compared to her peers, she takes longer to learn and master new language and reading related concepts.

Connie has received Tier Two reading interventions since the middle of first grade, including Title I reading support and Reading Recovery in which she made some progress but did not complete the program successfully within the allotted time. The Title 1 teacher reports that, although Connie has made some small gains, progress is very slow. Connie requires several "reteachings" of a lesson before she masters the skill.

Mr. Joel reports that Connie continues to struggle in reading and is falling further behind her peers. She has mastered first grade print concept standards (understanding organization and basic features of print and recognizing features of a sentence) but struggles with the phonological awareness and the phonics and word recognition standards especially in terms of knowing and applying phonics and word analysis skills. Connie does not consistently sound out words when she reads aloud, often replaces words that have the same beginning sounds (e.g., dog and dirt), and has difficulty with combining sounds and blends (e.g., "sh"). She struggles with fluently reading early first grade material, which appears to affect her ability to comprehend what she has read. Most other students in her second grade class are able to read grade-level text and complete reading activities independently.

Connie's parents report that they also have concerns about her progress in reading. In talking with Mr. Joel, they expressed concerns that Connie will get increasingly frustrated with learning to read and give up if she does not begin making more progress. After meeting with the team and discussing the interventions tried and the options available, Connie parents gave permission for her to be given a multi-factored evaluation to determine if she has a learning disability.

As part of the MFE, the team decided to formally evaluate Connie using the Wechsler Intelligence Scale for Children (WISC-III) and the Wechsler Individual Achievement Test (WIAT) with the following standard score results:

WISC-III

Performance IQ 107
Verbal IQ   89
Full Scale IQ   98

WIAT

Basic Reading	67
Mathematics Reasoning	91
Spelling	86
Reading Comprehension	74
Numerical Operations	101
Listening Comprehension	92
Oral Expression	90

The team used a failure of Response to Intervention approach in conjunction with the Ability-Achievement Severe Discrepancy model to determine if Connie has a learning disability. The team determined that Connie has a history of reading difficulties even after being provided effective classroom instruction and more intensive Tier Two interventions (Reading Recovery and Title 1). Her performance, visual and full scale intelligence assessment results indicated that Connie has an average IQ (performance 107, verbal 89, and full scale 98), while her basic reading academic achievement results were 67 and significantly below average (over two standard deviations or 31 points lower than her full scale IQ). After eliminating all other possible causes (hearing, vision, intellectual disability, or environmental factors) and determining she had received appropriate education, the team determined Connie had a learning disability.

Modifications

Modifications are necessary for some students to access the curriculum and to provide an appropriate education. Modifications change the curriculum, assignment, and/or assessments in some way that makes it more comprehensible to the student. These changes typically make the curriculum and expectations simpler than that of the students in general education. This could mean that the student is presented material at a lower reading or comprehension level if the general education text and materials are significantly above their ability level. It could mean that a student is provided a completely different curriculum that addresses more functional or daily living skills. Assignments can also be modified and could be shortened (e.g., answer two questions instead of five), changed in some way (e.g., draw a picture or sequence events rather than write an essay), or be completely different with different expectations (e.g., count coins rather than multiply decimals). Modifications can be made to assessments, such as shortened tests with fewer test questions; reducing the expectations, such as reducing the number of multiple-choice answers from four to two; or administering a different alternative assessment with different expectations.

The team needs to remember that many students with special needs can be successful in the general education curriculum alongside their peers without disabilities through accommodations. However, at times modifications may be needed. Accommodations allow students the supports needed to access the curriculum without the interference of their disability. While some students may require modifications, accommodations are less intrusive and should be considered first. Ultimately it is the needs of the students themselves rather than the disability that should determine what types of adaptations are necessary.

Instructional Strategies

Students with disabilities often need direct, specific, and concrete instruction for academic behavioral and functional tasks and skills. They tend to make more progress when given specific instruction and demonstrations on what to do and how to do it, with guided instruction, supports, and feedback. Direct instruction involves explaining the skill or knowledge the student is going to learn, teaching the skill or knowledge, modeling the skill or use of the knowledge, and having the student practice it while providing feedback as to what the student is doing well and what he or she needs to improve upon. The skill and knowledge are also reviewed to ensure the student maintains them and is able to build upon them (Polloway, Patton, Serna, & Bailey, 2013). Students with special needs may have problems generalizing skills and knowledge from one environment to another, such as from the resource room to the general education classroom or from the classroom to the real world. For example, a student may master the value of coins in the classroom but be unable to apply that knowledge in the school cafeteria. Providing direct instruction in these different environments and reinforcing the skills and knowledge may be essential to a student's education.

Direct instruction is often used for academic skills such as in math (e.g., multiplication, quadratic equations or geometry), language arts (e.g., phonics skills or determining parts of speech), science (e.g., parts of a flower or planets in the solar system), and social studies (e.g., causes of the Civil War or locating countries on a map), but it can also be used to teach behavioral and functional skills. Direct instruction can be used to teach a student how and when to raise her or his hand to ask a question, how to walk down a hall without disturbing other classes, how to ask a peer to play with her or him, or how to order from a menu or write a grocery list. It is important to remember that sometimes students with disabilities need direct instruction for skills that students without disabilities seem to understand without specialized instruction. A student with special needs may need direct instruction on how to request help from a teacher, how to ask a peer to borrow a pencil, how to join in a game at recess, or any number of other behavioral or functional activities. It is important for the team to look beyond academics in meeting the needs of students and providing the appropriate education.

5.2 APPLICATION CASE STUDY

Mrs. Peatree is an engaging ninth grade social studies teacher whose typical lesson involves lectures and PowerPoints. Students enjoy her class because she is a gifted storyteller. Parents appreciate her because she holds students accountable and sets high expectations. She expects her students to be engaged in class, take notes, and complete assignments that involve critically analyzing historic material and documents.

Carter is a student in Mrs. Peatree's class with a learning disability. Carter reads at a fourth grade level and has difficulty with spelling and handwriting but loves history.

1. List the possible areas that Carter might experience difficulties in Mrs. Peatree's class.
2. What information can Mrs. Peatree share with the team in regard to her class to help the team identify appropriate accommodations?
3. What are two types of presentation accommodations that might benefit Carter? How might these accommodations help?
4. What are two types of response accommodations that might benefit Carter? How might these accommodations help?
5. Are there other accommodations that may also be beneficial? If so, what and how are they beneficial?

Comprehension Check

1. Why is it important for the team to consider accommodations before considering modifications?
2. What are four different types of accommodations?
3. How can direct instruction improve the educational outcome for students with disabilities?

CHAPTER SUMMARY

IDEA disability categories are grouped into high- and low-incidence disabilities. The high-incidence categories make up 80% of students serviced under IDEA; the other 20% are low-incidence categories that typically involve a medical diagnosis. It is always important to remember that in order to receive educational services under IDEA, educational performance *must* be affected by a disability. Also, disabilities may not be due to a student's primary language.

High-Incidence Disabilities
Learning Disabilities (LD)

- ✓ Learning disabilities affect approximately 5% of the U.S. school population.
- ✓ An LD is seen when the student has difficulties processing, understanding, and/or using language.
- ✓ Evaluators must rule out vison, hearing, physical, or motor impairments, intellectual disabilities, emotional disturbances, or any environmental or cultural factors when determining LD.

✓ Two methods have been used to identify a child as having an LD.

- Ability-Achievement Severe Discrepancy model
- Documenting lack of a Response to Intervention (RTI)

✓ A combination of these two approaches may be used to determine an LD.
✓ Approximately 80% of students with LD experience difficulties in reading.
✓ Students with LD disproportionately live in poverty.
✓ Students with LD are twice as likely to be in foster care or experience homelessness.
✓ Black and Hispanic students tend to be overrepresented in this category, while whites and Asians are underrepresented.
✓ Two-thirds of the students with LD are male.

Intellectual Disability (ID)

✓ Intellectual disability has four main eligibility components.

- Cognitive ability
- Adaptive behavior
- Age of onset
- Effect on education

✓ Cognitive ability is measured through an IQ test, typically given by a school psychologist.
✓ Teachers and parents will observe and assess the student to determine strengths and areas of need in their adaptive behavior skills.
✓ Two hundred million people worldwide are thought to have an intellectual disability.

Emotional Disturbance (ED)

✓ An ED is when a student's mental health or behaviors interfere with her or his learning and/or participation in school.
✓ There are a range of behaviors and characteristics that may qualify a student as ED, causing this category to be more subjective than others.
✓ The team must determine if the problematic behavior has been happening for an extended period of time and occurs to a significant degree.

Speech and Language Impairment (SLI)

✓ SLIs affect a student's ability to communicate; this can be because of issues with:

- Articulation
- Fluency

- Voice (pitch or tone)
- Language

✓ Hearing problems cannot be the cause of the speech or language impairment.

Low-Incidence Disabilities

Autism

✓ Autism is a neurological disorder that affects three million people in the U.S.
✓ Autism is defined as a developmental disability significantly affecting verbal and nonverbal communication and social interaction—generally evident before age three—that adversely affects a child's educational performance.
✓ This category is diagnosed by a medical professional.
✓ Currently autism has no diagnostic subcategories; this is different from years past.

Deaf-Blindness

✓ Deaf-blindness affects about 40,000–50,000 people and 10,000 children in the U.S.
✓ Defined as *simultaneous* hearing and visual impairments.
✓ Deaf-blindness does not mean that a student has no vision and no hearing.
✓ Deaf-blindness co-occurs with other physical, medical, or cognitive disabilities up to 90% of the time.

Deafness

✓ Less than 1% of students served under IDEA are in the deafness category.
✓ Deafness under IDEA is considered to be a hearing impairment so severe that a child cannot process auditory information with or without amplification.
✓ Deafness does not affect a student's cognitive ability.

Hearing Impairment

✓ A hearing impairment that affects the child's education but is not covered under the deafness category.
✓ These students do have some degree of hearing.
✓ Hearing impairments do not affect a child's cognitive ability.

Multiple Disabilities (MD)

✓ MD accounts for approximately 2% of children served under IDEA.
✓ MD is a combination of more than one of the disability categories, not including deaf-blindness.
✓ MD typically affects more than a student's cognitive ability.

Orthopedic Impairment

✓ Approximately one percent of students have an orthopedic impairment.
✓ There are three main types of orthopedic impairments:

- Neuromotor
- Degenerative diseases
- Musculoskeletal disorders

✓ Students with orthopedic impairments may have greater difficulty navigating crowded hallways, need preferential seating, and take more time to write or come to the board.

Other Health Impairment (OHI)

✓ An umbrella category that catches all health impairments that are not formally discussed but affect academic performance.
✓ Focus on impairments that limit strength, vitality, or alertness, including a heightened alertness to environmental stimuli (ADHD).

Traumatic Brain Injury (TBI)

✓ Students with traumatic brain injury account for less than one-half of a percent of students with disabilities.
✓ A TBI does not apply to brain injuries that are congenital, degenerative, or induced by birth trauma.
✓ Traumatic brain injuries can influence:

- How a person moves, acts, thinks, and learns
- Social and/or emotional problems
- Cognitive issues
- Behavioral problems

Visual Impairment Including Blindness

✓ Visual impairments including blindness or any vision impairments that even with correction still adversely affect academic performance.
✓ Amblyopia is the most common type of visual impairment.
✓ This disability does not affect cognitive ability.

Developmental Delay

✓ This is not a required disability category; some states elect to use this as an additional category.
✓ Delays can be in one or more of the following areas:

- Physical development
- Cognitive development
- Communication development
- Social or emotional development
- Other developmental delays

Modifications and Interventions

✓ Accommodations are designed to allow students to learn or show their knowledge without the interference of their disability and without lowering expectations.

- An example of an accommodation may include extended time on an exam.

✓ There are four main accommodations a team should consider:

- The setting–potentially changing the student's environment.
- The time–when, where, or how long an assignment, lesson, or assessment takes place.
- The presentation–how information is presented to a student.
- The response–how the student will demonstrate his or her knowledge.

✓ Modifications lower expectations by making a student accountable for less.

- An example of a modification may include adding a word bank to an exam or making "fill in the blank" questions multiple choice instead.

✓ Modifications change the curriculum to make it more comprehensible to the student.
✓ Instructionally, students with disabilities tend to learn better with specific and concrete instruction. Progress is often made when there is direct instruction and demonstrations of what is expected.
✓ Direct instruction is often seen in the classroom for academic purposes but can also be utilized to teach behavioral ad functional skills.

Remember that IDEA mandates that students with disabilities are educated in their least restrictive environment. It is also important to note that the least invasive intervention should also be used. When possible, accommodations should be utilized before modifications to the curriculum. At all times, educators should allow students to learn and show their knowledge without the interference of a disability, as opposed to lowering expectations.

APPLICATION ACTIVITIES

1. Have the candidates use Venn diagrams to examine the similarities and differences in specific disability categories, such as learning disability and emotional disturbance, or learning disability and intellectual disability.
2. Have candidates research the possible causes of autism spectrum disorder or compare how the diagnostic criteria has changed from DSM-4 to DSM-5.

3. Provide the candidates with a simulation of what it is like to have certain disabilities. For example, have students write or play cards without using their dominate hand, have the candidates write a sentence with their eyes closed, or listen to a story with their ears plugged and then answer comprehension questions.
4. Have the candidates interview a teacher or parent of a child with a disability and discuss how the disability affects the child in everyday life.

REFERENCES

American Psychiatric Association. (2013). *Diagnostic and statistical manual of mental disorders: DSM-5*. Washington, DC: American Psychiatric Association.

Cortiella, C., & Horowitz, S. H. (2014) The state of learning disabilities (3rd ed.). New York, NY: National Center of Learning Disabilities.

Definition of Intellectual Disability. (2013). Retrieved on July 13, 2015, from http://aaidd.org/intellectual-disability/definition#.VaPoK_lVikp

Google. (n.d.). High-incidence disabilities. Retrieved from https://sites.google.com/site/inclusionresourcenote book/disability-areas/high-incidence-disabilities

Harris Interactive. (2011). *The MetLife survey of the American teacher: Preparing students for college and careers*. New York, NY: Metropolitan Life Insurance Company.

Individuals with Disabilities Education Act. (2004). 20 U.S.C. § 1400.

Intellectual Disability. (2015). Retrieved on July 13, 2015, from http://www.thearc.org/learn-about/intellectual-disability

Kehle, T. J., Bray, M. A., Theodore, L. A., Zhou, Z., & McCoach, D. B. (2004). Emotional disturbance/social maladjustment: Why is the incidence increasing? *Psychology in the Schools*, 41, 861–865.

Lambros, K. M., & Leslie, L. (2005). Collaboration between parents, school systems, and community resources in the management of the child with a learning disorder. *Pediatric Annals*, 34(4), 275–287.

National Consortium on Deaf-Blindness. (2007). Children who are deaf-blind. Monmouth, OR. Retrieved from http://documents.nationaldb.org/products/population.pdf

NICHCY. (2011). Speech & language impairments. Washington, DC. Retrieved from http://www.parentcenter-hub.org/wp-content/uploads/repo_items/fs11.pdf

NICHCY. (2012a). Deaf-blindness. Washington, DC. Retrieved from http://www.parentcenterhub.org/wp-content/uploads/repo_items/fs16.pdf

NICHCY. (2012b). Other health impairment. Washington, DC. Retrieved from http://www.parentcenterhub.org/repository/ohi/

NICHCY. (2012c). Visual impairments, including blindness. Washington, DC. Retrieved from http://www.parentcenterhub.org/repository/visualimpairment

NICHCY. (2014). Traumatic brain injury. Washington, DC. Retrieved from http://www.parentcenterhub.org/repository/tbi/

NICHCY. (2015a). Deafness and hearing loss. Washington, DC. Retrieved from http://www.parentcenterhub.org/repository/hearingloss/

NICHCY. (2015b). Intellectual disability. Washington, DC. Retrieved from http://www.parentcenterhub.org/repository/intellectual/

NICHCY. (2015c). Multiple disabilities. Washington, DC. Retrieved from http://www.parentcenterhub.org/repository/multiple/

Ohio Department of Education. (2011). *Accommodations manual: Selection, use, and evaluation of accommodations that support instruction and assessment of children with disabilities*. Columbus, OH: Ohio Department of Education.

Polloway, E. A., Patton, J. R., Serna, L., & Bailey, J. W. (2013). *Strategies for teaching learners with special needs* (10th ed.). Columbus, OH: Pearson.

Special Olympics. (2009). Status and prospects of persons with intellectual disability. Retrieved from http://www.specialolympics.org/uploadedFiles/LandingPage/WhatWeDo/Research_Studies_Desciption_Pages/Policy_Paper_Status_Prospects.pdf

Texas Council for Developmental Disabilities. (2013). Orthopedic impairments. Austin, TX. Retrieved from http://www.projectidealonline.org/v/orthopedic-impairments/

What Is Autism? (2015). Retrieved on July 13, 2015 from https://www.autismspeaks.org/what-autism

WHO. (2001). *The world health report 2001—Mental health: New understanding*. Geneva: New Hope.

6

EFFECTIVE STRATEGIES FOR COLLABORATION ACROSS GRADE LEVELS

Mary-Kate Sableski

Chapter Objectives

Following reading the chapter, students should:

1. Identify the six essential components for cross-grade level collaboration
2. Explain the special considerations for cross-grade level collaboration across grade bands
3. Describe the roles of content-area and specialist teachers in collaboration
4. Describe organizational structures to support cross-grade level collaboration

CROSS-GRADE LEVEL COLLABORATION

A wide array of philosophies, teaching approaches, and personalities likely exist among the teachers within any school building. The previous chapters discussed the processes schools follow to identify and support students with disabilities using the RTI and IEP processes. Understanding the characteristics of both high and low-incidence disabilities, and key ways to support students with these disabilities in the classroom, is critical to student success. A common vocabulary and set of understandings regarding "disability" are important components of the identification, assessment, and instruction process for supporting students with disabilities across the grade levels. Collaboration across grade levels to support transitions from grade to grade needs to be a primary consideration when teachers collaborate with one another.

Various definitions and characteristics of disabilities are used in schools, as the previous chapters articulated. Shared understandings about how disabilities are identified and remediated within the individual school or larger district are necessary. In schools in which a collaborative culture across the grade levels does not exist, students may transition from a classroom in which the expectations of the teacher and curriculum positioned the student as disabled, to a classroom in which the expectations shift and the disability is no longer readily apparent. Students can also move in and out of districts operating under differing sets of standards and expectations, causing inconsistent identification of disability from one context to the other. Response to Intervention, a process that was discussed in Chapters Three and Four, seeks to standardize definitions of disability across schools and districts, using common assessments and sets of expectations regarding success within a given curriculum to identify and remediate disability. RTI is one component to cross-grade level collaboration that helps to develop shared vocabulary, common understandings, and consistent support for all students as they transition throughout their school years.

Comprehension Check

1. Which processes are supported by cross-grade level collaboration?
2. How can cross-grade level collaboration facilitate consistent identification of disability in classrooms?

Case Study 6.1 contains an illustrative case study demonstrating the positive effects of cross-grade level collaboration.

6.1 ILLUSTRATIVE CASE STUDY

One school district found the benefits to cross-grade level collaboration when representatives from each school in the district came together for a year-long professional development experience focused on the implementation of the Common Core State Standards for the English Language Arts. The representatives joined the group with the understanding that a "train-the-trainer" approach would be used, in which the representatives would spend time engaging in in-depth study surrounding the standards, and then they would bring that information back to their colleagues in their individual schools.

When teachers discussed their instructional approaches, their eyes were opened to the differing philosophies and approaches of their colleagues in other schools and to the need to develop common understandings within and across the schools in the district. Two levels of cross-grade level collaboration emerged: within the schools and within the district. Time was set aside at each meeting for the teachers to talk with these groups, sharing ideas and resources and providing support. Out of this time, community was built among the teachers who facilitated the collaborative process.

School representatives brought back ideas from the professional development meetings to their colleagues, and conversations regarding ways to improve the articulation and connection of curriculum across the school were initiated. Teachers who were once unaware of what their colleagues were doing in classrooms down the hall concerning literacy instruction began to teach with their "doors open", deprivatizing their classroom practices and engaging in collaborative conversations regarding students and instruction.

After a few months of meetings, teachers began sharing in the sessions about the profound changes in their schools. In one school, teachers had formed a study group to examine how they could implement writing workshops across the grade levels. Another school implemented a Family Literacy Night as a result of the leadership of the teacher representatives. Teacher-led professional development sessions were initiated, which led to collegial relationships and conversations surrounding best practice instruction in the schools.

This case study is an example of the positive effects cross-grade level collaboration can have within a school and district. When this group of teachers deprivatized their practices, engaged in reflection as a group, and collaborated around shared goals centered in student learning, positive changes occurred.

ESSENTIAL COMPONENTS FOR CROSS-GRADE LEVEL COLLABORATION

Given the varying philosophies, instructional approaches, and personalities of the collective group of teachers in a building or district, cross-grade level collaboration is not always simple to achieve. The multiple and increasing pressures on teachers add to the complexity of the role of the classroom teacher, and cross-grade collaboration meetings can easily be seen as just another item in a long list of responsibilities, rather than an activity that can streamline and maximize instructional time. In this section, six essential components for cross-grade level collaboration will be discussed. These components have been identified in the research literature as important to achieving successful cross-grade level collaboration at the school and/or district level. When these components are included in collaboration plans, the likelihood of successful cross-grade level collaboration will be higher.

Time

Time is a precious commodity in most schools. It seems there is never enough time in a school day to accomplish the many goals of students, teachers, and administrators. Thus when presented with another meeting, task, or goal to squeeze into their already packed days, most teachers approach with caution and critical analysis of the merits of the proposal. Cross-grade level collaboration can have many benefits that will maximize time for teaching and learning, but in order for it to occur with success, teachers need to be provided with sufficient time to engage in deep, meaningful conversations surrounding the instructional practices implemented from grade level to grade level.

Setting aside time for collaborative work across grade levels takes careful planning, but it is a worthwhile endeavor. To maximize the impact of collaborative time on student learning, it is recommended to devote ten hours a week for teachers to engage in time to think and work with colleagues on instructional plans (Darling-Hammond, 2011). Further, it is recommended that teachers are provided with ten days per school year to engage in extended conversations and planning surrounding their instructional plans, specifically across grade levels. Schools are not typically designed to provide this amount of time for collaborative work between teachers, but the benefits of providing such time are clearly in the details. The National Center for Literacy Education (2012) found that only 40% of surveyed teachers received time to plan with colleagues more than once a month. Fifty-four percent of teachers received less than one hour during the school week to work with colleagues. Johnson (2014) identified time as the main reason collaboration was not scheduled across grade levels within one district. A second study completed by the National Center for Literacy Education (n.d.) found that teachers who engaged in collaborative planning regarding the implementation of the Common Core State Standards (CCSS) were more successful in implementing them with fidelity in their classrooms than those who were not engaged in collaborative planning. Recommendations that arose out of this study included more time for collaborative planning and professional learning to allow educators to design and use innovative teaching resources in aligning their curriculum to the CCSS. The National Center for Literacy Education provides an online database at www.literacyinlearningexchange.org to support teacher collaboration, specifically the type that occurs in teams from across a wide variety of grade levels and subject areas. The resources in this database are continually being updated to include recent examples of success in the area of literacy learning as a result of teacher collaboration. Clearly, time is of the essence where cross-grade level collaboration is concerned, and schools and districts need to pay careful attention to the need for devoted time for this level of collaboration.

Shared Goals

As discussed in Chapter One, any group, whether a team, a business, or a club, will be more successful when it develops shared goals to which it can work toward together. Schools are faced with numerous external goals from outside stakeholders, such as standards, assessments, and opportunities for funding. As a collaborative group of colleagues, teachers need to identify the shared goals they have that are grounded in the needs of their students and the specific culture of their school. Developing shared goals to which all the teachers in a school feel invested facilitates cross-grade collaboration.

To refer back to the Illustrative Case Study 6.1, this group of teachers found cross-grade level collaboration to be an effective way to improve their practice. Teachers, who came from different schools within the district, also found that the goals of one school were often different from the goals of another. These differences were due to a variety of factors, including the individual school culture, the needs of the students, the curriculum, the experiences of the teachers, etc. Gaining support from colleagues across the district was important, but until the teachers presented goals to colleagues from their school buildings, those goals were only shared by two teachers. Once the teacher representatives brought the goals to their colleagues, they had to engage in conversations regarding how the goals needed to shift to include the perspectives of all the teachers in the school. Schools that were able to develop shared goals within their individual buildings were able to engage in cross-grade collaboration in meaningful ways to incorporate consistent practices aligned with shared goals across the grade levels.

Where do shared goals come from? How does a group of very unique teachers unite around a common goal that will influence their instructional practices and the decisions they make in their classrooms each day? One of the ways in which shared goals are developed is by grounding them in the needs of the students. Backward design, in which planning begins with the end goal in mind, can result in conversations surrounding performance benchmarks teachers want students to demonstrate at the completion of each quarter, semester, grade level, or years in the school (Guskey, 2014). When teachers discuss what they believe an incoming first grade student should be able to do at the beginning of the school year, this can lead to conversations with the kindergarten teachers about how to best align instruction to support these skills. Conversely, when first grade teachers discuss what they believe their students should be able to do at the end of the first grade year, second grade teachers can weigh in on whether or not these expectations align with what they expect from the same students as incoming second grade students. Curriculum mapping conversations such as these lead to conversations about the collective goals of the teachers and where they can focus their efforts as a group to align instructional practices to meet these goals.

Student Centered

The shared goals determined by cross-grade level teams should be grounded in the needs of the students in the school. Each school and classroom is made up of students with unique needs, and effective teaching aligns methods and practices to meetings those needs on a daily basis. For cross-grade level collaboration to impact teaching and learning, the goals of the group should be aligned to the individual classroom goals of each teacher involved.

An effective teacher, before planning instruction, spends time getting to know the students in the group. Using assessments such as interest inventories, interviews, and surveys, teachers get to know their students' interests, backgrounds, and goals for their learning. In addition, teachers use academic assessments, both formal and informal, to understand their students' strengths and needs in the areas of reading, writing, and math. Teachers compile the data they receive from these assessments and design individual, small group, and whole group goals for the academic year based on the knowledge and skills students already possess and those they need to continue to develop. This is the basis for the assessment-instruction process, and it is detailed in Figure 6.1.

At the center of the figure is the student, who should remain the center of all conversations, both individual and collaborative, regarding assessment and instructional practices. Keeping the student at the center of conversations will increase the investment of teachers who gather as cross-grade level teams to plan vertical articulation of curriculum. Analyzing, discussing, and reflecting on student assessment data, as individual teachers do regularly in their classrooms to plan instruction, should be

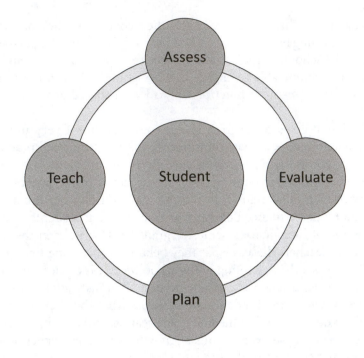

Figure 6.1 The Assessment-Instruction Process

a cornerstone component of cross-grade level conversations. "Teachers who analyze student work together are much more likely to be making significant changes in their teaching" (NCLE, n.d.). When given opportunities, through time and the development of shared goals, to examine student assessment data in collaborative, cross-grade level teams, teachers more frequently make changes in their instruction.

How should these conversations be structured, and where do teams begin to analyze the available data on student progress? As in any form of collaboration, cross-grade conversations should be grounded in the needs and the interests of the group. As stated earlier, one assumption is that these needs and interests are focused on student learning and their needs as learners across multiple domains. Research supports the notion of student-centered, cross-grade level collaboration and identifies shared accountability for student learning, shared decision making and actions focused on student learning, and clear definition of student outcomes as conditions for collaborative practice to build capacity in schools (NCLE, 2012). Grounding collaboration in evidence of student learning, utilizing multiple sources of data, examining data accurately, discussing data regularly with others, and assessing teaching actions in terms of their impact on student learning are the conditions for effective use of evidence in cross-grade level collaborative teams. As cross-grade level collaboration encourages teachers to open their doors and link arms with their neighbors, it can also help ground the school in its central mission to educate students.

Professional Learning

The components of time, shared goals, and a student-centered focus will serve to bring cross-grade level teams of teachers together regularly and for a common purpose. It is also important to consider the professional needs of the individual members of the group, however, just as the group develops shared goals surrounding student learning. Guskey (2014) reasoned that in order to plan meaningful professional learning experiences for teachers, planning must begin with the end goal of student learning. Keeping in mind the shared goals of the group and the outcomes desired for student learning is at the heart of planning meaningful professional learning experiences for any collaborative group. Professional learning communities among teachers is discussed in some detail in Chapter Seven.

As in our case study group of teachers, the motivations for joining the group were grounded in their own professional learning outcomes. The teachers in this group were motivated to collaborate with colleagues from across grade levels to increase their own knowledge and understanding of the CCSS for the English Language Arts. If the collaborative group did not provide time and structure for exploring these professional goals as a means to achieving the goals of the group, teachers would have lost interest and motivation to participate actively in the group. This chapter and others include discussions of the element of time and the challenges of arranging time for cross-grade level collaboration. Once that time has been arranged for teams, careful attention to the professional learning goals of the individuals will result in a greater stake in the goals of the group.

One approach to professional learning that is applicable in the context of cross-grade level teams includes collaborative inquiry (Palmisano, 2012). Collaborative inquiry maintains a focus on the collaborative process as critical to the learning of the individuals in the group. In cross-grade level teams, collaborative inquiry around the shared goals for student learning in the school can lead to productive, meaningful conversations surrounding shifts in instructional practices that may be needed vertically across the grade levels to meet these goals. Cross-grade level teams have the potential to become sources for learning with and from colleagues, grounded in organic, relevant goals. Collaborative inquiry in cross-grade level teams can push professional learning from a passive, de-contextualized individual endeavor to one of support, intention, coherence, and grounding in evidence.

The importance of situating professional learning within a collaborative context has been acknowledged in research. Engaging teachers jointly in locally situated, inquiry-based, longitudinal, and critical examinations of practice fosters meaningful, sustained changes in classrooms. The benefits of collaboration within a community of inquiry for supporting teachers' learning and practice revision are clear. Butler and Schnellert (2012) found that "engaging teachers in collaborative inquiry communities has potential to impact classroom practices in ways that benefit students" (p. 1216). A cross-grade level team can serve as a convenient community of inquiry, developed around a shared investment in student learning across the grade levels in the schools.

Reflection

Any endeavor worth pursuing requires deep and ongoing reflection to consider strengths and areas in need of change. Cross-grade collaboration, particularly in its beginning stages, requires teachers to reflect on which components are working well and which components may need to be revised, as teachers consider the needs of students across the grade levels in the school. Effective cross-grade collaboration includes more than conversations about transitioning students to new grade levels; it also includes deep conversations about instructional practices from grade to grade and how they can effectively be coordinated vertically across the grades.

A natural partnership can develop between teachers who teach a common grade level as they share similar students, curriculum, and instructional practices. Partnerships across grade levels, however, can provide support for teachers considering how to transition students from grade to grade. Peer debriefing is a process in which teachers form partnerships with another teacher to share their instructional practices, then reflect on the strengths and areas in need of change together. "Peer debriefing offers a way to help overcome isolation, sustain collaborative environments, increase retention and make dynamic improvements in classroom instruction" (Hail, Hurst, & Camp, 2011, p. 76). Teachers find that debriefing and reflecting with their colleagues on instructional practices and student needs is an invaluable part of teaching. When teachers share with colleagues beyond their grade-level teams, conversations surrounding curriculum articulation and student transitions are opened and supported. When peer debriefing is systematically utilized in a school to support reflection upon practice, it can be a useful tool for improving practice and developing supportive cross-grade level teams.

Maintaining a systematic focus on teacher reflection on cross-grade level collaborative teams is an essential component to the sustainability of these teams. The Plan/Act/Reflect cycle is an iterative cycle in which data gathered from practice feeds reflection with the team and continuous planning for action. In this cycle, teachers plan by thinking about the practice they want to study, act by considering how to work the practice into their instruction, and reflect by identifying how they know if the practice has worked. This cycle provides a framework for cross-grade level teams to identify common areas of concern regarding the vertical instruction in their school, to make a plan based on these concerns, and to reflect on the process as a team.

In the case study provided at the beginning of this chapter, one particular team of teachers identified writing instruction as an area in need of increased vertical articulation in the building. They met as a team of teachers and planned for key areas of practice they wanted to focus on related to writing instruction across the grade levels. Next, they took action by implementing these areas of practice in their classrooms. If they had stopped there, parting ways and retreating to the isolation of their individual classrooms and grade-level teams, the cycle would have stopped there and the articulation of writing instructional practices across the grade levels would have stagnated. In this case, however, the teachers formed a teacher study group, consisting of all the English Language Arts teachers in the building, surrounding writing instruction. Teachers from across the grade levels met monthly to share their practices, engaging in peer debriefing. They considered whether or not their practices were working to meet the goals they had identified as a team for their students and made plans for next steps. By engaging in peer debriefing and the Plan/Act/Reflect cycle, these teachers utilized reflection as a cornerstone component to their cross-grade level collaborative team.

Community

When teachers talk frequently with one another about their practices, the school community has the greatest potential for success (Smith & Bath, 2006). A strong school community leads to increased collaboration among colleagues who are comfortable sharing with one another, teaching in front of peers, and giving and receiving feedback. Community is both an outcome and a requirement of cross-grade collaboration. As cross-grade level teams come together, a foundation of trust and collegiality has to exist in order for teachers to trust one another. This foundation is built through the elements of time and shared goals, discussed previously. Finding a partner with whom one can share teaching practices can provide great support emotionally, intellectually, and practically. Schools that are designed to provide time and support for shared goals sustain the foundations of community, allowing collaborative teams, such as those that occur across grade levels, to flourish.

The teachers in the case study school wrestled with the foundations of community as they worked to develop a collaborative team across the grade levels. As in any school, teachers had formed unofficial partnerships with other teachers in the building based on a variety of reasons, including (but not limited to) personality, outside interests, and common philosophies of teaching and learning. Teachers who came together to form a professional learning community surrounding the writing instruction across the grade levels in their building had to work through barriers to build community within the team.

Comprehension Check

1. List the six essential components to cross-grade level collaboration.
2. Describe the assessment-instruction process. What component should be at the center of this process?
3. How can collaborative inquiry support collaboration across grade levels?

DEVELOPMENTAL AND AGE-LEVEL CONSIDERATIONS FOR CROSS-GRADE LEVEL COLLABORATION

Teachers who collaborate across grade levels support their students as they transition from one grade level to the next and from one school level to the next (e.g., from elementary to middle school). These considerations are important for any student and, in particular, students with special needs. Teachers are sometimes advised not to talk in the "teacher's lounge" about their students, to avoid "clouding" future teachers' perspectives on their incoming students. It is relevant to talk with other teachers about students and their specific needs when considering how to ease the transition from one grade level to the next and provide clear links between contexts. IEP goals do not change because a grade-level transition occurs, and student success will be enhanced when teachers communicate with one another about Response to Intervention and behavioral, family, or personal contextual issues that may be helpful in supporting the student in a new grade level. In the following sections, considerations for cross-grade level collaboration at each grade-level band will be discussed, specifically as they relate to the developmental and age level of the students.

Early Childhood Grades

The early childhood grade band includes preschool through grade three. Teachers in these grade levels typically teach in self-contained classrooms, sometimes with an aide or assistant. Special education teachers, speech therapists, occupational therapists, and other specialist teachers (e.g., reading specialists) are also involved at these early grade levels to support students' development and achievement in school. Collaboration among all of these professionals is a chief responsibility as young children enter school for the first time at the beginning of this grade band and progress to the end of the grade band, where they must be prepared for the demands of the intermediate grades.

A significant issue in the discussion surrounding early childhood transitions includes kindergarten readiness and the practice of "red shirting" children to sit out a year of school before beginning kindergarten. This issue is complex and nuanced and looks and sounds different depending on the context. The decision to "red shirt" a child in kindergarten can be made by the child's parents, the kindergarten or preschool teachers, or both. Multiple factors are considered in making this decision, including academic readiness, social readiness, and experiences in school. Preschool teachers plan curriculum and assessments to prepare children for kindergarten, and this information is used to determine the most appropriate transition to kindergarten for individual children. Some schools or early childhood centers have programs to facilitate this transition, called "early five" or "early kindergarten" programs. Teachers in these programs specifically gear curriculum to prepare students to transition successfully to kindergarten. Students are recommended for these programs based on performance in preschool, as well as academic and social assessments. Most students will continue on to traditional kindergarten at the end of the academic year. In some programs, the early kindergarten year can satisfy the kindergarten requirement for those children who are ready, based on progress throughout the year, to move on to first grade.

In one school, the introduction of an early kindergarten program resulted in new dialogue among the teachers regarding readiness for kindergarten and first grade, and how to most effectively facilitate this transition. The early childhood teachers at this school were looking for a solution to help support more successful transitions for those students who had completed two or more years of preschool but kindergarten screening measures demonstrated that they were in need of more academic or social development before being prepared to succeed in kindergarten. Young children develop quickly, and a student who does not appear to be quite ready for kindergarten can develop rapidly across the year as developmental milestones are achieved. This makes the decision of whether or not to send a child who is on the "bubble" to kindergarten or another year of preschool quite challenging, as teachers and parents cannot predict how the child will develop over the year. Teachers and parents at this school were looking for an option beyond the traditional "early five" program, which does not typically follow a kindergarten curriculum, therefore requiring the students to transition to kindergarten the following year. For some students, this is an appealing plan, but an option was needed for those students who were ready for more but needed some time to develop more fully in academic and social areas necessary for kindergarten.

The early kindergarten program was designed around a low teacher-student ratio (a cap of ten students was placed on the program), hiring an experienced and knowledgeable teacher to individualize the kindergarten curriculum, and admitting only students who had a "summer birthday". Summer birthdays are those birthdays from May through September, and children with summer birthdays are those most often mentioned for red shirting. The early kindergarten was designed to give parents and teachers one more year of development to decide when the student should begin first grade. At the end of the early kindergarten year, students are either placed in traditional kindergarten or first grade for the following year.

Decisions regarding kindergarten to first grade could not be made in isolation. The early kindergarten program required the collaboration of all of the early childhood teachers in the school to make decisions about student placements and transition. Preschool teachers identified students who met the age requirements and demonstrated qualities that showed they would benefit from the program. Kindergarten teachers flagged students who they noticed in kindergarten screening measures to be on the "bubble" and in need of just a little more time to develop. First grade teachers weighed in on the skills they were expecting of incoming first graders, helping to make those critical transition decisions. The early kindergarten program is an example of teachers working effectively together to support successful student transitions at the early childhood level.

Transition decisions in the early years of school are critical to the development of a solid foundation for future success for students. Teachers at the early childhood level must collaborate across grade levels to consider students' readiness for the academic and social demands of preschool through third grade. Decisions about grade retention in these early years of school are less impactful on the social and identity development of the student than they can be as students grow and become more a part of their peer group. When teachers consider the important elements of collaboration discussed in this book, coupled with the developmental and age-level considerations of students at the early childhood level, they provide students with supportive transitions across grade levels.

Middle School

The middle school grade band involves grades four through nine. Middle school is inherently a time of transition. During the middle years of school, students transition to acquire unique interests, talents, peer groups, and personalities, leaving behind the rapid development years of the early grades. Students in the middle grades are still developing and changing, but their development is less about growth milestones and more about becoming confident, capable individuals. Supportive transitions for students within this grade band must involve teacher teams who collaborate to meet the wide variety of personalities and needs of middle school students.

Middle schools are typically designed to foster collaboration among teachers. Content-area teachers specialize in one or two areas, and students begin to change classes to meet with these teachers. Teams of three to four teachers are formed to provide students with a "home base" within the larger middle school environment. These teams facilitate the transition from elementary to middle school for students who are facing significant developmental changes at the same time. Effective middle school teams work together to support the academic and social development of students as they make this transition. Middle school teams should consider the six elements of effective cross-grade level collaboration discussed previously to facilitate student success at the middle school level.

High School

High schools are traditionally organized according to content areas in which teachers form teams within specific departments according to their identified content areas. High school teachers can benefit from cross-grade level collaboration that also supports cross-curricular connections. For all students, but in particular for those in need of additional support, the initial steps to acquiring a skill may lie within the standards of one content area but grow and expand within the standards of another content area and across grade levels. For example, writing is an important skill in literacy, but it also applies to science, social studies, and even mathematics. High school is a time for students to transition from the supportive structure of school to prepare for college and careers as independent adults. Collaboration across grade levels in high school settings can provide effective transitions for students as they progress through their high school years. Students who witness this type of collaboration across grade levels and content areas will also benefit from participation in effective collaborative teams as they transition to college and careers following high school.

Comprehension Check

1. How can cross-grade level collaboration at the early childhood level support effective kindergarten transitions?
2. Describe the specific considerations of cross-grade level collaboration at the middle school level.
3. How do high school teachers implement cross-grade level collaboration to support student success?

Case Study 6.2 provides an example of the application of the various developmental considerations of cross-grade level collaboration.

6.2 APPLICATION CASE STUDY

In one school district, teachers meet on a weekly basis in cross-grade level teams to discuss the supports being provided to students on IEPs. In the meeting, teachers use multiple data sources to reflect on student successes, growth, and challenges. The goal of the meetings is to provide appropriate supports to students, adjusting each week based on evaluation of assessment results. Each teacher is responsible for coming prepared to the meeting with information about student progress in both academic and nonacademic arenas. Group participation includes equal input from each member concerning student support in the areas of classroom management, pedagogical and learning strategies. Teachers from across grade levels come together in these teams to support the success of individual students.

Divide into small groups based on early childhood, elementary, middle school, and high school interests. In these small groups, discuss the following questions the teacher teams described earlier might face:

1) What steps do the teams need to take to insure each member is responsible for his or her role and has his or her voice heard in the meetings?
2) How do the essential components for cross-grade level collaboration discussed in this chapter relate to the work of these teams?
3) List several topics that may be relevant to these teams at each grade-band level. What will be pertinent concerns for each developmental level?

Now, form new small groups with one representative from each grade level. Share the major points you discussed in your grade-band group with this new group. Identify any common themes in the groups to create a set of guiding principles for cross-grade level teams to consider in their work. Share these with the whole class.

ORGANIZATIONAL STRUCTURES THAT PROVIDE TIME NEEDED FOR CROSS-GRADE LEVEL COLLABORATION

Examination of the essential elements for cross-grade level collaboration reveals the major components to be considered as schools organize in ways to support collaboration across grade levels. Finding the time and space for collaboration is likely the most significant barrier facing any school. Specific structures that provide time needed for cross-grade level collaboration include professional learning communities and team planning time.

Professional Learning Communities

The Illustrative Case Study 6.2 describes a professional learning community that was designed to provide teachers with multiple levels of support to engage in collaboration. Professional learning communities provide the time and space for cross-grade level collaboration to occur, as teachers pursue topics of inquiry grounded in their interests and needs, not those specifically pertinent to their individual grade level. For example, a team of teachers in one school came together to study Writing Workshop (Atwell, 2014) as an instructional model, examining how this model could be implemented across all grade levels in their school to support students' writing development.

Professional learning communities can provide an outlet for cross-grade level collaboration within a school building, but they can also provide a bridge for teachers who need to expand beyond their school doors. In schools that are not able to arrange the time and space for professional learning communities to occur, teachers should locate sources in their local professional network, such as universities or professional development providers to engage in professional learning across grade levels (Berry, Daughtrey, & Wieder, 2009). Professional learning communities are discussed further in Chapter Seven.

Team Planning

Time, as has been discussed throughout this chapter, can be the biggest obstacle to achieving cross-grade level collaboration. Schools that attend to this important dimension will find that teachers are more effective when they can tap into the collective expertise of their peers (Berry et al., 2009). The concept of a team of teachers within a school attends to the essential components to cross-grade level collaboration discussed previously, specifically community and shared goals. Schools that are supportive of teachers working in cross-grade level teams need to provide time and space for team planning to occur. Teachers are typically given time to plan on their own in their classrooms, and this time should not just be "shifted" to become team planning time. Creative, flexible schedules are needed to allow time for teachers to plan individually, as grade-level units, and as cross-grade level teams. Vertical alignment of curriculum across grade levels is supportive of the structure of the Common Core State Standards, which articulates a clear vision across grade levels to achieve "college and career readiness". Collaboration in schools does not "just happen" spontaneously; teachers are busy and time is at a premium. Time for team planning at multiple levels is essential for teachers to engage in deep, collaborative discussions surrounding student learning. One recommendation is to provide 90 minute blocks of time for teachers to adequately wrestle with the critical issues facing them in the classroom (Berry et al., 2009). If teacher teams keep in mind the essential elements for cross-grade level collaboration, time, shared goals, community, student centered, professional learning, and reflection, teams will be able to influence curriculum development at multiple levels, as well as improve the teaching and learning across the school.

Comprehension Check
1. Describe how professional learning communities can help teachers to collaborate across grade levels.
2. What are some ways in which schools can provide time for team planning among teachers?

CHAPTER SUMMARY

Collaboration across grade levels is just as important as collaboration between teachers in the same grade level. In a culture where cross-grade collaboration does not happen, students who once utilized much needed supports may find themselves in a new grade with no support.

✓ There are six essential components for cross-grade collaboration to be successful:

- **Time**
- **Shared Goals**
- **Student Centered**
- **Professional Learning**
- **Reflection**
- **Community**

✓ **Time** is one of the most valuable commodities in schools. With ten seeming to be the magic number, it is recommended that educators set aside ten hours a week to think and work with colleagues on instructional plans, as well as ten days per school year to engage in extended conversations and planning surrounding their instructional plans, specifically across grade levels.

✓ Every team will be more successful when they have **shared goals.** These shared goals can be developed through backward design, or starting with the *end goal* in mind, and developing a plan for how to achieve these goals.

✓ Every cross grade-level collaborative relationship should have a **student-centered mind-set**. Effective teachers use assessments, interviews, surveys, etc., to understand the needs and interests of his or her students. This allows the educator to plan and teach his or her student more effectively.

✓ In order to keep vested interest in cross-grade collaboration, **professional learning** should take place. If the team does not provide the time and structure for exploring the interests of its members, motivation and interest to participate in the collaborative team will diminish.

✓ Cross-grade collaboration, particularly in its beginning stages, requires teachers to **reflect** on which components are working well and which components may need to be revised. Peer debriefing is once process that can help educators collaboratively reflect on their work.

✓ **Community** is both an outcome and requirement of cross-grade collaboration. As cross-grade level collaborative teams come together, a foundation of trust is built through the five other components to successful cross-grade collaboration. This allows educators to support one another intellectually, emotionally, and practically.

It is important to consider the age level and developmental level of children when collaborating across grade levels.

✓ **Early childhood** grade levels are considered preschool through third grade. It is at this point that many children are "red shirted", or held for a year before transitioning to the next grade. These grade retention decisions are relatively safe, as the child's social and identity development has a much smaller impact on the child at this young age.

✓ **Middle school** grades involve the fourth through ninth grades. At this stage, a child is not only transitioning through grade levels but also on a personal level through acquisition of interests, talents, peer groups, personalities, etc. Middle school, developmentally, becomes less about milestones and more about becoming confident, capable individuals.

✓ **High school** grades (tenth through twelfth) are a time when young adults begin to transition from a very supportive environment to a more independent environment. This will prepare children in high school for college or a career after high school.

Finding time and space for collaboration is most likely the most significant barrier facing any school. Two organizational structures that can provide the time needed for cross-grade level collaboration are *professional learning communities* and *team planning*.

✓ Professional learning communities are designed to provide teachers with multiple levels of support to engage collaboration, provide the time for cross-grade level collaboration, and allow teachers to pursue topics that meet their interests and needs.

✓ Team planning can be essential to cross-grade level collaboration, especially when the team has a strong community presence and shared goals. Teachers who are members of cross-grade level teams should not be asked to "shift" their planning time in their own classrooms to work on team collaborative efforts. Instead, flexible schedules are needed to allow time for teachers to plan for their individual classrooms, their grade-level units, and collaboratively on the cross-grade level.

APPLICATION ACTIVITIES

1. As a class, brainstorm possible scenarios that may be obstacles to cross-grade level collaboration. Use the essential elements for cross-grade level collaboration as a starting point. For example, one scenario might be a lack of time for collaboration. In small groups, develop and share skits illustrating each of these scenarios and invite responses concerning possible solutions to the obstacles from the class.

2. Meet with a team of teachers who are engaging in cross-grade level collaboration. This might be a professional development group or a curriculum team meeting in a school. Share the essential elements of cross-grade level collaboration discussed in this chapter with them, and ask them to share how these elements may or may not influence their work.

3. Interview a principal concerning how cross-grade level collaboration is included in the school. What are the major obstacles to cross-grade level collaboration in the school? What are some of the ways the staff has responded to cross-grade level collaboration? What have been the positive results of this collaboration?

REFERENCES

Atwell, N. (2014). *In the middle: A lifetime of learning about writing, reading, and adolescents*. Portsmouth, NH: Heinemann.

Berry, B., Daughtrey, A., & Wieder, A. (2009, December 1). Collaboration: Closing the effective teaching gap. Retrieved on January 1, 2015, from http://www.teachingquality.org

Butler, D., & Schnellert, L. (2012). Collaborative inquiry in teacher professional development. *Teaching and Teacher Education*, 28(1), 1206–1220.

Darling-Hammond, L. (2011). Soaring systems: High flyers all have equitable funding, shared curriculum, and quality teaching. *American Educator*, 34(4), 20.

Guskey, T. (2014). Planning professional learning. *Professional Learning: Reimagined*, 71(8), 10–16.

Hail, C., Hurst, B., & Camp, D. (2011). Peer debriefing: Teacher's reflective practices for professional growth. *Critical Questions in Education*, 2(2), 74–83.

Johnson, B. (2014, August 14). Deeper learning: Why cross-curricular teaching is essential. Retrieved on April 20, 2015, from http://www.edutopia.org

NCLE. (2012, May 28). Framework for building capacity. Retrieved on January 11, 2015, from http://www.literacyinlearningexchange.org

NCLE. (n.d.). Remodeling literacy learning together. Retrieved on January 1, 2015, from http://www.literacyin-learningexchange.org/sites/default/files/2014nclereport.pdf

Palmisano, M. (2012, May 18). Collaborative inquiry differs from traditional professional development. Retrieved on January 11, 2015, from http://www.literacyinlearningexchange.org

Smith, C., & Bath, D. (2006). The role of the learning community in the development of discipline knowledge and generic graduate outcomes. *Higher Education*, 51(2), 259–286.

7

OVERCOMING BARRIERS TO COLLABORATION

Stephen B. Richards

Chapter Objectives

Following reading the chapter, students should:

1. Identify various barriers to collaboration and consultation
2. Cite examples of conceptual, attitudinal, professional, and pragmatic barriers
3. Cite examples of how each of the types of barriers might be overcome

BARRIERS TO COLLABORATION AND CONSULTATION

In Chapter One, we discussed various principles and practices regarding collaboration. Among those were several barriers that bring to mind pragmatic issues in implementing collaborative processes. Chapter Six included numerous examples of cross-grade level teams of teachers collaborating in various ways and overcoming barriers. In this chapter, we elaborate on these barriers, provide additional examples, and cite how these barriers might be overcome. Throughout the text, there are many specific examples of how those involved in collaboration can and have addressed various problems that have arisen. In this chapter, we discuss in general how educators, administrators, and community leaders might address these pragmatic issues. In Chapter One, we noted that Welch (2000) and Taylor, Smiley, and Richards (2015) identified several barriers to collaboration. These included:

- Conceptual barriers
- Attitudinal barriers
- Pragmatic barriers
- Professional barriers

Within each of these categories, any number of issues and problems could arise, and of course these could arise in a combination of these categories simultaneously. Principles, practices, and barriers influence collaboration such that it may occur in different forms in different schools. In some schools, more informal, spontaneous collaboration may be valued, while in others, formal, planned collaboration is the only successful model (Taylor et al., 2015). In some instances (e.g., IEP teams), collaboration is required by law, and this is when respect is required if congeniality is not achievable. So long as teams can focus on the more positive examples of the principles and practices of collaboration, the barriers will be diminished (Taylor et al., 2015). This is important to remember as we discuss each category individually for convenience.

Conceptual Barriers

Schools and individuals develop their own concepts about how schools and teachers operate and the roles of teachers, professionals, families, and students (Welch, 2000). It is also worth noting that the development of new collaboration and consultation skills often takes time and substantial changes in people's roles and how the school operates to develop and improve (Niles & Marcellino, 2004). Being involved in collaborative teaming may very well require those involved to change attitudes about their roles and the school culture. Change often breeds anxiety, particularly when the change requires development of new knowledge and skill sets. Musanti and Pence (2010) suggested that resistance to change is nearly unavoidable and should be framed as a positive influence. For example, a teacher resistant to engaging in a co-teaching arrangement may, in fact, bring up various legitimate barriers, such as those discussed in this chapter and throughout the text. Professional development is a collaborative process that should result in learning through group exchanges, dialogue, and constant challenge (Musanti & Pence, 2010). These same authors stressed that teacher identity and knowledge are intertwined and significantly impact an individual's concepts about her or his place in educational and collaborative processes. For example, a special educator who has taught in a self-contained classroom is expected to shift to a more inclusive classroom arrangement for her students. This teacher may find that her lack of knowledge of inclusive practices and her present knowledge and skills in managing a self-contained classroom result in her concept as only a teacher in a self-contained classroom and generate anxiety and resistance to a shift in responsibilities.

Among other conceptual barriers is that funding does not always support collaboration. Therapists and other service providers may be under greater pressure to provide direct services to children to generate more funding (Hernandez, 2013). This may in turn reduce the use of the transdisciplinary consultation model of collaboration and may be more supportive of a multi- or interdisciplinary model of service delivery (these approaches are discussed in Chapter One).

In a study in the Netherlands, researchers found that among 411 primary level teachers in 49 schools that even the same foci of collaboration may result in different activities and outcomes in different schools (Doppenberg, den Brok, & Bakx, 2012). Qualitative factors affecting activities and outcomes include the depth of the collaboration, the intensity, etc. Also, certain types of collaboration such as joint work and exchange of knowledge may be more formalized through planned meetings, while other types of collaboration such as collegial support may be less formal and may occur less frequently as a result. Teachers also may collaborate more with other teachers working with the same grade-level students (or subject area perhaps) than with other teachers across the school in general. Finally, these authors also found that the more frequent collaborative learning activities among teachers occurred when the focus of collaboration was:

- Teaching a particular group of students.
- Implementing a new teaching strategy.
- Implementing new lesson materials.

(Doppenberg et al., 2012)

What is most important to our discussion is that conceptual barriers can be viewed in a general way, but the barriers one confronts in practice may be unique to the school culture, the structure and frequency of collaborative activities, and the desired outcomes of the collaborative processes. This is why throughout this text, we provide many examples of how collaboration may or may not be successfully implemented.

Attitudinal Barriers

Attitudinal barriers should not be construed automatically to mean an individual must possess a "bad" attitude. Rather, consider that one's attitudes about oneself, others in the work environment and community, and the expected roles of various professionals and community members are shaped by years of practice, experience, and the school culture. For example, Carr, Herman, and Harris (2005) pointed out that school cultures that narrowly define goals (e.g., "good" teachers are those who perform well on an observation checklist) also tend to have a narrow and limited focus on success. Similarly, schools or districts that focus goals on limited numbers (e.g., improving the skills of those lower performing teachers as opposed to improving the skills of all teachers) may find many in the schools or districts may perceive the goals are unrelated to them. Such limited goals may also too narrowly define what excellence is and have temporary impacts on the overall goal of improving learning (Carr et al., 2005). In turn, such conditions may very well lead to attitudes that are more individualized than collaborative (e.g., "I am being singled out as a poor teacher"; "I am obviously a great teacher because I wasn't identified for an improvement plan".).

Some professionals have a preference to work independently of others, an attitude often encouraged in U.S. society (Hernandez, 2013). It is necessary then to interweave professional development (knowledge and skill development) with exchanges with other inclusive teachers, dialogue about the changes to come, how those can be managed, and a shared responsibility for making the new arrangements work (Musanti & Pence, 2010). In turn, a change in attitude is a process, and recognizing this helps everyone better understand how to proceed and how to handle attitudinal barriers. Hernandez (2013) also emphasized many pre-service teachers are not well trained in collaboration skills, and a supportive school/professional culture is very helpful in helping novice teachers succeed in collaboration. Effective collaboration relies on organizational capacity and the contextual setting in which collaboration occurs (Hernandez, 2013). Best practice strategies for overcoming these barriers are discussed in a later section.

Pragmatic Barriers

Pragmatic barriers are often logistical in nature and significantly impact formal, planned collaboration, and consultation processes. Scheduling time for planning is typically a challenge, as well as the competing responsibilities of those involved (Welch, 2000; Taylor et al., 2015). Gajda and Koliba (2008) suggested, however, that merely creating space and time for teachers to interact is not sufficient to ensure good collaboration. While arranging space and time are obviously necessary, Gajda and Koliba (2008) stated that guidance for teachers and personnel on how to improve their dialogue, decision making, actions, and evaluation of outcomes are requisite as well. Several strategies for cross-level teams were included in Chapter Six that illustrate best use of time.

Administrators are often at the forefront of providing solutions to such pragmatic barriers. It is imperative to successful collaborative teams to have leaders who themselves demonstrate the skills they expect from other school personnel. Gajda and Koliba (2008) stressed that teachers are more likely to be engaged in collaborative activities when they experience and witness collaboration among administrators and faculty. These same authors noted that administrators must also be prepared to evaluate the quality of collaborative teams. This might occur through identifying and taking stock of teacher teams, reconfiguring teams as needed, using a rubric to evaluate the quality of the collaborative activities and outcomes, providing support and making revisions as needed, and, finally, celebrating and recognizing the achievements of collaborative teams (Gajda & Koliba, 2008).

Teachers, other personnel, and administrators can ensure that collaboration time is used wisely. Murawski (2012) offered the following suggestions specifically for co-teachers, but they are adapted here to apply to any collaborative team:

- Make sure there is a regularly scheduled time that is considered important to attend; in our experience, providing a common planning period for grade-level or content-area teams is one way to accomplish this.
- Find a relatively distraction-free environment; this is challenging, but, again, if there is a common planning period (or a period before or after school), this is helpful.
- Do not use too much of the time for rapport building; teachers should not spend most of the collaboration time simply sharing anecdotes or complaining.
- Make an agenda; if the collaborative team is only two people, then this responsibility can be rotated between them or done together. In larger collaborative teams, there may be a single, identified facilitator who distributes the agenda based on input from other team members or, again, the facilitator role can be rotated.
- Related to the previous point, it is often best to identify regular roles and responsibilities, at least for some duration of time, even if the team desires to change those roles among those members.
- Team members should decide during their planning time how to divide and conquer problems.

- Make sure a recorder keeps a list of concerns that are brought up, whether they relate to students' learning or the collaborative team; this way, the team can ensure that it is always addressing those identified concerns.
- Use the time for regular assessment and feedback; this assessment and feedback should focus both on the quality of the collaborative process as well as the identified outcomes to be accomplished.
- Document the planning done both in the formal time and setting, as well as during less formal opportunities; this allows the team to evaluate if perhaps too much time is being spent in informal opportunities and not in more formal settings with a specific agenda.
- A final suggestion by Murawski (2012) was specific to co-teaching and that co-teachers should discuss the "what" of teaching (e.g., standards, ideas, questions), the "how" of teaching (e.g., which co-teaching model to use), and the "who" (e.g., which students might need additional help or attention; what other personnel might be helpful).

When administrators, teachers, and other school personnel engage in planned and purposeful collaboration planning and implementation, they can systematically assess and evaluate whether their process is successful, in need of revision, or in need of a complete reconstitution of the plans, goals, responsibilities, etc. DiPaola and Walther-Thomas (2003) discussed building-level support from the principal and general education colleagues as very important in collaboration among general and special education teachers. Laine, Behrstock-Sherratt, and Lasagna (2011) pointed out three fundamental supports building-level leaders can provide to ensure a positive, collaborative, and productive school culture and environment including:

- Ensure that teacher workloads are reasonable.
- Provide a safe, clean, well-equipped school environment.
- Engage families and the community in meaningful and collaborative ways.

Pragmatic barriers are often cited as the greatest challenge to collaboration. In the final section in this chapter, leadership strategies to address pragmatic barriers are discussed. However, even when these barriers are addressed, teams may find they are confronted with professional barriers.

Professional Barriers

Another barrier to collaboration and consultation can be professionals themselves. Professional barriers are not entirely separate from the conceptual and particularly attitudinal barriers discussed earlier. Here we distinguish between those barriers and professional barriers. Professional barriers, for our purposes, include those barriers presented by one's professional education and training, licensure, and specified professional roles often understood through years of practice in a particular school or district.

Kochar-Bryant and Heisman (2010) discussed traditional roles of education professionals. Administrators have traditionally served as the individuals ultimately responsible for school functioning. This often led to a top-down management approach in schools. General education teachers traditionally were conceived as content experts who evaluated their own students' performance, and were often more isolated than collaborative. Special education teachers tended to teach more in isolation, designing instruction to meet the specific needs of learners with disabilities, and there was very little at stake in terms of ensuring progress through the general education curriculum. School counselors tended to provide academic advising and some counseling. School psychologists often acted primarily as psychometrists who focused on comparing students to national norms (Kochar-Bryant & Heisman, 2010).

Traditional professional roles may create barriers; feeling professional efficacy is important in overcoming professional barriers (Hernandez, 2013). Hernandez stated that "possessing a modicum of professional efficacy and a sense of competency" (p. 491) is critical in overcoming hesitancy and barriers to collaboration. Hernandez stressed that professional efficacy and capability "cannot be underestimated" as necessary ingredients for teachers to collaborate with one another and families. Conversely, a lack of a sense of efficacy and professional abilities may make the prospect of collaborating with other teachers appear to be a daunting or even intimidating task.

In one study in the United Kingdom, researchers investigated the impacts of pedagogical and physical space changes in a secondary school (Woolner, Clark, Laing, Thomas, & Tiplady, 2014). They noted two important areas of concern about changing educational practices. One was how changes would impact student performance and in turn how performance might affect the school's success. A second area of concern was related to organizational problems, time management, and how to work effectively within the entire school to improve learning outcomes (Woolner et al., 2014). These two areas of concern serve to illustrate the professional barriers teachers and leaders confront, as well as logistical issues, such as providing planning time.

Farris-Berg, Dirkswager, and Junge (2013) emphasized that teacher autonomy is important in facilitating school change. Empowered teachers also tend to be responsible and collaborative educators. Autonomy may be best practiced through community rather than in isolation. Autonomous teachers believe in collaboration for overall school success rather than individual success. While teachers confess collaboration can be challenging for many reasons, establishing a culture of interdependence among teachers and leaders, encouraging an open flow of ideas and suggestions from all constituents, being good listeners who strive to understand others' viewpoints, and valuing differences among educators are characteristics of autonomous teachers working in community (Farris-Berg et al., 2013). Empowerment is a key element to encouraging teams and team members to work together. In the following section, we discuss various strategies that have been successful in empowering educators and helping them overcome the myriad barriers to collaboration and consultation. Case Study 7.1 includes an illustration of various barriers to collaboration.

Comprehension Check

1. Provide examples of attitudinal barriers.
2. Provide examples of conceptual barriers.
3. Provide examples of professional barriers.
4. Provide examples of pragmatic barriers.

7.1 ILLUSTRATIVE CASE STUDY

Ms. Woodward and Ms. Henry are teachers at Majestic Middle School. Ms. Woodward has been teaching seventh grade English Language Arts for 13 years. Ms. Henry is in her second year working as a special education teacher. Both are assigned to the same seventh grade level team for planning, instruction, assessment, and support. They both work on a team with other seventh grade teachers who serve the same group of students.

Initially, Ms. Henry was enthusiastic about working with the general education teachers on the team. However, after the first two team meetings, she was feeling somewhat dismayed. First, two general education teachers stated that Ms. Henry was the resource room teacher and wanted to know when she was planning to serve the IEP students in their classes. When Ms. Henry suggested the possibility of co-teaching, the two teachers remarked, "We've always sent our students to the resource room. Why should we change?"

Second, when Ms. Henry asked if anyone was interested in co-teaching or another method of delivering services aside from the resource room, she was answered with, "Those students need their time with you. You are the one best trained to handle their issues. Besides, we're not certified to work with students on IEPs."

Finally, Ms. Woodward expressed she would be interested in co-teaching. She explained that while she was not a trained special education teacher, she believed she had learned many useful strategies to help students on IEPs and all learners in her classes. She also stated that she always felt that when her students were sent to the resource room in the past, the students were missing out on the learning occurring in her general education class. She stated, "I think two heads are better than one in planning and teaching."

Later, Ms. Woodward and Ms. Henry met with the school principal to ask for her support and to ensure they had mutual time for planning. The school principal liked their ideas so much, she decided to encourage all the grade-level teams to move toward co-teaching models.

OVERCOMING BARRIERS TO COLLABORATION AND CONSULTATION

Strategies that are used to overcome conceptual barriers may also be effective in overcoming attitudinal, conceptual, and professional barriers. Among these strategies are professional learning communities and university-school partnerships in pre-service teacher education. Duyar, Gumus, and Bellibas (2013) noted that teacher collaboration in schools also supports teacher's feelings of self-efficacy and job satisfaction. Also of particular importance are strategies used by educational leaders to support and encourage collaboration and consultation. Leadership strategies are especially necessary in addressing pragmatic barriers.

*Using Professional Development Learning Communities to Overcome
Conceptual and Attitudinal Barriers*

Professional Development Learning Communities (sometimes referred to simply as professional learning communities or PLCs) are commonly used today in schools. Examples were provided in Chapter Six related to cross-grade level teams. Similar entities include teacher communities of practice (Borg, 2012) or professional learning groups (Sheety & Rundell, 2012). Nevertheless, there is not universal agreement on what PLCs are, how they should be formed, or how they should be sustained (Dooner, Mandzuk, & Clifton, 2008). We will use the term PLCs to refer to these various team names.

Borg (2012) pointed out that PLCs (she used the term communities of practice) need system-level support to get a PLC up and running. First, members need time to develop collegial relationships, engage in professional development, share and gain knowledge, and achieve balanced workloads. Second, school leaders need to provide support and recognition. Creating time for PLCs, managing staffing, and providing release-time for collaborative planning are examples of direct support. Third, members of the PLC require a dedication to shared responsibility, negotiating differences, valuing group professional development, and openly recognizing successes (Borg, 2012). PLCs can take different forms depending on their overall purposes.

Thessin and Starr (2011) reported on one district's PLC development. The Stamford PLC Cycle includes the following steps:

- Inquiry–PLC members research instructional areas of focus.
- Analysis of data–available data are reviewed to identify learner-centered issues to be addressed.
- Examine student work samples to gain a clearer picture.
- Examine instructional practices–members observe one another teaching and provide feedback and debriefing.
- Student progress is assessed using common methods and areas for reteaching and review are identified.
- Members reflect on the teaching-learning cycle and establish an action plan to keep the PLC moving forward.

(Thessin & Starr, 2011)

Clearly, the Stamford PLC model is aimed at improving the assessment-learning cycle presented in Figure 6.1 in Chapter Six. Teachers benefit from a systematic approach to problems and having the support, knowledge, and skills available from other teachers. However, the Stamford model is just one example of a PLC.

Sheety and Rundell (2012) presented another model for a PLC (their term was professional learning group). In this model, the members each get opportunities to present a problem or issue. Other members get substantial time to provide feedback and suggestions to the learner who has presented the question or issue. The presenter then selects two suggestions for follow-up or implementation. The process is repeated eventually for each learner in the group (Sheety & Rundell, 2012). This model may include a focus on student learning outcomes, but the open-ended nature of the process allows members to present problems and issues not directly related to measurable student learning outcomes. For example, one group participant in this study asked about dealing with a learner answering a cell phone during school counseling sessions.

Still another model of a PLC focused on pre-service teacher growth and development. Rigelman and Ruben (2012) reported on PLCs that included teacher education candidates, mentor K–12 teachers, and university faculty. These PLCs could also be nested to include PLCs for teacher candidates, mentor teachers, or university faculty. The triad model used in this study is supported by research and has implications for teacher education to develop and sustain collaboration and consultation skills (Rigelman & Ruben, 2012).

Pre-service Teacher Preparation to Overcome Professional Barriers

PLCs are certainly one model for developing collaboration skills that assist pre-service (and mentor) teachers to overcome professional barriers, such as their specific licensure area. PLCs are often cited as one of the better methods for overcoming such areas among practicing teachers. However, for pre-service teacher education candidates, clearly an aim is for them to be prepared to collaborate upon entering the teacher profession. That may not always be the case. For example, some general education pre-service teachers might point out that because they teach a content area (e.g., middle school math, high school science) that they are not prepared to work with students with disabilities or other learning issues, such as poor reading comprehension or English Learners. Some special education pre-service teachers might point out that they are best prepared to provide individualized instruction and interventions and are not well prepared to co-teach in content-area focused general education classrooms. These types of professional barriers can be overcome to a large extent in the teacher education program.

Richards, Hunley, Weaver, and Landers (2003) reported on a study in which 47 secondary pre-service candidates and 30 special education pre-service candidates worked collaboratively in their teacher education program. Candidates in both licensure areas received training in collaborative processes, disability simulation activities to generate awareness of the learning and physical issues experienced by students with disabilities, training in collecting data on student outcomes, and training in instructional and curriculum adaptations. Candidates spent approximately 14 hours in university-based training activities and 28 hours in school-based activities. Candidates were provided a ten-step process to frame their collaborative work including:

- Present a problem for your learner and define that problem in observable, measurable terms.
- Collect and summarize baseline data gathered in relation to the problem.
- Determine a performance standard (criterion for success) to gauge learner outcomes.
- Determine the discrepancy between baseline results and the performance standard.
- Write a specific, observable, measurable, ambitious, and realistic objective for the learner.
- Hypothesize why the learner is underperforming.

- Brainstorm potential interventions based on your hypothesis.
- Implement an intervention.
- Monitor student progress on the objective.
- Determine the effectiveness of the intervention.

(Richards et al., 2003)

Results from this study suggested such organized activities both support positive attitudes toward collaboration among teacher education candidates and support development of collaboration and problem-solving skills (Richards et al., 2003).

As noted earlier, Rigelman and Ruben (2012) reported on a triad model during student teaching to support collaboration and develop collaboration skills. These authors outlined three design principles for a PLC that supports collaboration and skill development. The first principle is to establish PLCs. This model included multiple PLCs that included pre-service candidates engaging with one another, engaging on a team with a mentor teacher, and engaging on a team that included a university faculty member. These nested PLCs encouraged candidates to focus on student learning. Candidates commented about being flexible, taking risks, communicating with others, and reflecting regularly about their teaching. Rigelman and Starr's second principle involves connecting theory and practice. Implementation of a PLC that involved field-based work encouraged candidates to apply in schools what they were learning at the university. The third design principle occurs in application activities working with students. The candidates learned the importance of encouraging and supporting student thinking and learning.

In both the Richards et al. and Rigelman and Starr studies, the importance of candidates working together with supportive faculty and applying their skills in real teaching settings is demonstrated. To overcome professional barriers related to licensure in particular, teachers should be engaged in their professional education programs to collaborate and recognize and use the knowledge and skills of peers and more experienced mentors. However, for PLCs to succeed in K–12 schools or university-school collaboration, leaders must provide supports that "free up" individuals to interact, learn, and engage.

Leadership Strategies for Overcoming Logistical Barriers

Leadership strategies can work in at least two ways. One is to support the development and maintenance of collaborative team processes. The second is to remove logistical barriers that prevent or impede that development and maintenance.

The importance of leadership in school organizations toward the development and maintenance of collaborative teams was illustrated in a study in Sweden. Ohlsson (2013) reported on the work and reflections of three teacher teams in three different schools. The first team was in a school where there was an explicit effort to promote collaborative teamwork and that effort was supported by the school headmaster. The second team was also in a school where the headmaster supported team organization with the intent to build collaboration among teachers. A third team was in a school where there was no team-building process at work nor were their organizational development efforts to building collaboration. The first team, which had the more explicit and focused organizational and leadership support, also had members who expressed interdependency among team members and a joint task orientation. The second team members described themselves as a team, although not as strongly as the first team. The third team, which had no organizational and leadership support, expressed that collaboration was rare and most teacher work was done independently. Several members also indicated that the team was not important in their learning, although they did interact with some other individual team members. To be sure, the overall success of the teams also depended on the collaboration skills and commitments of its members, but it also appeared the more explicit the leadership support, the more successful was the team (Ohlsson, 2013).

In a study in the Netherlands, Honingh and Hooge (2014) found that there tends to be more collaboration in Dutch primary than secondary schools. Similarly, teachers in primary schools tend to perceive more leader support than their secondary counterparts. However, secondary teachers reported being more satisfied as to their participation in instructional and curriculum decisions than the primary teachers. These same authors suggested that perhaps it was more the preparation of secondary teachers (i.e., more content area focused) that led to their perceived increased participation in instructional and curriculum decision making. One potential pragmatic issue at work could be that if collaborative teams are organized by content areas, this may diminish school-wide collaboration efforts (Honingh & Hooge, 2014). Interestingly, these authors also found that having time for collaboration was less important than having additional conditions in place to structure the use of the time (Honingh & Hooge, 2014). In Chapter Six, we provided strategies for how secondary-level teams could collaborate across grade levels.

It would appear that good leaders engage in five actions that serve as catalysts for building and supporting collaborative work among teachers (Carr et al., 2005). These five actions include:

- Critical analysis of the initial state of affairs and ongoing analysis that involves self-analysis by a school leader, analysis by colleagues, and analysis by external reviewers.
- Advocacy for collaboration personally and to internal and external constituencies. Leaders visibly support collaboration at the district level, with the Board of Education and in the community. Leaders also model collaboration and its support and focus on developing additional advocates.
- Leaders obtain, leverage, and allocate resources to support collaboration. Scheduling and budgeting are two important areas where support can be clearly demonstrated.
- Leaders actively work at facilitating collaboration. They provide the scheduling, resources, professional development, and other in-service needed to develop and sustain collaborative teams.
- Leaders monitor the progress of collaborative teams. They identify short- and long-term measures to provide feedback and provide a basis for revision and change of procedures and practices.

(Carr et al., 2005)

In the following chapters on co-teaching, you will read about various strategies used by educators to develop and sustain this important method of collaboration in a variety of co-teaching models. Co-teaching itself can provide opportunities for creating PLCs and leadership support, as well as demonstrate to pre-service candidates how co-teaching benefits students and encourages collaboration knowledge and skill development. In Case Study 7.2, you will find an application example of the strategies discussed in this chapter.

7.2 APPLICATION CASE STUDY

Ms. Fahrnbach is a principal at Carlie Middle School. She has recently become concerned that the collaboration teams in her school have not been working well. These teams were organized by teaching content areas and each had a special educator assigned to the team consisting of general education teachers in math, science, social studies, or language arts. Ms. Fahrnbach is beginning to rethink if organizing collaborative teams by content area was such a good idea. In the spring, she wants to begin planning for a reorganization of her teams. She wants there to be more school-wide collaboration across teaching content areas.

1. Decide who Ms. Fahrnbach might include on her own leadership team to reorganize the collaboration teams.
2. Brainstorm some possible ways in which collaborative teams might be reorganized to support her wishes for there to be more school-wide collaboration across teaching areas.
3. Write a specific mission or goal for the collaborative teams to achieve once reorganized.
4. Write down three ways in which Ms. Fahrnbach can demonstrate support for collaborative teams in the school.
5. Write down three possible barriers to the success of reorganized teams.

Comprehension Check

1. What are the possible functions of various PLCs?
2. Discuss at least one model for a PLC.
3. Identify strategies/activities to encourage development of collaboration skills in pre-service teachers.
4. What are the five actions leaders may take to develop and support collaborative teams?

CHAPTER SUMMARY

Four main areas of problems and issues that arise can be categorized at conceptual, attitudinal, pragmatic, and professional barriers.

It is important to know that:

✓ Different outcomes and activities may be the result of groups who have the same collaborative goals.
✓ Collaborative exchanges may occur through more formal, planned meetings or less formal exchanges.
✓ Research shows more collaboration occurs when the focus of collaboration was:

- Teaching a particular group
- Implementing a new teaching strategy
- Implementing new lesson materials

Conceptually, individuals develop their own thoughts and opinions about the way a school should operate.

✓ Being part of a collaborative relationship may cause the need for some individuals to change their previously held beliefs about how a school should operate.
✓ This change can often breed anxiety. Since resistance to change is nearly unavoidable, it should instead be framed as a positive influence.

Attitudinally, one's attitude about oneself, others in the work environment, and expected roles of group members are shaped by years of practice, experience, and school culture. Attitudinal barriers should not be confused with meaning an individual has a "bad attitude".

✓ Schools that have narrowly defined goals also tend to have a narrow and limited focus on success.
✓ Narrowly focused goals can be perceived by many as "not pertaining to me" and lead to attitudes that are more individualized and less collaborative.
✓ Some professionals have a tendency to want to work independently. This is often an attitude seen in the U.S. culture. It is necessary to then interweave professional development with other teachers to promote collaborative relationships.

Pragmatic barriers are often logistical in nature. They can significantly impact formal, planned collaboration and consultation processes. However, merely creating space and time for collaboration to take place is not sufficient. Here are some important factors to remember to overcome pragmatic barriers:

✓ Leaders should demonstrate the skills they expect from their school staff.
✓ Ensure there is a regularly scheduled time that is considered important to attend.
✓ Find a distraction-free environment for collaboration.

✓ Do not use too much time for rapport building; focus on the issue at hand—creating an agenda to support efficiency.

✓ Identify regular roles and responsibilities of group members.

✓ Keep a record or list of responsibilities and outcomes.

✓ Remember to evaluate both the quality of the collaboration process and the outcomes or goals created.

✓ Ensure teacher workloads are reasonable; there is a safe, clean, and well-equipped work environment; and families are also engaged in meaningful and collaborative ways.

Professional barriers are not entirely separate from conceptual or attitudinal barriers; however, there are some distinguishing factors. Generally, professional barriers are ones presented by professional education and training, licensure, or specified professional roles.

✓ Lack of professional efficacy may make the task of collaboration with others seem daunting or intimidating.

✓ Teacher autonomy and professional efficacy are important for fostering school change. Empowered teachers are often responsible and collaborative educators.

Professional Development Learning Communities are commonly used in today's school to help overcome conceptual and attitudinal barriers. These PLCs need system-level support.

✓ Members of PLCs need time to develop relationships, engage in professional development, share and gain knowledge, and achieve balanced workloads.

✓ School leaders should provide support and recognition of PLCs.

✓ Members of PLCs must share responsibility, negotiate differences, value group development, and openly recognize success.

✓ There are several models of PLCs; any of which may be utilized to fit best with any group of professionals.

✓ Strong leaders engage in five actions that serve as catalysts for building and supporting collaborative relationships.

• Critical analysis of the initial state of affairs and ongoing analyses
• Advocacy for collaboration personally and to internal and external constituencies
• Obtain, leverage, and allocate resources to support collaboration
• Actively work at facilitating collaboration
• Monitor the progress of collaborative teams

APPLICATION ACTIVITY

1. Attend campus meetings. Afterwards, ask the facilitator how she/he organizes, leads, and follows up meetings. Compare how different facilitators work.

REFERENCES

Borg, T. (2012). The evolution of a teacher community of practice: Identifying facilitating and constraining factors. *Studies in Continuing Education*, 34(3), 301–317.

Carr, J. F., Herman, N., & Harris, D. E. (2005). *Creating dynamic schools through mentoring, coaching, and collaboration*. Alexandria, VA: Association for Supervision and Curriculum Development.

DiPaola, M. F., & Walther-Thomas, C. (2003). *Principals and special education: The critical role of school leaders*. Gainesville, FL: Center on Personnel Studies in Special Education.

Dooner, A. M., Mandzuk, D., & Clifton, R. A. (2008). Stages of collaboration and the realities of professional learning communities. *Teaching and Teacher Education*, 24(3), 564–574.

Doppenberg, J. J., den Brok, P. J., & Bakx, A.W.E.A. (2012). Collaborative teacher learning across foci of collaboration: Perceived activities and outcomes. *Teaching and Teacher Education*, 28, 899–910.

Duyar, I., Gumus, S., & Sukru Bellibas, M. (2013). Multilevel analysis of teacher work attitudes: The influence of principal leadership and teacher collaboration. *International Journal of Educational Management*, 27(7), 700–719.

Farris-Berg, K., Dirkswager, E., & Junge, A. (2013). *Trusting teachers with school success*. Lanham, MD: Rowman & Littlefield.

Gajda, R., & Koliba, C. J. (2008). Evaluating and improving the quality of teacher collaboration. A field-tested framework for secondary school leaders. *NASSP Bulletin*, 92(2), 133–153.

Hernandez, S. J. (2013). Collaboration in special education: Its history, evolution, and critical factors necessary for successful implementation. *US-China Education Review B*, 3(6), 480–498.

Honingh, M., & Hooge, E. (2014). The effect of school-leader support and participation in decision making on teacher collaboration in Dutch primary and secondary schools. *Educational Management Administration & Leadership*, 42(1), 75–98.

Kochar-Bryant, C.A., & Heisman, A. (2010). *Effective collaboration for educating the whole child*. Thousand Oaks, CA: Corwin.

Laine, S., Behrstock-Sherratt, E., & Lasagna, M. (2011). *Improving teacher quality: A guide for education leaders*. San Francisco, CA: Jossey-Bass.

Murawski, W. W. (2012). 10 tips for using co-planning time more efficiently. *Teaching Exceptional Children*, 44(4), 8–15.

Musanti, S. I., & Pence, L. (2010). Collaboration and teacher development: Unpacking resistance, constructing knowledge, and navigating identities. *Teacher Education Quarterly*, Winter, 2010, 37, 73–89.

Niles, W. J., & Marcellino, P. A. (2004). Needs-based negotiation: A promising practice in school collaboration. *Teacher Education and Special Education*, 27, 419–432.

Ohlsson, J. (2013). Team learning: Collective reflection processes in teacher teams. *Journal of Workplace Learning*, 25(5), 296–309.

Richards, S. B., Hunley, S., Weaver, R., & Landers, M. F. (2003). A proposed model for teaching collaboration skills to general and special education preservice candidates. *Teacher Education and Special Education: The Journal of the Teacher Education Division of the Council for Exceptional Children*, 26(3), 246–250.

Rigelman, N. M., & Ruben, B. (2012). Creating foundations for collaboration in schools: Utilizing professional learning communities to support teacher candidate learning and visions of teaching. *Teaching and Teacher Education*, 28(7), 979–989.

Sheety, A., & Rundell, F. (2012). A PLG (professional learning group): How to stimulate learners' engagement in problem-solving. *Online Submission. US-China Education Review*, 5, 497–503.

Taylor, R. L., Smiley, L. R., & Richards, S. B. (2015). *Exceptional students: Preparing teachers for the 21st century* (2nd ed.). New York, NY: McGraw-Hill Education.

Thessin, R. A., & Starr, J. P. (2011). Supporting the growth of effective professional learning communities districtwide: Teachers do not magically know how to work with colleagues; districts must support and lead that work if PLCs are to live up to their potential. *Phi Delta Kappan*, 92(6), 48.

Welch, M. (2000). Collaboration as a tool for inclusion. In S. E. Wade (Ed.), *Inclusive education: A casebook and readings for prospective and practicing teachers* (pp. 71–96). Mahwah, NJ: Erlbaum.

Woolner, P., Clark, J., Laing, K., Thomas, U., & Tiplady, L. (2014). A school tries to change: How leaders and teachers understand changes to space and practices in a UK secondary school. *Improving Schools*, 17(2), 148–162.

8

CO-TEACHING MODELS

Mary-Kate Sableski

Chapter Objectives

Following reading the chapter, students should:

1. Discuss the rationale for co-teaching
2. Describe the characteristics of co-teaching
3. Describe the six co-teaching models
4. Apply the co-teaching models to practical examples
5. List the conditions necessary for successful co-teaching partnerships

WHY CO-TEACHING?

Co-teaching currently represents a major aspect of the collaborative efforts among teachers working with students with disabilities in inclusive settings, but it can be used with any diverse group of students. It can be successfully implemented with students with mild to severe disabilities and with young children, as well as students at the secondary level. Proponents of co-teaching stress that it takes advantage of the unique knowledge and skills each teacher brings to the classroom. Co-teaching requires that teachers plan to use their classroom space to best meet the needs of all students and to work collaboratively to plan lessons, use materials, and monitor student progress. Co-teaching is generally defined as two educators sharing space and materials to collaboratively plan and provide instruction to a group of diverse students (Mastropieri, Scruggs, Graetz, Norland, Gardizi, & McDuffie, 2005; Brown, Howerter, & Morgan, 2013).

Co-teaching as an instructional model was originally developed to support the education of students with special needs in general education classroom settings

(Murawski & Dieker, 2004; Magiera, Smith, Zigmond & Gebauer, 2005; Sileo & Van Garderen, 2010; Graziano & Navarrete, 2012). Over 61% of students with disabilities ages 6 through 21 years are educated over 80% of the school day in the general education setting as the least restrictive environment (U.S. Department of Education, 2010). Co-teaching is a natural evolution of the components of IDEA and the least restrictive environment (LRE) in which students with disabilities are educated within the environment that meets their needs with the least amount of restrictions on their access to typical settings. This legislation was reinforced by the No Child Left Behind Act, which emphasized the need for all students to make Adequate Yearly Progress (AYP), and introduced accountability measures for all stakeholders in the education of students with and without disabilities. The introduction of the Common Core State Standards in 43 U.S. states has further stipulated that all students should be taught to read texts of grade-level complexity to prepare for the demands of college and career (Shanahan, 2015). Co-teaching is an instructional method that is supportive of reform efforts and legislation aimed at increasing student achievement (Murawski & Hughes, 2009; Graziano & Navarrete, 2012).

Co-teaching can have a positive impact on student learning, meeting not only the needs of students on IEPs, but of all learners in the classroom (Wilson & Michaels, 2006). Despite what is known about its potentially positive effects on student learning, many teachers do not feel prepared to engage in this practice. Thus it is important that teacher candidates consider the components of co-teaching as part of their preparation for teaching and working effectively with colleagues. Among the factors identified as critical to the implementation of co-teaching, several remain salient throughout the research. These critical factors include administrative support, professional development or training, time for collaborative planning, and mutual willingness to engage in co-teaching on the part of all partners (Taylor, Smiley, & Richards, 2015). Co-teaching has been described as akin to a professional marriage (Kohler-Evans, 2006), in which cooperation and flexibility are important components for a successful, supportive relationship. Effective co-teaching partnerships, in which students with and without disabilities are equally served within one classroom environment by equal teaching partners, do not just "happen". Administrative support is essential to match two willing partners who compliment one another's strengths and weaknesses and then to provide training and professional development to enable teachers to collaborate and communicate effectively and successfully to benefit their students. Dedicated time for planning and collaboration opens up space for the real work of co-teaching to occur, including collaborative lesson planning, assessment, and differentiation. Most importantly, as in a marriage, the two participants should be willing and motivated to work together. Teachers who are given support, time, and training to co-teach will be more motivated to take on such a challenge because of the benefits they know it can have for their students.

While co-teaching arises from the need for special and general education teachers to collaborate, it is worth noting that co-teaching need not be restricted to the merging of efforts of these professionals only. Co-teaching could involve related services personnel (e.g., speech and language pathologists), reading specialists, English language teachers, and even two general education teachers. The focus of the discussions in this chapter will be the co-teaching relationships between a general and a special education teacher, but these models can easily be applied to any equitable partnership between two qualified teachers.

Keep in mind, co-teaching is a planned, purposeful use of two professionals to deliver instruction to a diverse group of students in the same physical space (Friend & Cook, 2000; Witcher & Feng, 2010). There are several defining characteristics of co-teaching:

Co-teaching involves *two professionals.* Co-teaching involves interactions among *peers* as professionals; co-teaching is not based primarily on the interaction of a professional and a paraprofessional. Although a well-trained paraprofessional can occasionally be involved in co-teaching, a paraprofessional is not typically responsible for planning, delivering, monitoring, revising, and evaluating instruction.

Co-teaching involves *jointly delivering instruction.* Co-teaching is sometimes misconstrued to be one teacher delivering instruction and the other monitoring or assisting students (with disabilities in many cases). While this model can represent co-teaching at a basic level, continued use of such a model is less productive and in a very real sense may still create a "separate" group for instruction anyway.

Co-teaching is used with a *diverse student population.* Co-teaching should allow for professionals to better address the needs of all students, both as a group and individually, regardless of whether they are on IEPs or not.

Co-teaching involves *sharing classroom space.* The two teachers should both have space and feel the classroom is "theirs" for co-teaching to be successful. If one teacher maintains complete control over the space and materials, collaboration is difficult to achieve. Each professional must be willing to give up some autonomy and control.

In this chapter, we will present models of co-teaching to consider and provide practical applications of these models to classrooms. Within each of these models, the specific roles of the general education and the special education teachers will be discussed. In effective co-teaching partnerships, it is often difficult to tell which teacher is addressing the needs of the students with special needs. These partnerships are equitable, supportive, and collaborative, and they are the essence of co-teaching at its best. Case Study 8.1 provides an illustrative case that describes the potential co-teaching has for impacting student learning.

Comprehension Check

1. Define co-teaching.
2. What are the defining characteristics of co-teaching?
3. What do teachers need in order to engage effectively in co-teaching?

8.1 ILLUSTRATIVE CASE STUDY

Feeling the pressure of state and federal mandates to insure all students were successful on standardized tests, as well as prepared for college and career beyond the classroom, the Northfield School District decided to implement co-teaching at multiple levels throughout the district. After carefully examining student performance results on state tests, the staff learned that students with disabilities were performing significantly lower than their regular education peers and demonstrating significant deficits over time. Students with disabilities were failing to make Adequate Yearly Progress at the same rate as their peers who participated in the regular education environment.

After much discussion among the staff, co-teaching was identified as a method that held the potential to positively impact the learning of students with disabilities. The district staff knew they needed to meet the specific needs of students with disabilities in a setting that supported these needs, using highly skilled instructors to deliver specific, rigorous instruction. They also wanted to provide an environment that was supportive to the development of positive identities and self-esteem for all students.

Once co-teaching was identified as the model to implement, administrators contacted a local university to provide professional development in the form of in-service trainings to all teachers interested and willing to engage in co-teaching. Teachers were specifically invited to attend the training by administrators who saw them as someone with the skills, disposition, and expertise to engage in co-teaching. Volunteer co-teaching teams were formed at all levels (elementary, middle, and high school).

Collaborative planning time was arranged for the co-teaching teams, including supported summer planning time and time during the school week for the teams to engage in ongoing planning. Professional development was also provided throughout the year to support individual teams of co-teachers as they developed a professional relationship in the classroom.

Co-teaching teams engaged in multiple forms of co-teaching, making decisions about which model to use based on their grade levels, teaching backgrounds, and student needs. Drawing on the knowledge they gained regarding co-teaching during the professional development sessions and the ongoing planning and support they received throughout the year, they adjusted the models of co-teaching they applied until they found the mix of models that worked for the teachers and the students.

At the end of the first year of implementation, the co-teaching teams reflected on the process of co-teaching, identifying factors that went well and factors that were in need of change for the following year. Initial data from the first of student assessments indicated that students with disabilities were increasing their performance on key measures, and they were engaged with regular education curriculum. Plans for continuing to refine the co-teaching process, adding to the amount of teams, and monitoring student progress are in place, and the Northfield School District is off and running with co-teaching (Magiera, Simmons, Marotta, & Battaglia, 2005).

SIX CO-TEACHING MODELS

Definitions of co-teaching are consistently accepted as the cooperative instructional effort of general and special education teachers to meet the needs of all students within the general education environment. Although definitions are consistent, the application of co-teaching across settings can take on many forms (Sileo & Van Garderen, 2010; Solis, Vaughn, Swanson, & McCulley, 2012). Six models of co-teaching have been widely cited in the literature on co-teaching (Friend & Cook, 2000; Sileo & van Garderen, 2010; Taylor et al., 2015). Each of these models is discussed in the following sections and includes examples of how they may be applied in a school setting. It is important to remember that the application of any of these models in a classroom should be based on a number of factors, including a close and careful evaluation of the multiple contextual factors of the administrators, general education teachers, and special education teachers involved in the implementation of co-teaching (Reeve & Hallahan, 1994). In addition, not one co-teaching model will be appropriate for all classrooms all the time. Co-teachers need to carefully consider lesson objectives and student learning needs for each lesson to determine what model(s) their co-teaching should involve to be most successful (Dieker & Murawski, 2003). Co-teaching is derived from the word, "cooperative", meaning that at its core, co-teaching models are dependent on the cooperation of all involved for the model to have a positive impact on student learning and success.

One Teach, One Observe

In the one teach, one observe model, one teacher teaches and the other observes during instructional times (Friend & Cook, 2000). The teachers can switch these roles as needed. The observing teacher may be gathering data on the performance or behavior of a particular student (Sileo & Van Garderen, 2010). For example, while one teacher instructs the students in social studies and then administers a weekly test, the other observes a student with a learning disability to see if she is paying attention, on task, taking notes, and able to work through the test without assistance. In another situation, the observing co-teacher would be focused more on the other co-teacher. For example, the observing teacher could, on request, observe the instructing co-teacher to gather data on who is being called on to answer questions, how much time is being spent on each learning activity, and whether the instructing co-teacher is providing clear examples of concepts being taught. The one teach, one observe model involves less planning, less communication, and less collaboration between the co-teachers than some of the other models (Friend & Cook, 2000). It is also probably not best as a "permanent" model of co-teaching but used more on an as-needed basis.

One of the main concerns in co-teaching interactions between a special educator and a general educator includes the equitable sharing of responsibility for the teaching within the lessons. In the *one teach, one observe* model, the teacher who teaches the class will naturally be seen as the authority figure and the teacher in the classroom, while the observer takes on a background role (Friend & Cook, 2000). When teachers decide to implement this model, consideration needs to be given to the purpose of the co-teaching relationship. If the purpose is to support the teaching of individual teachers or monitor the progress of individual students, this model would be an appropriate choice. In this model, teachers have the opportunity to analyze student work

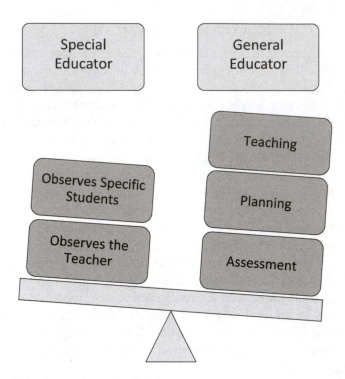

Figure 8.1 One Teach, One Observe Co-teaching Model

collected during instruction, allowing for analysis of student learning as the lesson is being taught (Bessette, 2008). To maximize the experience and expertise of both teachers to benefit student learning, however, teachers might consider one of the other models of co-teaching as a supplement or replacement for the *one teach, one observe* model. Figure 8.1 describes the one teach, one observe model of co-teaching.

One Teach, One Drift

The one teach, one drift model places less emphasis on co-planning, communication, and collaboration than some of the other models (Friend & Cook, 2000). This model is similar to the one teach, one observe model in that one of the co-teachers assumes the greater responsibility for planning and delivering instruction. The drifting co-teacher may move about the classroom, manage student behavior, observe students work, and provide assistance to students as needed. In this model, co-teachers share the same space and students, but they also share more in-classroom management responsibilities than in the one teach, one observe model. For example, the drifting teacher may be involved in ensuring students are on task, following directions, and completing assignments. There may also be a need on the drifting teacher's part to communicate with the other co-teacher concerning the curriculum, instruction, and assessment of students.

This model has also been referred to as the "one teach, one assist" model of co-teaching, to describe the assistant role often assumed by the special education teacher in the classroom (Scruggs, Mastropieri, & McDuffie, 2007). It is also one of the most commonly observed in classrooms (Bessette, 2008). In theory, either teacher can take on the "assisting" role, but in practice, it is typically the special educator who adopts this role. This can occur for a variety of reasons; one of the most commonly cited being the content-area knowledge of each teacher. Particularly at the middle and secondary levels, teachers are often highly trained in their specific content area, while the special education teacher is more specifically prepared to address learning differences and disabilities in a classroom setting. When this model is used as a way for the special education teacher to provide assistance to the classroom teacher, the benefits of co-teaching are not maximized. At the end of this chapter, there will be a discussion of some of the conditions necessary for successful co-teaching. In general, valuing and maximizing the expertise and experience each teacher brings to the classroom and the significant collaborative contributions each can make to student learning are essential for the success of any of the co-teaching models discussed in this chapter. In the "one teach, one drift/assist" model, the expertise of the special education teacher should not be relegated to the role of teacher's assistant, but rather it should be used as a way to enhance and extend the content instruction to all students in the classroom. Figure 8.2 describes the one teach, one drift model.

These first two models, *one teach, one observe* and *one teach, one drift* may be most comfortable for co-teachers as they embark on the collaborative process. They require less commitment but still provide opportunities to build trust, respect, and a sense of

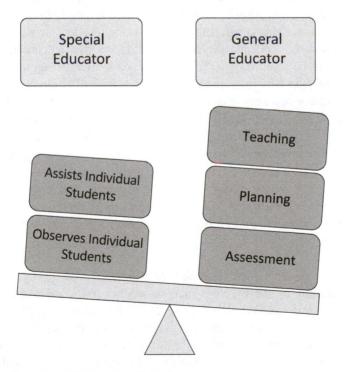

Figure 8.2 The One Teach, One Drift Co-teaching Model

community. The next three models of co-teaching to be discussed (station teaching, parallel teaching, and alternative teaching) are considered regrouping models of co-teaching in which students are re-grouped in some format within the regular classroom for specialized or remedial instruction. These regrouping models help to address the RTI model discussed in Chapters Three and Four. Specifically, these regrouping models will help to address Tier Two, in which students are expected to receive specialized instruction within the regular classroom environment (Murawski & Hughes, 2009).

Station Teaching

The station teaching model involves the co-teachers planning and instructing a portion of the lesson content in stations through which the students move (Friend & Cook, 2000). For example, in a lesson where teachers are instructing students on addition with carrying, one co-teacher may instruct her students on the use of manipulatives to solve the problem, while the other co-teacher instructs her students on how to write down the mathematical computations for the problems. A third station may allow students to engage in a mathematics game that reinforces prior learning. As each co-teacher concludes her portion of the lesson, the groups of students at each station move to the next station so that all students complete the activities in each station. In this model, co-teachers must communicate to co-plan the lesson and the instructional content, materials, and strategies each will use. They share the same space and students, curriculum and goals, and must collaborate regarding classroom management techniques and how students are assessed. This model represents a significant leap in the collaborative process, because now the co-teachers must truly work together to be successful. This model is commonly found among teachers working with younger children, although the example given of working on math problems may not be appropriate to this population (e.g., preschoolers or kindergartners).

Heterogeneous, flexible grouping of students is one of the conditions necessary to help make station teaching more successful. Students quickly identify when one group has been labeled as the intervention group and associate the special education teacher's station with intervention. Station teaching presents an opportunity for the special educator and the general educator to truly share roles so that the students do not see the special educator as only present to assist a handful of students but there to provide different learning opportunities for all. Station teaching also invites each teacher to contribute ideas to the lesson that represent their individual teaching style and goals for the students, all centered on consistent content. Figure 8.3 describes station teaching.

Parallel Teaching

The parallel teaching model involves each co-teacher planning and instructing students on the same material (Witcher & Feng, 2010). Each teacher presents information to a smaller heterogeneous group of students in the class. The smaller teacher-student ratio created by two learning groups allows for greater discussion, interaction, and closer supervision (Friend & Cook, 2000). Parallel teaching is best used for review of learning rather than initial instruction. For example, each co-teacher could review

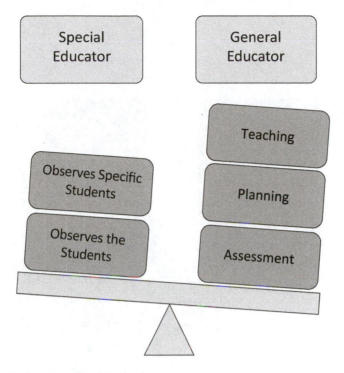

Figure 8.3 Station Teaching Co-teaching Model

with her group for an upcoming test, go over key concepts and definitions, and review notes. This model requires co-teachers to be comfortable with the content and to plan together what and how the material will be taught (Friend & Cook, 2000). Parallel teaching also allows for the application of each co-teacher's distinct teaching style, as the constant is the material, not the way in which it is delivered to student. Along the same lines, parallel teaching opens up space for teachers to design lessons to meet the specific learning needs of the students in their group, rather than adapting a whole group lesson.

An example of parallel teaching includes its use with English Language Learners in the context of a regular classroom. ELLs are not necessarily on IEPs and do not always require the services of a special education teacher; however, students learning English may require additional support to navigate the content as they learn English. In a parallel teaching model, two teachers may assume responsibility for half the class, with the students learning English homogeneously grouped. Teachers would teach the same content to both groups, but they would use different teaching methods to help the English Language Learners make connections between the content, providing time to read about the material in their first language, use hands-on materials to build understanding, or allow greater time to discuss the material in English with the teacher. Parallel teaching, in this case, allows for consistent content to be taught to students with different learning needs (Aliakbari & Bazyar, 2012). Figure 8.4 describes parallel teaching.

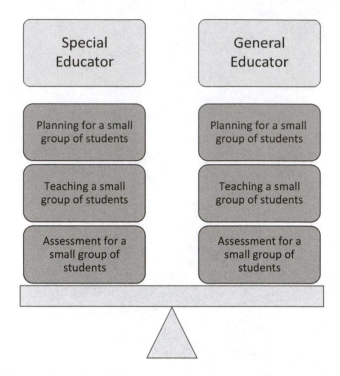

Figure 8.4 Parallel Teaching Co-teaching Model

Alternative Teaching

The alternative teaching model involves each co-teacher planning and instructing the students. In this model, each teaches a separate heterogeneous group of students. While one co-teacher works with a group for a specific purpose, the other co-teacher works with the remainder of the class (Friend & Cook, 2000). For example, one co-teacher might take a group of students who have fallen behind due to absences and reteach material missed while the remainder of the class works on another activity under the other co-teacher's supervision. As another example, the first co-teacher could take her group and pre-teach material the whole class will be learning in the next lesson or the next day. When using this model, it is important that one of the groups does not become a homogeneous group of students with disabilities who are regularly pulled aside for remedial instruction, particularly when taught exclusively by a special education teacher. This is important so that the teachers do not create a static "special education group" in the classroom, discouraging inclusive education. In this model, co-teachers must co-plan the instruction and materials for each group. They should be sharing the same space and the same students over time, both managing the classroom, both familiar with the curriculum and goals, and both sharing how students are assessed (Friend & Cook, 2000).

Attention to heterogeneous grouping and equitable sharing of teaching roles is critical in alternative teaching, similarly as it is to station teaching, discussed previously. Fountas and Pinnell (1996) discuss the use of a "three-ring circus" model to

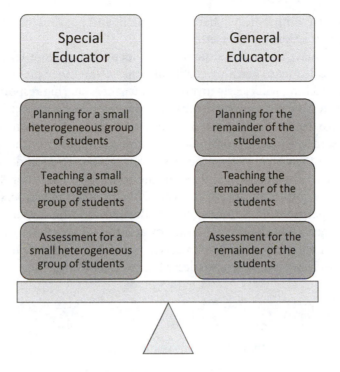

Figure 8.5 The Alternative Teaching Co-teaching Model

provide flexible, differentiated instruction to students in elementary classrooms. In one of the "rings", a small guided-reading group occurs, led by one of the teachers. In another ring, students work in pairs to read and discuss a text. In a third ring, another teacher could work with individual students who need one-to-one instruction in a particular skill area. The type of instruction that occurs within each ring can vary and shift, depending on the needs of the students within each particular lesson. In this example of station teaching, both teachers share equitable responsibility for the content of the lesson and the success of the students. Students know that they will move flexibly within groups and across stations, and they see both teachers as guides for their learning. Figure 8.5 describes alternative teaching.

Team Teaching

In team teaching, co-teachers take equal responsibility for all aspects of the classroom: management, planning, preparing materials, delivering instruction, and assessing student learning outcomes (Friend & Cook, 2000). This model is the most collaborative. In team teaching, students may not distinguish between which co-teacher is a special educator and which is a general educator, as the co-teachers regularly change roles, each taking the lead or jointly sharing teaching responsibilities. In team teaching, "the general educator is the content specialist, while the special education team members are the learning specialists" (Lindeman & Magiera, 2014, p. 41). Team teaching is considered the "gold standard" for co-teaching, as it is heavily dependent on the ability of the co-teachers to communicate, share roles equally, and put student learning first and foremost in the relationship (Bessette, 2008).

Carefully evaluate classroom situations self-identified as team teaching, as many times what is called team teaching is actually one of the other previous models discussed. Team teaching will clearly involve both teachers sharing responsibility for the delivery of the lesson, tag teaming the instruction. Team teaching requires more planning time, more trust and collegiality, and more communication than any of the other models. "In team-teaching arrangements, the equity and parity of the team members is obvious from their roles within the classroom" (Villa, Thousand, & Nevin, 2004, p. 49). Team teachers include two desks in the room, two names on the door, both names on parent communications, etc. The differences in the teachers' backgrounds and areas of expertise will be observable only during planning sessions, during which the content expertise of the general educator and the differentiation expertise of the special educator will work in tandem to develop a lesson to meet the needs of all of the students in the classroom. Figure 8.6 describes team teaching.

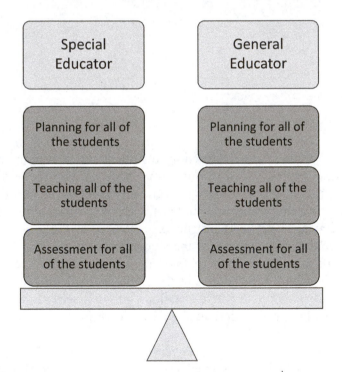

Figure 8.6 Team Teaching Co-teaching Model

Comprehension Check
1. What are the six models for co-teaching?
2. What are the advantages and disadvantages for each model?
3. Describe appropriate applications of each model.

CONDITIONS FOR SUCCESSFUL CO-TEACHING

Multiple factors should be considered when schools implement co-teaching. These factors were mentioned at the beginning of this chapter. Now that the six models of co-teaching have been discussed, consider the following conditions necessary for any co-teaching configuration to be successful. Case Study 8.2 is an application case study to describe the interaction of these critical factors within co-teaching partnerships.

8.2 APPLICATION CASE STUDY

One of the co-teaching teams within Northfield School District at the middle school level, which was not a part of the initial year of implementation, began their co-teaching relationship with excitement and trepidation. Ms. Dooley and Mr. Nugent both had several years of teaching experience and had been in the district for their entire teaching careers. Ms. Dooley was the content teacher, specializing in math and science. Mr. Nugent was the special educator, and he had been teaching reading intervention in a resource room prior to the co-teaching partnership.

The two teachers experienced a number of successes during their first year as co-teachers, but they also faced several challenges. Since they had not been a part of the initial year of implementation in the district, they were missing the initial push of support and enthusiasm and often felt they were navigating the waters of co-teaching on their own. Specifically, the challenges they faced included:

- *Collaborative Planning.* Although specific time for co-planning had been set aside by the district, the teachers found it often overtaken by distractions. For example, Ms. Dooley was a part of a district curriculum committee and was often called away for meetings during the co-planning time for that meeting. As this continued to occur, Mr. Nugent began to use the co-planning time to meet with parents or hold IEP meetings, as he did not want to waste the free block of time in the day. Slowly, the co-planning time was not prioritized by either teacher, and tension arose between them over the best use of the time.
- *Equity of Roles.* Both Ms. Dooley and Mr. Nugent brought different teaching styles to the partnership, and they struggled to reconcile those differences at times. Although the coaches they had from the local university as a part of their professional development plan helped them to see each other's styles as strengths and as a way to provide differentiated instruction to students, they often disagreed over the best way to meet a particular student's needs or to communicate challenging content. Without the weekly planning time as a reliable event to discuss those issues, tension continued to build over how to reconcile different teaching styles to support student learning.

In small groups, discuss the dilemma for Ms. Dooley and Mr. Nugent. Imagine that you are a colleague in the building who has built a successful co-teaching partnership during the previous school year.

1. What advice would you give the co-teachers regarding how to prioritize the co-planning time allocated to them?
2. How would you suggest they reconcile the differences in their teaching style to maximize student learning?
3. Which model of co-teaching do you think Ms. Dooley and Mr. Nugent might be most successful applying at this point? Why?

Administrative Support

A primary need identified by teachers who engage in co-teaching includes the importance of support for the partnership from school administration (Scruggs et al., 2007). Administrator support for co-teaching can come in many forms, from the initial introduction of the concept to the team, to the provision and participation in professional development to develop co-teaching skills (Walsh, 2012). It is ideal if administrators not only arrange for professional development related to co-teaching but also participate in the professional development to understand the multiple layers and skills involved in effective co-teaching partnerships. Chapter Seven included some strategies for administrative support.

Another area in which administrators can be supportive of co-teaching is through student assignments (Bouck, 2007). Co-teaching between a general and special educator should not be seen as an "excuse" to place all students on IEPs in one classroom. This is an inappropriate application of inclusion and does not provide for the least restrictive environment for most students. Appropriate ratios of students on IEPs in a single classroom have been identified at 30% per class (Nierengarten, 2013). Administrators can provide support through scheduling the day in such a way as to allow multiple opportunities for co-taught classes so that this ratio can be maintained.

Professional Development

Reading and discussing the six co-teaching models described in this chapter is an important step forward in the ability to apply these models in the future. Implementing co-teaching effectively involves a deep knowledge of the multiple factors involved in co-teaching, including an understanding of the models it can take on in classrooms (Solis et al., 2012). Successful co-teaching depends upon an in-depth understanding of the process and a willingness to continue to learn about how to engage in it successfully (Dieker & Murawski, 2003). Co-teaching is significantly different from the traditional "one teacher per classroom" model, so to expect educators to understand and implement it without specific instruction in the pertinent knowledge and skills is inappropriate (Friend, Cook, Hurley-Chamberlain, & Shamberger, 2010). Professional development surrounding effective communication skills, cooperative lesson planning, content specific strategies, and instruction for students with disabilities is an essential component to successful co-teaching partnerships.

Co-teachers should participate in professional development and training for co-teaching together as a team (Scruggs et al., 2007). Joint participation in learning about co-teaching will help to develop shared understandings, consistent ideas, and a common vocabulary about co-teaching that will enhance the co-teaching relationship in the classroom (Magiera, 2014). General education teachers need training on inclusion, and the special educator on the team can provide insight into the material for the general educator based on experience (Santoli, Sachs, Romey, & McClurg, 2008). Similarly, special education teachers may need training on content specific material or strategies for the co-taught classes, and by participating in this training as a team, the general and special educator have a greater chance of using a common set of vocabulary and principles related to the content in their teaching (Nierengarten, 2013). As discussed in Chapter Seven, professional learning communities for co-teachers could be an excellent model for professional development.

Collaborative Planning Time

It almost goes without saying that collaborative planning time is critical for successful co-teaching. If two teachers simply show up in a classroom, ready to teach their own lesson, disaster will surely strike in the form of disorganized instruction and missed opportunities for learning. "Merely assigning two teachers to a classroom is not sufficient to meet the intensity and individualization as mandated by the No Child Left Behind and Individuals with Disabilities Education Improvement Act of 2004" (Scheeler, Congdon, & Stansberry, 2010, p. 92). Once a co-teaching partnership has been established, a close and careful look at the daily, weekly, and monthly schedule of the school should be conducted to identify opportunities for consistent collaborative planning time for the co-teachers (Arguelles, Hughes, & Schumm, 2000; Dieker & Murawski, 2003; Bouck, 2007; Scruggs et al., 2007; Nierengarten, 2013). One recommendation is to provide co-teachers with regularly scheduled common planning time during the week (Simmons & Magiera, 2007).

Middle school arrangements seem to work well to arrange for common planning time for successful co-teaching (Santoli et al., 2008). In a typical middle school, teachers are arranged into teams to support students at one grade level. Within these teams, block scheduling is often employed, opening up larger spaces of time in the day for collaborative planning within teams. Interestingly, a meta-analysis of the research on co-teaching revealed that co-teaching is occurring with high frequency in elementary and high school settings, but not as frequently in middle school settings (Murawski & Swanson, 2001). Elementary and high schools that are already using co-teaching or plan to implement it in the future would be advantaged by examining middle school daily schedules as a model to locate time for collaborative planning among co-teachers.

Co-teachers can use collaborative planning time in a variety of ways, and the more well developed the co-teaching relationship is, the more fluid the use of this time becomes. Initially, a structure and purpose to each meeting will be important to plan lessons and discuss pertinent issues related to student learning, teaching approaches, assessment, etc. Co-teachers need to consider the use of space in their arrangement, including the physical space, instructional space, and management or discipline space (Bouck, 2007). Collaborative planning time is a space in which the co-teaching relationship develops and strengthens over time, and it is essential to a successful partnership.

Willingness

Administrative support, professional development, and collaborative planning time all can "lead the horse to water", so to speak, but only a willingness to participate in co-teaching will make teachers want to participate. Co-teaching will only be successful as a partnership if the participants are willing and self-motivated to engage in the practice (Bouck, 2007; Scruggs et al., 2007; Conderman, Johnston-Rodriguez, & Hartman, 2009). The first and most important component of co-teaching involves this willingness to participate in a practice that will initially push a teacher beyond the comfort zone and provide challenges, but with significant payoff, for both teaching and learning.

Co-teaching as a form of collaboration can have multiple levels of positive impact on instruction. Collaboration, of which co-teaching is one form, "encourages teachers to move beyond reliance on their own memories and experiences with schooling and toward engagement with others around important questions of teaching and learning" (Goddard, Goddard, & Tschannen-Moran, 2007, p. 892). Teachers can learn new strategies and improve their instructional practices (Pratt, 2014). When teachers co-teach, particularly at the beginning stages, they have the opportunity to observe their colleague teaching and provide and receive feedback on their teaching. Once a successful co-teaching relationship is established within a school, willingness to participate in further co-teaching partnerships may increase as teachers see the impact on instruction and the opportunity to share new ideas with colleagues.

Communication within the co-teaching partnership is paramount (Gately & Gately, 2001; Conderman et al., 2009). Effective communication is built on deep knowledge of the partner teacher, understanding his or her teaching style, behavior management style, and other aspects of professional behaviors. Well-developed co-teaching relationships are marked by teachers who communicate openly and effectively with one another, providing feedback, sharing responsibilities, and using communication skills to move the relationship forward. Needs of students and the instructional task at hand are placed ahead of personal preferences and conflicts. This level of communication involves a willing commitment on the part of both co-teachers and represents a high degree of professional behavior and engagement. The compatibility of the co-teachers is also a component of effective communication, and the degree to which the teachers' personalities and teaching styles compliment one another's should be considered when arranging for co-teaching partnerships (Scruggs et al., 2007).

Equity of Roles

Co-teaching has been described as ". . . a highly complex relationship in which the teachers had to negotiate their roles" (Bouck, 2007, p. 48). When teachers think about how to share instructional roles, three components remain constant: joint planning, joint instruction, and joint evaluation (Jang, 2006). The issue of how to effectively share roles within a co-teaching partnership is an important one to consider before engaging in co-teaching (Harbort, Gunter, Hull, Brown, Venn, Wiley, & Wiley, 2007).

Responsibility for student learning through lesson planning and assessment should be equitably shared between both teachers. Kurz and Paul (2005) recommend that traditional "special education" occur within the context of co-teaching situations in which both teachers have a general education background, "but one of them would have more extensive knowledge of working with children and adolescents with specific disabilities" (p. 22). This is consistent with the mandate included in the IDEA legislation that all special education teachers be "highly qualified" in the content areas in which they are teaching. Such a qualification is achieved through advanced course work and passing a state level exam, but it can be difficult to achieve for all of the content areas in which a special education teacher might teach. Particularly at the secondary level, co-teaching can work to pair a teacher highly qualified in content with one specialized in disabilities who also has strong general education knowledge. "When special education teachers are co-teaching, they are, in theory, collaborating with a highly qualified teacher" (Bouck, 2007, p. 47). However, the assumption cannot be that the general education teacher is the lead teacher while the special education teacher simply fills in the peripheral roles. The co-teaching models described in this chapter emphasize the equitable sharing of responsibilities for teaching and learning across both partners.

Teachers need to consider the roles they must take on within a classroom and use co-teaching as a way to address more of them within a single lesson. Bouck (2007) identified eight different roles teachers can potentially take on within a lesson, and co-teaching can lessen the demands on a single teacher by dividing the responsibilities between two people. Co-teaching has the potential to lessen the amount of time any one teacher has to spend on student discipline or behavior management, because as the saying goes, "two eyes are better than one" (Murawski, 2006). By varying instructional styles within a co-taught classroom, teachers can equitably share roles and meet the diverse learning needs of all of the students in their classroom, while also keeping students more actively engaged and on task.

CHAPTER SUMMARY

Co-teaching affords the ability for teachers to work with students with disabilities in a general education classroom or the least restrictive environment. Currently, over sixty percent of students with disabilities are in a general education classroom over 80% of the day.

- ✓ Co-teaching can benefit not only students on IEPs but also general education students.
- ✓ Co-teaching has been described as "a professional marriage."
- ✓ While co-teaching arose from the need for special and general educators to collaborate—co-teaching does not always have to happen between these two types of educators. For instance, speech and language pathologists may also develop a co-teaching relationship.

For "co-teaching" to occur, there are a few defining factors that should be present:

- ✓ Co-teaching involves *two professionals*
- ✓ Co-teaching involves *jointly delivering instruction*

✓ Co-teaching is used with a *diverse population*
✓ Co-teaching involves *sharing classroom space*

Currently there are six different models of co-teaching. It is important to remember that the application of just one co-teaching model may not be appropriate in all classrooms or even for all lessons delivered in one classroom.

✓ *One teach, one observe* is the model in which the general educator teaches during the instructional time and the other co-teacher observes the rest of the classroom. The teachers may switch roles as needed, and the observing teacher may monitor the students' progress or collect data on academics or behavior.

✓ The *one teach, one drift* method allows one co-teacher to move around the classroom to manage student behavior, observe students work, and provide assistance as the other co-teacher completes the educating, planning, and assessment of the students.

✓ *Station teaching* involves co-teachers planning and instructing a portion of the lesson in stations in which students move and learn. Co-teachers in this model share the same space, the same students, and should be familiar with the curriculum and goals of the school. This is the first truly collaborative model in co-teaching.

✓ *Parallel teaching* involves each co-teacher planning and instructing students on the same material. Each teacher may educate smaller, heterogeneous groups of students. This model of co-teaching is best suited for review rather than instruction.

✓ In *alternative teaching*, each co-teacher takes a separate heterogeneous group of students. It is important that the group pulled aside is not homogenous and populated by students with disabilities but instead is a group of students who have, for instance, fallen behind due to absences.

✓ In the *team-teaching* model, co-teachers take equal responsibility for all aspects of the classroom: management, planning, preparing materials, delivering instruction, and assessing student learning. This is considered by many to be the best form of co-teaching. This model requires more planning time, trust, and communication; however, the outcomes of this model are incredibly beneficial for both educators and students.

A successful implementation of co-teaching requires several things: administrative support, professional development or training, time for collaborative planning, and mutual willingness to engage in co-teaching on the part of all partners in order to succeed.

✓ *Administrator support* of co-teaching may come in many different forms. It starts from the initial introduction of the concept of team teaching and moves all the way through continual professional development to strengthen co-teaching teams.

✓ **Professional development** is a must to continually grow as an educator and co-teaching team. Learning effective communication skills, cooperative lesson planning, content specific strategies, and differentiated instructional plans are a few key areas to develop.

✓ **Collaborative planning time** is essential for educators to be organized, fluid, and successful in a classroom.

✓ **Willingness** to engage in co-teaching is essential. Collaboration takes at least two people; an unwillingness to participate in a collaborative relationship will cause a co-teaching model to fail almost immediately.

APPLICATION ACTIVITIES

1. Observe or interview actual co-teaching teams. If no co-teaching teams are available to observe in your area, view videos of co-teaching online. Reflect on which models you observed and the advantages/disadvantages you noticed. Which of the characteristics of co-teaching discussed in the chapter did you see in action?

2. In pairs or small groups, develop co-teaching plans by pairing with an intervention specialist or general education licensure candidate, or by pairing with similar or the same licensure areas. Remember, co-teaching need not always be considered a collaborative team process among general and special education teachers.

3. Plan and deliver a mini lesson in a classroom or in the university classroom with your co-teaching partner from the previous exercise. Reflect on the rewards and challenges to co-planning and teaching teams. Link your reflection to the characteristics and models of co-teaching discussed in this chapter. Consider the grade-level indicators appropriate to your licensure band/content area.

REFERENCES

Aliakbari, M., & Bazyar, A. (2012). Exploring the impact of parallel teaching on general language proficiency of EFL learners. *Journal of Pan-Pacific Association of Applied Linguistics*, 16(1), 55–71.

Arguelles, M. E., Hughes, M. T., & Schumm, J. S. (2000). Co-teaching: A different approach to inclusion. *Principal*, 79(4), 48, 50–51.

Bessette, H. J. (2008). Using students' drawings to elicit general and special educators' perceptions of co-teaching. *Teaching and Teacher Education*, 24, 1376–1396.

Bouck, E. C. (2007). Co-teaching . . . not just a textbook term: Implications for practice. *Preventing School Failure: Alternative Education for Children and Youth*, 51(2), 46–51.

Brown, N. B., Howerter, C. S., & Morgan, J. J. (2013). Tools and strategies for making co-teaching work. *Intervention in School and Clinic*, 49(2), 84–91.

Conderman, G., Johnston-Rodriguez, S., & Hartman, P. (2009). Communicating and collaborating in co-taught classrooms. *Teaching Exceptional Children Plus*, 5(5), 2–17.

Dieker, L. A., & Murawski, W. W. (2003). Co-teaching at the secondary level: Unique issues, current trends, and suggestions for success. *The High School Journal*, 86(4), 1–13.

Fountas, I. C., & Pinnell, G. S. (1996). *Guided reading: Good first teaching for all children*. Portsmouth, NH: Heinemann.

Friend, M., & Cook, L. (2000). *Interactions: Collaboration Skills for School Professionals*. Boston, MA: Pearson.

Friend, M., Cook, L., Hurley-Chamberlain, D., & Shamberger, C. (2010). Co-teaching: An illusion of the complexity of collaboration in special education. *Journal of Educational and Psychological Consultation*, 20(1), 9–27.

Gately, S. E., & Gately Jr, F. J. (2001). Understanding coteaching components. *Teaching Exceptional Children*, 33(4), 40–47.

Goddard, Y. L., Goddard, R. D., & Tschannen-Moran, M. (2007). A theoretical and empirical investigation of teacher collaboration for school improvement and students achievement in public elementary schools. *Teachers College Record*, 109(4), 877–896.

Graziano, K. J., & Navarrete, L. A. (2012). Co-teaching in a teacher education classroom: Collaboration, compromise, and creativity. *Issues in Teacher Education*, 21(1), 109–126.

Harbort, G., Gunter, P. L., Hull, K., Brown, Q., Venn, M. L., Wiley, L. P., & Wiley, E. W. (2007). Behaviors of teachers in co-taught classes in a secondary school. *Teacher Education and Special Education*, 30(1), 13–23.

Jang, S. J. (2006). Research on the effects of team teaching upon two secondary school teachers. *Educational Research*, 48(2), 177–194.

Kohler-Evans, P. A. (2006). Co-teaching: How to make this marriage work in front of the kids. *Education*, 127, 260–264.

Kurz, N., & Paul, P. V. (2005). Toward an inclusive teacher education program. *Journal of Teaching and Learning*, 3(2), 15–27.

Lindeman, K. W., & Magiera, K. (2014). A co-teaching model: Committed professionals, high expectations, and the inclusive classroom. *Odyssey: New Directions in Deaf Education*, 15, 40–45.

Magiera, K., Simmons, R., Marotta, A., & Battaglia, B. (2005). A co-teaching model: A response to students with disabilities and their performance on NYS assessments. *SAANYS Journal*, 34(2), 1–5.

Magiera, K., Smith, C., Zigmond, N., & Gebauer, K. (2005). Benefits of co-teaching in secondary mathematics classes. *Teaching Exceptional Children*, 37(3), 20–24.

Mastropieri, M. A., Scruggs, T. E., Graetz, J., Norland, J., Gardizi, W., & McDuffie, K. (2005). Case studies in co-teaching in the content areas: Successes, failures, and challenges. *Intervention in School and Clinic*, 40(5), 260–270.

Murawski, W. W. (2006). Student outcomes in co-taught secondary English classes: How can we improve? *Reading and Writing Quarterly*, 22(3), 227–247.

Murawski, W. W., & Dieker, L.A. (2004). Tips and strategies for co-teaching at the secondary level. *Teaching Exceptional Children*, 36(5), 52–59.

Murawski, W. W., & Hughes, C. E. (2009). Response to intervention, collaboration, and co-teaching: A logical combination for successful systematic change. *Preventing School Failure*, 53, 1–9.

Murawski, W. W., & Swanson, H.L. (2001). A meta-analysis of co-teaching research. *Remedial and Special Education*, 22(5), 258–267.

Nierengarten, G. (2013). Supporting co-teaching teams in high schools: Twenty research-based practices. *American Secondary Education*, 42(1), 73–81.

Pratt, S. (2014). Achieving symbiosis: Working through challenges found in co-teaching to achieve effective co-teaching relationships. *Teaching and Teacher Education*, 41(July 2014), 1–12.

Reeve, P. T., & Hallahan, D. P. (1994). Practical questions about collaboration between general and special educators. *Focus on Exceptional Children*, 26(7), 1–11.

Santoli, S. P., Sachs, J., Romey, E. A., & McClurg, S. (2008). A successful formula for middle school inclusion: Collaboration, time, and administrative support. *RMLE Online: Research in Middle Level Education*, 32(2), 1–13.

Scheeler, M. C., Congdon, M., & Stansberry, S. (2010). Providing immediate feedback to co-teachers through bug-in-ear technology: An effective method of peer coaching in inclusion classrooms. *Teacher Education and Special Education*, 33(1), 83–96.

Scruggs, T. E., Mastropieri, M. A., & McDuffie, K. A. (2007). Co-teaching in inclusive classrooms: A meta synthesis of qualitative research. *Council for Exceptional Children*, 73(4), 392–416.

Shanahan, T. (2015). What teachers should know about common core. *The Reading Teacher*, 68(8), 583–588.

Sileo, J. M., & Van Garderen, D. (2010). Creating optimal opportunities to learn mathematics: Blending co-teaching structures with research-based practices. *Teaching Exceptional Children*, 42(3), 14–21.

Simmons, R. J., & Magiera, K. (2007). Evaluation of co-teaching in three high schools within one school district: How do you know when you are truly co-teaching? *Teaching Exceptional Children*, 3(3), Article 4.

Solis, M., Vaughn, S., Swanson, E., & McCulley, L. (2012). Collaborative models of instruction: The empirical foundations of inclusion and co-teaching. *Psychology in Schools*, 49(5), 498–510.

Taylor, R. L., Smiley, L. R., & Richards, S. (2015). *Exceptional students: Preparing teachers for the 21st century* (2nd ed.). New York, NY: McGraw-Hill Higher Education.

U.S. Department of Education (2010). Retrieved from https://www2.ed.gov/offices/OSERS/OSEP/Research/OSEP97AnlRpt/wp/section3.doc

Villa, R. A., Thousand, J. S., & Nevin, A. (2008). *A guide to co-teaching: Practical tips for facilitating student learning*. Thousand Oaks, CA: Corwin Press.

Walsh, J. M. (2012). Co-teaching as a school system strategy for continuous improvement. *Preventing School Failure*, 56(1), 29–36.

Wilson, G. L., & Michaels, C. A. (2006). General and special education students' perceptions of co-teaching: Implications for secondary-level literacy instruction. *Reading and Writing Quarterly: Overcoming Learning Difficulties*, 22, 205–225.

Witcher, M., & Feng, J. (2010). Co-teaching vs. solo teaching: Comparative effects on fifth graders' math achievement. Presentation, Mid-South Educational Research Association Annual Conference.

9

OTHER MODELS OF COLLABORATION

Mary-Kate Sableski

Chapter Objectives
1. Describe the transdisciplinary model of consultation
2. Describe how this model relates to multidisciplinary and interdisciplinary models of consultation
3. List the practices involved in consultation
4. Identify key principles of consultation

Collaboration is a style of working and interacting with others (Cook & Friend, 2010) and can take many forms. Sometimes co-teaching is just not a feasible option or is not necessary. In the latter case, this may be due to students who are successfully included in most respects but tend to experience difficulties in one area of a class or are experiencing a temporary problem. In other words, the use of a full co-teaching model is not necessary or is not available. Instructional decisions should always be made with the student at the center of the discussion, over the needs of the teachers or collaborative team. In nearly all instances, however, the use of co-teaching is beneficial so long as the collaborative teaming is effective, respectful, and based on the successful characteristics of collaboration discussed throughout this book. This tenet reflects the belief that co-teaching need not always be focused on the inclusion of students with disabilities.

Consultation, as it relates to teaming, involves key stakeholders in a child's education coming together to communicate, collaborate, and coordinate services to meet a student's unique needs. Consultation in schools can follow a **multidisciplinary, interdisciplinary,** or **transdisciplinary** model of teaming. This model requires team members to be willing to share their expertise with other team members and for all team members to be willing to engage in **role release**. Role release requires team members to be willing to learn from other team members and to be willing to engage in activities based on that learning. For example, an intervention specialist faculty member may need to learn how to support activities of daily living for a student that are developed and initiated by an occupational therapist. The intervention specialist faculty may be primarily responsible for the actual implementation of those activities with the occupational therapist acting as a consultant. Another example could include a general education teacher who monitors the behavior of a student who has exhibited emotional disturbance. A school psychologist, counselor, or psychiatrist may have worked with a student who is having a difficult time and experiencing depression. General education teachers could learn what signals or signs from the student (e.g., oral or written comments, behavior, interactions with peers) that could indicate an improving or worsening condition. The general education teachers would be primarily responsible for monitoring the student with the psychological professional providing consultation as to any additional course of action. This model is in contrast with the **multidisciplinary** and **interdisciplinary** model of collaborative consultation. All three of these models will be discussed in greater depth later in this chapter.

It is important to remember that consultation is dependent on the voluntary nature of the relationships and trust among team members. School consultation is voluntary and involves one professional assisting another to address a problem concerning a third party (Friend & Cook, 2012). Team members must rely on each other for input and guidance. Consultation becomes more difficult when team members perceive one person is "in charge" and dictating to others what they should do or how they should behave. This is a more hierarchical relationship that may not be sustainable over time.

Collaborative consultation involves a careful negotiation of the professional roles and courtesies necessary for productive working relationships between colleagues. Collaboration does not occur immediately once a team is assembled; rather, teams should follow an iterative process of establishing norms and learning how to work together effectively. Friend and Cook (2012) indicated the following steps in the consultation process:

a. Entry–professionals (and perhaps caregivers) agree the consultation process is needed and begin the building of trust and respect
b. Problem identification–the team members establish a goal for the consultation
c. Planning–decisions are reached regarding how best to achieve the identified goal
d. Intervention–the implementation of the plan
e. Evaluation–the ongoing and summative assessments of the effectiveness of the intervention
f. Exit–the ending of the consulting relationship

It is clear from these steps that consultation is not typically thought of as a permanent arrangement, although some of the barriers to collaboration, described in Chapter One, may necessitate such a relationship. Again, a common difficulty with such a "permanent" arrangement is that the relationship may be less voluntary and less of a "two-way street." The professional responsible for *step d* presented earlier may very well become resentful at being told by another professional what he/she must do. The consultant should always be respectful and mindful of any constraints experienced by the consultee. Similarly, the consultee should act in good faith and carry out the plan as agreed. Collaborative consultation in any form requires nuanced, give-and-take relationships that keep the student at the center of the discussion at all times.

Comprehension Check

1. What is the transdisciplinary model of teaming?
2. What is the definition of consultation?
3. What are the steps in the consultation process?
4. What are some potential pitfalls of using consultation as a more "permanent" arrangement?

ELEMENTS OF COLLABORATIVE CONSULTATION

School collaboration can be thought of in terms of six distinct elements (Dettmer, Thurston, & Dyck, 2005). These include system, perspective, approach, prototype, mode, and model. Case Study 9.1 describes collaborative consultation as it relates to these key elements. The following section will then discuss each of these elements as it relates to school teams.

9.1 ILLUSTRATIVE CASE STUDY

Southtown Elementary School is a preschool through fifth grade building. The school's philosophy has encouraged an inclusive, multi-age curriculum that has led to teaming by all staff.

One team includes two general education teachers and one assistant teacher, who have been part of the team for three years. This year an ELL teacher, a reading specialist, and a special education teacher have also joined the team.

This team serves the kindergarten and first grade classrooms. There are 40 students across two classrooms at this grade level, and the team is intended to support the needs of all of these students. All members of the team provide instruction to the students, with the specialists providing instruction to the students whose needs match their areas of expertise.

One distinguishing factor of this team is the fluidity of the roles of each team member. For example, the school includes a high percentage of ELL students, so the ELL teacher would have a large caseload of students if left on her own. However, since the needs of the students expand beyond their language needs and can include areas in reading or learning disabilities, the special education teacher and the reading specialist will sometimes serve the ELL students, as well.

The team will often divide students into small groups, with each teacher taking responsibility for one of the groups. The groups are heterogeneous and dynamic, meaning that their membership changes based on the lesson being taught, the skills required, and recent assessment data.

The team engages in co-planning two times a week in order to facilitate these fluid, flexible dynamics. The school schedule has been designed to support this co-planning time within the school day for the team members. This also allows the team to invite other specialists to consult on specific student needs as needed. Depending on the year, if there is a student with specific needs requiring a specialist, that person would be included in all aspects of team planning and teaching, as appropriate for the situation.

The entire school is organized into teams, so a philosophy of collaboration pervades the school environment. To this end, teams are often fluid across the school. A student's specific needs drive the membership of the team. In addition, colleagues from different teams are often heard in the workroom discussing particular students and their specific needs.

On the kindergarten/first grade team, one consultant the team frequently employs is a dyslexia specialist. This teacher has received advanced training in multisensory teaching methods and is able to observe students, provide short-term remediation within the classroom, and make a recommendation for further testing for dyslexia. This teacher "floats" around the school, providing consultative services across grade levels, moving in and out of teams as necessary.

System

In collaborative consultation, or teaming, a **system** refers to the many parts of the team serving one common purpose, the student. These "parts" include anyone who educates the student, for example, teachers, parents, support personnel, other caregivers, etc. This term also refers to the multiple contexts, or **systems**, in which a student is educated. For example, a student is educated at home, at school, in a medical setting, in extracurricular settings, etc. Consideration of the systems at play in the collaborative process is an important element of teaming.

In the case study example, the system in which the team operated was an elementary school in the specific grades of kindergarten and first. The components of the team were the educators serving the students. Parents and students were not part of this particular team's system, although as the case study indicated, they could be invited to participate as needed.

Perspective

The **perspective** of the team refers to the thought or viewpoint from which the team operates. For example, the team might take a *purchase* perspective and choose to accept or reject consultation from service providers as they deem appropriate. Or, the team may take a *doctor-patient* perspective in which the service provider is the diagnostician and prescriber but not the actual provider of the service. This occurs when a classroom teacher consults with a special educator on a specific need of a student for diagnostic and prescriptive advice. Finally, a team can take a *process* perspective in which the consultant becomes a part of the process to observe, identify, and remediate the need with the student. In this final perspective, the consultant is a part of the team process. This process perspective is most often seen in schools because of the collaborative, efficient nature of it as a way to bring multiple perspectives together to serve students.

In the case study example, the perspective relies on a process perspective. The team functions as a dynamic system, inviting consultants in as necessary, but these consultants become a part of the team to serve the students' needs. The consultants flow in and out of the core team as needed. These needs are determined by the core team, based on the areas of expertise each of them brings to the team context. In the case study, the team would need consultants for PT, OT, SLP, etc., as all members of the team are educators.

Approach

The **approach** of the team refers to the steps taken to work with one another to meet a student's needs. This approach can be *formal*, in which collaborative consultation occurs within a team meeting or as part of an IEP conference. It can be *informal* when it occurs more spontaneously. For example, the teacher's lounge at lunchtime can be one site for an informal approach to consultation, as would email exchanges or phone conversations. When two teachers exchange notes about a student in the hallway, or a classroom teacher runs into a specialist at the grocery store and inquires about a student's needs, informal consultation has occurred. Both approaches serve to shape the way in which a collaborative team operates to meet student needs.

In the case study example, the approach was formal, as the team was an official system within the school. However, because of the dynamic relationships of the members of the team and the longevity of their collaboration, informal approaches were also taken. The case study described the teachers' conversations in the workroom with members of other teams to receive advice about student needs. This is an example of the informal approach to collaboration that often occurs in schools.

Prototype

In consulting, a **prototype** refers to the pattern according to which the consultation occurs. Typically, a consultant will define the problem, isolate the contextual variables that contribute to the problem, and offer interventions to remediate the problem (Dettmer et al., 2005). In a collaborative team in a school, the consultant might be a special educator, a medical specialist, or a community member knowledgeable about an issue affecting the child. The consultant joins the team, gathering information through observation and conversation about the problem. The consultant should also refer to assessment data gathered by the team or gather specific assessment data needed to identify the problem. Next, the consultant will identify what is occurring in the school or home environment, or factors affecting the child that are contributing to the problem. Finally, the consultant will offer intervention plans to address the problem.

In the case study example, the dyslexia specialist is an example of the prototype of the team in action. The dyslexia specialist acts as a consultant on an as needed basis and is not a permanent member of the team. However, this teacher is seen as a part of the team in that she understands the system, perspective, and approach of the team and can effectively slide in and out of its operations to support a specific student.

Mode

The manner in which the collaboration occurs is referred to as the **mode**. A consultant might work directly with the student or work only with the team, providing recommendations for instruction. For example, a consultant may take on tutoring tasks within the classroom or work with the student on specific life skills outside the regular classroom. Or, a reading specialist may meet with the team to provide recommendations on reading intervention programs appropriate for the student's specific needs but will not provide the actual instruction.

In the case study example, the mode of collaboration was very fluid and dynamic. There is one core team that serves the kindergarten and first grade students as a whole, but consulting members are often invited in on a temporary or a more long-term basis, depending on the needs of the student and the team.

Model

A model is a representation of a real entity, designed to help shape actual practices. There are several models that school teams can use to guide their work as a group. Any model used should involve interchangeable roles among members of the team, depending on the needs of the student and the context. The model that is the focus of this chapter is the **collaborative consultation** model. In this model, all members of the team are seen as equal partners with diverse expertise (Dettmer et al., 2005). Members of the team work together to solve problems, disagree constructively, and communicate in a nonhierarchical format. **Parity** is a key word used to describe the equal, supportive relationships among the members of a team using this model. All members of the team provide instruction to the student using their expertise and skills to meet the specific needs. In other models, not all members of the team contribute instructionally to the student's needs. The collaborative consultation model is used in the transdisciplinary approach, which will be discussed in the next section.

In the case study example, parity and collaborative consultation are critical components to the successful implementation of the team across the school. One factor that made this successful includes the commitment to teaming across the school, so that teaming to support student needs is seen as just "what we do" in the school and not as a function only of the special educators or those who co-teach.

Comprehension Check

1. List the six elements of collaborative consultation.
2. Define the collaborative consultation model.
3. Compare and contrast an informal team approach and a formal team approach.

MODELS OF COLLABORATION

The case study example described a school in which the administration had decided to implement teaming across all grade levels and classrooms. As a result, there were several different teams functioning within the school, applying fluid principles of collaboration and teaming as was appropriate for the situation. The following sections will describe three different collaboration models schools often follow in forming teams and collaboration.

Multidisciplinary

Multidisciplinary teams are loosely formed groups of professionals who consult with one another on the educational needs of a student. This model of collaboration aligns with a medical, pull-out model of instruction, as teams do not function as a unit to support a student in the least restrictive environment; rather, the classroom teacher or the special education teacher maintains primary responsibility for the coordination and delivery of instruction to the student but may collaborate intermittently with other professionals and specialists based on the student's needs.

In a multidisciplinary team, assessment is done in isolation, and results are not automatically shared with others who work with the students. This practice assumes that only those specifically trained in the discipline can assess and intervene (Hernandez, 2013). Educational planning is then challenging to complete when all of the teachers who work with the student are not aware of the full picture of the student's assessment data.

The primary function of multidisciplinary teams is to implement evaluation and placement procedures for students with disabilities. Multidisciplinary teams consist of a wide variety of individuals. Each member works independently and the team only meets as needed. Family members meet with each team member alone (Raver & Childress, 2014). Multidisciplinary teams involve the least amount of collaboration and communication on the part of members of the team.

As an example, a multidisciplinary team would include a regular education teacher, a special education teacher, and an ELL teacher meeting to coordinate services for the ELL students in the classroom. Not every ELL student will need special education services, so the teachers would provide their individual perspectives on the students' needs as identified by their assessments and then make decisions about who should provide instruction to the students based on their identified needs. Once these decisions are made, the team would not meet again until re-evaluation would be necessary. Teachers would provide their instruction without necessarily coordinating this instruction with the other teachers, conducting their own assessments to monitor and document progress.

Interdisciplinary

Interdisciplinary teams follow a similar structure to the multidisciplinary teams, but there is a higher degree of collaboration and communication on the part of the team members. These teams meet more frequently than multidisciplinary teams to discuss student progress and coordinate instruction. Interaction between team members occurs within the meetings but not in the delivery of service (Raver & Childress, 2014). The special education teacher is typically the case manager for an interdisciplinary team, acting as the coordinator of the team meetings and services provided to the students.

Interdisciplinary teams can perpetuate the idea that students with severe disabilities attend school to receive therapy, as each member of the team is seen as providing an isolated service to the child. A physical or occupational therapist may provide the instruction during the school day but in a separate setting with which the classroom or special education teacher has little interaction. The professionals would discuss the services at team meetings but would not interact to provide the services.

An example of an interdisciplinary team would be a team of teachers with a common prep period who meet together as needed to coordinate services for a student. This is also known as an Intervention Assistance Team (IAT). The common planning period and the increased accountability to the team members distinguish an interdisciplinary team from a multidisciplinary team.

Transdisciplinary

In a transdisciplinary model of collaboration, there is "collective responsibility for the creation and implementation of the educational and therapeutic plan. No individual is solely responsible for the progress and development in any particular skill area" (Hernandez, 2013, p. 485). Transdisciplinary teams are interactive and dynamic, as specialists interact to provide services in a coordinated manner to students. The integral nature of the collaboration between team members necessitates training and professional development in effective communication and collaboration as part of a transdisciplinary team to help it function effectively (Hong & Reynolds-Keefer, 2013). The family and the child are the focus of a transdisciplinary team and there are benefits to families in the form of efficiency and consistency of services (Raver & Childress, 2014).

Three Phases

There are three phases in bringing a transdisciplinary team together (Kaczmarek, Pennington, & Goldstein, 2000). Phase 1 involves organizing the team. This depends on the systems in place in the school to support teaming and what approach the team would like to take. A transdisciplinary team is marked by flexible roles with each member of the team and all team members sharing in the service delivery to the student. Phase 2 involves facilitating the team process. This is a critical step in the formation of an effective transdisciplinary team, as teachers need training and professional development to learn the theory behind transdisciplinary teaming, effective tools for communicating within the team, understanding of the various roles of team members, and they must become well versed in the shared vocabulary of the team. In Phase 3, the team is developed and implemented in the school to serve students. Once the team is up and running, it is important that schools constantly reevaluate the team process, beginning again with Phase 1 and moving through the three phases as necessary to improve the outcomes for students. Figure 9.1 details the three phases in building a transdisciplinary team.

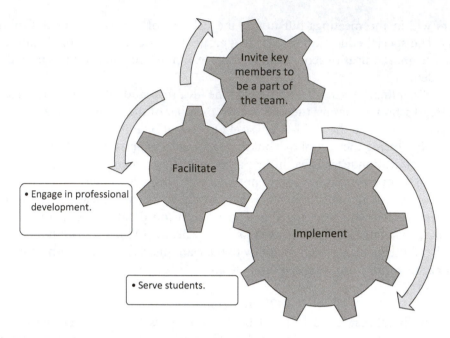

Figure 9.1 The Three Phases in Building a Transdisciplinary Team

Multiple Components

Due to the high degree of collaboration and communication that must occur to make a transdisciplinary team function effectively, multiple components should be considered throughout the transdisciplinary team process. The components of a transdisciplinary team will be discussed in the follow sections but are also detailed in Table 9.1.

Regular Meeting Schedule

Regular meetings are critical for the successful operation of a transdisciplinary team (Domik & Fischer, 2011). For transdisciplinary teams to function effectively there needs to be a high degree of communication, cooperation, and collaboration. This can only occur through adequate time for the team to meet and discuss the issues facing the team.

Table 9.1 Components of a Transdisciplinary Team

Component
Regular Meeting Schedule
Inclusive
Efficient Goal Development
Trust and Communication
Administrative Support
Role Release
Arena Assessment

Inclusive

Transdisciplinary teams should be inclusive of all providers who wish to contribute to the success of the student. Additionally, participation in the team should be voluntary when possible. Conditions for both of these components to occur need to be built throughout the school environment, but a context in which transdisciplinary teams can be successful should be professionally supportive of diverse viewpoints, include faculty who are motivated to work for the success of students with others, and encouraging of team collaboration.

Efficient Goal Development

Within a transdisciplinary team, efficient goal development for students should be a priority. What marks a transdisciplinary team from another model of collaboration is the crossing of boundaries of all service providers. IEP goals should be developed collaboratively and efficiently, keeping in mind the overall picture of assessment of the student's needs rather than the individual interpretations of each provider. Efficient goal development will make achieving the goals more realistic, rather than scattered and isolated goals that are related but separate across contexts as in the other models of teaming. For example, if a student has speech and language issues that are also affecting his reading fluency, these goals should be coordinated across the SLP and the reading specialist. Coordination of services in support of these goals can then occur, which will be more meaningful and purposeful for the student.

Trust and Communication

Trust and communication among team members are essential components to a transdisciplinary team (Domik & Fischer, 2011; Hernandez, 2013). Compatibility, both personally and professionally should also be considered when forming a transdisciplinary team (Domik & Fischer, 2011). As was stated previously, a school culture that supports collaboration among faculty will be supportive of the major components of transdisciplinary teams. Teachers who are compatible on multiple levels will be more suited to working together on a team. This process does not always occur naturally but must be supported and facilitated through professional development, faculty retreats, and social experiences.

Administrative Support

Related to the issue of compatibility and trust, administrative support (Spencer, 2005; Domik & Fischer, 2011) is a critical component of transdisciplinary teams. A transdisciplinary team must have the full support of administration to be successful, if for no other reason than the sheer logistics and coordination of faculty requires the support at the administrative level to occur. However, administrative support for the team to acquire resources for assessment and instruction at a transdisciplinary level is paramount. Transdisciplinary teaming can look distinctly different from traditional notions of teaming, so clear administrative support for this model of collaboration will allow the teachers to be successful. In the case study example, transdisciplinary teaming occurred at a school-wide level, indicating administrative support across the board for the concept. In a school in which transdisciplinary teaming may be more isolated, administrative support will be essential to its success.

Role Release

Transdisciplinary team members blend or share roles to create parity in the roles of each member of the team (Hernandez, 2013). Specialists interact to create an intervention plan for students, which distinguishes transdisciplinary teams from multidisciplinary or interdisciplinary teams. Role release is also called "role sharing" because of this collaborative, interactive exchange of roles within a team (Raver & Childress, 2014). Role sharing creates a regular and systematic sharing of knowledge and skills across disciplines within a team.

Role release has been described as including five distinct stages as professionals grow more accustomed to sharing roles and responsibilities equally with team members. These stages include *extension*, in which team members first become more educated about their own discipline, either through professional development, additional course work, or other forms of study. Next, team members go through *enrichment*, in which individuals learn about other disciplines so that they can knowledgeably share roles with other professionals on the team. In the *expansion* stage, team members share ideas with each other to develop intervention plans and build trust and communication. *Exchange* involves team members in implementing integrated assessment and intervention plan, combining the efforts of everyone on the team, and involving an extensive amount of trust and communication to coordinate efforts. Finally, role release involves *support*, in which team members consult regularly to monitor the implementation of the intervention plan, and make any changes necessary as determined by assessment data. Figure 9.2 describes the stages of role release in more detail (Woodruff & McGonigel, 1988; Stepans, 2002; Boyer & Thompson, 2014).

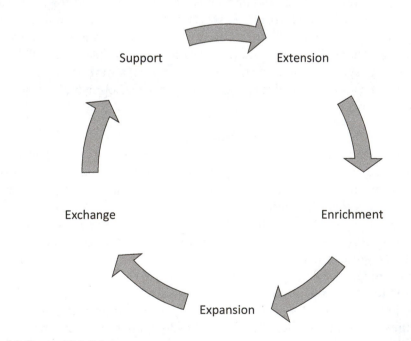

Figure 9.2 Stages of Role Release

Arena Assessment

Arena assessment is a unique concept to transdisciplinary teaming. In this approach to assessment, one member of the team acts as the facilitator of the evaluation process. Information from assessments is then shared with all members of the team to inform the collaborative intervention plan. In other forms of teaming, individual team members conduct assessments to inform unique disciplines. For example, the reading specialist and the SLP might administer different assessments to understand the student's needs in the area of language and reading. The data from these assessments is likely similar, however, and can inform each other and strengthen the intervention plan. Arena assessment is episodic, in that it captures one moment in time, as opposed to isolated assessments which may occur over a longer window of time (Grisham-Brown, 2000). Teams would want to consider this fact when interpreting data, as one moment in time could include a variety of contextual factors that would influence assessment outcomes, including student illness, classroom contexts, or family situations. Team members jointly complete arena assessments, thus emphasizing the involvement of all team members in the evaluation process to interpret data across assessments and develop a strong intervention plan.

Comprehension Check

1. Describe the three models of collaboration discussed in this section.
2. Discuss the three phases involved in forming a transdisciplinary team.
3. List the components of a transdisciplinary team.

TEAM MEMBER ROLES

A team, whether it is formed according to a transdisciplinary, interdisciplinary, or multidisciplinary model, can be made up of a variety of individuals, and the factors in determining team membership were discussed previously in this chapter. In the following sections, roles of common team members will be discussed as they apply to any of the three models described in this chapter. It is important to remember when forming a team that more is not always better when building a team. An ideal team includes only enough team members as needed to meet the needs of the child (Grisham-Brown, 2000; Spencer, 2005). Before reading this section, study the Application Case Study 9.2 to consider the multiple roles needed on a collaborative team.

9.2 APPLICATION CASE STUDY

Brandon is a sixth grade student who has multiple disabilities. Brandon has cerebral palsy and uses a walker. Brandon is also cognitively delayed, with an IQ of 62. A speech impediment is also a disability for which Brandon receives support. Brandon is being raised by his grandmother and has no brothers or sisters. As a young child, a family crisis caused him to move with his grandmother, away from his mother, to a new city.

The least restrictive environment in which Brandon is educated is a self-contained special education classroom for most of the day. Brandon participates in inclusion in "specials" classes, including art, music, physical education, and home economics. Sixth grade is the first year of middle school for Brandon, meaning he is transitioning to a new building within the district. The transition to the new building also involves a reexamination of the composition of the collaborative team that supports Brandon.

Form small groups within the class and discuss who you would consider inviting to be a part of the collaborative team to support Brandon's transition to middle school. Consider the following questions as you discuss the team:

1. Who would be the critical members of the team to support Brandon?
2. What roles would team members need to play to most effectively support Brandon's educational progress?
3. What other considerations does Brandon's case present to a collaborative team?

Family Members

Family members are the most important members of the team, as they know the child and his or her background best (Spencer, 2005; Raver & Childress, 2014). Family members should be included in the evaluation process and implementation of the intervention plan to the greatest extent possible, dependent on the school context and the needs of the family. Chapter 5 in this text discusses the roles of family members in the collaboration process. A school team might also include other family members or family friends at the discretion of the family. For example, a family might invite an aunt who is a special education teacher in another district to sit in on team meetings to provide informed insights into how the team can meet the needs of the child.

Educator

A team will of course include both general and special educators who are responsible for providing instruction on a daily basis to the student. In a multidisciplinary or interdisciplinary team, the special educator might be the primary provider of instruction to the student. In an interdisciplinary team, the roles are more fluid and may change based on a variety of contextual factors. As team members, educators should try to be thoughtful, knowledgeable, compassionate, and provide leadership in areas related to coordination of instructional services (Eccleston, 2010). In addition to the general and special educator, educators can include the reading specialist, gifted specialist, dyslexia specialist, etc. Depending on state licensures and district resources, educators can include anyone who is responsible for the educational aspects of the intervention plan.

Therapists

Therapists, such as the speech-language pathologist, physical therapist, or occupational therapist will be members of the school team, depending on the needs of the child. In a multidisciplinary or interdisciplinary team, therapists would work independently, consulting with the team to develop the IEP and monitor student progress periodically. In a transdisciplinary team, the therapists would interact more often with the members of the team, meeting on a regular basis and sharing roles (role release) with other members of the team to implement the intervention plan. Therapists play an important role on school teams due to their specialized knowledge, which compliments the knowledge base of the educators and family members to meet the wide variety of special needs children might present.

Medical Personnel and Other Professionals

Medical personnel, mental health professionals, tutors, or other professionals relevant to the needs of the child might also be included on a team. In any model of teaming, these professionals would play a more consultative role, floating in and out of the team process as necessary to meet the needs of the child, as in most instances these professionals would not be employed by the school. In a transdisciplinary team, these professionals might still participate in arena assessment, but their assessments would be much more specific and not as closely related to the educational assessments provided by the team. These team members play an important role in educating the whole child and might be invited by the family, the special educator, or might elect to join the team based on their work with the student. It is important to remember what was previously stated regarding the need to include only essential personnel on a team; however, including these other professionals can greatly enhance their ability to provide services to the student, whether those services occur within or outside of the regular school day.

Comprehension Check

1. What are the considerations in inviting people to be members of a collaborative team?
2. What are the benefits to inviting other service providers to be a part of a collaborative team?
3. What are some of the roles other service providers might take on within a collaborative team?

CHAPTER SUMMARY

At times co-teaching is not a feasible option or necessary in every situation. During these times, collaboration can be utilized through consultation. Consultation involves key stakeholders in the child's education who come together, keeping the child's best interests at the center of the conversation.

✓ Collaboration does not occur as soon as a team is formed. Instead collaboration develops through the process of consultation.
✓ The first step of consultation is *entry*. This is when the stakeholders agree that a consultation process is necessary.
✓ The second step of consultation is *problem identification*, or developing goals.
✓ The third step of consultation is *planning*. During this step, phases are identified that will allow the team to best achieve the identified goal.
✓ The fourth step of consultation is *intervention*—or the implementation of the plan.
✓ The fifth step of consultation is *evaluation*. This is an ongoing process of summative assessments to determine the effectiveness of the intervention.
✓ The sixth step of consultation is *exit*—or the ending of the consulting relationship.

Just as there are six steps to the consulting relationship, there are also six aspects or distinct elements to a collaborative consultation. These six elements are:

✓ **System**. The system refers to two things, the first being the many parts of the team that is serving one common purpose—the student. The second being the multiple contexts in which the student is educated (e.g., home, school, extracurricular activities).
✓ **Perspective**. The perspective of the team refers to the thoughts or viewpoints in which the team operates. This can either happen through a *purchase* perspective or through a *doctor-patient* perspective.
✓ **Approach**. Approach refers to the steps taken in order to work collaboratively to meet a student's needs.
✓ **Prototype**. Prototype refers to the pattern according to which the consultation occurs.
✓ **Mode**. The manner in which the collaboration occurs is considered the mode; this can look like a consultant working directly with the student, only working with the team, or just providing recommendations.
✓ **Model**. A representation of the working collaborative process is considered to be the model. Different models are used to help shape the consulting relationship.

Multidisciplinary teams are loosely formed groups of professionals who consult with one another on the educational needs of a student.

✓ These teams are typically aligned with a medical, pull-out model of instruction.
✓ This model is not designed to keep a child in the least restrictive environment.
✓ All assessment is done in isolation, and results are typically not shared with all stakeholders in the child's education. This makes the multidisciplinary model the least collaborative model.

Interdisciplinary teams follow a similar structure to multidisciplinary teams but have a slightly higher degree of collaboration.

✓ Collaboration occurs within meetings; however, it does not happen in the delivery of service.

✓ This model of consultation is common among different specialists in a school setting. For example, a speech pathologist, occupational therapist, and teacher may meet to discuss a child's special services; however, each will serve the child individually.

✓ In many schools, Intervention Assistance Teams (IAT) are considered to be interdisciplinary teams.

Transdisciplinary teams are a group of interactive, dynamic specialists who provide their services in a coordinated manner. There are three phases to the transdisciplinary collaborative team.

✓ Phase one: organizing the team.

✓ Phase two: facilitating the team process.

✓ Phase three: the team is further developed and implemented in order to best serve students.

✓ Transdisciplinary teams should have:

- A regular meeting schedule
- Be inclusive
- Efficient goal development
- Trust and communication
- Administrative support
- Role release
- Arena assessment

✓ Inclusiveness in a team will allow all providers who wish to contribute the opportunity to enable the success of students.

✓ Efficient goal development strategies should be a priority if a team will succeed. All goals should be developed collaboratively rather than individually.

✓ Trust and communication are essential components to a transdisciplinary team. Compatibility should always be considered when forming a team.

✓ A transdisciplinary team must have full administrative support to be successful, if for no other reason than to ensure logistically a team is able to function.

✓ Role release involves members of a team bending and sharing roles to create parity. Role release has been described in five distinct stages:

- Extension
- Enrichment
- Expansion
- Exchange
- Support

No matter how a team is formed, it can be made up of a variety of individuals. There are some common team members in an educational setting who have common roles.

✓ *Family members* could be considered the most important members of the team. These members know the child and his/her background. These members are also able to see the child outside of an educational setting.

✓ *Educators* can include both general and special education members. These individuals are responsible for providing instruction on a daily basis to the student.

✓ *Therapists* in an educational setting can include specialists, such as the speech-language pathologist, physical therapies, or occupational therapist. These members of the team will vary depending on the needs of the child.

✓ *Medical and other personnel* will include any medical, mental health, tutors, or other professionals relevant to the child's needs. These professionals may play a more consultative role to meet the needs of the child.

APPLICATION ACTIVITIES

1. In small groups, review and present on the three basic team models: multidisciplinary, interdisciplinary, and transdisciplinary. Compare and contrast the models. Have you experienced in your observations the use of any or all the models? What might be the circumstances when each are used, including the possible benefits and limitations?

2. Summarize in small groups one of the six elements of consultation discussed. Present the information, including a description of the element and an application to a situation you have observed in the field.

3. Interview a teacher and/or related services provider *or* invite one or more to the university class. Prepare an interview questionnaire in advance. The interview should address the consultation process, its benefits, and its challenges. Inquire about the steps in consultation, the nature of the relationship among the consultant and consultees and how they problem solve any issues that arise. Also address why the consultation was/is used and if it is a temporary or permanent relationship. Reflect on the responses of the interviewees.

REFERENCES

Boyer, V. E., & Thompson, S. D. (2014). Transdisciplinary model and early intervention: Building collaborative relationships. *Young Exceptional Children*, 17(3), 19–30.

Cook, L., & Friend, M. (2010). The state of the art of collaboration on behalf of students with disabilities. *Journal of Educational and Psychological Consultation*, 20, 1–8.

Dettmer, P., Thurston, L. P., & Dyck, N. J. (2005). *Consultation, collaboration, and teamwork for students with special needs* (5th ed., pp. 35–66). Boston, MA: Allyn and Bacon.

Domik, G., & Fischer, G. (2011). *Transdisciplinary collaboration and lifelong learning: Fostering and supporting new learning opportunities* (pp. 129–143). New York, NY: Springer Heidelberg Berlin.

Eccleston, S. T. (2010). Successful collaboration: Four essential traits of effective special education specialists. *The Journal of International Association of Special Education*, 11(1), 40–47.

Friend, M., & Cook, L. (2012). *Interactions: Collaboration skills for school professionals* (7th ed.). Boston, MA: Pearson.

Grisham-Brown, J. (2000). Transdisciplinary activity assessment for young children with multiple disabilities: A program planning approach. *Young Exceptional Children*, 3(2), 3–10.

Hernandez, S. J. (2013). Collaboration in special education: Its history, evolution, and critical factors necessary for successful implementation. *US-China Education Review B*, 3(6), 480–498.

Hong, S. B., & Reynolds-Keefer, L. (2013). Transdisciplinary team building: Strategies in creating early childhood educator and health care teams. *International Journal of Early Childhood Special Education*, 5(1), 30–44.

Kaczmarek, L., Pennington, R., & Goldstein, H. (2000). Transdisciplinary consultation: A center-based team functioning model. *Education & Treatment of Children*, 23(2), 156–172.

Raver, S. A., & Childress, D. C. (2014). *Family-centered early intervention*. Baltimore, MD: Brookes Publishing.

Spencer, S. A. (2005). Lynne Cook and June Downing: The practicalities of collaboration in special education service delivery. *Intervention in School and Clinic*, 40(5), 296–300.

Stepans, M. B. (2002). The role of the nurse on a transdisciplinary early intervention assessment team. *Public Health Nursing*, 19(4), 238–245.

Woodruff, G., & McGonigel, M. J. (1988). Early intervention team approaches: The transdisciplinary model. In J. B. Jordan (Ed.), *Early childhood special education: Birth to three* (pp. 164–181). Reston, VA: The Council for Exceptional Children.

10

RELATED SERVICE PROVIDERS

Mary-Kate Sableski and Catherine Lawless Frank

Chapter Objectives

Following reading this chapter, students should:

1. Explain how the need for related services is determined
2. List several related service providers
3. Describe the roles of related service providers in schools
4. Discuss how related service providers work with school teams to provide services to students

RELATED SERVICES DETERMINATION

IDEA requires schools to provide students with disabilities a free and appropriate education, as well as the needed supports, both academic and nonacademic, to most effectively serve these students. These needed supports are referred to as *related services*. These supports could include speech and language services for a student who has difficulties articulating specific sounds, occupational therapy for a student with difficulties holding a pencil, counseling for a student or family in crisis, or for any number of other services or supports a student needs in order to obtain an appropriate education ("Related Services", 2010). IDEA (Sec. 300.34) defines related services as:

> transportation and such developmental, corrective, and other supportive services as are required to assist a child with a disability to benefit from special education, and includes speech-language pathology and audiology services, interpreting services, psychological services, physical and occupational therapy, recreation, including therapeutic recreation, early identification and assessment of disabilities in children, counseling services, including rehabilitation counseling, orientation and mobility services, and medical services for diagnostic or evaluation purposes.

Related services also include school health services and school nurse services, social work services in schools, and parent counseling and training.

It is important to remember that the definition provides examples of possible related services and not an exhaustive list of all related services. Other services may be necessary, but not mentioned, and still covered under IDEA. These services are provided at no cost to qualifying students ("Related Services", 2010).

Related services do not cover surgically implanted devices such as cochlear implants, pacemakers, or insulin pumps. While the implanted devices may not be covered under IDEA, services that support the surgically implanted device may qualify for coverage. For example, if a student has a cochlear implant, ensuring that the external portion of the implant is turned on and working would be considered a related service. If this student also needs speech and language services, an interpreter, and/or assisted technology, those services would qualify as well. Having a surgically implanted device does not negate the necessity for other special education or related services ("Related Services", 2010).

Determining if a student qualifies for related services is done during the eligibility assessments for special education (see Chapter Four). During this assessment process, a student should be evaluated on all areas of her or his suspected disability. This includes any related service areas, whether the related service area is commonly associated with the disability category or not. For example, if a student is suspected of having mobility issues and the suspected disability category is a physical impairment, then the student must be assessed for physical therapy services at the time of evaluation. This is also true for a student suspected of having a learning disability. If the student is suspected of having a learning disability and a mobility issue, then the student must also be screened for physical therapy, even though physical therapy is not commonly associated with learning disabilities. A student may also qualify for related services under Section 504 if she or he has a qualifying disability, even if that disability does not qualify for special education under IDEA ("Related Services", 2010).

If a student qualifies for related services, the services are specified on her or his IEP or 504 Plan. It is the team's responsibility for determining the appropriate goals and amount of service needed to achieve those goals. The team must also decide what type of services will be provided, when the services begin, where the services will take place, and how often and for what duration the services will be provided ("What are", n.d.).

The team must decide if services will be direct or indirect. In direct services, the therapist or other professional will administer the therapy or service (e.g., counseling) one-on-one or directly to the student. For an indirect service, the therapy or service is provided by a teacher, parent, paraprofessional, or other professional under the guidance or consultation of the therapist ("What are", n.d.). For example, an occupational therapist may work directly with a student providing the therapy and supports necessary for the student to independently perform the activities of daily living. An occupational therapist could also provide indirect services to a student by consulting with the student's teacher on supports or equipment he or she can use in the classroom to improve the student's ability to perform necessary tasks.

The team should also consider when the services are to be provided. Many related services, such as occupational and physical therapy have better results when provided in the student's natural environment at a naturally occurring time. For example, if a student is receiving support from an occupational therapist for handwriting, then the student is more likely to benefit from the therapy if it is provided when and where the student typically uses handwriting (e.g., Language Arts class or more specifically writing class) as opposed to a time and place where handwriting is not typically necessary (e.g., music class).

The team must also determine where the services will be provided. Will the student remain in the general education classroom and receive the service, either directly or indirectly, within this context? Will the student receive pull-out services in which the services are provided in another room or area of the school? The answer to this question is also dependent on the type of services provided. Some services are more appropriately provided in a general education class than others. Speech and language services are more easily and appropriately provided in a general education classroom than many counseling services. Related services should be provided in the least restrictive environment possible; however, the general education classroom is not always appropriate ("What are", n.d.)

The team must then decide when the related services will begin, how often and for how long they will be delivered. This is dependent on the needs and goals of the individual student.

Related service providers are not mandated to be members of the IEP team under IDEA; however, including these providers within the team will prove beneficial for the student receiving services ("Related Services", 2010). Related service providers have an area of expertise that is typically not present in other team members, and their input is essential to providing the supports a student with disabilities needs to meet her or his academic and nonacademic needs.

RELATED SERVICES PERSONNEL

In the following sections, we discuss many of the related services available to students with disabilities with a focus on the service providers of the most common services, namely speech and language therapy, occupational therapy, physical therapy, psychological services, and school social work services.

Speech-Language Pathologists

Speech-language pathologists (SLP) provide critical services to students with communication disorders. Speech-language pathology services are related services to help students who have difficulty with communication skills perform learning and school-related tasks. Speech-language professionals and speech-language assistants provide these services in accordance with state regulations to address the needs of children and youth with disabilities affecting either speech or language. IDEA defines this related service as:

  (i) Identification of children with speech or language impairments;
  (ii) Diagnosis and appraisal of specific speech or language impairments;

(iii) Referral for medical or other professional attention necessary for the habilitation of speech or language impairments;

(iv) Provision of speech and language services for the habilitation or prevention of communicative impairments; and

(v) Counseling and guidance of parents, children, and teachers regarding speech and language impairments.

Speech-language pathology services are long-standing related services in IDEA. They are also crucial in the education of many children with disabilities. More than one million children are served under the disability category of "speech or language impairments" alone, according to the *25th Annual Report to Congress* (U.S. Department of Education, 2003).

A speech-language disorder could be the primary disability for a student, or it may be related to another disability category. For example, in addition to primary special education services for a disability such as autism, a student might receive additional services for speech and language concerns. When speech-language impairments are the sole disability addressed in the IEP, then speech-language impairment becomes a disability category; but when the IEP is designed for another disability primarily, speech and language pathology acts as a related service.

Qualified Providers

Speech-language pathologists earn graduate degrees in a related field from accredited university programs. Many SLPs have undergraduate degrees in education or communication, but this is not a requirement. Licensing requirements vary by state, but most require graduation from a program accredited by the Council on Academic Accreditation in Audiology and Speech-Language Pathology.

Speech-language pathologists in schools are qualified to work with students in early language and literacy development. Training as an SLP provides skills in building and reinforcing relationships between early spoken language and early preliteracy abilities; addressing difficulties involving phonological awareness, memory, and retrieval; teaching children to use tactile-kinesthetic and auditory cues in reading and writing; analyzing how the language demands of textbooks, academic talk, and curriculum may stress a student's capabilities at different age and grade levels; and conducting analyses of written language, including spelling, to generate interventions that match the needs of individual students.

Services Provided

The role of the SLP on the IEP team will change with the degree to which speech and language impairment is affecting the student as compared to other disabilities. If speech and language impairments are the primary disability, the SLP will be a primary member of the team. When speech and language impairments are a secondary disability, then the SLP must work effectively with the team to develop an IEP.

Speech-language pathologists provide a range of services, adjusting the menu of options to meet the needs of students and context. SLPs provide support for communication and swallowing problems, such as articulation issues, including how sounds are pronounced and put together to form words. Children may say one sound for another, leave out a sound, or have problems saying certain sounds clearly. For example, a common problem is with the "liquid" consonant sounds of /l/ and /r/, and SLPs will provide exercises and awareness of the place and manner of articulation in the mouth to remediate these articulation issues.

Issues with articulation can lead to problems with reading and writing through the grade levels. For this reason, another service SLPs provide relates to language, specifically vocabulary concepts and grammar. The pragmatics of language, including social communication, such as how to take turns, how close to stand to someone when talking, how to start and stop a conversation, and how to follow the rules of a conversation, are another area in which SLPs provide support. SLPs will also provide services related to language discourses, including voice, how we sound when we speak, and stuttering, also called a fluency disorder, or how well speech flows. Issues with thinking and memory, also called cognitive communication, including problems with long-term or short-term memory, attention, problem solving, or staying organized, can also be addressed through the work of an SLP. Difficulty with feeding and swallowing, also called dysphagia, can make it hard for children to do well in school and may lead to other health problems. The services provided by SLPs, therefore, are wide ranging in scope. As a related service, the focus of a speech-language pathologist is to support the speech and language development of students as either a primary or secondary disability category. Table 10.1 summarizes the services provided by a speech-language pathologist. Case Study 10.1 provides an illustration of related services provision.

Table 10.1 Services Provided by SLPs

Speech Pathologists provide support for:
• Communication problems, including articulation
• Language concerns such as vocabulary and grammar
• Pragmatics of language including: how to take turns, how to engage in a conversation, and appropriate standing distance from someone else during a conversation
• Services related to language discourse such as voice and fluency disorders
• Cognitive communication concerns including: thinking and memory, problem solving, and attention
• Swallowing and feeding issues

10.1 ILLUSTRATIVE CASE STUDY

Courtney is an eight-year-old child who was born with cerebral palsy that affects both her gross and fine motor functioning. Courtney has received special education services since shortly after birth, first through her community early intervention agency and later through her public school district. While she has made improvements in her fine and gross muscle ability, her PT and OT are vital members of her collaborative IEP team.

While Courtney is mobile, she walks with the aid of a walker. Her PT, Pat McKinley, works with her one-on-one to improve her flexibility and coordination through the use of exercises and stretches. Courtney's teacher collaborated with Pat on the optimal room arrangement for Courtney to maneuver her walker and build her muscle tone. Pat has also taught Courtney's teacher stretches Courtney and the rest of the class can do daily to enhance the muscle tone of the entire class. Pat also ensured that Courtney's teachers and the school nurse were trained on the appropriate way to assist Courtney in using her walker and developing an evacuation plan in case of an emergency.

Courtney's OT is Scott Wilson. Scott's main occupational goals for Courtney include object manipulation and hand-eye coordination. Together, Scott and Courtney work on dexterity, such as grasping objects, handwriting, and holding books and other supplies. Scott worked with Courtney's teacher to ensure she had the appropriate and needed supports and proper accommodations, adaptive materials, and assisted technology to help Courtney in accessing the curriculum and being fully included in the school environment.

Besides providing regular updates on Courtney's progress, Pat and Scott consult and provide support to both her teachers and her parents. They work collaboratively with the team and Courtney's parents to develop the goals and provide the therapy that will allow Courtney to be as independent and successful as possible.

Comprehension Check

1. When are speech and language impairments considered a disability category versus a related service?
2. Name the services a speech pathologist could potentially provide for a student.
3. Describe a speech pathologist's role as assessor, team member, and intervention provider.

Occupational Therapist

An occupational therapist (OT) specializes in assisting students in performing activities of daily living (ADL) in both academic and nonacademic areas. OTs analyze the school environment (e.g., classrooms, cafeteria, playground . . .) and recommend and/ or provide the supports and modifications to help students overcome barriers and fully participate in all aspects of the school day ("What are", n.d.).

According to IDEA in §300.34(c)(6), occupational therapy is defined as:

(i) Means services provided by a qualified occupational therapist; and
(ii) Includes—

(A) Improving, developing, or restoring functions impaired or lost through illness, injury, or deprivation;

(B) Improving ability to perform tasks for independent functioning if functions are impaired or lost; and

(C) Preventing, through early intervention, initial or further impairment, or loss of function.

("Related Services", 2010)

Suppose Jaidyn is a student with a disability who has a deficit in her fine motor abilities. As part of her free and appropriate public education as stated on her IEP, she may receive services from an OT. The OT may help Jaidyn with picking up and positioning her pencil correctly to write and draw legibly. The OT may also work with Jaidyn on the appropriate grasp to button her coat or provide the appropriate supports to allow Jaidyn to hold an eating utensil properly. The OT is working to improve Jaidyn's ability to perform ADL tasks independently.

Qualified Providers

An OT or an occupational therapist assistant (OTA) may provide occupational therapy. An OT holds a graduate degree, while an OTA holds an associate's degree and works under the supervision of an OT. Both an OT and an OTA must pass a national certification exam in order to provide occupational services ("What are", n.d.).

Services Provided

Both OTs and OTAs work with students to increase their independence in ADL in order to increase their participation in school, learning, and extracurricular activities. OTs may work one-on-one with students (e.g., self-care or proper pencil grip), support post-high school transition (e.g., support student's ability to perform job related tasks), and address other sensory, motor, or cognitive needs (e.g., tie a shoe or manipulate a game or puzzle pieces)(AOTA, 2013).

OTs collaborate with team members to recommend instructional strategies and interventions to increase student participation. They may work with school personnel on ways to adapt the school environment (e.g., playground equipment) to make it more accessible for all students. OTs may consult with teachers to recommend specific supports (e.g., specialty scissors), assistive technology (e.g., computer access equipment), classroom adaptations (e.g., seating arrangements), and instructional strategies to increase student attention (e.g., sensory or motor breaks) (AOTA, 2013).

Physical Therapy

Physical therapy focuses on improving a student's posture, movement, and muscle strength. This therapy is provided to students with deficits in gross motor skills that limit their ability to participate in school and the learning process. Physical therapy is defined under IDEA as "services provided by a qualified physical therapist" [§300.34(c)(9)] ("Related Services", 2010).

Qualified Providers

Either a physical therapist (PT) or a physical therapist assistant (PTA) can perform physical therapy. A PT has completed a graduate degree program in physical therapy, while a PTA has completed an associate's program and works under the supervision of a PT. Both PTs and PTAs must hold national and state licenses to perform physical therapy in the school environment ("What are", n.d.).

Services Provided

PTs and PTAs may work one-on-one with students on a variety of skills that help develop posture, muscle strength, and mobility, such as running, walking, skipping, throwing a ball or climbing. PTs also help to enhance coordination, balance, and flexibility in order to increase a student's mobility and independence ("Physical Therapy", n.d.). They may support students on more specific school tasks, such as using appropriate posture or seating positions at a desk, maneuvering in the cafeteria and carrying a lunch tray, transferring in and out of a wheelchair or walker, or transitioning between classes in a given amount of time. PTs and PTAs may also assist students with transition or work-related skills at places of employment or in the community to help develop or support the physical skills needed to perform job and community-related tasks ("Examples of", n.d.)

PTs and PTAs may collaborate with teachers on developing seating arrangements for the classroom or recommend strategies and supports that facilitate posture (e.g., seat wedges or therapy balls), mobility (e.g., a posterior walker or raised desk), and muscle strength (e.g., lying stomachs on the floor to read or writing on a vertical surface).They collaborate to develop plans for supporting a student on field trips or in extracurricular activities. PTs and PTAs may also be responsible for providing professional development and training on how to safely lift and transfer a student or on the purpose and use of specialized equipment. PTs and PTAs may work with other team members and school personnel to develop school evacuation plans or programs that promote the physical well-being of students ("Examples of", n.d.).

Psychological Services

Psychological services are designed to promote the mental health and behavioral well-being of students. Psychological services are defined under IDEA §300.34(c)(10) as

  (i) Administering psychological and educational tests, and other assessment procedures;
 (ii) Interpreting assessment results;
(iii) Obtaining, integrating, and interpreting information about child behavior and conditions relating to learning;
 (iv) Consulting with other staff members in planning school programs to meet the special educational needs of children as indicated by psychological tests, interviews, direct observation, and behavioral evaluations;
  (v) Planning and managing a program of psychological services, including psychological counseling for children and parents; and
 (vi) Assisting in developing positive behavioral intervention strategies.

A school psychologist or other qualified professional such as school counselors or social workers can provide psychological services. This section will focus on the role of the school psychologist, and in the following sections, the role of the school social worker ("Related Services", 2010).

Qualified Providers

School psychologists have completed course work in both psychology and education. They hold a graduate degree in school psychology and either a state license or certificate depending on the requirements in the state in which they work. They may also be nationally certified through the National School Psychology Certification Board (NSPCB) ("What are", n.d.).

Services Provided

School psychologists work with students to provide counseling and behavioral supports. They may work one-on-one or in small groups with students who have difficulties with social skills, behavior management, or developing relationships with teachers or peers. They may provide counseling to students, and possibly parents or families, who have family issues or are in crisis. Academically, they may assist students in developing appropriate study skills such as time management or organization and facilitate academic interventions. School psychologists also assess individual students to determine their strengths and areas of need, especially for eligibility purposes ("What are", n.d.).

School psychologists are an integral part of many school teams. They help to determine the student's eligibility for special education and may be responsible for conducting individualized intelligence tests and interpreting the results; performing student observations, screenings, and interviews; and administering other formal assessments. They collaborate on district or building leadership teams to develop school-wide positive behavioral support programs or on pre-referral intervention teams to provide positive behavioral supports for individual students. They may work on a crisis management team to ensure a school's preparedness and facilitate crisis response and other programs to advance the mental health of students ("Related Services", 2010).

Social Work Services

School social workers use their knowledge in child development and family dynamics to address social and psychological concerns that may be interfering with students' progress in school ("What Does", n.d.). Social work services in schools are defined under IDEA in §300.34(c)(14) as:

   (i) Preparing a social or developmental history on a child with a disability;
  (ii) Group and individual counseling with the child and family;
 (iii) Working in partnership with parents and others on those problems in a child's living situation (home, school, and community) that affect the child's adjustment in school;
 (iv) Mobilizing school and community resources to enable the child to learn as effectively as possible in his or her educational program; and

(v) Assisting in developing positive behavioral intervention strategies [§300.34 (c)(14)].

(Related Services, 2010, http://www.parentcenterhub.org/repository/iep-relatedservices/ #psych)

Qualified Providers

School social workers may hold either a bachelor's or graduate degree depending on the state in which they work. Each state also has its own accreditation, licensure, and/ or certificate requirement. School social workers can also hold a more specialized certificate through the National Association of Social Workers.

Services Provided

In working with individual students or small groups, school social workers provide counseling, intervention, and support services to help students cope with stressful situations, crisis, and/or family troubles. They may also help students develop anger management, conflict resolution, or other behavioral skills, as well as decision making, relationships, and social skills ("What does", n.d.).

School social workers can help the team better understand family and community factors that affect a student's performance in school. They may provide the link between schools, families, and community resources. They may collaborate within teams to develop school-wide behavioral supports systems, crisis intervention plans, and other support services to help meet the emotional and physical needs of students. School social workers may work on teams to determine eligibility for special education services by gathering background information such as the social and developmental history of a child or they may assist in transition planning ("School Social Work", n.d.; "What does", n.d.).

Other Related Services in Schools

Schools employing the consultation model of service delivery in which service professionals are invited as "consultants" to participate in IEP meetings and service plan implementation in schools based on the specific needs of the students (see Chapter Eight) rely on a variety of related services. Since the services utilized in schools will vary with the specific needs of the students, there are no federal definitions under IDEA for these services. It would be impossible to provide an exhaustive list of all possible services in a school, so the following sections will provide examples of some of the services frequently used in schools to meet the needs of the students. Decisions regarding other related service professionals to consult with will be made by the intervention team and will be directly related to the identified disabilities and IEP goals for individual students. Table 10.2 summarizes the other related services commonly called upon in schools to provide services to students.

Assistive Technology

Assistive technology (AT) is a service that enables a student to communicate and participate fully in the school day. Commonly used devices include computers, access

Table 10.2 Commonly Used Related Services

- Assistive technology
- Audiology services
- Counseling services
- Early identification and assessment of disabilities
- Interpreting services
- Medical services
- Orientation and mobility services
- Parent counseling and training
- Recreation services
- Rehabilitation counseling services
- School health services
- Transportation services

systems, and specialized software (Murchland & Parkyn, 2011). Assistive technology devices are provided to students based on the content of their IEP goals. Well-equipped schools provide AT services to evaluate the student's need for a device; select, fit, adapt, repair, or replace the device as needed; facilitate the services for a student who uses a device; and provide training or technical assistance to the student and others involved in the use of the device (Huntinger, 1994). Assistive technology is a constantly changing, evolving field, so even the specific service professionals called in to consult with the team will change depending on the device and its intent. Service providers for AT might include the occupational therapist, speech-language pathologist, or intervention specialist.

Audiology Services

Just as a speech-language pathologist will provide support related to speech and language impairments, a school audiologist helps a student with hearing loss or an auditory processing disorder to navigate curriculum. Audiologists are trained to provide a variety of services, such as fitting and maintaining technology; providing in-service training, consulting, and guidance to support personnel, teachers, and families; participation in IEP meetings; diagnosing or assessing hearing loss and auditory processing disorders; implementing hearing loss prevention programs; assessing students' functional classroom performance; conducting a hearing screening; and assessing classroom acoustics for students who have hearing disorders (Mattson, 2001). Clearly, audiology services are highly specific and require extensive training. In addition, the needs of students related to audiology will be nuanced and unique to each person. Since audiology services are a long-standing service in schools, it is important that schools consult with an audiologist who is trained to work in schools and support curricular needs.

Counseling Services

Increasing numbers of students deal with anxiety, depression, ADHD, and related disorders every day. Increased awareness of symptomology, improvements in diagnoses, as well as the destigmatization of seeking out therapeutic services are all factors that have led to an upswing in the amount of cases of childhood mental and emotional disorders (Centers for Disease Control and Prevention [CDC], 2013). School counselors work with all students, including those with disabilities. School counselors take on numerous roles in schools and should be aware of the types of services students receive. School counselors work with a student in counseling to address issues that interfere with his or her educational success, including anxiety- and depression-related concerns. Counselors communicate with families and other agencies, as well as assist general educators in inclusive settings with issues related to behavior and classroom management. Counselors also work with students on postsecondary transition planning, such as the transition to work or college. Most schools have a counselor on staff who can provide these services on a consistent basis throughout the school year.

Early Identification and Assessment of Disabilities

In school settings that include young children, early identification and assessment is an important related service provided to help identify disabilities as early as possible. A lack of swift assessment and intervention can result in academic challenges later in life (Lange & Thompson, 2006). Young children who are suspected of having a disability receive services under the disability category of developmental delay. Though the suspected disability is still being evaluated and may not be identifiable, the need for services and intervention is imperative at this young age. An IEP team can establish a written plan, as part of the IEP, to outline the process to undertake to help identify that student's disability, while the student continues to receive support and services to facilitate developmentally appropriate progression toward individual and curricular goals.

Interpreting Services

Students who are deaf or hard of hearing utilize this related service so that they can access the curriculum. Oral language, cued language, or sign language transliteration services and transcription services are all included under interpretation services. Students who are deaf-blind may also require related interpretation services. This related service is highly dependent on the unique needs and experiences of the individual student and the limitations and affordances of the school context ("Classroom Interpreting", n.d.).

Medical Services

Medical services provided by a licensed physician to determine a child's medically related disability and the need for special education and related services are considered related services. Medical treatment and intervention is not included in a school service plan, thus medical services qualify as a related service when used for diagnostic or evaluation purposes only (Bigby, 2004).

Orientation and Mobility Services

Students who are blind or have low vision will access orientation and mobility services (O&M) to help them navigate the school and classroom environment. These services are provided as needed for students who are blind or have low vision and will occur on a consultative basis. O&M specialists can teach skills such as how to navigate one's environment or how to travel independently throughout the community (Neal, Bigby, & Nicholson, 2004)

Parent Counseling and Training

Parent counseling and training is an important related service that should be considered in the overall plan of delivery of services. This related service is geared toward assisting parents to better understand the special needs of their child and to assist them with information that can help their child be more successful in academic and other environments (e.g., home, community). A wide variety of professionals such as special education teachers, therapists, or behavior specialists may provide this service depending on the specific areas of need. In addition, this service might be provided in a group setting in which parents learn about disabilities and support options along with other parents (Colorado State Department of Education, 2002).

Recreation Services

Just as early identification services are important for young children, this service gains importance as students grow older and become more involved in out-of-school activities. Assessment of both in-school and out-of-school leisure activities for students is an important component of this service as students learn to use their free time in productive ways. Therapeutic recreation involves the use of sports, games, arts and crafts, music, dance, drama, and non-traditional recreational activities to improve or maintain the physical, mental, and emotional well-being of students who receive special education services. Therapeutic recreation specialists assist students with disabilities to participate in in-school and out-of-school activities to the fullest extent possible (Etzel-Wise & Mears, 2004).

Rehabilitation Counseling Services

From early identification to recreational services, students require different sets of related services across their educational career. School teams can arrange for these related services to support students' changing phases of development and prepare them to confidently enter the post-school world. Vocational rehabilitation services focus on career development and preparing students for employment, independence, and integration into the school, work, or community groups of which they will be a part beyond their PK–12 school years. These services, though identified as ancillary services, are critical components to preparing students to successfully transition out of secondary school (Mattson, 2001).

School Health Services

School health and nursing services can be critical related services for some students who have medical conditions requiring constant monitoring and support, such as asthma or diabetes. Such services might include medication administration, ensuring that students with disabilities have a written emergency plan for such things as medical emergencies (e.g., asthma attack, seizure), and for nonmedical emergencies (e.g., evacuation in case of fire, tornado procedures). Wheelchairs, walkers, assistive devices, and other necessary equipment require careful planning and support for the medical and emergency situations that might arise in a school setting. Coordination of school health services when designing a service plan will insure the safety of the student at school (Bigby, 2004).

Transportation Services

Planning for the transportation needs of students with disabilities should be a component of the service plan. How a student with a disability travels to and from school as well as in and around school buildings is crucial to successful participation in the curriculum and activities of the day. This service should also consider any necessary specialized equipment for travel. A student's disability may present a challenge in traveling to school in the same manner as other students, in which case transportation may be an appropriate related service. Transportation is an example of a related service that takes into account the residual details of the educational adaptations provided by the IEP. Educators and other members of the team must consider these details as part of the overall picture of successfully and meaningfully educating a child with disabilities (Mattson, 2001).

Comprehension Check

1. Decisions regarding other related service providers to consult with will be based on what factors?
2. What sort of services are audiologists trained to provide?
3. Describe the function of a school counselor.

Roles of Related Service Providers

The roles of a related service provider in a school can take on multiple forms, including assessor, intervention provider, curriculum designer, evaluator, resource specialist, researcher, and team member. The service providers can act as *assessors*, in that they screen students, using reliable and valid assessment tools, in their specific area of specialties to determine students' strengths and areas of need. Using this data, the service provider works with the team to decide whether a student is eligible for services and develop appropriate IEP goals and objectives.

Once assessments are in place and an IEP is developed, the related service provider takes on the role of *intervention provider*. In this role, the service provider works with students to meet their individual needs and goals. As the interventions are implemented, the service provider must also *evaluate* student progress toward those goals and communicate progress to the other team members.

The related service providers may also help to develop curriculum, design programs, and choose textbooks, supports, and other materials that help children learn and participate in school. As *curriculum designers*, service providers will research effective therapies, methods of instruction, or other supports and accommodations to enable the student to meet their goals. The service providers also act as *resource specialists*, providing resources and information to students, staff, and parents to help them understand the student's disability and its impact on learning and participating in school. A service provider is a *researcher*, engaging in original research and reading existing literature to continue to fine-tune his or her practice.

One of the most important roles of a service provider is that of a team member. Service providers must be effective collaborators to ensure that students receive the support, therapy, and services needed to have the greatest impact on their growth and learning. Table 10.3 summarizes the services provided by speech-language patholo-gists in schools.

Service providers are critical members of school communities, as they have the specialized knowledge and experience needed to identify related service needs and provide the help that students need to build and remediate those needs. The roles and services they provide help children build the skills they need to succeed in school and in life. Case Study 10.2 provides an opportunity to apply your knowledge of related services.

Table 10.3 Roles of a Speech-Language Pathologist in Schools

- *Assessor*–using assessments to determine whether or not a student is eligible for services
- *Intervention provider*–implementing interventions catered to the specific needs of the student
- *Evaluator*–measuring progress of student and making sure interventions are supporting IEP goals
- *Curriculum designer*–inform curriculum design for students
- *Resource Specialist*–providing resources to students, staff, and parents about specific disorders and the impact on learning
- *Researcher*–constantly reevaluating intervention strategies and updating them based on the most current research
- *Team member*–essential to providing the most effective interventions for students

---

10.2 APPLICATION CASE STUDY

Thomas is a new student in the third grade at Fairhaven Elementary School. He has recently moved into the area with his family, which includes one older sister and two younger brothers. Thomas's father is a car salesman, and his mother is a seamstress. Thomas was on an IEP in his former school for autism and speech-language impairments. Past records indicate he performs adequately in most areas at grade level, but he struggles with comprehension of text. He is able to use speech in a fluent manner but is not always socially appropriate.

The IEP team gathers at the beginning of the year to evaluate Thomas's current IEP goals and make plans for the delivery of services at the school. Ini-tially, the IEP team includes the classroom teacher, the parents, and the speech-language pathologist. After the first meeting, however, the team decides to add several related service professionals to the team. One of those professionals is a recreational therapist, to address concerns that Thomas has difficulties participating in after-school activities such as Boy Scouts and Lego League due to his social language delays. Thomas's parents expressed concern that Thomas had not been allowed to participate in those activities at his old school, and the team at Fairhaven wanted to address that right away.

Another service professional who was invited to consult with the team was the school counselor. Thomas's delayed social skills have caused concern that he may also be developing social anxiety and early signs of depression as a result of not being included in social activities.

Finally, the team discussed options for educating Thomas's parents on autism and community-based options available to them, such as respite care, since they are new to the community. While in the meeting, Thomas's parents displayed signs of stress and worry about the influence of Thomas's disability on their other children and on their family life. With two jobs and three other children, Thomas's needs were beginning to detract from the strong family unit they desired. A respite coordinator will be invited to the next meeting, and the counselor offered to bring information on support groups and other community resources.

1. What questions will you have for the rest of the IEP team?
2. What step has the team missed in the process of inviting the other service personnel to the meeting?
3. Discuss what one of Thomas's IEP goals should be, specifically related to his social skills. How would this goal then be monitored throughout the school year?

CHAPTER SUMMARY

In a school there are many different professionals working collaboratively to ensure that students receive a free and appropriate education. Supports students receive from these professionals can be academic or nonacademic. These supports are referred to as related services. The related services that children with disabilities qualify for will be specified on the IEP or 504 Plan. Important facets to remember of these related services include what type of services will be provided, when the services begin, where the services will take place, and how often and for what duration the services will be provided.

Speech and Language Pathologists (SLPs)

✓ Provide services to students with communication disorders.
✓ SLPs may be responsible for:

- Identification, diagnosis, and appraisal of specific speech or language impairments
- Referral for medical or other professional attention

- Provision of speech and language services
- Counseling and guidance of parents, children, and teachers

✓ Training of an SLP focuses on skills in:

- Building and reinforcing early spoken language and early preliteracy skills
- Addressing phonological awareness, memory, and retrieval
- Teaching tactile-kinesthetic and auditory cues
- Analyzing language demands of the curriculum
- Conducting analysis of written language

✓ SLPs may also help children with vocal, swallowing, or articulation problems.

Occupational Therapists (OT)

✓ OTs specialize in assisting students in performing activities of daily living
✓ OTs may be responsible for:

- Assisting or restoring functions impaired through illness, injury, or deprivation
- Improving abilities to perform independent living tasks
- Preventing further impairment or loss of function

✓ OTs may work one-on-one with a child, in a team, or provide the tools children need to assist themselves.
✓ OTs may provide support to teachers by suggesting specialized tools for children with disabilities or training teachers how to use specialized tools.

Physical Therapists (PT)

✓ PTs specialize in improving a student's posture, movement, and muscle strength.
✓ PTs are generally involved in gross motor actions and may be responsible for:

- Mobility
- Flexibility
- Coordination
- Balance
- Gait

✓ PTs may also be a valuable educational resource for educators by providing trainings and professional development sessions on how to safely lift and transfer students with disabilities.

Psychological Services

✓ Psychological services are designed to promote the mental health and behavioral well-being of students.
✓ Those who provide psychological services may be responsible for:

- Administering assessments, tests, and interoperating results
- Obtaining, integrating, and interpreting information about child behavior and aspects of the child's learning
- Collaborating with other staff members in planning school programs to meet the special educational needs of children
- Planning and managing a program of psychological services
- Consult with and counsel teachers and caregivers
- Assist in developing positive behavioral intervention strategies

✓ Psychological services can be provided by a school psychologist or other qualified professional such as school counselors or social workers.
✓ These service providers may also work with families in crisis or with children to develop social and behavioral skill training.
✓ School psychologists are integral members of the school, as they help determine a student's eligibility for special education, determine a student's areas of strength or weakness, and assist in developing appropriate academic interventions.
✓ School psychologists may also perform student observations, collect data on a student, and screen and interview students, as well as interoperate results from tests and assessments.

Social Work Services

✓ School social workers use their knowledge in child development and family dynamics to address social and psychological concerns.
✓ These service providers may be responsible for:

- Preparing a social or developmental history
- Group and individual counseling
- Working in partnership with parents and others on problems in a child's living situation
- Mobilizing school and community resources
- Assisting in developing positive behavioral intervention strategies

✓ When working with small groups, school social workers provide counseling, support to help students cope with a variety of issues, and/or assist with a crisis or family troubles.
✓ These service providers may be very helpful aiding educators in a student's family and community history or issues.

Several other commonly used related services include:

✓ *Assistive technology services*, which allow a student to communicate and participate fully.

✓ *Auditory services*, which assist a student who has hearing loss or auditory issues.

✓ *Counseling services*, which assist students who may be struggling with ADHD, anxiety, depression, or related issues.

✓ *Early identification and assessments of disability services*, which ensure swift assessment and intervention in order to prevent more severe academic challenges later in life.

✓ *Interpreting services*, which may be utilized by students who are deaf or hard of hearing so that they may fully access the curriculum.

✓ *Orientation and mobility services*, which teach children who are blind or have low vision to access and travel independently in the community.

✓ *Parent counseling and training*, which is geared toward assisting parents to better understand the special needs of their child.

✓ *Recreation services*, which teach after-school and out-of school leisure activities and the importance of utilizing time in productive ways.

✓ *Rehabilitation counseling*, which is an organization of services from early identification to recreational counseling aimed at supporting a child through development and into post-school life.

✓ *School health services*, which can include medication administration, creation of medical or nonmedical emergency plans, and support for medical equipment in a school.

✓ *Transportation services*, which provide the planning and actual transportation for students with special needs.

REFERENCES

The American Occupational Therapy Association (AOTA). (2013). *What is the role of the school-based occupational therapy practitioner?* [Brochure]. Retrieved from http://www.aota.org/-/media/Corporate/Files/Practice/Children/ParentsBrochure.pdf

Bigby, L. M. (2004). Medical and health related services: More than treating boo-boos and ouchies. *Intervention in School and Clinic, 39*(4), 233–235.

Centers for Disease Control and Prevention. (2013, May). *Morbidity and mortality weekly report: Mental health surveillance among children- United States 2005–2011.* Atlanta, GA: The Office of Surveillance, Epidemiology, and Laboratory Services, Centers for Disease Control and Prevention (CDC), U.S. Department of Health and Human Services.

Classroom Interpreting. (n.d.). Classroom interpreters—what does an educational interpreter do? Retrieved from http://www.classroominterpreting.org/Interpreters/role/

Colorado State Department of Education. (2002, September). *Parent counseling and training: A related service under the Individuals with Disabilities Education Act. Guidelines for Colorado parents and educators.* Retrieved from https://www.cde.state.co.us/sites/default/files/documents/cdesped/download/pdf/guidelines_pct_oct02.pdf

Etzel-Wise, D., & Mears, B. (2004). Adapted physical education and therapeutic recreation in school. *Intervention in School and Clinic, 39*(4), 223–232.

Examples of how physical therapists or physical therapist assistants help students (n.d.).Retrieved from http://iris.peabody.vanderbilt.edu/module/rs/cresource/q1/p02/#content

Huntinger, P. L. (1994). State of practice: How Assistive technologies are used in educational programs of children with multiple disabilities. A final report for the project: Effective Use of Technology to Meet Educational Goals of Children with Disabilities. Washington, DC: Office of Special Education and Rehabilitative Services.

Lange, S. M., & Thompson, B. (2006). Early identification and interventions for children at risk for learning disabilities. *International Journal of Special Education*, 21(3), 108–119.

Mattson, N. (2001). *Related services*. News Digest 16, Washington, DC: US Department of Education, Office of Educational Research and Improvement, Educational Resources Information Center.

Murchland, S., & Parkyn, H. (2011). Promoting participation in schoolwork: Assistive technology use by children with physical disabilities. *Assistive Technology*, 23, 93–105. Retrieved from http://dx.doi.org/10.108 0/10400435.2011.567369

Neal, J., Bigby, L., & Nicholson, R. (2004). Occupational therapy, physical therapy, and orientation and mobility services in public schools. *Intervention in School and Clinic*, 39(4), 218–222.

Physical Therapy. (n.d.). Retrieved from http://cerebralpalsy.org/about-cerebral-palsy/treatment/therapy/physical-therapy/

Related Services. (2010, September). Retrieved from http://www.parentcenterhub.org/repository/iep-relatedservices/#psych

School Social Work. (n.d.). Retrieved from National Association of Social Workers website: http://www.social-workers.org/practice/school/default.asp

U.S. Department of Education. (2003). Retrieved from https://www2.ed.gov/about/reports/annual/osep/2003/25th-vol-1-sec-1.pdf. What are related services for students with disabilities and how are they provided? (n.d.). Retrieved from http://iris.peabody.vanderbilt.edu/module/rs/cresource/q1/p02/#content

What are some of the most common related services used in schools? (n.d.). Retrieved from http://iris.peabody.vanderbilt.edu/module/rs/cresource/q2/p07/#content

What does a school social worker do? (n.d.). Retrieved from Elementary Support Services website: http://www.lkgeorge.org/webpages/esupportservice/sw.cfm?subpage=1338948)

11

STUDENT COLLABORATION

Mary-Kate Sableski

Chapter Objectives

Following reading of this chapter, students should:

1. Provide a rationale for student collaboration
2. Discuss the differences between cooperative learning and collaborative learning
3. List the eight key principles for student collaboration
4. Describe several models for student collaboration

STUDENT COLLABORATION

The benefits of collaboration have been highlighted throughout this text, but the focus has been on teacher collaboration to support student learning. This chapter will focus on how teachers can utilize student-to-student collaboration, or peer collaboration, to maximize student learning. Given the dominance of ever-evolving technologies and social networking, as well as the emphasis on collaborative skills in the Common Core State Standards, it is imperative that teachers prepare students to be effective collaborators within and beyond the classroom. Collaboration for students living and working in a digital society is one of the "Four C's of Education" ("The 4CS", n.d.), along with communication, critical thinking, and creativity. Chapters Three and Four discussed the use of RTI as a way to structure interventions to meet student needs. Student collaboration can be a component of Tier One, as it is a classroom modification with potential to impact student learning in positive ways. Active engagement during authentic, collaborative learning tasks can benefit all learners and increase student motivation (Nastasi & Clements, 1991). Collaborative groups bring the benefits of peer support to the center of the learning process (Slavin, 1990; Lave & Wenger, 1991).

Learning within a social context is different from learning independently, thus special consideration needs to be given to the design of collaborative learning tasks in an inclusive classroom. Simply placing students in groups and assigning a task will not help students learn the essential skills needed to collaborate effectively. Student collaboration provides a social context in which students can learn material in collaboration with a peer, given appropriate support, scaffolding, and modeling. When two people collaborate to solve a problem, each brings his or her own perspective to the context. Vygotskian sociocultural theory describes collaboration as leading to cognitive change when peers develop a shared or intersubjective understanding of the situation (Bearison, Magzamen, & Filardo, 1986; Gauvain & Rogoff, 1989; Tudge, 1992; Tudge, Winterhoff, & Hogan, 1996). Student collaboration with their peers has been called *peer pedagogy* (Ching & Kafai, 2008), due to the instructional nature of the interactions between peers during student collaboration. In this type of group work, which has also been called **peer scaffolding**, peers have the opportunity to teach each other, taking on some of the instructional responsibilities of the teacher. Adopting these advanced skills requires strategic instructional decisions by the teacher to help groups work effectively to raise the level of knowledge of each member of the group.

Special education teachers can use student collaboration to help their students meet critical IEP goals, as collaborative groups provide "ready-made" contexts for differentiation. The socialization required of student collaboration can provide opportunities to teach social skills and goals, as well as an opportunity to meet academic goals. In collaborative work, students take on the role of the teacher, becoming experts in the area of study and scaffolding content for their peers. Empowering students with special needs with "expert" status and instructional responsibilities for the members of a collaborative group can have positive benefits instructionally and socially. Peer relationships tend to shift within the context of collaborative groups as peers see one another from a new perspective (Henry, Castek, O'Byrne, & Zawilinski, 2012). For example, a struggling reader develops knowledge about a topic and reading skills through a collaborative interaction, which may also lead to a feeling of empowerment and confidence (Henry et al., 2012).

Collaborative learning has many benefits for all students. It has been shown to have a positive effect on student learning over individual, competitive situations (Johnson & Johnson, 1990; Slavin, Hurley, & Chamberlain, 2003). Collaborative learning can meet more learning style needs within a classroom than direct instruction (Shindler, 2004). Interpersonal skills that are critical for later personal and professional success can be learned. Collaborative learning can be a powerful tool toward building community, practicing conflict resolution skills, learning to consider others' needs, and exploring how to be an effective team member (Watson & Battistich, 2006). Collaborative learning also has the potential to increase student engagement and motivation over more individual, direct approaches to instruction.

In this chapter, student collaboration will be discussed in terms of its application to inclusive settings. Settings in which teachers also collaborate with one another to support student learning can be particularly supportive of models of student collaboration. In the following section, **cooperative learning** will be compared to **collaborative learning**. These two terms are related but distinct in their application to student learning. Next, the principles of collaborative learning will be discussed, followed by a highlighting of the predominant models of collaborative learning among students.

Comprehension Check
1. List two benefits to collaborative learning for students in inclusive settings.
2. Why is collaborative learning an essential skill for today's students?
3. What is the role of the teacher in collaborative learning experiences?

COOPERATIVE LEARNING VERSUS COLLABORATIVE LEARNING

Cooperative learning and collaborative learning are similar terms that are often used interchangeably. Despite some fundamental differences, these approaches do share many common characteristics. Both approaches involve students working with peers on a learning task in a small group. Social constructivist theories of learning, in which knowledge is built through group work, are at the center of each approach. Understanding group communication skills as well as individual roles within the group are essential foundational pieces for both approaches to be successful. Just as when teachers engage in collective work, there is a qualitative difference in the nature of the group work when individuals *collaborate* versus when they *cooperate* to accomplish a goal. Throughout this text, collaboration has been used to describe the highly interactive, mutually supportive work in which teachers engage to support student learning. The same is true of student collaboration in the classroom, in that collaboration involves students interacting and supporting one another to reach their individual and collective learning goals. As this description implies, cooperative learning differs from collaborative learning in key ways.

Cooperative Learning

Cooperative learning is widely employed in K–12 classrooms. Technically, cooperative learning includes any form of instruction in which students are working together for a purpose (Shindler, 2009). However, successful cooperative learning in a classroom requires more than just placing students in a group and letting them work at a task together. Mutual interdependence, collective problem solving, and striving for a common goal are characteristics that mark a group activity as cooperative learning (Webb et al., 1995; Johnson, Johnson, & Holubec, 1998). The emphasis in cooperative learning is on the group process and how the group works together in pursuit of a common goal. The role of the instructor in cooperative learning is to provide structure for the learning experience, monitor the group process and provide feedback, and assess the final outcome according to a set of criteria. In cooperative learning, the instructor plays an important role in facilitating the group process and product (Rockwood, 1995). Cooperative learning is an appropriate method for foundational knowledge that students need to acquire in a domain.

An example of cooperative learning would be a literature circle group in a classroom. In a literature circle, students either select or are assigned a book to read as a group. Roles are assigned to each student within the group, designating their area of responsibility for the discussions about the book. One student might take on the role of "discussion director" and pose questions for the group to discuss. Another student might take on the role of "vocabulary detective" and highlight challenging new vocabulary words in the reading selection. Groups engage in periodic discussions about the book and then work together to produce a final synthesis of the book in the form of a skit, creative project, or essay. Teachers are involved in monitoring the group discussions and evaluating the group discussion process, as well as the submitted product at the conclusion of the reading of the book. Literature circles begin as a tightly controlled cooperative learning experience. As students become more accustomed to the roles and responsibilities of the group, they take on greater responsibility for the flow of the group and its outcomes.

Collaborative Learning

Collaborative learning is an evolution of cooperative learning, in that cooperative learning lays the foundation for more intricate group interactions within collaborative learning. Collaborative learning is truly a give-and-take and may be described as a sophisticated version of cooperative learning. In collaborative learning, the social development of the group is a priority. There is an increased emphasis on sharing outcomes with others and the social constructive nature of learning. However, collaborative group work includes independent assignments and accountability that are completed in consultation with other students working on a similar task or goal. Collaborative learning helps students to prepare for the world of college and career, in which they will be accountable for their own responsibilities but will also have to work in conjunction with others to achieve their goals. In a sense, cooperative learning, with its emphasis on individual roles and the group process, lays the foundation for the dynamics of collaborative relationships. Teachers who provide collaborative group opportunities for their students should consider their previous experience in cooperative learning as preparation for the work of collaborative learning. In addition, an eye toward the next steps the students will take in group work will help teachers to structure effective collaborative learning experiences for students.

An example of collaborative learning would be an inquiry group in a science classroom. The group would brainstorm essential questions about a topic of study and determine an area of study based on these questions. Each member of the group would be responsible for researching a different aspect of the question, but the group would support one another throughout the process through periodic meetings, sharing of resources, and brainstorming of ideas. In alignment with class expectations, the group would determine the product that they submit at the conclusion of the study. The teacher would float in and out of the group to participate in the inquiry and assist with any conflicts or issues. The group would use its previous understanding of effective group communication and processes to focus on the larger goal of generating knowledge about its area of inquiry.

In this chapter, cooperative and collaborative learning models will be discussed interchangeably, with an emphasis on collaborative learning models. Due to the closely related nature of these terms, and the need for teachers to strategically select elements of cooperative and collaborative learning in their lesson planning to meet the needs of their students, it can be difficult to tightly distinguish between these terms when discussing their application in the classroom. In the following section, principles of student collaboration will be discussed to clarify the application of this approach in the classroom. Case Study 11.1 will provide an illustration of the differences between cooperative and collaborative learning.

Comprehension Check

1. List two similarities between cooperative and collaborative learning.
2. List two differences between cooperative and collaborative learning.
3. What are the considerations in choosing which approach to implement in the classroom?

11.1 ILLUSTRATIVE CASE STUDY

Mr. Thursby is spending his planning period wrestling with the upcoming unit he will be teaching on the environment to his seventh grade science class. Reviewing the chapter in the science textbook reminded him of the multiple layers of content he will need to cover within this one unit. Mr. Thursby decides to set up a meeting with Mrs. Mason, the sixth grade science teacher, to discuss the unit. He also hopes that she can shed some light on what the students learned about the environment during the previous school year so that he can be sure to plan his content to build on what the students already know. "There is so much content here and a lot of important issues to discuss", he shares, "I just want to help them take the information and apply it to their own lives."

Mrs. Mason suggests he design a cooperative learning activity for the students to engage in the content. She suggests he divide the chapter up into manageable sections and ask the students to work together to research each area and share it with the class through an oral presentation. Mr. Thursby likes the cooperative element to this activity, but he would like to provide the students with a more authentic way to apply the content to their own lives.

Back in his classroom, Mr. Thursby reads several news articles about environmental issues affecting the local community. Reading these important pieces, he recognizes the need for his students to be able to connect what they are learning about in science class with these community-related issues.

The final unit becomes a collaborative one, in which students work together to not only research an issue but to make an applicable connection to the community issues affecting their lives. Students not only work together to learn about an issue, but they also collaborate to provide new knowledge and experiences to make their community a better place to live.

PRINCIPLES OF STUDENT COLLABORATION

Student collaboration can be distinguished from cooperative learning by the way in which the group takes responsibility for the learning and produces outcomes. There are several principles of student collaboration that will be discussed in the following sections. Again, it is important to remember that cooperative and collaborative learning among students are closely related. Many of these principles also apply to cooperative learning, although this discussion will focus on their application to collaborative learning contexts. As always, teachers are the ultimate decision makers in their classrooms and should determine which of these principles apply to the interactive learning experiences they wish to design for their students. Collaborative teams of teachers should also consider how the principles align with the individual learning goals of the students they teach.

Size

In Chapter Nine, the size of teacher collaborative teams was described as including only those members essential to meeting the needs of the student. More is not always better when it comes to collaboration at any level. When forming collaborative groups of students, three to four members is ideal for an effective process. Even a pair of students can work as a collaborative group. However, groups larger than three or four should only be employed when there is a clear purpose for the additional members. For example, a long-term project such as organizing an event or studying a community issue, with involvement from the school community, community leaders, professionals in the field, etc., may require multiple subtasks to complete. Additional group members may be required to form subgroups and complete the tasks. The essential piece to remember is the decision-making process that goes into determining the size of collaborative groups, as teachers consider the purpose of the group, the tasks set before them, and the experiences of group members with cooperative or collaborative learning.

Composition

The composition of collaborative groups is an important consideration as teachers implement collaborative learning in their classrooms, and it should be based on a variety of factors. Collaborative groups can be formed randomly, numbering students off in a fixed pattern to produce a group of mixed abilities, styles, and goals. Groups can also be formed according to similar abilities, goals, or learning styles. In this latter formation, students are grouped on the basis of similar ability in an academic area, a predisposition toward a certain learning style, or similar academic or IEP goals. These groups allow students to work collaboratively at a pace that is comfortable for them. This can allow students of lower ability to act as leaders within a group of similar ability. Forming mixed-ability groups intentionally selects students based on ability, learning style, or goals to insure an even representation across groups. This formation can allow for rich learning between students, but it can also position students as natural leaders based on ability alone. Students of lower ability may feel marginalized by the higher ability students in the group. Mixed groups allow for students of different learning styles or with different goals to collaborate in support of one another and to be exposed to students who learn differently from themselves. Finally, groups can be self-selected by students, in which teachers allow students to form their own groups based on their preferences. This formation can have obvious disadvantages in that some students will not be "selected" first to be in a group and will be left out. It can also have advantages in that students work with those with whom they feel most comfortable. Selection of the group formation should be made based on the goals for the lesson and the experiences students have in working in cooperative and collaborative groups.

For example, a third grade inclusive classroom implementing collaborative groups to complete a study of the solar system would need to consider the prior experiences students have had throughout the school year in cooperative learning to prepare them for the study. Next, the teacher would want to consider the goals of the lesson and the group composition that would most appropriately help students to meet these goals. If the goal is for each student to contribute equally to an in-depth planet study, then the teacher might want to consider intentionally mixed-ability groups to provide balance and diversity of roles.

Roles

Transitioning students from cooperative to collaborative groups requires that they are able to take on varying roles within a group, depending on the composition of the group and the goals of the task. Assigning students specific roles, as in the literature circle example provided previously, is an example of cooperative learning. For a group to be collaborative, roles should be more fluid and dynamically taken on by members based on the needs of the group. However, particularly when working with young students or students of varying abilities, defining roles within a group should be a decision a teacher makes as the lesson is planned. **Interdependence** is an important component to collaborative groups, and it requires students to become reliant on one another in order to be productive and successful in achieving a common goal. By taking on new and different roles in collaborative groups, students learn to rely on each member of the group in productive ways. Pre-teaching the ways in which collaborative groups function through modeling and mini-lessons prior to engaging in the group process can help students understand the importance of each person's role within a group.

For example, prior to forming collaborative groups for the inquiry project discussed previously, the teacher might choose to spend 15 minutes each day modeling a different role within a collaborative group. It could also be helpful to have a small group of students act out the different roles within a group scenario in front of their classmates. Scenarios might model conflict, leadership, communication, or another aspect of the group process. Then, the students in the class can debrief the modeling and discuss how it applies to the roles they might take on within their groups. The important piece to emphasize in collaborative learning is the fluid, dynamic assigning of roles that occurs.

Norms

For any group to function effectively, it is important to establish norms that will govern the interactions of the group. In a collaborative group within a classroom, this might include respecting one another, allowing every person a turn to talk, taking turns completing tasks, etc. Collaborative groups can establish their own norms for their group, or these can be developed as a class. These can again build on the prior experiences students have had working in cooperative groups, in which there has likely been more defined expectations of roles and responsibilities provided by the teacher. Collaborative group norms should come from the students, just as the knowledge and the product does, as well.

In one example, a fifth grade class worked together with their teacher to establish norms for group work at the beginning of the year, and these were placed on a poster in the classroom. When the class formed mixed-ability collaborative groups to work on a social studies project, however, one group found that they were not able to accomplish much during the time frame allotted to them to work together in class. Since this was a mixed-ability group, the group included students who were gifted, as well as one student with autism with multiple IEP goals related to socialization and turn taking. The special education teacher encouraged the group to have an additional conversation about the group norms, and develop a list that would be unique to the group. The group used the class list of group norms, and added more specifics to some of the guidelines to further define how their particular group would operate. Specifically, the group discussed the issue of shared leadership at length, helping to define who would take on leadership roles at what points in the group process. In addition, the group developed the class norm about turn taking to make the expectations more clear, both for the student who struggled with this procedure as well as for the rest of the group to understand what was expected.

Time and Task

Collaborative groups are intended to operate according to open and fluid processes. The group members take on different roles as needed and develop group norms based on the composition of the group and the task at hand. In a classroom, however, teachers need to set forth some guidelines concerning the amount of time groups will have to meet and work, as well as how the task will be evaluated and defined. In conjunction with the modeling and mini-lessons regarding norms and roles, teachers should also spend time discussing how the group will organize its time. Teachers can arrange for certain days of the week, or time periods each day, based on the school and class schedule in which the groups can work. Depending on the level of experience with cooperative and collaborative learning the group brings, the teacher can assist the students in developing a schedule for accomplishing the task within the specified time frames.

In addition to time, the type of task or product the students are asked to produce is an important consideration in forming collaborative groups. This will also inform the composition of the group, the size of the group, and potentially the roles members take on within the process. In general, groups should discuss the product organically, determining what product they will produce based on the composition of the group and the goal of the activity. Teachers will want to structure these experiences for groups, providing scaffolding and supports as appropriate for the group members' experience with collaborative learning. Teachers will also want to provide guidelines and expectations for the product commensurate with the group composition and experience. When expectations are clear and explicit, cooperative group work can flourish (Shindler, 2009).

For example, a sixth grade class studying conservation might form collaborative groups to investigate issues of interest related to this topic. Prior to forming the groups, the teacher would review and discuss with the class the goals of the project and provide guidelines for the time allotted for the project and the possible products that would align with the learning goals. If the class has not had any experience working in collaborative groups, this process will involve a week or more, as well as whole-class modeling and discussion. If the class is experienced in working in collaborative groups, this process may be a brief overview of the schedule and the goals for the project. Time and task are adjusted to meet the needs of the class.

Classroom Context

No classroom is just like another, and the tangible and intangible differences in class-room contexts influence the instructional activities that occur. A tangible difference might include the number of students who are on IEPs in the classroom, influencing the differentiation that would need to occur within collaborative groups. Another tangible difference could include the type of scheduling the school follows, particularly at the middle school or high school level. Block scheduling, in which students remain with one teacher for multiple periods in a row, allows for extended time for collaborative group work. Physical space would be another tangible difference in a classroom, including established space for independent and group work to occur. If students are expected to work in groups outside of structured class time, establishing physical space within the school that encourages group work is a tangible example of a context supportive of collaboration.

Intangible differences in classroom contexts are related to the tangible differences but contribute more to the climate of the classroom, rather than to the physical space or time available for collaboration. For example, the investment of the teacher in scaffolding and preparing students to engage in collaboration will influence to what degree it is built into lesson plans. The level of teacher collaboration that exists within the classroom will also be an intangible influence on the classroom context for collaboration. If teachers are engaging in team teaching for example (see Chapter Six), students would see a consistent, daily model of collaboration to emulate in their own work. Teachers should give careful consideration to the tangible and intangible components of the classroom context when designing collaborative learning experiences for students.

Assessment

Collaborative work can be challenging to assess, as it involves contributions from all members of the group in different forms. A common thread throughout these characteristics of collaborative group work has been the need for teachers to consider the goals of the activity and the composition of the group in designing the collaborative learning experience. This is also true of assessment. Decisions about assessment of collaborative work should be made based on the goals of the learning activity and the collaborative experiences and skills of the group members.

Assessment procedures should be explicitly communicated at the outset so that students understand how they will be evaluated. Students can be involved in the development of the assessment rubrics, but teachers should clearly identify which components will be individually evaluated and which will be assigned a group grade. When assigning a group grade for any component of collaborative work, teachers should be transparent about how the grade will be assigned and clearly explain why the group grade is justified. Groups may also require additional support to divide up roles and responsibilities to insure equal contributions from each member of the group. Individual grades can be assigned for individual contributions to the over-all team product, raising the level of personal responsibility group members have in developing the team product.

One important component of collaborative group assessment is the opportunity for students to provide feedback on their peers' contributions to the final product. Using a standard form, as in Figure 11.1, students can provide their impressions of the individual efforts of team members. Asking students to provide feedback on the group process increases the level of accountability the group members feel for the process and also serves as a continuous improvement tool for the group itself and the collaborative group work as a whole in the class. Students should also evaluate their own contribution to the product, raising personal accountability and helping students to understand how to improve their own collaborative efforts. Remember, one of the benefits to engaging in collaborative work with students in the first place is to help them become more effective collaborators beyond the classroom and school doors, so opportunities for self-evaluation are important components of assessment in collaborative learning.

Group members' names	This person has contributed to the group project by ...	Concerns I have about this person's participation are ...	I can help this person by ...
Annie	Organizing the group	She needs to contribute more to the final project.	I can remind her of the tasks that need to be completed.
Patrick	Completing the PowerPoint	He is not completing tasks on time.	I can work with the group to make a list of deadlines.
Nora	Doing outside research	She has not found very many resources.	I can ask the teacher to help us find more resources.
Me	Editing and revision	I don't know enough about punctuation.	I can ask another group member for help.

Figure 11.1 Cooperative Group Evaluation Form

Role of the Teacher

The teacher in a collaborative classroom really becomes the "lead learner", rather than the teacher. The role of facilitator becomes important and critical as students learn to take on the norms and habits of working collaboratively. The teacher can model collaborative skills with other teachers, professionals, parents, and students. The teacher should also model what collaborative learning looks and sounds like, providing students with a visual representation and role model for the goals of collaborative learning. In developing collaborative groups, the teacher has to walk a careful line between structuring and monitoring the groups effectively, while also allowing groups to function independently, discussing points, disagreeing, agreeing, and coming to group consensus. The classroom context, both at the tangible and intangible levels, is the first responsibility of the teacher. When a strong classroom community has been created, and students feel safe and valued in the classroom, collaborative learning can flourish.

In relation to the principles already discussed, the role of the teacher involves: 1) clearly specifying the goals of the lesson, 2) developing heterogeneous groups, 3) clearly explaining the expectations of the learning and behavior of the group, 4) monitoring the effectiveness of the group, and 5) evaluating student achievement and group effectiveness (Stainback & Stainback, 1996). The emphasis here is on the critical role of the teacher in creating and sustaining a collaborative culture within the classroom. In the many puzzle pieces that must be in place in order for collaborative learning to work effectively in a classroom, the teacher is the final, critical piece to complete the puzzle.

Comprehension Check

1. List the eight characteristics of collaborative learning.
2. What is an ideal size for a collaborative group?
3. Discuss the tangible and intangible differences in classroom contexts. What is the role of the teacher in creating a collaborative classroom context?

MODELS OF STUDENT COLLABORATION

In the previous sections, definitions of cooperative and collaborative learning were discussed, as well as the fundamental principles for effective student collaboration. Engaging students in collaboration is clearly more than forming groups, assigning a task, and leaving them to their own devices. Taking into consideration the goals of the activity and the experiences of the students will serve to build a foundation for successful collaboration among students. Providing scaffolding and support for students as they take on the habits of effective collaborators is critical to preparing students for lifelong collaboration beyond the classroom. Figure 11.2 describes the ways in which these models build on one another to provide less and less structure to the collaborative experiences, helping students take on the collaborative skills and apply them to new situations.

Cooperative learning: Lays the groundwork for collaborative learning. The group process and how members work together to achieve an end goal are the focus of cooperative learning. It is often used in the process of teaching foundational knowledge.

Collaborative learning: The emphasis of collaborative learning is the social development of the group. This type of learning helps students to become responsible for their own work, yet within the context of working with others.

Figure 11.2 Building on the Models for Cooperative and Collaborative Learning

In this section, several models of student collaboration will be introduced. These are only some examples of the form student collaboration might take in a classroom. Keep in mind that an effective teacher will adjust these models to meet the unique needs of students as they learn about and through collaboration with their peers. Case Study 11.2 includes application of these models to classroom situations.

11.2 APPLICATION CASE STUDY

Which model is best? In the following examples, select the best model to match the vignette.

1. As part of a unit on the Civil War, sixth grade students are asked to read a nonfiction article about the role women played in the war. The article is quite lengthy and contains many text features and structures.
2. Fourth grade students are working to improve their oral reading fluency, specifically their ability to read with expression. They are expected to read several short texts aloud with expression to practice this skill.
3. Fifth grade students are studying fractions in a math unit. The math class is generally grouped by ability, but every Friday the groups come together to explore the new concept together.
4. As part of a unit on citizenship and government, students express interest in learning more about key aspects of government. Interests vary across the class but can generally be grouped into several larger categories.
5. A unit on immigration has led to big questions about immigration in today's society, including its implications for the economy. Though the unit is over, students still would like to learn more and explore these big questions.

Name one of the models of student collaboration for each of the scenarios and justify your answer with support from the text and your experiences. Discuss your responses with a group of classmates.

Peer Learning

Learning with peers is one of the most observable benefits to collaborative learning. When students work effectively in collaborative groups, they can be seen sharing ideas, strategies, and expertise with one another to produce an authentic product.

Peer learning is not limited to groups working together on a shared product. In peer learning, collaborative groups can be formed for the specific purpose of peers taking on the role of the teacher. Peer learning groups should be flexible, formed based on areas of expertise and understanding on the part of students to clarify or extend content taught in class. For example, this strategy might work well in a class that includes several English Language Learners who understand the content, but are struggling with the vocabulary of a math lesson. In a peer learning group, peers who have a good understanding of the vocabulary would work with the ELL students to explain the vocabulary. This process benefits not only the ELL students' math vocabulary knowledge in English but also allows the peers to revisit the mathematical concepts, gaining deeper understanding through explaining the terms and working through the concepts with the ELLs (Elbers & de Haan, 2005).

Cross-Grade Level

Implementation of cross-grade level collaboration is largely dependent on the context of the school. Multiple grade levels with existing collaborative structures between teachers need to be in place in order for cross-grade level collaboration among students to occur. Additionally, students who are asked to engage in cross-grade level collaboration should have some preparation for the norms of collaborative learning. Particularly when an older student is paired with a much younger student, the older student will need to lead and model the collaborative learning experience. This arrangement presents opportunities for both students to learn more about how to collaborate, building from their present understandings at their own level and pace. For example, a frequent pairing involves a kindergarten student with an older "buddy" from eighth grade. When these two students come together, the older student will need to draw from previous experiences working collaboratively to model and structure the time for the kindergarten child. Cross-grade level collaboration among students is frequently used to give an older student an opportunity to teach a younger student, mutually benefiting both students academically and socially.

Jigsaw

In a jigsaw model, students have opportunities to work in multiple levels of collaborative groups surrounding an area of study. Students form groups to read or study one specific area of a topic. For example, in a study of the food guide pyramid, one group would read an article or complete a study about grains, one about protein, one about fruits, one about vegetables, and so on. After the group has gathered information and become "experts" in the area, new groups are formed with one representative from each of the original groups in each. So the new groups would be made up of one member of the grain group, one from the protein group, one from the fruit group, one from the fruit group, etc. In these new groups, students are responsible for teaching their group members about their food group. Finally, the new group completes a synthesizing product together, developed in collaboration with the teacher using the guidelines for assessment discussed earlier.

In jigsaw groups, students have to employ collaborative skills at multiple levels and in new contexts, so the teacher should plan to implement jigsaw groups only after considerable time has been spent working in more basic collaborative groups. Time spent working first in the peer learning groups described earlier would be advantageous prior to engaging in the jigsaw model. Mini-lessons and modeling of the strategies involved in jigsaw groups, such as how to effectively present information in a way others can understand, would also be important pieces of the process. This model can be differentiated to meet the needs of students with special needs or who may have difficulties working at this high level of collaboration. For example, two, rather than one, representative may be included in the new groups to provide a "buddy" when the groups are re-formed. Jigsaw presents many opportunities for teaching students about researching and presentation skills, as well as working effectively with a variety of people in new groups.

Inquiry Groups

Inquiry groups are collaborative groups formed to explore an area of interest. Inquiry groups represent a significant shift in the collaborative process, as they involve less structure from the teacher and more latitude in the direction of the learning on the part of the students. Inquiry groups are formed based on interest, with some eye to heterogeneity from the teacher and consideration of any special needs. When engaging in inquiry groups, student involvement in determining the schedule, structure, final product, and assessment process takes on greater meaning, as the inquiry group should be student driven. Teachers who have provided appropriate levels of scaffolding and support by engaging in peer learning, cross-grade-level collaboration, and jigsaw groups with students will have prepared students to engage in this next level of collaborative learning.

An example of an inquiry group would be students ranking areas of interest brainstormed by the class related to a study on the Great Depression. Students would rank their preferences for study, then the teacher would form the groups based on these preferences and the skills of the students. The class would then discuss the possibilities for product and assessment, working with the teacher to establish guidelines based on the goals of the lesson. The teacher would model and provide structures for the groups to use in dividing up responsibilities, determining a schedule, and completing the final product. The teacher is still very involved in monitoring the inquiry groups, but their level of independence as a collaborative group is significantly increased from the previous three models.

Project-Based Learning

Project-based learning, also called problem-based learning, places students in heterogeneous, collaborative groups to work on an authentic problem or project. In this type of collaborative learning, students should share the teacher's role for instruction, as they work to complete a project using the varying strengths of the group members (Ching & Kafai, 2008). This is a much more complex model of collaborative learning and requires that the students take on significantly more control of the learning process within the group than in the previous models. In PBL, the teacher is much more facilitator than leader, setting the stage, monitoring the process, and providing the appropriate scaffolding as the groups require to be successful. PBL should not be assigned to a group without significant time and attention invested in preparing students to work collaboratively and function as a group.

An example of project- or problem-based learning would be a class, out of a study on government, deciding on an issue of local concern in their community that they wish to bring to the local government's attention through presentation at a town hall meeting, a meeting with the mayor, an op-ed in the newspaper, etc. The key component to PBL involves the authentic product that occurs at the end of the study in which the students feel invested and motivated to engage. Students would form groups, taking on different components of the issue to research and present on, and the teacher would provide structure and resources throughout the study to keep the group functioning effectively. Engaging in collaborative assessment is a critical component of PBL, as the groups work together to evaluate their process and product at both an individual and group level.

Web 2.0

The proliferation of interactive technologies available via the Internet has revolutionized opportunities for student collaboration. Social media, interactive Internet sites, wikis, and online software programs have opened space within classrooms for students to collaborate within and beyond their classroom doors in innovative and, seemingly endless, ways. Table 11.1 describes some of the options available in wikis, social media, and online software programs to use as collaborative learning support in the classroom.

Wikis

A wiki is an online tool for creating a website that does not require programming skills or advanced knowledge of web development. Wikis have become a widely used tool in education, particularly at the college level. However, wikis also have applications to K–12 classrooms because of the numerous opportunities they present for collaborative learning. Wikis are constructivist in nature, supporting organic, student-constructed learning experiences. Within a wiki environment, students can work collaboratively to take notes, evaluate one another's process and product, or create a product together. As with any technological tool, however, careful thought and planning needs to be given to the how and why of implementation of the wiki in

Table 11.1 Some Options Available for Online Learning

- *Wikis*–A wiki is a collaborative website in which users can add, edit, and organize content. Wikipedia is the most popular website used. Other public wiki examples include Catawiki, Wikitionary, and Open Street Map.

- *Social Media*–Social media connects classroom learning to the real world. Sites such as Twitter and Facebook allow for collaboration at all hours of the day and to any place in the world, with access to new information in real time.

- *Online software programs*–Programs such as Blackboard Collaborate allow individuals to work together through an online learning platform and include features such as high definition video and audio, as well as file sharing. Other programs such as Asana provide a unified team space that allows members to track important tasks, information, and overall progress.

support of collaborative learning for it to be truly effective (Chang, Morales-Arroyo, Than, Tun, & Wang, 2011).

Social media

Facebook, Twitter, Instagram . . . these are all social media sites with which today's students are intimately familiar and use on a daily basis for personal and social use. These sites are increasingly finding their way into classrooms as tools for collaborative learning. As more and more K–12 schools adopt one-to-one technology for their students, the use of these platforms as tools in the classroom is likely to continue to rise. Social media in the classroom presents logistical challenges, including privacy issues, pragmatic issues, and logistical issues, but its power as a tool to help students collaborate holds promise for educators.

Social media is inherently familiar and motivating to students. Collaborative learning should always be grounded in authentic links to how collaborative skills will benefit students beyond the classroom, and the use of social media in student's daily lives makes it a natural resource to use to bridge this gap (Junco, Elavsky, & Heiberger, 2013).

Online software programs

Online software programs need to be introduced and structured according to the specific skills required of the program so that students can be successful in their use (Miller & Benz, 2008). These programs can act as the more knowledgeable other and support social and collaborative learning in the classroom (Cicconi, 2014). Students are increasingly being asked to use technology tools as a way to demonstrate their understanding in high-stakes testing environments, so experience using online software programs in collaboration with others will provide the structure and support needed for them to apply these skills to school contexts.

The teacher's role within Web 2.0 collaborative technologies is significantly different from that of the more traditional, in-classroom facilitation (Abdu, De-Groot, & Drachman, 2012). The teacher has to account for the many possibilities presented by the technological tools and the advantages and disadvantages present in each. Anticipating the need for new norms of behavior within collaborative learning is another important component of the teacher's role when using technology as a tool for collaboration. Web 2.0 tools have the potential to move student collaboration beyond the classroom doors, both literally and figuratively. As teachers work to prepare students who are prepared for a collaboration-based workplace, developing skills for collaboration within technological environments is an imperative.

Comprehension Check

1. List the benefits of working with peers.
2. Describe how a jigsaw model works.
3. What are some benefits and advantages of using social media in collaborative learning?

CHAPTER SUMMARY

Student collaboration can be an integral part of Tier One support in an RTI model. Active engagement during authentic, collaborative tasks can benefit all learners in the classroom, as well as increase student involvement. Student collaboration should not be confused with cooperative learning, although they do have many things in common—including:

- ✓ Both involve students working with peers on learning a task in a small group.
- ✓ Both are based on social constructivist theories.
- ✓ For both approaches to be successful, students must understand group communication rules, as well as individual roles in the group.
- ✓ Both involve mutual independence, collective problem solving, and striving for a common goal.

Collaborative Learning

- ✓ Collaborative learning is considered an evolution of cooperative learning.
- ✓ In collaborative learning, there is an increased emphasis on sharing outcomes with others.
- ✓ When forming collaborative groups, groups of three to four students are ideal.
- ✓ Collaborative groups can be formed randomly in a fixed pattern to produce a mixed group based on similar abilities/interests, or chosen by the students themselves.
- ✓ Roles in a collaborative group are more fluid. Roles can be dynamic and changed depending on the needs of the group.
- ✓ It is important that members of a collaborative group already understand the norms and rules that govern the interactions of a group. However, members may create and define norms for their specific group depending on the needs of the group.
- ✓ In a classroom setting, teachers will still need to set times and guidelines for when the group should meet and collaborate.
- ✓ Teachers should be very clear on how the students in a collaborative group will be assessed, both as a group and individually. This assessment should take into account the goals of the learning activity and the experiences/skills of the group.
- ✓ When implementing collaborative groups, a teacher becomes "the lead leader" rather than teacher.
- ✓ A teacher should model collaborative skills for his or her students.

Models of Collaborative Learning

Peer Learning

- ✓ Not limited to groups working together on a shared project.
- ✓ Should be formed with the goal of peers seeking to take on the role of "teacher".
- ✓ Should be flexible groups with the understanding of clarifying or extending content taught in class.

Cross-Grade Level

✓ This collaboration is largely dependent on the context of the school.
✓ Older students are able to model and teach younger students in content area, socialization, and how to collaborate.

Jigsaw

✓ Students have an opportunity to work in multiple levels of collaborative groups surrounding one area of study.
✓ A student will become an expert in one area of content, with other students becoming experts in the same area; they will then transition to a new collaborative group where they will teach the content they have learned. At the same time they will learn from other students who have become experts with separate content in the same area of study.
✓ When this collaborative process is done, all students should be well versed in all content in the same area.

Inquiry Groups

✓ Students form a collaborative group based on an area of interest.
✓ These groups involve less structure from the teacher and more latitude in the direction of the learning on the part of the students.

Project-Based Learning

✓ Also called problem-based learning.
✓ Heterogeneous in nature, this group works on an authentic problem or project.
✓ This group requires the students to take on significantly more responsibility for learning.

Web 2.0

✓ These types of groups utilize technology to collaborate and educate. These groups can utilize several different technological mediums including:

- Wikis
- Social Media
- Online software programs

APPLICATION ACTIVITIES

1. Divide up into groups and chose one of the models of collaborative learning listed in this chapter. As a group, design a project demonstrating the

concepts of the model. Discuss potential roadblocks to the implementation of this model and any factors needed for consideration in the planning of the project.

2. Meet with a teacher who has experience in implementing collaborative learning projects. Gather information on his or her experience, including successes and challenges he or she has faced in the process. What have they found to be most helpful? What has proven to be their biggest obstacle? What do they wish they had known when first attempting to implement collaboration models?

3. Within groups, design some sort of learning aid that demonstrates the difference between cooperative and collaborative learning. This can include a visual representation, metaphor, or some sort of interactive activity that provides an experimental exercise that demonstrates the groups understanding of these two learning styles.

REFERENCES

Abdu, R., DeGroot, R., & Drachman, R. (2012). Teacher's Role in Computer Supported Collaborative Learning. In *Proceedings of the 7th Chais Conference for Innovation in Learning Technologies* (pp. 1-6). Raanana, Israel: The Open University of Israel.

Bearison, D. J., Magzamen, S., & Filardo, E. K. (1986). Socio-cognitive conflict and cognitive growth in young children. *Merrill-Palmer Quarterly*, 1982, 51–72.

Chang, Y. K., Morales-Arroyo, M. A., Than, H., Tun, Z., & Wang, Z. (2011). Collaborative Learning in Wikis. *Education for Information*, 28, 291–303.

Ching, C. C., & Kafai, Y. B. (2008). Peer pedagogy: Student collaboration and reflection in a learning-through design project. *Teachers College Record*, 110(12), 2601–2632.

Cicconi, M. (2014). Vygotsky meets technology: A reinvention of collaboration in the early childhood mathematics classroom. *Early Childhood Education Journal*, 42(1), 57–65. .

Elbers, E., & de Haan, M. (2005). The construction of word meaning in a multicultural classroom. Mediational tools in peer collaboration during mathematics lessons. *European Journal of Psychology of Education*, 20(1), 45–59.

Gauvain, M., & Rogoff, B. (1989). Collaborative problem solving and children's planning skills. *Developmental psychology*, 25(1), 139.

Henry, L. A., Castek, J., O'Byrne, W. I., & Zawilinski, L. (2012). Using peer collaboration to support online reading, writing, and communication: An empowerment model for struggling readers. *Reading & Writing Quarterly*, 28(3), 279–306.

Johnson, D. W., & Johnson, R. T. (1990). *Learning together and alone: Cooperative, competitive, and individualistic learning* (3rd ed.). Boston, MA: Allyn & Bacon.

Johnson, D. W., Johnson, R., & Holubec, E. (1998). *Cooperation in the classroom* (7th ed.). Edina, MN: Interaction Book Company.

Junco, R., Elavsky, C. M., & Heiberger, G. (2013). Putting twitter to the test: Assessing outcomes for student collaboration, engagement and success. *British Journal of Educational Technology*, 44(2), 273–287.

Lave, J., & Wenger, E. (1991). *Situated learning: Legitimate peripheral participation*. New York, NY: Cambridge University Press.

Miller, R. L., & Benz, J. J. (2008). Techniques for encouraging peer collaboration: Online threaded discussion or fishbowl interaction. *Journal of Instructional Psychology*, 35(1), 87–93.

Nastasi, B. K., & Clements, D. H. (1991). Research on cooperative learning: Implications for practice. *School Psychology Review*, 20(1), 110–131.

Rockwood, H. S. III (1995). Cooperative and collaborative learning. *The National Teaching & Learning Forum*, 4(6), 8–9.

Shindler, J. (2004). Teaching for the success of all learning styles: Five principles for promoting greater teacher effectiveness and higher student achievement for all students. Retrieved on October 9, 2008, from Paragon Consulting website: http://web.calstatela.edu/faculty/jshindl/ls/

Shindler, J. (2009). Effectively managing the cooperative classroom. In *Transformative classroom management*. San Francisco: Wiley. Retrieved from http://web.calstatela.edu/faculty/jshindl/cm/TCM%20TOC%20 final.htm

Slavin, R. E. (1990). *Cooperative learning: Theory, research, and practice* (Vol. 14). Boston, MA: Allyn and Bacon.

Slavin, R. E., Hurley, E. A., & Chamberlain, A. (2003). Cooperative learning and achievement: Theory and research. *Handbook of Psychology*, 177–198.

Stainback, S.B.E., & Stainback, W. C. (1996). *Inclusion: A guide for educators*. Baltimore, MD: Paul H. Brookes Publishing.

The 4CS research series. (n.d.). Partnership for 21st Century Learning. Retrieved from http://www.p21.org/ our-work/4cs-research-series

Tudge, Jonathan R. H. (1992). Vygotsky, the zone of proximal development, and peer collaboration: Implications for classroom practice. In L. C. Moll (Ed.), *Vygotsky and education: Instructional implications and applications of sociohistorical psychology* (pp. 155–172). New York, NY: Cambridge University Press.

Tudge, Jonathan R. H., Winterhoff, Paul A., & Hogan, Diane M. (1996). The cognitive consequences of collaborative problem solving with and without feedback. *Child Development*, 67(6), 2892–2909.

Watson, M., & Battistich, V. (2006). Building and sustaining caring communities. In C. M. Everson & C. S. Weinstein (Eds.), *Handbook of classroom management: Research, practice, and contemporary issues* (pp. 253–279). Mahwah, NJ: Lawrence Erlbaum.

Webb, N. M., Troper, J. D., & Fall, R. (1995). Constructive activity and learning in collaborative small groups. *Journal of Educational Psychology*, 87, 406–423.

12

EFFECTIVE INTERPERSONAL INTERACTIONS

Catherine Lawless Frank

Chapter Objectives

Following reading the chapter, students should:

1. Determine the components of interpersonal communication
2. Identify the steps and skills needed for active listening
3. Understand nonverbal communication and its impact on interpersonal communication

INTERPERSONAL COMMUNICATION

Interpersonal communication is the means by which a person conveys a message to another person or group of people, no matter the setting, group, or topic. Interpersonal communication can be talking to friends about plans for the weekend, asking a professor a question, teaching a class, negotiating with a police officer about a speeding ticket, or explaining assessment results to an emotional parent. It is an exchange of information in which one person, the speaker, sends information, both verbally and nonverbally, and another person or group of people receives it. The receiver(s) or listener(s) then interpret both the verbal and nonverbal message. The interpersonal communication is successful if the receiver of the information understood and interpreted the message in a manner in which the sender intended (Dziak, 2015). This is not a simple process. Interpreting a message involves a degree of subjectivity, which is influenced by context of the situation and the receiver's thoughts, mind-set, knowledge, feelings, and experiences. Two people may hear the same message and interpret it completely differently (Comstock, 2015b).

Interpersonal communication is composed of both verbal and nonverbal communication. Verbal communication encompasses the words or spoken language used to send a message. Nonverbal communication comprises all other aspects of the message that do not involve language. Nonverbal communication is made up of nonverbal cues, such as physical appearance, body movement or language, facial expressions, posture, adornments, personal space, touch, and smell. While both verbal and nonverbal communications are subject to misinterpretation, interpreting nonverbal communication tends to be more difficult and more subjective. Nonverbal communication does not rely on words and often relies only on the interpretation of the receiver, but both verbal and nonverbal components are important parts of interpersonal communication (Dziak, 2015). Nonverbal communication may, however, also involve sign language, which then includes linguistic messages as well.

Mediated Communication

While this chapter will focus mainly on face-to-face communication, it is important to understand that interpersonal communication can also be mediated and facilitated through the use of an electronic device such as a computer or cell phone (e.g., emails, text messages, social media, or video conferencing). Mediated communication is invaluable to educators because of the distance and time it saves in sending and receiving messages. The communicating partners do not have to be present to communicate and can send a message that is received at a later time by the recipient. The recipient can then respond to the message when it is convenient for him or her or even choose not to respond at all. A parent can email a teacher in the morning about homework concerns, and a teacher can read and address that email at lunchtime. A special education teacher can text a general education teacher over the weekend to arrange a meeting for Monday after school. A teacher can email her or his lesson plans to the principal on Thursday so he or she can review them on Friday. An IEP team can video conference with a medical professional about the supports and services that are most appropriate for a student's education. Mediated communication is vital to saving time and allowing communication to occur without being in the same space and at a time that is convenient to all parties (Codington-Lacerte, 2013; Dziak, 2015).

While the use of mediated communication can be invaluable for parents and educators, it cannot replace the benefits of face-to-face interactions in building collaboration. While time is a benefit to mediated communication, it is also a disadvantage. Mediated communication often lacks the ability to send and receive information in current time and provide immediate feedback. If a parent has a question and emails the teacher, the parent must wait until the teacher accesses the email and responds before receiving an answer. While this process can be immediate, it can also take several hours or even days. With face-to-face communication, the question can be answered almost immediately, because all parties are in the same place at the same time (Codington-Lacerte, 2013; Dziak, 2015).

Mediated communication does not have the advantage or support of nonverbal cues in helping to decipher the emotions or importance that a person attributes to a message. The receiver may attribute emotions or importance to a message that the sender did not intend, or the receiver may not attribute an emotional significance to a message that the sender did intend. Mediated communication typically relies on language alone without the support of nonverbal cues to relay the emotion or significance attached to a message, causing confusion and miscommunications (Codington-Lacerte, 2013; Dziak, 2015).

Face-to-Face Communication

Face-to-face communication is direct interpersonal communication because the communication occurs between the partners at the same time and in the same space. A parent can ask a question and a teacher can respond to it almost immediately and further exchanges can clear up any additional questions or confusion. Both parties can use the nonverbal cues of the other to facilitate comprehension not only of the message but also the emotions and importance attributed to the message (Dziak, 2015). Successful face-to-face communication relies on a person's verbal abilities, active listening skills, and nonverbal cues in order to be successful.

Successful direct communication relies on a solid, clear command of the language and appropriate word choice. A solid, clear command of the language consists of vocabulary, pronunciation, and grammar, which are necessary for the listener to be able to clearly decipher the spoken word. Appropriate word choice is necessary for the listener to understand and identify with the spoken word. Word choice is defined as using words and phrases that are suitable for the given audience. For example, discussing assessment results with a school psychologist could involve different word choices than discussing assessment results with a parent. While solid and clear command of the language is necessary for both occasions, word choice is also important to communicate a meaningful message. With a school psychologist, a special education teacher may be able to use terms such as norm-referenced, raw score, or standard deviations; using these phrases with parents may cause confusion. Rephrasing the terms into more common language such as "compared to other people" for norm-referenced, "the number correct" for a raw score, and "above or below average" for standard deviation may be more appropriate word choices to use with parents or others not familiar with standardized assessments. A school psychologist may have the assessment background needed to comprehend norm-referenced, raw score, or standard deviation but a parent may not. This is especially important in education where specific acronyms and terminology are common (e.g., IEP, RTI, SLD, progress monitoring). Collaboration requires that all team members feel equally important and, therefore, appropriate word choices that are comprehensible for all are necessary to ensure that all members feel included and valued. It may be difficult to feel like an equal member of the team when other team members are using words, acronyms, and phrases that are uncommon and unknown.

In the next two sections of this chapter, we will be examining the other two components of direct interpersonal communication, active listening skills, and nonverbal cues.

Comprehension Check

1. What are the components of interpersonal communication?
2. How does mediated communication differ from direct or face-to-face communication?
3. How are time and distance both an advantage and disadvantage to mediated communication?

Active Listening Skills

An essential element in the communication process is listening, because without listening no real communication can occur (Comstock, 2015b). Listening is more than just hearing. Hearing is the physical process of obtaining a message. Listening is the active process of hearing but also includes attending to a message with the intent of understanding and interpreting it. Hearing, or obtaining the message, is involved in listening, but listening is more than hearing. A person can hear well and be a poor listener. Actively listening requires the receiver to hear a message, interpret it, reflect upon it, and provide feedback to the speaker in order to acknowledge or clarify the message (*Merriam-Webster* online dictionary, Downs, 2008; Comstock, 2015a).

Steps of the Listening Process

Active listening is more than just being polite and demonstrates through actions and words that the receiver is interested and engaged in the communication process (Hoppe, 2006). Active listening shows that the thoughts, ideas, and feelings of the speaker are important and valued. It is essential in building professional and personal relationships and in the collaborative process.

Active listening is a six-step process that demonstrates through words and actions that a person is focused on the speaker, open to the message, reflecting on and clarifying what is being said, able to summarize key points, and able to provide an appropriate response. While active listening can be beneficial to employ in everyday conversations with friends, peers, and family members, it is especially effective in emotional situations and conflict resolution (Comstock, 2015a).

The first step in the active listening process is to focus on the speaker. Oftentimes there are many distractions, both internal and external, that interfere with effective communication. These distractions make it harder to focus and effectively communicate. If possible, find a quiet location to conduct conversations and focus on the speaker's verbal and nonverbal message while ignoring other noises, conversations, and internal thoughts. Pay attention to the speaker and remember the objective is to listen, understand, and connect. It is also important to remember that nonverbal cues must also demonstrate that a person is interested in and focused on the speaker. Looking around the room, reading an email, or multitasking tells the speaker that the listener is not focused and other things are more important than her or his message. This breaks down the collaborative process. A person's body language should demonstrate that he or she is engaged and focused. If it is culturally appropriate, make eye contact and lean forward to show interest. A smile and nod of the head may also demonstrate listening while providing encouragement to the speaker (Hoppe, 2006; Comstock, 2015a).

The second step in active listening is to be open and receptive to the message. This does not mean that the receiver agrees with what the speaker is saying. It does mean that judgment needs to be suspended and that the receiver is willing to listen to the speaker to understand her or his point of view. The intent should not be to judge the speaker but to gain information, knowledge, thoughts, feelings, and insights. Being open and receptive is especially important in tense situations where emotions are high or people are upset. Being open and receptive does not demonstrate agreement but does demonstrate empathy as well as a sense of respect for the other person's ideas and thoughts (Hoppe, 2006).

In active listening, the third step is to reflect and paraphrase both the verbal and nonverbal message of the speaker. This step involves listening not just to the words but also to the emotions and nonverbal cues of the speaker to interpret the meaning of the message. Nonverbal cues may provide greater insight into the significance, intent, and emotions the speaker attaches to the message. This step involves interpreting the speaker's nonverbal cues and feelings, then verifying that interpretation through paraphrasing the key verbal and nonverbal points. Statements like "Let me make sure I have this right . . ." and "What I think you are saying is . . ." allow the listener to demonstrate her or his engagement and command of the message. Phrases like "You seem pretty concerned about this, let me make sure I understand what you are saying . . ." allow the listener to not only paraphrase the verbal message but also the emotions attributed to it. Reflecting and paraphrasing allows the speaker to correct any miscommunication early in the conversation (Hoppe, 2006; Comstock, 2015a).

Step four in active listening is to ask questions to clear up any confusion and/or to gain more information or insight. Asking open-ended questions allows the speaker to clarify or expand upon a message. Open-ended questions like "I am a little confused. What did you mean by . . ." or "I think I may have missed something. What did you say about . . ." can be used to clarify information. Questioning may also assist the speaker in further thinking about, reflecting, and expanding upon her or his message, which may illicit further insight and engagement in the topic. Who, what, where, when, and why questions, such as "Who do you think should be involved?" or "What do you think about . . ." can help in delving deeper into the topic (Hoppe, 2006).

Restate and summarize the main idea of the message is step five in active listening. Restating a message does not mean that the listener necessarily agrees with what was said but that she or he is attending to and understands the message being communicated by the speaker. This also allows the speaker to again clear up any confusion. Statements like "Let me make sure I understand this. Your main concern is . . ." or "Your idea is to . . . Correct?" demonstrate ways the listeners can restate and summarize key points (Hoppe, 2006).

At this point in active listening, the listener has focused on the speaker, been open to the message and reflected upon it, clarified any confusion, and restated the key points. Now it is time to reply. The final step in the process is to provide a response and share ideas, thoughts, and feelings. Active listening is not passively absorbing information but an active process that demonstrates attentiveness, ensures comprehension, and requires providing a response. This is when the listener shares her or his views and possibly collaborates and works toward a solution. Statements like "While I understand that you think this . . . this is what I think" and "I like your idea to . . . What if we . . ." provides the listener a chance to summarize key points as well as provide insight (Hoppe, 2006). Case Study 12.1 provides an example of active listening.

12.1 ILLUSTRATIVE CASE STUDY

Mrs. Anita Lincoln (Anita) is a special education teacher.
Mrs. Linda Johnson (Linda) is a student's (Sean) parent.

Anita is sitting at her desk after school completing some paper work.
Linda bangs on the door and says, "Can I speak with you?"
Anita replies, "Sure. Have a seat." Anita turns off her monitor and turns to face Linda.

Linda: "Sean has too much homework. It takes him twice as long to complete homework as it does his friend Johnny, and he always seems to have more. It is unfair. Sean wants to go out and play, but he can't because he spends all afternoon doing homework."

Anita: "It sounds as if you are upset. Let me see if I have this correct. I think you are displeased because Sean has more homework than Johnny, and it takes Sean longer to complete his homework than it takes Johnny. Correct?"

Linda: "Yes, I am upset. Sean has a learning disability, so it takes him longer to do his homework. Because he is slower to complete assignments at school, teachers seem to think it is ok to send all the incomplete work home as homework. Sean ends up with more work to do than his classmates, and it takes him forever. It is not fair. How is he supposed to be able to play if all he is doing is schoolwork? I spend half my evening helping him because he cannot do it by himself. I don't get it."

Anita: "Ok. I think I understand. You think Sean has too much homework. Sean has difficulty with the homework and you help him. So both you and Sean spend a lot of time on his homework."

Linda: "Yes, he has a lot of homework and I have to help. But he has more homework than Johnny."

Anita: "Do you think Sean could do the homework independently, without your assistance?"

Linda: "Well, maybe some of it, but I do not think he can do all of it."

Anita: "Ok. What parts do you think he can do independently?"

Linda: "I guess the math. He seems to get that, except maybe with word problems. He cannot do the science, though. He cannot read the textbook. It is too hard for him to read it, so then he cannot answer the questions."

Anita: "So he can do the math, except the word problems, but he cannot do the science, correct?"

Linda: "I know he has more homework because he has trouble completing assignments in class, and I know Johnny does complete his assignments. But it is still not fair."

> *Anita:* "So you are ok with the amount of math homework Sean has?"
> *Linda:* "Yes."
> *Anita:* "You are concerned about the science homework. Correct?"
> *Linda:* "Yes."
> *Anita:* "What if we meet with Mrs. Cleveland, Sean's science teacher, and see what we can work out? I think between the three of us we can figure out how to provide Sean more supports in science so he can complete his assignments in class. Would it help to include Sean in on the meeting?"
> *Linda:* "Yes, I think it would be a good idea to include Sean. And thank you."
>
> Anita arranges a meeting for Mrs. Cleveland, Linda, Sean, and herself for tomorrow after school.

If this process is part of a longer discourse, it may be beneficial to ask the speaker to provide a summary of the key points at the end of the conversation to ensure both the speaker and the listener equally understand the topic and the decisions that were made. A concluding summary of key points allows a final chance to ensure comprehension and clarify any misinformation (Hoppe, 2006).

It is important to remember nonverbal cues when engaging in active listening; following the steps of active listening without the appropriate nonverbal cues defeats its purpose. Appropriate body language and other nonverbal cues can support the process, while inappropriate ones can destroy it. Looking around the room, reading an email, or writing a note during a conversation contradicts active listening and may lead the speaker to believe her or his thoughts, opinions, and emotions are not important to the listener. Sighing, yawning, or looking at a watch may imply that the listener is not interested or actively engaged. Body language and nonverbal cues are important and should convey attentiveness and engagement. Remember is it not just what you listen to but how you listen to it that is important (Comstock, 2015a).

Verbal and nonverbal communication can also be misinterpreted when working with people of different cultural backgrounds. Active listening can help in these situations to avoid confusion and allow for clear communication (Hoppe, 2006).

Active listening is a valuable skill to use in everyday life with family, friends, and peers. It is even more valuable to use in the collaborative process when working with coworkers, students, and parents—especially in culturally diverse or emotional situations. Listening is an important part of building effective relationships and makes the speaker feel that she or he and the message are important to the listener. This is essential to the collaborative process and ultimately provides a stronger, more cohesive education for students (Hoppe, 2006; Comstock, 2015a).

Barriers to Active Listening

There are barriers to implementing active listening. Like any new skill, it requires practice and a potential change of mind-set. Teachers often spend a great deal of time in college classes and professional development learning how to plan, present, and teach a lesson. In comparison, they spend little, if any, time learning how to listen. Active listening is a learned skill and not an innate one. It takes effort and a willingness to learn and implement, but its assistance to the collaborative process is invaluable (Hoppe, 2006; Comstock, 2015a).

It can be hard for a listener to be quiet and focus rather than interrupt the speaker with his or her own thoughts and ideas or to ignore internal and external distractions. This is especially hard to do if the listener is busy, preoccupied, or disagrees with what the speaker is saying. Oftentimes individuals may be quick to respond without taking the time to reflect and truly understand another person's message. Active listening requires a person to be silent, reflect on the message, and summarize it before forming a response. Being silent and reflecting before responding may feel unnatural or be difficult, but doing so may provide the knowledge and insight needed for true communication and collaboration (Hoppe, 2006).

Active listening may seem like it requires more time. Just as time is a barrier to the collaborative process (see Chapter One), time is also a barrier to active listening. It may seem more time efficient to assume the ability to multitask when listening or make assumptions about a speaker and the message; however, doing so often hinders the communication process. Teachers may feel as if there is not enough time to actively listen when there is planning, grading, and a list of other jobs to complete. While it may not seem like it at the time, active listening can save time by heading off potential misunderstandings and conflicts before they arise. Taking time to listen demonstrates to the speaker her or his importance and clarifies comprehension, which often saves time that would later be spent correcting misinterpretations and miscommunications (Hoppe, 2006; Comstock, 2015a).

One of the roles of the special education teacher is to be a manager, which often means assuming a leadership role. One barrier to active listening is assuming that to be a manager one needs to be knowledgeable and decisive. Active listening is part of effective management and does not negate a manager's ability to lead or be decisive. Active listening builds cohesion, which enhances leadership. People in leadership roles may be tempted to refute a statement or argument rather than being open to another's point of view, but active listening allows others to express their thoughts and fosters a more collaborative approach to management (Hoppe, 2006). Suppose a special education teacher makes a decision to rearrange the schedule of a paraprofessional, which causes the paraprofessional to be upset. Active listening to the paraprofessional's concerns does not diminish the special education teacher's role as a manager. The special education teacher does not need to agree with the arguments; however, by employing active listening, the paraprofessional can feel her or his input is valued and important no matter what decision is made. Remember that responding is part of the process. In that response, the special education teacher can state why the decision or changes were necessary, can further the discussion until a mutually agreed upon decision is reached, or agree with the paraprofessional's argument. None of those possible outcomes at all diminishes the special education teacher's role as manager. Even if the final decision does not include the paraprofessional's input, by employing active listening, greater rapport has been established and the paraprofessional may feel validated rather than ignored or unimportant. The process shows that the paraprofessional's opinion matters and does not diminish the role of the special education teacher.

Active listening may be especially challenging when it involves mediated communication or is not face-to-face. Mediated communication tends to be more impersonal than direct communication and typically does not provide nonverbal cues to assist in comprehension, especially comprehending emotions. Although it can be more challenging, it is important to remember that the steps of active listening can still be used in mediated communication to help avoid confusion and miscommunication (Hoppe, 2006).

Comprehension Check

1. What are the six steps of active listening?
2. Why is active listening an important skill for collaboration?
3. What are some of the barriers to employing active listening?

Nonverbal Cues and Communication

Nonverbal communication is a form of communication that does not involve words or language (except in the case of sign language) and is often the primary way humans communicate emotions, moods, sarcasm, and attitudes. It is what people often use to form judgments or impressions of others. Nonverbal communication may send an intentional and deliberate message (e.g., a smile when you greet a person or shaking an index finger at a child in trouble) or unintentional and accidental message (e.g., a yawn in the middle of a meeting or a person blinking her or his eyes when telling a lie). For our discussion, we refer to the nonverbal communication associated with verbal messages and not to sign language.

While a person can be aware of the nonverbal messages she or he sends, either intentional or not, a person may not always be aware of these messages. People are often unaware of their nonverbal communication and how the receiver perceives and interprets it. Nonverbal messages are more subtle and vulnerable to more subjective interpretation than verbal communication, which tends to be more direct and more easily clarified with a question or follow-up. Nonverbal communication is often considered to be a more authentic expression of a person's feelings or emotions than verbal communication (Fontenot, 2014).

For example, suppose Sue tells Beth that she is excited about running five miles with Beth at 6 a.m. tomorrow morning . . . then rolls her eyes. The verbal message is that Sue is excited to get up early and go running, but the nonverbal message (eye roll) could communicate sarcasm. This may be interpreted as Sue is not really excited. In this case, the nonverbal message was more likely deliberate and indicated her true feelings about running a far distance early in the morning with Beth. Sue says she is excited, but Beth could interpret her nonverbal communication to mean that Sue is really not excited. Beth is more likely to believe Sue's nonverbal communication as opposed to her verbal communication. It is also possible that Sue intended a completely different message with the eye roll or even no message at all. Sue may have rolled her eyes to mean that she was impatient with the question because Beth had asked it three times before. Or Sue could have intended no message with the eye roll but had something in her eye that she was trying to get out. Without verbal clarification, the nonverbal communication is often left to the listener to interpret based on best judgment.

Assume at 6 a.m. the following morning Sue gets up to run with Beth. Sue tells Beth that she is wide awake and slept well the night before, but when Beth looks at her eyes, they look a little red and the skin underneath her eyes is puffy. This time, Sue's verbal message is that she is well rested, but the unintentional impression Beth may form is that Sue is actually tired based on her red puffy eyes. Sue's red puffy eyes are her unintentional nonverbal communication that Beth may use to form an assumption that Sue is tired no matter what Sue's verbal message says. Beth is more likely to believe Sue's eyes than her words. Unless Beth comments on her impression, Sue may not know that Beth really believes that she is tired. Sue may have no idea that her eyes look tired or that that Beth believes she is tired, especially since Sue's verbal communication stated that she was well rested.

In this chapter, the term sender will refer to the person sending the nonverbal communication or nonverbal cues. The receiver will be the person receiving and interpreting the nonverbal information.

It is important for educators to be aware of nonverbal communication and cues and how they impact a person's impression of others and others' impressions of them. The impressions formed by nonverbal cues influence the feelings, thoughts, and attitudes the receiver has about the sender, which ultimately affects how well or effectively they work and collaborate together. If that impression, especially if it is a first impression, is favorable, then the desire to work and collaborate together may be stronger than if the impression is unfavorable. It is important for educators to know the different types of nonverbal cues and reflect on how they are used to form impressions.

Nonverbal Cues

Nonverbal communication is made up of nonverbal cues, the nonlinguistic behaviors of a person that communicate information and are often used by others to form an impression. These cues potentially communicate a great deal of meaning that the sender may or may not have been aware of or ever intended (Fontenot, 2014). Studies have shown that it takes as little as one-tenth of a second to use nonverbal cues to form an impression about a person based on facial appearance alone. If a person is given more than a tenth of a second to form an impression, that additional time only strengthens the initial impression rather than altering it (Rholetter, 2013). In the earlier example, Beth formed an impression of Sue based on her facial appearance (red, puffy eyes). If Beth spent a longer time looking at Sue, she would be more likely to find additional evidence to support her assumption that Sue is tired rather than find evidence that she looks wide awake, even after Sue tells Beth she is well rested.

Some nonverbal cues are visual in nature and can be detected through a person's sight. Visible cues include a person's physical appearance, body language or movement (kinesics), adornments or material possessions, and use of personal space. Physical appearances are the way a person looks and includes features such as hair color, the shape and size of a person's nose or mouth, skin complexion, and even a person's height or body type (Hall, 2012; Fontenot, 2014). The receiver uses these nonverbal cues or features to form an impression about the sender without the sender saying a word. People with blond hair may leave a different impression than people with brown hair. A receiver may judge the ancestry of the sender based on a large nose or pale, freckly complexion. The impression made by a tall, muscular male tends to be different than that made by a small, petite female. A person's height and physical size are often used to determine a person's power and status and are considered to be important components of a person's physical appearance in regard to impressions formed by nonverbal cues. Taller people are usually perceived as having more status than shorter people, and attractive people are typically seen as more persuasive than those who are not as attractive (Fontenot, 2014).

Visible nonverbal cues also include kinesics or how a person moves or uses the body. This can be broken down into three different types: gestures, facial expressions, and posture. Gestures are unconscious or conscious movements that can have multiple types of meaning that positively or negatively impact a message. Gestures can even provide a substitution for a verbal message (e.g., a wave to signal hello). Gestures can be used to illustrate a point (e.g., "The fish I caught was this big," accompanied with a hand gesture to demonstrate the size of the fish), to help explain a concept (e.g., "It is shaped like this," with a gesture indicating a shape), or to display an emotion (e.g., both hands covering your mouth to indicate suspense or fright). Gestures can also be used to help control a conversation or regulate turn taking (e.g., hold a hand up to indicate a person should stop talking or that you have something you want to say). Gestures are often times culturally specific. The gesture for "ok" in the U.S. may have a different, less attractive meaning in other parts of the world (Fontenot, 2014). It is important for educators to be aware of the gestures they use and how they impact, accentuate, or detract from a message.

While an upward turn of the mouth for a smile or a downward turn for a frown are common examples of facial expressions, they are just two of the many nonverbal messages conveyed through the facial muscles. Facial expressions are nonverbal cues that convey a message through the use of the mouth, eyebrows, forehead, head tilt, and eyes. A furrowed brow can be interpreted as a scowl or that a person is unhappy or not pleased. A furrowed brow accompanied by a head tilted to the side could be interpreted as someone is confused. Looking someone in the eye sends a different message (e.g., confidence) than avoiding eye contact (e.g., shyness or having something to hide). In fact, humans have approximately 90 muscles in the face that are capable of producing over 250,000 facial expressions (Hall, 2012; Fontenot, 2014). Aligning facial expressions to verbal messages is an important component of effective communication. A teacher smiling at a parent to welcome her or him into the classroom supports a hospitable, collaborative atmosphere. A teacher smiling at a joke told by the class clown while interrupting a lecture is likely to reinforce the class clown's behavior and is not likely to support the teacher's verbal message to be quiet during class.

Another type of kinesics is posture or how a person holds the body while standing or sitting. It is not uncommon to hear a parent tell a child to stand up straight, and while straight posture is important for relieving strain on a back, it also provides a nonverbal cue about a person. The nonverbal cues provided by posture can be interpreted differently if a person's back is rounded or straight. A straight back with shoulders back can be a sign of confidence, while rounded back and hunched shoulders can be seen as lacking confidence, lazy, or indifferent (Hall, 2012; Fontenot, 2014). A person with a rounded back and eyes cast down often communicates a completely different message than a person with a straight back and eye contact or even a rounded back and eye contact. The posture of the spine contributes an important component to the overall impression formed by the receiver.

Visible nonverbal cues also include personal space or the area surrounding a person that they consider theirs, where encroachment into this space feels uncomfortable (Fontenot, 2014; Google online dictionary). The distance a person sits or stands from another person communicates a message without the use of words. A close friend or family member standing, sitting close, or touching a person could make the person feel comfort or as if they share a bond. A stranger sitting or standing that closely could make a person feel anxious or uncomfortable. It is important to remember that a person's desired amount of personal space is often culturally related. While sitting or standing close in some cultures may feel uncomfortable, in other cultures it may be considered the norm. Holding hands, hugging, touching, or even kissing an acquaintance is not uncommon in many cultures, but may be considered a violation of personal space in others.

A person's adornments or material possessions are also used as a cue to form an impression. The clothing a person wears, the size of her or his house, or type of car are all cues that convey a message about the sender (Hall, 2012; Fontenot, 2014). For educators, their clothing choices and manner of dress tend to impact the impression parents and coworkers have of them and has more impact than other adornments, such as a type of car or home. Dressing professionally often sends the message that the teacher is serious and confident, while less professional clothing may convey a more relaxed or less serious impression.

Nonverbal cues can also be auditory and include the sounds a person makes (e.g., sigh, yawn) and the quality of her or his voice, accent, tone, or pitch. There are many different ways sound can be used to impact a message. Imagine someone with a deep voice and another with a high-pitched voice. Or imagine a person with a strong accent from Brooklyn, New York, or Boston, Massachusetts. Impressions about a person can be formed based solely on the sound of their accent or emphasis in their speech. Think of how many different accents or ways there are to emphasize the phrase "oh my gosh" and the different impressions each one makes. Messages and impressions are also influenced by rate of speech, use of pauses, silence, and tone of voice. Imagine a person who rushes through a speech as opposed to one who speaks at a slower rate or uses dramatic pauses. While the words and intended message in both situations may be the same, the actual message and impressions they provide about the speaker may be completely different (Hall, 2012; Fontenot, 2014).

It is important to remember that nonverbal cues form an impression, especially when used to form first impressions, but these impressions are not always accurate. Nonverbal cues do not necessarily provide an indication of a person's true character; and some people are better at forming accurate impressions than others. There are also many cultural and personal differences that impact the use of nonverbal cues

(Rholetter, 2013). It is important for educators to be aware of this and consider the impact these cues have on the collaborative process.

Other Considerations about Nonverbal Communication

Just as verbal cues can be misunderstood or misinterpreted, so too can nonverbal cues. Nonverbal cues can lead to even more uncertainty because they are subtle, subject to interpretation, and people often are not aware of their impact. Three things to keep in mind about nonverbal cues and communication are the difference between nonverbal behaviors and nonverbal communication, the rules that guide nonverbal communication, and the cultural influences of nonverbal communication (Fontenot, 2014).

The first thing to remember is that nonverbal behaviors are considered different than nonverbal communication. Nonverbal communication is designed to communicate a message, while nonverbal behaviors are not. For example, failing to look someone in the eye when speaking to them can be a form of nonverbal communication or it can be simply a nonverbal behavior. If a person fails to look someone in the eye while speaking to them, it could mean that they are shy or that they have something to hide. Those are both forms of nonverbal communication. A nonverbal behavior would be not looking a person in the eye due to the position of the sun behind the other person's head making it too bright to look her or him in the eye. In this case, not looking someone in the eye is a nonverbal behavior with no communicative intent behind it. Sometimes what is interpreted as a nonverbal cue is really a nonverbal behavior with no communicative intent. How the action is interpreted, as nonverbal communication or nonverbal behavior, is up to the receiver unless clarified by the sender (Fontenot, 2014).

The second thing to keep in mind about nonverbal communication is that is it guided by hidden rules. These rules are unwritten and arbitrary. They are also rarely taught and most often learned through modeling and observing others. The rules of nonverbal communication can also change depending on the situation or setting. For example, while at times it may be socially acceptable to stare or watch another person (e.g., watching a play, watching a professor teach a lesson), at other times it is considered not socially unacceptable (e.g., staring at somebody in line or a person in a wheelchair). Certain facial expressions are also appropriate at certain times and considered inappropriate at others. It is socially acceptable to smile and laugh at a birthday party but not at a funeral. Likewise, it is not appropriate to frown or be visibly unhappy at a birthday party. It is socially acceptable to stand close enough to touch a stranger in a crowded elevator but not socially acceptable to stand close enough to touch them in a long line. When and where it is acceptable to watch another person, smile or frown, or stand near a stranger is guided by arbitrary rules that are rarely taught but assumed that a person should know and follow (Fontenot, 2014).

A third characteristic of nonverbal communication is that culture greatly affects nonverbal communication. Nonverbal communication that is acceptable in one culture may not be acceptable in another. In some cultures, looking a person in the eye while they are speaking is a sign of disrespect, while in other cultures, not looking a person in the eye when they are speaking is a sign of disrespect. Some cultures bow their heads upon greeting, while others shake hands. Some cultures have a small area of personal space, while other cultures find that smaller personal space uncomfortable. Some cultures are louder and more boisterous or use gestures that other cultures may find rude or disrespectful. Touching in some cultures is a part of casual conversation, while in others it is reserved for more intimate or close relations (Fontenot, 2014). There are many variations to the cultural norms of nonverbal communication, making it imperative for educators to be aware of how they impact communication.

Misinterpreting nonverbal cues based on any of these three characteristics can lead to unintended impressions or emotional reactions and break down communication. It is important to remember that people judge and are judged by their nonverbal communication and cues. These cues may be completely unintentional but have a large impact on communication and the impressions formed. Nonverbal communication is subjective, guided by unspoken rules, and influenced by culture. As educators, it is important to realize how this communication impacts the impression we form of others and the impression that others form of us. Nonverbal communication can benefit or hinder the collaborative process through the interpretation of the receiver. Case Study 12.2 provides an opportunity to apply your knowledge.

12.2 APPLICATION CASE STUDY

Olivia is a special education teacher in an elementary school. While her students love her and her enthusiasm, her coworkers find her to be loud, boisterous, and difficult to work with. In meetings and in conversations in the hall, Olivia tends to speak loudly, often drowning out other voices or disrupting other classes. Teachers complain that they do not like co-teaching with her because she is so loud she takes over the class. Olivia is very knowledgeable and passionate about working with students but is rarely approached by other teachers for input, ideas, or to collaborate on a project.

1. What types of nonverbal cues is Olivia sending?
2. How are those cues being interpreted?
3. What suggestions could you give Olivia to help her become a communicator and collaborator?

Comprehension Check

1. What is nonverbal communication?
2. How can understanding nonverbal cues be beneficial to the collaborative process?
3. What are three things to remember about nonverbal communication?

CHAPTER SUMMARY

Interpersonal communication is the means by which a person conveys a message to another person; this can be done both verbally and nonverbally. When communicating, it is important to be cognizant of the message you send and if the message is received successfully. Unsuccessful interpersonal communication can lead to the breakdown of a collaborative relationship.

- ✓ Verbal communication encompasses the words or spoken language used to convey a message.
- ✓ Nonverbal communication includes all other aspects of the message that do not involve language.
- ✓ Interpersonal communication may occur face-to-face or be mediated through the use of an electronic device.

Mediated Communication

- ✓ Many times interpersonal communication is mediated via electronic device. Communicating in this manner is convenient, as those communicating do not need to share the same space or time to convey messages.
- ✓ Relaying information in this way may take days, weeks, or may never happen.
- ✓ Immediate feedback is possible but does not always happen.
- ✓ Lack of nonverbal cues allow for a greater chance of miscommunication and frustration.

Face-to-Face Communication

- ✓ Face-to-face communication can be seen as cumbersome. Having to share the same time and space may be seen as a disadvantage, but face-to-face communication allows for the ability to send and receive information immediately.
- ✓ Nonverbal cues are present and may result in better understanding of the message.
- ✓ Those communicating must find an appropriate time and space where all parties can meet.

Successful Communication

- ✓ Successful communication relies on verbal abilities, active listening skills, and nonverbal cues.
- ✓ Appropriate word choice and vocabulary can allow a message to be conveyed clearly. Using unfamiliar words or jargon in a school meeting may confuse parents and cause them to feel unequal as a team member.
- ✓ A six-step process called active listening is beneficial for successful collaboration. The six steps to active listening are:

  - *Focus on the speaker*—remain distraction free.
  - *Be open and receptive to the message*—this does not mean you need to agree with the message.

- *Paraphrase both the verbal and nonverbal message*—this will let the other party know the listener understood the message.
- *Ask questions*—this will clear up any confusion the listener may have.
- *Restate and summarize the main idea*—this does not mean the listener agrees with the message, but understands the main idea.
- *Provide a response*—share any ideas, feelings, or thoughts.

✓ Active listening may take more time initially, but saves time, headaches, and confusion through ensuring successful communication.
✓ Remember to remain culturally aware when communicating as not to provide verbal or nonverbal ques that may cause confusion.

Nonverbal Communication

✓ Nonverbal communication lends itself to greater subjective interpretation.
✓ Can be seen as a more authentic expression of a person's feelings.
✓ Nonverbal communication can include physical appearance, kinesics, material possessions, and use of personal space.
✓ Kinesics can be broken down into three separate parts:

- Gestures
- Facial expressions
- Posture

✓ Nonverbal communication may also be the sound a person makes such as a sigh or yawn.

APPLICATION ACTIVITIES

1. Have candidates watch a scene from a movie or show with the sound turned off or muted. Have candidates interpret what is going on through nonverbal cues alone. Discuss as a class what different interpretations they formed, the basis of those interpretations, and their impressions of each of the characters.
2. Role-play difference nonverbal cues. Choose a phrase such as "I am happy to see you" or "Isn't the weather beautiful?" and in pairs see how many different ways those phrases can be said using different nonverbal cues. Have the receiver state the messages that he or she interprets from the different approaches.
3. Have candidates observe an IEP or other team meeting. Throughout the course of the meeting, ask candidates to document the types of nonverbal cues and/or steps of active listening they observe. Candidates can then reflect on how the nonverbal cues and/or steps of active listening impacted the interpersonal communication.

REFERENCES

Codington-Lacerte, C. (2013). *Face to face interaction*. Hackensack, NJ: Salem Press Encyclopedia.
Comstock, N. W. (2015a). *Active listening*. Hackensack, NJ: Salem Press Encyclopedia.
Comstock, N. W. (2015b). *Critical skills: Communication*. Hackensack, NJ: Salem Press Encyclopedia.
Downs, L. J. (2008). *Listening skills training*. Danvers, MA: ASTD Press.

Dziak, M. (2015). *Interpersonal communication*. Hackensack, NJ: Salem Press Encyclopedia.

Fontenot, K. A. (2014). *Nonverbal communication and social cognition*. Hackensack, NJ: Salem Press Encyclopedia of Health.

Hall, J. A. (2012). *Nonverbal cues and communication. Encyclopedia of social psychology.* Thousand Oaks, CA: Sage.

Hoppe, M. (2006). *An ideas into action guidebook: Active listening: Improve your ability to listen and lead.* Greensboro, NC: Center for Creative Leadership.

Rholetter, W. (2013). *First impression (psychology)*. Hackensack, NJ: Salem Press Encyclopedia.

13

WHEN THINGS GO AWRY
Managing Conflict

Stephen B. Richards

Chapter Objectives

Following reading the chapter, students should:

1. Identify the causes and costs of conflict among teams
2. Identify strategies for managing conflict among teams
3. List and explain the various steps in due process procedures

THE CAUSES AND COSTS OF CONFLICT

In Chapter Twelve, you read and learned about effective communication. Effective communication skills can be instrumental in avoiding conflicts when each individual is understood, respected, and encouraged to participate in collaborative teaming. In Chapters Eleven through Sixteen of this text, you will read how to develop and maintain positive working relationships with families and community members. However, even with the best of intentions, conflicts will arise and almost inevitably in any long-term collaboration. By identifying the causes of conflict that commonly arise and using strategies for managing those conflicts, the general or special education teacher is likely to encourage the sustainability of ongoing relationships and productive teaming. These strategies are relevant to working with teams, including professionals, families, and/or community members. Managing conflict, unfortunately, tends to be a skill that develops over time and with experience and practice in application of the skill (Girard & Koch, 1996). In other words, managing conflict successfully tends to be the result of engagement in conflict. Caspersen (2014) pointed out that conflict can be useful even when it is inevitable. However, when it is not managed well, it can be quite destructive (Caspersen, 2014).

By anticipating that conflicts will arise and by being knowledgeable about when and how to apply principles for resolving those conflicts, you can be better prepared to handle most situations. Remember, there are problem-solving principles and steps that have been discussed in earlier chapters that are related to the use of collaborative teams to address a student, school, or district problem. In this chapter, we are referring to resolving conflicts that arise in those problem-solving efforts. Many strategies such as effective planning, facilitating of team meetings, and communication skills can go a long way toward preventing conflict.

Caspersen (2014) pointed out that conflict is not necessarily "bad." However, Dana (2001) indicated there can be considerable costs to unresolved conflict including:

- It can create costs. For example, if a school district pays for in-service activities that are then not used due to team conflicts, there is an actual monetary cost.
- It wastes time. People involved in conflict who are not working toward a resolution are wasting time in meetings and likely wasting time outside of meetings "stewing" about the conflict.
- It can lead to bad decisions. Team members are interdependent in their decision making, and conflict may lead to members seeking decisions not for the benefit of the team or its constituents, but rather to satisfy a personal agenda. Families are likely to have personal agendas, and this can be quite appropriate, as they are the ultimate caregivers of students.
- If the conflict is severe, one or more members may transfer schools or move to another district. Family members may withdraw from participating in team activities. At worse, schools and families may have to begin a mediation process that is discussed at the end of this chapter.
- Leaders may have to restructure teams to avoid conflicts among members. This often leads to less efficient and effective teams.
- Sabotage may occur if team members become so interpersonally conflicted they actually seek to derail any efforts of others.
- Team members are quite likely to lose motivation when there is unresolved conflict.
- Finally, team members may miss work to avoid conflicts or may actually suffer physical ailments as a result of the stress of conflict (Dana, 2001).

How might one begin to resolve conflicts? There is considerable literature from business and education as to how to manage conflicts. Girard and Koch (1996) suggested that to address conflict, one must consider the "stance" of the individuals involved (and they must consider their own stances). One's stance may serve to generate conflict. The first component of a person's stance is her/his position. A positional stance that focuses on achieving a specific, desired outcome leaves little room for compromise and negotiation (Girard & Koch, 1996). For example, if one team member in a co-teaching situation insists that she always be the lead teacher and the other teacher serve in a "helping" role, the only resolution is that either she gets her way or not (at least most of the time). A second aspect of position is one's interests. Interests are the personal motivations of the team members. For example, the teacher who wishes to always be the lead may believe her students will not achieve as well if she relinquishes the lead teacher role at all. Her interests can present good arguments for why she holds the position she does. However, her interests also tend to close the door to conflict resolution. The third component of position is one's needs. Psychological needs are often at work in conflict. Our lead teacher may have a need to feel in control and to have her classroom activities be conducted only in the manner she deems best. Again, focusing on satisfying one's needs can close the door on conflict resolution (Girard & Koch, 1996).

Conflict is "good" or "bad" depending on the reactions of those participating in the team process. Everyone should expect that conflict will likely arise at some point in his/her teaching career. Knowing what leads to conflict and the steps to resolve or manage it are paramount to successfully collaborating, not only with teams, but with individuals as well. Carr, Herman, and Harris (2005) pointed out that nearly all teams will experience conflict. Many educators are not trained to see the potential benefits from conflict, yet often effective solutions and strategies emerge from the resolution of conflicts (Carr et al., 2005). Carr et al. also identified typical reasons why conflicts might arise early in a collaborative team effort. These include:

- Clearly articulated purposes and goals for the team have not been expressed.
- Meeting times are not realistic or meetings are cancelled or changed without sufficient notice. This can be especially detrimental to family participation.
- Team members may harbor long-term resentments toward one another.
- Team members' personalities may not complement each other. Their personalities need not be quite similar, but should work in harmony to achieve team goals and outcomes.
- Team members were not selected thoughtfully and with care toward who was really needed for the team to make progress and succeed.
- Individual team members have very different expectations of one another and the team as a whole.

(Carr et al., 2005)

Many of the types of problems discussed here are also addressed in Chapter Seven, "Overcoming Barriers to Collaboration and Consultation", and in various other chapters addressing strategies for effective collaboration and consultation. A distinction here is that conflict may emerge over a limited number of team members or perhaps one or two members are "pitted against" the rest of the team. These types of conflicts require the use of specific strategies, particularly when managing conflicts with families and community members.

There may be other specific reasons you could list that lead to conflict, although the ones cited are relatively common ones that occur among team members. Remember, the investment and stance of team members can affect how they respond to conflict. Parents/caregivers can have tremendous investment in the outcomes of interventions associated with their student such that they have strong opinions about what is or is not appropriate (Carr et al., 2005). Team members clearly will have different personality types, different experiences in collaboration, and different knowledge and skill levels in collaboration. These are other reasons that might lead to conflict. The ways in which conflict is managed can vary among the different team members.

> **Comprehension Check**
> 1. What are possible costs/outcomes of conflict?
> 2. What are the causes of conflict? Can you give examples?

MANAGING CONFLICT

As expressed earlier, it is recognized that conflict may have benefits when it is managed appropriately. Conflicts can result in strengthened interpersonal relationships, better cultural understanding, improved communication, negotiation, and listening skills, and certainly in better decisions and more resilient teams. For conflict to result in such desirable outcomes, strategies must be used that promote resolution. Such outcomes may not occur if left to happenstance.

In general, there are several principles to managing conflict at any grade level among teams. Girard and Koch (1996) suggested the following steps. First, the parties must agree to negotiate. Each party is likely to have her/his stance as referenced earlier, but each must be willing to come to the table. It is necessary to obtain a commitment from team members to at least try to resolve their conflicts.

Second, team members must gather various points of view (Girard & Koch, 1996). The effective communication skills discussed in earlier chapters are important at this stage in particular. Varying viewpoints on what the conflict is, what are its origins, and how it might be resolved are clearly going to be different among team members. Using active listening skills is critical to getting all the viewpoints out on the table without casting judgment or blame.

Third, team members need to find common interests (Girard & Koch, 1996). Although there are bound to be differences in viewpoints, getting them out on the table may allow team members to identify where their common interests lie. Rather than perceiving the situation as a win or lose proposition, finding common interests may result in a win-win orientation for team members.

Fourth, team members need to create win-win options (Girard & Koch, 1996). If members in conflict believe that no one is getting her/his way entirely and that each or all parties are gaining some recognition and action based on their viewpoints, they are much more likely to resolve their conflicts.

Fifth, team members need to evaluate the options identified (Girard & Koch, 1996). Evaluating options must occur in the context of the overall agreed upon goals and purpose of the team. Again, the options should not result in win-lose circumstances or conflicts are bound to fester, even if a particular conflict is resolved.

Finally, team members should reach an agreement (Girard & Koch, 1996). The agreement should renew the team members' commitments to fulfilling the team's purpose and achieving the desired goals. The agreement should also discourage actions that are based on personal agendas. Case Study 13.1 presents such an example of the implementation of these principles.

13.1 ILLUSTRATIVE CASE STUDY

The seventh grade level team at Mathes Middle School has reached a point of conflict among members. The overall goals of the team and its purpose are to identify, implement, and evaluate strategies to improve students' writing skills. Initially, the team functioned quite well as the focus was on the English Language Arts (ELA) teachers. The team identified, implemented, and evaluated strategies that ELA teachers could use in their classrooms that would support writing across the curriculum. The ELA teachers were excited initially about working toward helping the seventh grade students to be better writers in the content areas of math, science, and social studies. However, over time the ELA teachers began to feel that they were doing all the work. When these feelings were first presented at a team meeting, the response of several content teachers was that writing instruction was the job of the ELA teachers.

The team used the principles identified by Girard and Koch (1996). First, the team members agreed to have a meeting and try to reach some kind of a resolution. It was clear to everyone, regardless of their own personal feelings, that the team members were losing their motivation and focus and the long-term outcome would not likely benefit the students. Second, at the meeting, all members expressed their viewpoints. They all agreed to take no more than two minutes and not to interrupt or comment on others' viewpoints. The team met again and identified where the common interests were. All agreed that improving students' writing skills was in everyone's best interest. They decided they could begin with an understanding that that was the aim.

Team members met again to discuss options. One possibility was that the ELA teachers would continue the writing instruction. A second option was that the content areas teachers would take on the responsibility for teaching students' writing skills. Each of these was viewed as a win-lose option for one group or the other. Everyone agreed that having the ELA teachers continue to devote time in their classes to improve content area writing was desirable, but also that the ELA teachers would provide in-service on encouraging writing in each content area and suggestions for writing activities and evaluating writing in content areas. In this way, all team members were directly invested in students' learning outcomes. Also, the ELA teachers could eventually pare back instruction on content area writing and focus on other areas of the ELA curriculum. Content-area teachers would eventually become more proficient in encouraging and monitoring writing skills relevant to their own teaching areas. All team members agreed that this option would likely continue the team's momentum and improve students' writing skills.

Finally, the team wrote out an agreement as to who was responsible for what, timelines for implementation and evaluation of the agreement plan, and, finally, when to meet to discuss and revise the plan as needed. No one on the team felt she/he got exactly what she/he wanted, but each team member felt the team was back on track and working well together again.

The 13.1 case study illustrates how conflict can work for the positive. Achinstein (2002) suggested that conflict with reflection offers opportunities for change. Furthermore, "To engage in conflict and question one's beliefs with the possibility of deep change is fundamentally a positive and hopeful act rather than a problematic one ..." (p. 450) (Achinstein, 2002).

In order to achieve positive outcomes from conflict, school leaders need to be prepared to step to the fore (Somech, 2008). School principals should provide in-service in conflict resolution and assure various team members possess conflict resolution skills (Msila, 2012). Principals themselves should be adequately trained in conflict management (Msila, 2012). Teacher leaders trained in conflict management are fundamental to having successful collaborative teams in schools (Msila, 2012). Principals and other school leaders may initially need to be active in forming teams, identifying team goals, ensuring they meet and address their respective goals, and monitoring team progress and functioning (Somech, 2008). However, there are other actions school leaders should take. They may need to redesign the workplace to provide time and resources for planning. They may need also to encourage high goal and task interdependency (i.e., team members must work together to promote their common good) (Somech, 2008). High goal and task interdependency helps team members realize they have a vested interest in the success of other team members rather than personal success only (Somech, 2008).

Teacher education programs should develop programs in preparing pre-service teachers to participate in collaborative teams and manage conflict as well. Such programs need to provide teacher education candidates with the skills and knowledge to develop and maintain positive relationships and to prevent and manage conflicts that do arise (Bradley & Monda-Amaya, 2005). Teachers, although often engaged in independent work and evaluated on their individual performance, should understand that high goal and task interdependency can be beneficial (Dettmer, Knackendoffel, & Thurston, 2013). Given the increasing responsibilities of teachers, the need to collaborate and work together becomes increasingly necessary to survive and thrive (Dettmer, Knackendoffel, & Thurston, 2013).

Despite the best efforts of team members, conflicts can erupt in ways that appear to be unmanageable by the team members. In the case of professional teams, the school leaders may need to intervene as already noted. However, in the case of conflict among school personnel and families of students with disabilities, there are specific steps that must be followed under IDEA. School personnel may sometimes refer to this circumstance "as going to due process." More precisely, all the steps in place under IDEA to implement Response to Intervention, progress monitor, refer a student for a multifactor evaluation, the individual assessments given, the determination of eligibility, and the implementation of the agreed upon IEP are all steps in due process. The point of due process is to ensure that families are involved in and informed about their student's entry and continued involvement in special education and that all steps are conducted fairly and without discrimination. Families and school personnel may not always reach agreement on what is an appropriate education; what services, accommodations, modifications, or assistive technology is needed; and what is the student's least restrictive environment (among other possible areas of conflict). When this occurs, IDEA provides specific due process procedures to follow to ensure fairness for all parties. Again, Chapters Fourteen through Sixteen specifically address how to work constructively with families to avoid these circumstances.

Comprehension Check

1. What are the six steps outlined by Girard and Koch (1996) for managing conflict?
2. What steps might principals or school leaders need to take in resolving conflict?
3. What are some possible areas of disagreement among school personnel and families that might lead to conflict requiring due process proceedings?

DUE PROCESS PROCEDURES

In IDEA, there are provisions for managing conflict systematically when an IEP team cannot resolve differences between the school and the family. Free appropriate public education (FAPE) is typically at the heart of such conflicts. Taylor, Smiley, and Richards (2015) summarized the proceedings available.

Initially, parents or schools may request a mediation hearing. A neutral third party is involved who can work with both parties. Costs can be quite high for due process proceedings, and schools will often prefer this mediation process to actual due process hearings and reviews. The parties to the conflict may enter into a resolution session in attempts to develop a written, binding agreement to resolve the issues. Unless both the school and family waive the right to mediation, this step is required prior to more legally formal proceedings (Taylor et al., 2015). Hearing officers at this step are concerned with whether a student is not receiving FAPE, if the student's caregivers were not able to participate in decision making regarding FAPE, or if the student is being deprived of educational benefits (Taylor et al., 2015). Specific procedures under IDEA are discussed in the following paragraphs and are summarized from the U.S. Department of Education Office of Special Education Programs (2006, http://idea.ed.gov/explore/view/p/,root,dynamic,TopicalBrief,16).

- Due process complaints must allege a violation within two years (depending on when the family or school knew or should have known about the violation). The aggrieved party must request a hearing within that same time frame. Families may be exempted from the deadline if the school misrepresented or withheld information.
- Both parties must be notified. State Education Agencies must have provisions for assisting families in filing due process complaints.
- Schools must respond to families' filing complaints with information about whether the school will or will not take action and explain why or why not including data used in the decision. There are specified timelines for this step.

- Schools must convene a resolution meeting with the family that includes relevant IEP team members and the Local Education Agency (LEA—which is typically the school district) representative who has decision-making authority. Schools may not include an attorney unless families also bring an attorney. As mentioned earlier, the purpose of this meeting is to reach a written agreement resolving the conflict.
- If a resolution is not reached within a specified time frame, the parties will present their "cases" to an impartial hearing officer. Attorneys may be present and a court recording is made of the hearing. At this hearing, the hearing officer will listen to testimony and review evidence and render a decision with a specified time frame.
- If a resolution is not reached following this hearing, the State Education Agency will provide a review of the local hearing and render a decision.
- Finally, if a resolution is not reached after the state review, either party may file a civil court action. Ultimately, either party can be made responsible for paying the other's attorney's fees. Thus, the monetary costs of going through all the due process proceedings can be staggering.

The overall purpose of due process proceedings is to ensure fairness in a timely manner. It is typically not in the best interest of either schools or families to progress through all the proceedings available. Resolving the conflict at the mediation stage is desirable in most instances and that is why this step was added to IDEA from early reauthorizations of the law. Ultimately, using the strategies discussed in Chapters Twelve, Fourteen, Fifteen, Sixteen, and Seventeen are much preferable to these more legal remedies to conflict. Nevertheless, educators need to be aware that due process procedures for conflict resolution are available and are implemented from time to time. Case Study 13.2 provides for application of conflict management knowledge.

13.2 APPLICATION CASE STUDY

The IEP team for Treavor Baldwin met a few days ago. Certain members of the team from the school personnel had disagreements about the services for Treavor. Treavor's parents had several concerns that reflected the disagreements among the school personnel. Unfortunately, by the end of the IEP team meeting (it was the first annual review of Treavor's initial IEP), Treavor's parents and school team members were not prepared to sign the IEP and agree to implementation. Treavor is in the third grade and has been identified to have specific learning disabilities in reading (word recognition, fluency, and comprehension) as well as in writing (phonetic spellings, poor legibility, poor punctuation, limited vocabulary in sentence use).

Conflict arose during the discussion of where services would be provided and what was Treavor's least restrictive environment. Some school team members felt Treavor needed to spend more time in a resource room setting for small group and individualized instruction in reading and writing. These school team members believed Treavor would need up to two hours per day in the resource room. In order to free up that much time in Treavor's schedule, it was suggested that he have more limited time in "specials" such as art and music.

Other school team members felt that one hour per day at the maximum was sufficient, and they were concerned that Treavor would be missing too much time from his general education class and specials as well. Treavor's parents did not want Treavor regularly scheduled to be served in the resource room at all. He had had all services delivered in the general education classroom for his initial IEP. District achievement testing did suggest Treavor had lost some ground, so to speak, in comparison with his peers (i.e., they were making more progress in reading and writing than Treavor, and the gap between his skills and his peers' was growing somewhat wider).

Assume you are in a position to influence the team and its workings.

1. What step(s) would you take to resolve the conflict without due process proceedings?
2. What might be some win-win options for the parties involved?
3. What steps would need to be taken if the conflicts could not be resolved within the IEP team?

Comprehension Check
1. What is the purpose of a resolution meeting?
2. What are the next steps if a resolution meeting is not successful?
3. What are some reasons for why schools might want to avoid due process proceedings regarding conflicts with families?

CHAPTER SUMMARY

Managing conflict when it arises is an invaluable skill, especially when working in a school system. Unfortunately, successfully managing conflict is a skill that develops over time through experience and practice. Conflict, which inevitably occurs, can be rather constructive if handled appropriately, or it can be destructive when it is not.

✓ There are considerable downfalls to not resolving conflict, including:

- It can create unnecessary costs
- It can waste time
- It can lead to poor decisions
- Members may request to transfer schools or move districts
- Leaders may need to restructure teams to avoid more conflict

- Sabotage may occur if team members become interpersonally conflicted
- Team members may lose motivation
- Team members may miss work to avoid conflict

✓ In order to address conflict successfully, mediators may need to consider three parts:

- The stance–this is the position of those in conflict. A positional stance focuses on achieving a specific goal or outcome
- The interests–These are the personal motivations of team members
- The needs–Oftentimes psychological needs are at work during conflict

✓ Educators are not always trained on the benefits that can occur through solving conflict. Some of the issues that may cause conflict and, therefore, be solved are:

- Clearly stated goals and purposes for a team have not been expressed
- Meeting times are not realistic or change without notice
- Team members may harbor long-term resentment toward one another
- Team members' personalities may not complement one another
- Team members were not selected thoughtfully or with care
- Individual team members may have different expectations

Managing Conflict

✓ To manage conflict, parties must first agree to negotiate.
✓ Second, team members must gather various points of view; communication is key during this step.
✓ Third, team members must find common interests.
✓ Fourth, team members need to create win-win options.
✓ Fifth, team members need to evaluate the options identified.
✓ Finally, team members need to reach an agreement.

Who Is Responsible?

✓ In order to achieve positive outcomes from conflict, school leaders should be prepared and willing to step in and assist with mediation.
✓ School principals should also provide in-service training for conflict resolution. This may highlight to teachers why conflict resolution is important for a safe and welcoming work environment.
✓ Lead teachers should be well versed in conflict resolution and model these skills for other teachers.

Conflict between Schools and Families

✓ When there is conflict between schools and families, IDEA outlines specific steps that must be followed—you may hear this referred to as "going to due process".
✓ Initially, a school or family may request a mediation hearing when there is a disagreement on what is an appropriate education. The mediator should be an impartial third party.

✓ If both parties waive their rights to a mediation hearing or the conflict is not resolved in the mediation hearing, an impartial hearing officer then investigates three issues:

- If the student is receiving a free and appropriate education
- Whether or not the caregivers were able to participate in the decision making regarding FAPE
- Whether or not the student is being deprived of educational benefits

✓ If a resolution is not reached with the assistance of a hearing officer, the conflict will then move to the State Education Agency. This agency will review the local hearing and render a decision.

✓ If a resolution is still not reached with the State Education Agency, either party may file a civil court action.

✓ Remember that it is more beneficial and cost effective to manage conflict during the mediation phase.

APPLICATION ACTIVITIES

1. Have students take the Myers-Briggs Inventory. This will provide them with feedback on how their personalities and how they respond to others. Have them discuss how this feedback might impact them as team members involved in conflict.

2. Students write a reflection paper concerning a conflict in which they were involved. The conflict could involve one-to-one conflict or conflict within a group/team. Students should address how they felt about their conflict, what stance they assumed, whether the conflict was resolved, and what steps were used if the conflict was resolved. If not, reflect on why the conflict was unresolved. Reflect on whether there were positive outcomes of the conflict.

3. Randomly assign students to teams of four to six. Designate one person as the facilitator, one as a timekeeper, and one as a recorder. Assign the students to research models of conflict management among K–12 students to create a multimedia presentation. At the conclusion of the project, ask the students to identify what steps they took to accomplish the project. Ask the students to use the steps identified by Girard and Koch (1996) if they experience any conflicts of significance. Regardless, ask each team to identify how they resolved any conflicts that arose and how they avoided conflict if none occurred. Have teams discuss different strategies for resolving conflicts and for avoiding conflicts.

REFERENCES

Achinstein, B. (2002). Conflict amid community: The micropolitics of teacher collaboration. *Teachers College Record*, 104(3), 421–455.

Bradley, J. F., & Monda-Amaya, L. E. (2005). Conflict resolution: Preparing preservice special educators to work in collaborative settings. *Teacher Education and Special Education: The Journal of the Teacher Education Division of the Council for Exceptional Children*, 28(3–4), 171–184.

Carr, J., & Herman, N., & Harris, D. E. (2005). *Creating dynamic schools through mentoring, coaching, and collaboration.* Alexandria, VA.: Association for Supervision and Curriculum Development.

Caspersen, D. (2014). *Changing the conversation: The seventeen principles of conflict resolution.* New York, NY: Penguin Books.

Dana, D. (2001). *Conflict resolution mediation tools for everyday worklife.* New York, NY: McGraw-Hill.

Dettmer, P., Knackendoffel, A., & Thurston, L. (2013). *Collaboration, consultation, and teamwork for students with special needs* (7th ed.). Boston, MA: Pearson.

Girard, K., & Koch, S. J. (1996). *Conflict resolution in the schools: A manual for educators.* San Francisco, CA: Jossey-Bass.

Msila, V. (2012). Conflict management and school leadership. *Journal of Communication,* 3(1), 25–34.

Somech, A. (2008). Managing conflict in school teams: The impact of task and goal interdependence on conflict management and team effectiveness. *Educational Administration Quarterly,* 44(3), 359–390.

Taylor, R. L., Smiley, L. R., & Richards, S. B. (2015). *Exceptional students: Preparing teachers for the 21st century* (2nd ed.). Boston, MA: McGraw-Hill.

U.S. Department of Education Office of Special Education Programs (2006). Retrieved from http://idea.ed.gov/explore/view/p/,root,dynamic,TopicalBrief,16

14

UNDERSTANDING FAMILIES

Jackie M. Arnold

Chapter Objectives

Following reading the chapter, students should:

1. Name the four subsystems of families
2. Cite the seven family functions
3. Identify barriers to family participation as identified by parents and school personnel
4. Cite examples of how those barriers might be overcome

PRINCIPLES OF DEFINING FAMILIES AND FAMILY FUNCTIONS

Families are an essential element and basic unit to the fabric of our society. As our society becomes more diverse so also does what constitutes a student's family. As educators, we must have an inclusive view of the fabric that makes up the student's family rather than assuming a viewpoint in concert with previous particular notions about what is a family and how it should work. This is not to say that a person's cultural beliefs or values about families are invalid. It does mean that the assumption should not be made that one's beliefs and values are the *only* valid ones regarding family. School leaders and teachers need to value each child with an understanding of that individual's and his or her family's lived experiences, culture, language, and other factors impacting the child's education (Boske & Benavente-McEnery, 2012). It is important to remember that one can accept another individual's perspective on family without *agreeing* with that perspective. It is also important to remember that family dynamics change over time in individual families as well as in society as a whole.

Family by Definition

So what defines a family? By definition a family is the basic unit of society in which a group of individuals coexist to meet a group's needs as well as individual needs collectively. The United Nations Convention on the Rights of the Child defines family as "the fundamental group of society and the natural environment for the growth and well-being of all its members and particularly children" (UNICEF, 1989, p. 1). This statement is a reminder of the fundamental importance of the family in a child's learning and development (Miller, Colebrook, & Ellis, 2014). Families are critical members of collaborative teams and often may be the primary determinants of whether a student's education is successful based on the families' notions of success.

However, the concept of family has changed dramatically since the 1950s when the traditional husband, wife, and children unit dominated perceptions of what is a family. Today's families can have diverse and multiple characteristics that go far beyond that 1950s stereotype. Keep in mind that today's families are likely to be impacted by various economic and social challenges. For example, thirty-five percent of U.S. children are currently living in a single-parent household (Kids Count Data Center, 2015) and twenty-two percent of children under the age of 18 are living in poverty. It is estimated that five percent of families have a child with a disability. These factors impact the family dynamics as stress is placed both upon the internal and external relationships and experiences of each member.

Though negative stereotypes exist for families who form a different fabric than that of the "traditional family", many families are formed out of individuals who share a commitment to meeting the needs of their group and who may be committed by blood, marriage, legal ties, or otherwise (e.g., two unmarried adults of the same sex who raise children together in the same household). Across cultures and countries, the basic desire for a good life for children is universal among functioning families, regardless of why they are committed to one another (Fiedler, Simpson, & Clark, 2007).

Family Systems

A family unit, in the broadest context, is made up of members who are influenced by factors both internal and external to the family. For example, the presence of a disability in a child will impact all family members. Similarly, bad economic times tend to affect most families' members. Clearly, the school experiences of children will be an external factor on the family system. How these factors influence a child will be directly impacted by the family subsystem the child lives within. Turnbull, Turnbull, Erwin, Soodak, & Shogren (2015) outlined four family subsystems. The four family subsystems are marital partner subsystem, the parental subsystem, sibling subsystem, and extra-familial subsystem. We have summarized those subsystems in the following paragraphs.

Four Family Subsystems

In the **marital partner subsystem**, marital partners or significant others function as marital partners. These adults have needs and roles they play with one another as well as in the context of the family as a whole. They make family plans, provide support for one another, enjoy recreation together, and share intimacy (Turnbull et al., 2015).

The ***parental subsystem*** includes adult primary caregivers and the children. These caregivers are not always biological or adoptive parents. In interacting with children, parents/caregivers serve as counselors, disciplinarians, educators, financial providers, and more (Turnbull et al., 2015).

The ***sibling subsystem*** includes children (related by blood or not) within the family unit. Siblings may function as supporters, rivals, friends, and so on. Siblings also sometimes assume the role of caregiver and function more as a parent than as a child (Turnbull et al., 2015).

Finally, the ***extra-familial*** (or extended family) subsystem includes members of the family living outside of the home as well as community members who interact with the family members. This subsystem could include teachers, church members, community professionals, and relatives or other significant persons in the life of the family. Clearly, the various roles played in this subsystem are considerable depending on who is interacting and the overall purpose (Turnbull et al., 2015).

What may be most important for educators to remember is that some families will have substantial support within this subsystem, while others will have little or no support in such a subsystem. In the latter case, the family may need to develop or be encouraged to participate with supportive subsystem members, such as school or other community personnel.

Comprehension Check

1. What is your definition of a family?
2. Name the four subsystems of families.
3. Describe the elements to these four subsystems.

FAMILY FUNCTIONS AND INTERACTIONS

Family functions are the tasks families must engage in to meet their collective and individual members' needs. These functions would include economic needs, daily care needs, socialization needs, recreational needs, self-definition needs, affection needs, and educational and vocational needs (Turnbull et al., 2015).

Family Functions

Inherent to society today, all families have ***economic needs***. In this regard, all families must contend with obtaining and spending money (Peterson & Green, 2009). Failure to meet financial needs tends to place tremendous stress on a family system (http://hrsbstaff.ednet.ns.ca/kbmact/six_functions_of_the_family.htm, n.d.). Parents/caregivers may find they have little time or energy to devote to other roles when financial needs demand their attention for much of their days and/or nights. Financial issues may also exacerbate other existing family issues (Fiedler et al., 2007).

Families also must attend to ***daily care needs*** (Turnbull et al., 2015). Some families have tremendous needs in this area, particularly with some children with more severe disabilities (Fiedler et al., 2007). This may be the most important "routine" function in any family. Parents/caregivers can become exhausted by meeting these needs. Also, when the family system is relying on a single parent/caregiver, the demands are increased on that individual. This can also affect the roles of siblings, particularly older ones who may have to assume some of these responsibilities (Turnbull et al., 2015).

While perhaps not an absolute necessity, *socialization needs* are important in the quality of life of a family system (http://hrsbstaff.ednet.ns.ca/kbmact/six_functions_ of_the_family.htm, n.d.). For example, a family with a child with a serious emotional disturbance or other severe disability could mean that member's and other members' socialization needs are not being met or only in a limited way (although it would be wrong to assume this is the case for all or even most families with children with disabilities). Meeting socialization needs may be linked to the extra-familial (or extended family) subsystem (Turnbull et al., 2015). Some families, as in all these functions, may benefit from formal or informal supports from schools and community agencies.

When *recreational needs* are met, this enhances the quality of life for family members. Families are frequently able to meet many or all of these needs within their own internal systems (marital, parental, sibling), but again, they may rely considerably on the extra-familial system. Socialization and recreational needs are often intertwined and met through the same activities (Turnbull et al., 2015).

Self-definition needs provide ways in which each family member defines him or herself as an individual as well as a family member (Turnbull et al., 2015). Parents'/ caregiver's identities may be greatly influenced by the performance of the children in school (Fiedler et al., 2007). While educators tend to be more concerned with a student establishing a school and personal identity, parental identity might also benefit from involvement in school-based teams and activities and collaborating with school personnel (Staples & Diliberto, 2010).

Affection needs are ways in which each family member has opportunities to know they are loved unconditionally, and this may be expressed through both verbal and nonverbal actions (Peterson & Green, 2009; Turnbull et al., 2015). School personnel should also understand when such needs are not met, children may display unwanted behaviors indicative of distrust, hostility, negative self-image, or emotional problems (http://hrsbstaff.ednet.ns.ca/kbmact/six_functions_of_the_family.htm, n.d.). As teachers, we rarely have access to the "whole story" of a family and its members. Also bear in mind that some families may resist the efforts of school personnel to be involved in this area of need (e.g., in health and sex education).

Finally, families have *educational and vocational needs*, and this is the area of need most directly concerning and addressed by educators. As educators, we are charged with making these needs a high priority in the life of each student. However, we must also recognize that with a family system, competing needs may lead to relegation of these needs to lower than the priority that we attach to them. A collaborative relationship with parents (or even good faith efforts at establishing one) is more likely to encourage making these needs a higher priority in a family with other competing needs (Staples & Diliberto, 2010; Turnbull et al., 2015).

Comprehension Check

1. Name the seven family functions.
2. List an example for each of the family functions.

Effective Family Interactions

Critical to family relationships are the ways in which the family interacts with each other (http://hrsbstaff.ednet.ns.ca/kbmact/six_functions_of_the_family.htm, n.d.). Effective interactions within families have certain characteristics. First, communication should be clear and open. Any messages that are sent should have appropriate content and feeling. Additionally, roles and responsibilities should be clear but maintain flexibility to address changing situations. Children need to have clear boundaries, but members must also understand changes in time and circumstances may lead to adjustments in each individual's role (Peterson & Green, 2009). It is important for family members to accept limits and resolve their conflicts. The needs of individuals are not denied, nor are they always considered paramount to the needs of all other family members at all times. Resolution is sought with overall commitment to one another and the family throughout the process. In families with effective interactions, intimacy is present and is not based on control by one family member over another. Intimacy is not demanded nor withheld as a means of exerting control over others. Finally, families with effective relationships balance change and stability. Family members have a predictable structure on which they can rely but also are able to adapt to changes that demand changes in family roles (Turnbull et al., 2015).

This section has provided a foundation for understanding families and the ways in which families function and interact. It is important that you understand these family basics so as to have context for the issues that arise in collaborating with families. It is important that future teachers not use this information to "diagnose" family problems or assume a role as an expert on families. It is even more important that this information not be used to judge or condemn family members. Different cultures (e.g., religious sects) may have specific guidelines into what is a family, how families interact, and the roles family members assume. It is important to use the information to understand the stresses and successes that students and their families experience that influence student performance and behavior.

Comprehension Check

1. What is a family?
2. What are the four subsystems of families?
3. What are the needs of families? What are some potential negative impacts of each need when it is not being met?
4. Provide indicators that families are having successful interactions.

BARRIERS TO FAMILY INVOLVEMENT

We have discussed families, how family systems work, family functions, and how family systems can exist along continua that encourage or discourage family members' growth, and indicators of successful family interactions. In Chapter One, we discussed barriers to effective collaboration. Next we explore the collaborative relationship among families and school personnel. Specifically, we will review the barriers to family involvement in education that may differ from those confronting educators. These barriers can emanate from family or professional issues. In Chapter Seventeen, we will review specific strategies to encourage family-school collaboration.

Barriers to family involvement in a child's education can be varied. In this section, we will examine three major barriers. But it is also important to remember that professionals may generate barriers to family involvement. Thus it is also important to examine three additional barriers to involvement that have been identified by professionals

Barriers to family participation that have been identified by parents include logistical barriers, communication barriers, and lack of school understanding. In this section, we will also discuss suggestions for overcoming these barriers.

Logistical Barriers

We have discussed logistical barriers throughout this text as significant, and it is no different for families. These barriers involve complications that families may have arranging time away from home or work. These barriers can be a serious problem for some parents when invited to meetings, conferences, or other school activities (Best & Dunlap, 2012). School personnel should be particularly sensitive to loss of wages that may be invoked for parents/caregivers in order to be involved in a collaborative meeting. Time is often cited as the single greatest barrier for parents (National PTA, n.d.). School personnel may be able to ease this barrier by:

- Arranging meeting times convenient to parents
- Offering to provide transportation to the meeting
- Offering child care during the meeting
- Ensuring meetings are conducted efficiently and time is not wasted

Communication Barriers

Barriers may also develop from communication problems, especially when families do not share the same cultural or socioeconomic backgrounds of school personnel (National PTA, n.d.). The language and speech of school personnel (e.g., vocabulary usage) may differ to a significant degree with parents/caregivers. Families also have different communication styles and effectiveness, as previously discussed in this chapter. The response of educators to those styles can also present communication difficulties. For example, school personnel should be careful not to interpret loudness as aggressiveness or reticence as a lack of caring. Families and school personnel need time to get to know one another. School personnel might ease the communication barrier by:

- Avoiding the use of jargon or vocabulary that is inaccessible or difficult for parents/caregivers.
- Providing an interpreter as needed or inviting a parent advocate to assist the parents/caregivers.
- Using effective listening skills and checking your understanding of the meaning of what parents/caregivers are telling you.
- Using effective communication skills (listening, nonverbal, and verbal) to build rapport and clarify your message.

Barriers Resulting from Misunderstandings

Finally, barriers may develop when there is a lack of understanding of schools (National PTA, n.d.). School districts and individual schools tend to be somewhat complex organizations with both written and unwritten policies, as well as professional and personal agendas on the part of personnel. Families may be overwhelmed by or simply unfamiliar with the complex ways in which a school and its personnel "work" (National PTA, n.d.).

Also, some parents/caregivers did not have the best experiences in schools themselves (Best & Dunlap, 2012). They may have not been seen as high achievers, could have had behavioral issues, or may have been bullied. Any previous negative experiences may leave them feeling awkward, insecure, intimidated, or even angry when interacting with school personnel as a matter of their personal history as well as any current issues regarding their child. Families whose cultural/linguistic and/or socioeconomic backgrounds differ from the majority of school personnel may also feel vulnerable and lead to diminished involvement (Best & Dunlap, 2012). To overcome this barrier, school personnel could:

- Ensure school personnel are educated about how to communicate with families from all backgrounds.
- Provide a parent advocate to assist the parents/caregivers in navigating the system and interacting with school personnel.
- Examine current practices to determine what the school may be doing to encourage or discourage family involvement (Best & Dunlap, 2012), especially if there is a notable difference in the cultural/ethnic and/or socioeconomic background of many families and the school personnel.
- Provide in-service to parents/caregivers to help them better understand the system, their rights, and how to be involved.
- Use technology to reach out to parents (e.g., newsletters, emails, websites, faculty webpages, homework help pages, etc.) but be mindful that some, if not many, families may not have access to and/or be comfortable with computer technology—provide in-service to parents in accessing technology.
- Recognize that any "negative" communications about their child are likely to invoke emotional reactions from parents—be sure to include positives in

communicating with parents and make some communications specifically to be positive only (Fiedler et al., 2007).
• Recognize that families can be an educational resource (National PTA, n.d.).

In Case Study 14.1, you will read an illustrative case study. As you read, identify the various positive examples of principles and practices of collaboration and consultation with school colleagues and with families.

14.1 ILLUSTRATIVE CASE STUDY

Mrs. McDonald is a first year teacher who has been assigned to teach second grade. She is new to the area and is unfamiliar with the community. Mrs. McDonald wants to get to know her families better. Consequently, she invites each family to complete a survey in which she asks the following:

Tell me about your parenting style.
How do you feel about your child's school?
What concerns do you have for your child this year?
How would you describe your relationship with your child?
What limitations might you have this year in supporting your child?

Before sending her survey out, Mrs. McDonald shares her idea and a draft of the survey with her principal and with the school counselor. The school is situated in an area that has a high population of military families and as such there are many families who transfer into the school and out of the school throughout the year. The principal and counselor share this information with Mrs. McDonald. They also share that because so many families move throughout the year, it is hard to get to know them personally and to build collaborative relationships. They encourage Mrs. McDonald to send her survey home to her new class in both print and electronic form to accommodate all parents. They set a date and time to get back together to go through the surveys.

After two weeks, Mrs. McDonald is thrilled to have all but one survey back. She decides to call her remaining family and verbally communicates with this last family on the phone to gather their information and input. After collating her data, Mrs. McDonald meets with her principal and counselor to review the information.

As a team, the three educators quickly identify that many of the families have economic needs and are working multiple jobs. The families identify concerns that they cannot spend a significant amount of time helping with homework, as they struggle to meet economic and daily care needs. The families clearly illustrate their love for their children and their intentions that the school will provide not only a strong education for their child but strong friendships.

This team decides to respond proactively by sharing the overall themes with the other teachers during a staff meeting. At that time, the team discussed the implications for how they can continue to collaborate proactively with their families. They decide to implement the following components to support their families:

- Limit requests for during the school day activities
- Communicate with parents' about integrative educational opportunities
- Reach out to parents during after-school pickup times
- Continue to communicate and collaborate in both print and electronic forms

Barriers Identified by Professionals

School professionals have identified barriers to family involvement as well. The first of these barriers is related to personnel perceptions about parents/caregivers, while the other two are directly related to professionals themselves.

Parental Apathy

First, parental or caregiver apathy can be a major obstacle to involving families in a child's education. This perception of professionals may be exacerbated when there are cultural/linguistic and/or socioeconomic differences between the majority teacher culture and that of families. However, Pugach, Johnson, Drame, and Williamson (2012) point out that this perception may often be overstated by teachers. There are multiple reasons why this perception might exist. As discussed previously, parents/caregivers may have had negative school experiences and avoid interactions now as they expect them to be negative. It may also be that parents/caregivers may believe they have little influence or power in processes related to school and simply "give up" on trying. Additionally, some cultures perceive teachers as highly respected professionals not to be contradicted, and teachers may be perceived as knowing what is best and, therefore, parents/caregivers may feel it is "not their place" to collaborate. Finally, what school personnel perceive as apathy may simply be exhaustion from other demands in life (Fiedler et al., 2007).

Professionals might combat their perceptions of family apathy by:

- Reducing or eliminating any bias or preconceived notions about parental/caregiver involvement.
- Ask about what type of support might be available within your district to support families that are overwhelmed by other demands (e.g., transportation, time away from work) that hinder family involvement (National PTA, n.d.).
- Ensure parents/caregivers are given a voice in meetings and participate in decisions to the degree they are comfortable (Turnbull et al., 2015).
- Check to ensure in advance, during, and/or after any meetings that parents/caregivers understand the team process and their participation is taken seriously (National PTA, n.d.; Pugach et al., 2012).

Time Constraints

A second barrier that educational professionals cite would be in the area of time constraints, as it is in virtually all collaborative processes. Educational professionals, like families, also have limited time for collaboration and encouraging the collaboration of families in school. Teachers who are asked to attend meetings outside of regular school hours may be constrained by their own family obligations. This barrier might be overcome by:

- Being as creative as possible in scheduling meetings and using other methods of communication (e.g., by phone, by email, by mail, through other technology tools)—this can also help to make any face-to-face meetings as efficient as possible.
- Checking with school administrators for ways in which teacher time constraints can be reduced (e.g., providing substitute teacher during meeting time). Scheduling meetings well in advance to allow for the aforementioned communications to take place prior to the meeting (e.g., parental/caregiver input, completion of paper work, explanation of the process, advising of rights, etc.).

(Best & Dunlap, 2012)

Lack of Professional Expertise

Finally, a third barrier identified by educational professionals would be their concern for their own professional expertise. Some educators may feel they lack the skills and knowledge to interact effectively with and support families. This may be especially true with families of different cultural/linguistic backgrounds (National PTA, n.d.). Obviously, providing in-service training is a major method for overcoming this barrier. Also, the understanding and utilization of effective communication skills can be helpful (Fiedler et al., 2007).

Although there are significant barriers, at times, to the involvement of families in collaborative processes, educators should believe they have a duty to encourage involvement and to learn how to support families in these efforts. Pugach et al. (2012) point out that, too often, schools send a hidden message that parental/caregiver participation is not required or even desired. This occurs through how meetings are scheduled and conducted. This may also occur through how the input or suggestions of parents/caregivers are treated. It could also occur through a lack of effort to provide any supports to families who are having difficulty with demands such as transportation that hinder their involvement. Educators can also present an attitude that they are unwilling to give of their own time outside of strict duty hours to accommodate parental/caregiver participation. Teachers can also treat any parent/caregiver who disagrees with school decisions or input as a troublesome team member whose input is not welcome. In short, there are many ways in which schools and families can succumb to barriers and simply not try to overcome them. Case Study 14.2 includes an opportunity to apply your knowledge. In Chapter Sixteen, we will address how to use family conferences and meetings to encourage parental/caregiver input.

14.2 APPLICATION CASE STUDY

Assume you are a third grade teacher and your principal tells you that in your upcoming new class you have two families that have been very challenging in the past. One mother has been very "over involved" and demands to walk her child to the classroom every day to help her unpack. She also frequently has lunch with the class and writes the teachers for constant updates on how her child is doing in class, both academically and socially.

Additionally, you have a family with a child who will be in your room who has demonstrated considerable learning difficulties. The previous teacher spent the entire year trying to meet with the family to start special education testing for the child, but was completely unsuccessful communicating with them regarding their child's needs and obtaining their permission for an evaluation for eligibility for special education and related services.

Divide your own classroom (college/university classroom) into pairs or small groups and consider and discuss each of the following:

1. What are the possible barriers that might be in place for each situation?
2. What strategies would you utilize to collaborate with each family?
3. What resources might you call upon to support your collaboration with each family?
4. What outcomes would you develop for each family?

Return to a large group and compare your pair/small group responses. Were different ideas to support the families generated? Were different principles, practices, and barriers identified in different pairs/small groups?

Comprehension Check

1. What are three barriers identified by parents/caregivers for their involvement in school?
2. What are some strategies for overcoming each barrier?
3. What are three barriers identified by professionals for involving families in school?
4. What are some strategies for overcoming each barrier?

CHAPTER SUMMARY

Families, an essential element and basic unit to the fabric of our society, have become ever diverse in the past few decades. It is import as educators that we have comprehensive knowledge of how family systems work with and without our schools.

The Family Unit

✓ Each family may have a different perspective of whom and what a family unit is and does. It is important to note that one can accept another's view of a family without agreeing with his or her definition.

✓ Our working definition of a family is "the fundamental group of society and the natural environment for the growth and well-being of all its members and particularly children".

✓ Currently, there are four family subsystems:

- The marital partner subsystem
- The parental subsystem
- The sibling subsystem
- The extra-familial subsystem

✓ **The marital partner subsystem** includes the adults as well as the needs and roles they play in context to the family as a whole.

✓ **The parental subsystem** includes both the adult caregivers as well as the children in a family. It is important to note that the adult caregivers do not need to be biologically related or even the adoptive parents.

✓ **The sibling subsystem** includes all children within the family unit. Again, it is important to note that members of the sibling subsystem do not need to be biologically related.

✓ **The extra-familial subsystem** includes all other members who are important to the family. These can be family friends, congregation members, community professionals, other relatives, etc.

Family Needs

✓ **Economic needs** involve obtaining and spending money in an efficient way. Negative associations with this need may exacerbate already negative relationships in the family.

✓ **Daily care needs** include daily tasks such as cooking, cleaning, transportation, laundry, etc. As children in the family grow older, they may assume some of these responsibilities.

✓ **Socialization needs include** interactions with members outside of the immediate family, perhaps with members in the extra-familial subsystem. These needs may not be absolutely necessary, but they do affect the quality of life for the family.

✓ The quality of life is also increased when **recreational needs** are met. These needs may be met by the immediate family but can also rely heavily on members in the extra-familial family subsystem.

✓ **Self-definition needs** are ways in which each family member can define him/herself as an individual who fits into the family, much like a puzzle piece to the whole.

✓ **Affection needs** are ways in which each family member has opportunities to know that they are loved unconditionally and may be expressed through verbal and nonverbal actions.

✓ **Educational and vocational needs** are most directly connected to educators. Through a collaborative relationship with parents/caregivers, it is more likely educators can make educational and vocational needs a high priority.

✓ **Effective family interactions** are critical to family functioning. Families need to communicate as well as manage roles and conflicts effectively.

Barriers to Family Involvement in Education

✓ **Logistical, communication,** and **lack of school understanding** are all barriers to a collaborative relationship that have been identified by caregivers.

✓ **Logistical barriers** may be overcome through:

- Arranging meeting times convenient to parents
- Arranging meetings at the family's home or a closer location instead of school
- Offering to provide transportation to the meeting
- Offering child care during the meeting
- Ensuring meetings are conducted efficiently and time is not wasted

✓ **Communication barriers** may be overcome through:

- Avoiding the use of jargon or vocabulary that is inaccessible or difficult for parents/caregivers
- Providing an interpreter as needed or inviting a parent advocate to assist the parents/caregivers
- Using effective listening skills and checking your understanding of the meaning of what parents/caregivers are telling you
- Using effective communication skills (listening, nonverbal, and verbal) to build rapport and clarify your message

✓ **Lack of school understanding barriers** may be overcome through:

- Providing a parent advocate to assist the parents/caregivers in navigating the system and interacting with school personnel
- Examining current practices to determine what the school may be doing to encourage or discourage family involvement, especially if there is a notable difference in the cultural/ethnic and/or socioeconomic background of many families and the school personnel
- Providing in-service to parents/caregivers to help them better understand the system, their rights, and how to be involved
- Using technology to reach out to parents (e.g., newsletters, emails, websites, faculty webpages, homework help pages, etc.) but being mindful that some, if not many families may not have access to and/or be comfortable with computer technology—provide in-service to parents in accessing technology
- Recognizing that any "negative" communications about their child are likely to invoke emotional reactions from parents, be sure to include positives in communicating with parents and make some communications specifically to be positive only
- Recognizing that families can be an educational resource

✓ **Parental apathy, time constraints,** and **lack of professional expertise** are all barriers to a collaborative relationship that have been identified by educators.

✓ **Parental apathy** may be overcome through:

- Reducing or eliminating any bias or preconceived notions about parental/ caregiver involvement, particularly when this becomes an excuse for lack of effort on the part of the professional to encourage family involvement— check if your perception of parents/caregivers who are involved is that of "troublemakers"
- Asking about what type of support might be available within your district to support families that are overwhelmed by other demands (e.g., transportation, time away from work) that hinder family involvement
- Ensuring parents/caregivers are given a voice in meetings and participate in decisions to the degree they are comfortable
- Checking to ensure in advance, during, and/or after any meetings that parents/caregivers understand the team process and that their participation is taken seriously

✓ **Time constraints** may be overcome through:

- Being as creative as possible in scheduling meetings and using other methods of communication (e.g., by phone, by email, by mail, through other technology tools)—this can also help to make any face-to-face meetings as efficient as possible
- Checking with school administrators for ways in which teacher time constraints can be reduced (e.g., providing substitute teacher during meeting time)
- Scheduling meetings well in advance to allow for the aforementioned communications to take place prior to the meeting (e.g., parental/caregiver input, completion of paper work, explanation of the process, advising of rights, etc.)

✓ **Lack of professional expertise** can be overcome through professional development and in-service training.

APPLICATION ACTIVITIES

1. Have candidates reflect on how their own family's subsystems changed or remained stable from their own early childhood into young adulthood (or older in the case of "non-traditional" candidates). Have candidates reflect on how changes in family subsystems affected them as a family member and the impact on their school experiences. Candidates could also reflect on how they believe the supports needed for a child member of a family change as the child develops into a young adult.
2. Have students reflect on the various needs they have experienced in their own family systems. Have them prioritize the needs in terms of which were more important growing up and currently. Have them compare how the needs might

have changed in priority over time. If they are willing, have candidates compare and contrast how different families prioritize needs differently. Candidates could also reflect on *how* needs were met in their own families (e.g., socialization, recreation, educational needs). They could again reflect on how the means by which needs were met changed over time and/or how different families go about meeting these needs.

3. Invite parents/caregivers to participate in a panel discussion to explore how different families attend to different family needs and their priority within different families. Includes questions about different family subsystems and the ways in which school can collaborate with families to support their needs and break down any barriers.

REFERENCES

Best, J., & Dunlap, A. (2012). *Student achievement beyond the classroom: Engaging families and communities.* Denver, CO: Mid-continent Research for Education and Learning.

Boske, C., & Benavente-McEnery, L. (2012). Culturally and linguistically diverse students: Tapping into the Strengths of Families. In A. Honigsfeld & A. Cohan (Eds.), *Breaking the mold of education for culturally and linguistically diverse students* (pp. 75–83). Lanham, MD: Rowman & Littlefield.

Fiedler, C. R., Simpson, R. L., & Clark, D. M. (2007). *Parents and families of children with disabilities: Effective school-based support services.* Upper Saddle River, NJ: Pearson. Retrieved on October 26, 2015, from http://hrsbstaff.ednet.ns.ca/kbmact/six_functions_of_the_family.htm (n.d.).

Kids Count Data Center. (2015). Children in single-parent families. Retrieved on June 12, 2015, from http://datacenter.kidscount.org/data/tables/106-children-in-single-parent-families?loc=1&loct=2#detailed/2/2–52/false/36,868,867,133,38/any/429,430

Miller, G. E., Colebrook, J., & Ellis, B. R. (2014). Advocating for the rights of the child through family-school collaboration. *Journal of Educational and Psychological Consultation,* 24(1), 10–27.

National PTA (n.d.). Barriers to parent involvement: Roadblocks and detours. Retrieved on October 26, 2015, from http://www.leadershipcharlotte.org/wp-content/uploads/2011/01/Barriers_to_Parent_Involvement.pdf

Peterson, R., & Green, S. (2009). Families first: Keys to successful family functioning family roles. *Virginia Cooperative Extension.* Retrieved on October 25, 2015, from https://vtechworks.lib.vt.edu/handle/10919/48301

Pugach, M. C., Johnson, L. J., Drame, E. R., & Williamson, P. (2012). *Collaborative practitioners, collaborative schools* (3rd ed.). Denver, CO: Love Publishing.

Staples, K. E., & Diliberto, J. A. (2010). Guidelines for successful parent involvement: Working with parents of students with disabilities. *Teaching Exceptional Children,* 42(6), 58–63.

Turnbull, A., Turnbull, R., Erwin, E. J., Soodak, L. C., & Shogren, K. A. (2015). *Families, professionals, and exceptionality* (7th ed.). Upper Saddle River, NJ: Pearson.

UNICEF. (1989). *Convention on the rights of the child.* Retrieved from http://digitalcommons.ilr.cornell.edu/cgi/viewcontent.cgi?article=1007&context=child

15

STRATEGIES FOR EFFECTIVE FAMILY COMMUNICATION AND COLLABORATION

Jackie M. Arnold

Chapter Objectives

Following reading the chapter, students should:

1. Name the essential elements to consider when planning a family conference
2. Cite important considerations inherent in a successful family conference
3. Identify strategies after a conference to facilitate family involvement
4. Understand ways to communicate with families
5. Define strategies to promote family involvement

PRINCIPLES OF FAMILY COLLABORATION

Previous chapters, such as Chapter Two, have defined and illustrated steps for scheduling and conducting collaborative tasks. In particular, strategies for developing and conducting committee meetings were presented. Those steps are valid and useful, but in those chapters, the focus centered upon teams primarily involving professionals, although parents/caregivers might also be involved. In this chapter, the content is specifically on collaborative meetings involving parents/caregivers and especially for encouraging their involvement in school.

Family conferences are a primary and essential way in which family involvement can be encouraged. It is critical for teachers to build collaborative, healthy connections between the school and the family for the sake of all participants (Staples & Diliberto, 2010). The ways in which the school and the family interact can directly impact the student. Families may feel welcomed and included or they may feel that they are not valued or included based upon their experiences and satisfaction. As discussed in Chapter Fourteen, no two families are alike (Boske & Benavente-McEnery, 2012), so it is crucial that schools develop trust and identify the type of role a family would prefer to have regarding their child's education (Turnbull, Turnbull, Erwin, Soodak, &

Shogren, 2015). While some families would prefer to have consistent and direct inclusion in the decision-making process, other families may prefer less responsibility following a philosophy of "letting the experts take the lead." Schools should consider these different approaches and respect a family's philosophy. Keeping these different perspectives in mind will help in the process of collaboration and conference planning.

Essential Elements to Planning a Family Conference

Family conferences are a critically important component to building a collaborative relationship with families. The ways in which conferences take place vary in relation to the age of the child, time of the year, and dynamics of the family. This section will detail some of the ways in which conferences may take place and how to plan for them.

Some conferences may be planned as school-wide events, such as school open house nights. These conferences are important, as they can reach multiple families at one time. They can also be beneficial, as many families are more comfortable in a group context rather than an individual context.

However, many times it is critical to have a family conference focused upon just that family and their child. Conferences can be held with families for a variety of purposes and most importantly they should not only be held for negative reasons or interactions. Typically, conferences can have four main purposes (Pugach, Johnson, Drame, & Williamson, 2012). First, a teacher may hold a conference to exchange information about the home and school environments. This type of conference allows each of the members to build a relationship and understand each other better. By equally sharing information, all individuals can come to know and appreciate the other's context. A second reason for having a conference is to develop rapport and commitment to the student's development. Taking time to meet together (either face-to-face or virtually) to build collaboration and reconnect regarding a student's progress will help everyone know and support that child's development. A third reason to hold a conference would be to enhance working together to promote the student's development and to discuss progress. To help every child throughout the year, it is critical to stay in touch with families, updating them on their child's progress and what might be done to help facilitate the child's development in all areas, not just academically. Finally, it is sometimes necessary to hold a conference to mediate any concerns or problems that arise. There are times that miscommunications, issues, or other related conflicts need to be discussed and resolved for the good of all involved. Although it may seem easier to avoid this type of conference, it is critical to work through conflict for collaborative relationships to flourish.

Certainly other reasons for conferencing could also be considered. However, most such conferences are generally focused on outcomes related to the student family member. Still, in-services, support groups, and planning how parents/caregivers can participate in school activities are a few examples of other reasons for conferencing.

Planning for the Conference

For a successful conference, planning is of critical importance. There are three basic steps in the conferencing process: planning for the conference, conducting the conference, and follow-up. Each of these basic steps includes several substeps advisable for a successful conference.

When planning for a conference, it is important to consider how to notify those involved, all that should be done to prepare, and to consider arrangements that should be made prior to actually conducting the conference.

Notification

In the notification process, key family members should be notified well in advance that a meeting is going to occur. In fact, written notification is required by IDEA for certain meetings (e.g., Individualized Education Program meetings). Family input on the day and time of the conference is recommended when feasible. The teacher or person responsible for the planning should check to see if there are any barriers to attendance. If there are any barriers, these should also be addressed to support the family needs. The invitation itself should be nonthreatening and encourage family participation. If the family members are non-English speakers or understand another language more readily, the notification should be made in that language. Remember, under IDEA, this is a requirement. It is advantageous to follow a written notification with a personal phone call.

Preparation

Educators should review any pertinent information or data needed. All members of the conference team should be knowledgeable about the child's current achievement levels and progress, especially regarding any areas of concern. Preparation should include organizing examples of the student's work as needed to illustrate any important elements to be discussed in the conference. Members of the conference should devise an outline of points of discussion and decisions that need to be made. The conference preparation, if possible, should incorporate input from family members (including the student, as appropriate) and from other professionals as needed prior to the meeting. If helpful, give parents a list of activities to be conducted (e.g., checking the child's hearing aid battery, collecting data on how much time the student spends on homework) or information that should be obtained (e.g., paper work, prescription drug side effects).

Arranging the Environment

The way in which the environment is arranged can send clear messages, either positive or negative. To send a clear, collaborative message to your participants, ensure that the room is comfortable, affords privacy, and includes ample seating for adults. Make sure the arrangement of seating does not place all school professionals across a table from family members, suggesting some adversarial purpose. Be prepared and ready to go when the family members arrive. Greet them warmly and let them know how much you appreciate their time and commitment to their child. Be sure potential for interruptions is limited. Make sure the temperature and other elements for physical comfort are arranged. For example, you may want to ensure that drinking water is available. Having tissue available in the event of emotional reactions is a good idea. Make sure an interpreter or parent advocate is present as needed. Even having a known individual (e.g., a paraprofessional familiar with the family) present can be helpful.

Conducting the Conference

Upon completion of the conference preparation, the educator is now ready to hold the conference. Keep in mind that clear, effective, kindly communication is the key foundation for a successful conference. While the conference should be planned for efficiency, the plan should not be so rigid as to disallow for discussions and reasonable variance from the plan. A quality conference will have flexibility and will accommodate the family members' needs throughout the time of the meeting. It is also important that everyone involved is aware and knowledgeable of cultural influences on how family members might participate. In our experience, IEP team meetings were scheduled by one assistant principal 30 minutes apart. During one meeting, the student's mother broke down crying and explaining she wasn't sure she could continue taking care of her son with severe disabilities. She wasn't sure what she should do or how to proceed. The assistant principal appeared to be concerned with the time rather than the significant problem being experienced by the mother. Fortunately, other team members refused to rigidly adhere to the schedule in order to help the mother problem solve the situation and set a procedure in place to assist her in investigating possible living arrangements for her son.

Consider involving the student in the conference if appropriate. Student-led conferences can be engaging and rewarding for everyone, as it provides an opportunity for the student to take responsibility for the learning and the communication of he or she has grown thus far. A student-led conference will also provide an opportunity for the student to communicate his or her needs and future goals (Brown & Knowles, 2014).

Make Introductions

Before the "heart" of the conference begins, take a little time for everyone to introduce themselves and to try and make everyone as comfortable as possible. Be aware that in some cultures, "getting down to business" can be a sign of rudeness. As needed, take some time for informal conversation to help everyone relax and feel welcome. This is particularly important at initial meetings where it is important to build rapport and trust with the family.

Incorporate Input

If at all possible, provide time for the family members to speak as early in the conference as possible and provide time for the family to participate throughout the conference, as often as possible. Professionals at the conference should not make pronouncements or opinions until the end. Always try to end a conference by asking the family members if there is anything they would like to add.

Throughout the conference it is important to use effective listening skills as well as open nonverbal cues and verbal interactions as discussed in earlier chapters. All educators should respond empathetically if family members open up about issues or problems that are confronting their family or child.

Any professional information shared during the conference should begin with a positive note. Use positive examples of student work or personal anecdotes that illustrate some positive aspects of the student, particularly if the conference is going to involve addressing more negative concerns and issues. Watch family members' reactions to comments and adapt accordingly (e.g., provide more specifics, allow for questions or comments, or end the conversation more quickly). Address more negative aspects after positive ones.

The conference is an ideal time to make an intervention plan as needed. Tasks to be accomplished should be clearly outlined as well as who will be responsible for those tasks, how and when progress will be determined should be discussed, and the plan for a follow-up meeting, if possible, should also be addressed. Identify someone to take notes throughout the conference and throughout the development of the intervention plan.

Finally, end the conference by summarizing the highlights of the meeting and the plans made. It is important to make sure family members and professionals have another opportunity for questions or comments before adjourning. Thank the family for their involvement in the conference and offer to be available if they should have concerns they think about later.

After the Meeting

Often it is easy to have the conference but let the important elements "slip away" or go unimplemented. To prevent this from happening, consider the following important steps. First you may wish to review with the student the outcomes of the meeting whether he/she attended or not, assuming you have parental/caregiver consent to do so. Clearly, in some instances, the subject matter of the conference may not lend itself to such a review.

Make sure to take the time to review the outcomes of the meetings with other professionals or stakeholders who were not able to attend and who have a need to know those outcomes. Complete minutes of the meeting and a detailed outline of the plans made. Distribute these to all appropriate parties. If an intervention plan was developed, be committed to communicating the plan with anyone who should know about the elements and what the outcomes might be. Communicate the action items and any critical next dates. Make sure you maintain a permanent record of all such meetings, minutes, and plans. Remember, these become a part of the student's record as well, so be sure the language and materials included are professional in wording and appearance.

Finally, take time to reflect and evaluate how the conference went. Was it a collaborative effort on the part of all? Were effective communication skills used? Were rapport and trust present or at least in the process of being built? Were collaborative team members satisfied with the outcomes and if not, why so? Assess both the strengths of the conference and what might have been done to improve the process and product.

Be sure to follow up on the plan, with the persons responsible for various tasks, with any data to be collected, and to ensure the follow-up conference is planned and conducted. Remember, a follow-up meeting to celebrate a successful intervention can be just as important as one to revise a plan or devise a new plan because there is a lack of progress. Case Study 15.1 illustrates how these various tasks may be conducted.

15.1 ILLUSTRATIVE CASE STUDY

Mrs. Peters is a third grade teacher who needs to have a conference with one of her new families. The student in her class, Michael, has joined the group later in the school year and after a week Mrs. Peters is starting to have some concerns. Michael is struggling to make new friends and has been in trouble in the cafeteria twice this first week. Mrs. Peters does not yet have Michael's school records from his previous school, but she has noticed that Michael does not yet seem at the same academic level as the other third graders in the room.

Mrs. Peters begins by preparing for the conference. She writes a note home to the family asking if they can meet at any time that is convenient for the parents. In the note she sends a form with questions designed to gather more information about Michael and to help Mrs. Peters prepare for the conference. On the form she asks the family:

Tell me about Michael's strengths.
What goals do you have for Michael this year?
Do you have any concerns for Michael's transition to our school?
In what ways do you think Michael learns best?
What would you like me to know about Michael?
Is there anything specific you would like to discuss when we meet?

Before sending home her request to meet with the family, Mrs. Peters shares her plan and form with her principal and the school counselor. She asks if either of them might be available to attend the conference to help make the family feel welcome and to share any additional resources that could be helpful as they transition to the area. They agree to attend and appreciate the form that she has created to gather more information about Michael before the conference time. Mrs. Peters sends home the note and form with Michael. She waits three days, and upon not hearing back from the family, follows up with a phone call. Michael's mom is apologetic about not responding yet, as she has been overwhelmed settling into their new house. Together they set a time that is convenient for Michael's parents, and she promises to send in the form tomorrow.

Upon receiving the form, Mrs. Peters's learns that Michael's parents are concerned for his academic and social transition as well. Michael did not want to move from his previous home and has been acting out. He also shut down academically at his previous school when he found out about the move. Mrs. Peters shares this information with her principal and school counselor. Mrs. Peters also has Michael take a reading and writing performance assessment to gather a preliminary idea of his academic levels. They all attend the meeting to support Michael and his family. During the conference, they discuss everyone's concerns regarding Michael's academic and social transition and develop the following action plan. Michael's family will be given a mentor family with a son Michael's age to help ease his transition to the school and to help build his social network. Mrs. Peters will carefully monitor Michael's performance in class with the intervention specialist's input to attend to Michael's needs. The school counselor will meet with a small group during lunch to help Michael as he makes friends.

Before the conference ends, Mrs. Peters schedules a convenient date and time for everyone to meet again in six weeks to determine how the plan is going and to see what Michael needs next. Mrs. Peters discovers that emails are easier for Michael's family. After everyone leaves, Mrs. Peters summarizes the notes taken during the conference and emails them out to the group with a reminder of their determined next meeting date and time.

This section of the chapter discussed specific steps and strategies for conducting family conferences. The process should be planned, conducted, and followed up in a way that encourages family involvement. Professionals should also be willing to accept whatever level of involvement a family provides, at least initially, and promote increased involvement as appropriate. Professionals should be aware of cultural/linguistic differences that could enhance or derail the process and be prepared to adapt to those differences. Using effective communication and conflict resolution skills may be needed, and teachers should review these prior to and after conferences to reflect on personal and team success in these areas. Professionals should also provide any assistance they can to help families overcome any barriers that prevent or limit involvement. But what are other strategies aside from conferences to promote family involvement? The next section of this chapter will address this important area.

Comprehension Check
1. What steps should be taken in preplanning a collaborative family conference?
2. What steps should be taken in conducting a collaborative family conference?
3. What steps should be taken in follow-up to a collaborative family practice?

ADDITIONAL WAYS TO COLLABORATE WITH FAMILIES

It is important that educators incorporate other communication ideas throughout a school year and beyond that are not specifically related to conferences. This section will provide strategies to encourage families to collaborate in the educational process, as well as attending school events and volunteering at school.

Communicating with families (aside from specific conference-related communications) is important in maintaining a collaborative relationship. Educators need multiple strategies for written communication, for unplanned meetings, and for group family meetings. Remember to utilize the previous information for suggestions regarding telephone contacts and activities related to technology options. These are also relevant for encouraging family collaboration.

Written Strategies

Communicating in writing has several advantages. Remember that any written materials must be appropriately translated for a family as needed. The first advantage inherent to written communication is that most family members are literate and can read the materials and notes sent home. Written communications also do not require technologies that a family may not have, such as email. Second, because such communication is frequently transported by the student, the student is aware that the parents/caregivers and the school are in regular communication. Third, written communication results in an ongoing record of issues, concerns, and successes being discussed. Finally, written communication frequently forces the writer to consider carefully the words chosen and the tone of the message. While lack of the nonverbal and verbal cues can sometimes lead to confusion about a message, most writers are aware that a written communication should be accurate, clear, and as specific as possible, with minimal emotional wording—especially if the communication is one addressing a difficult issue.

There are several types of written communication that an educator could use to build conversations with families, including handbooks, handouts, newsletters (Turnbull & Turnbull, 2001; Staples & Diliberto, 2010; Pugach et al., 2012), and daily communications (LeBel, Chafouleas, Britner, & Simonsen, 2012).

Handbooks

Student handbooks are important for schools in specifying policies and procedures (e.g., dress codes, attendance policies). As an educator, it is important to develop a supplemental handbook specific to the class that includes personnel, homework procedures, information about technology usage or technology communications (e.g., webpage), lunches, snacks, etc., as appropriate. The language should be simple, forward, and easily understood. The handbook should be attractive and professional looking. Always remember to provide a translated version for any family that may need the handbook in a different language.

Handouts

Handouts are typically about a specific topic or concern, such as an upcoming field trip, a community resource, or special school event. Handouts can encourage family involvement when the following are considered. Make sure the handout is designed attractively and is easy to read. The handout should focus on family interests. For example, you may create a handout for a special ethnic event or occasion. It is always beneficial if the students themselves can be involved or if one or more family members can be involved in their preparation as appropriate. Remember, handouts can be individualized by highlighting or starring information for a particular family.

Newsletters

Newsletters, like handbooks, can be developed for an entire school, an entire grade-level team, or a specific class. There are several elements to keep in mind when creating a newsletter. Whenever possible, use drawings, quotations, or essays written by students. It is also collaborative to include birthday and special accomplishment announcements. Include information about special events that your families might want to know are taking place in the near future. Provide your families updates on ongoing projects or long-term assignments. It is also helpful to incorporate information about community agencies/services and/or school services. Families may also appreciate information about support groups, in-services, or workshops for parents/caregivers. Finally, as with handouts, involve students and family members in the preparation of the newsletter whenever appropriate and possible.

Daily Communications

Letters, notes, and dialogue journals are communications that can be adapted to family-specifics and can be used daily when needed. This type of communication allows for building rapport and trust among family members and educators. These types of communications should not be used exclusively for discussing some problem area. They should regularly be used to celebrate success and applaud effort. Dialogue journals do have the advantage of creating a record of communication over time and generally are not as easily misplaced as a letter or note. In such types of regular communication, it is wise to involve families in deciding who will be communicating in the journal, how often, what types of information should be included, and whether the journal's contents should be open or restricted in terms of who may or may not review its contents. Regular communication through letters, notes, or journals tends to support family involvement and increase participation in face-to-face meetings when necessary.

Report Cards, Grading, and Progress Reports

Report cards, grading, and progress reports are formal ways of communication sent to families of all students (with the exception of students who have reached the age of majority and are their own legal guardians). There are many viewpoints on how to grade or judge progress, what grades should mean, what should be included in grading criteria and decisions, and what should be the consequences for poor and/or excellent grades. There is no single viewpoint that has all the answers for grading. However, remember that reports to families should, as always, be collaborative and helpful to the child's educational progress. Remember when communicating about a child's progress to include positive feedback as well as any negative feedback. Any communication about the student's progress should be accurate and factual and less opinion based. It is important to focus on performance rather than the student him or herself. For example, state that the student's math performance is problematic rather than that the student is poor in math. There may be times when progress communication needs to be more regular than the school-wide requirements (LeBel et al., 2012). Be responsive when some families and students need more frequent information and feedback. It is also important to consider performance in a variety of tasks and not just tests and quizzes. Finally, consider collaboration among professionals in determining overall progress. Provide an opportunity for everyone who works with the child to give input regarding his or her overall performance.

Occasional Messages

Occasional messages can be specific messages about student successes and can encourage rapport and collaborative relationships. Certificates, "happy grams", "good news" postcards, and other such positively oriented written communications provide reinforcement for students and parents/caregivers alike.

A word of caution is in order when considering written communications. Educators should have another professional or adult review any formal message to be sent (newsletter, letter, form, etc.) to ensure the message is clear, accurate, and free of writing errors. Even when communicating with less formal methods, such as dialogue journals, teachers should be careful that their writing is error free to the greatest extent possible. Also, teachers may need to have their building administrator review communications such as class newsletters, announcements, etc., as required by policy and common sense. Finally, always be careful if a portion of the communication is designed to invoke humor or convey a personal feeling. Be careful to consider if the message could be construed in any way other than how it is intended.

Additional Ways to Communicate and Collaborate

It is critical that educators continually strive to find new, effective ways to communicate with families. Additional strategies that encourage family involvement might include unplanned meetings, group family meetings, and innovative usage of technology (Grant, 2011; Turnbull et al., 2015)

Unplanned meetings take place when parents or caregivers may drop by school, see you in the grocery store or at a school event, or call you at home. These types of meetings may invoke more intense feelings and emotions than might otherwise be revealed when all parties have the opportunity to plan what they are going to say or do. To be best prepared for such impromptu encounters, try to decide in advance where and when it is appropriate to respond to such communications. However, know that this is highly flexible based upon the topic and the family. There may be times and places that impromptu collaboration is appropriate and times where it is not. Gather the advice of other professionals regarding how they handle such situations. Also try to identify any issues that are off-limits for such encounters (e.g., a service that is agreed to and included on a written IEP) and whether the issue must be addressed in a formal meeting.

Talk to the school administrator regarding his or her preference on how to handle difficult or problematic encounters as soon as possible. If you do have an impromptu meeting with a family that develops into a concern, make sure to document this with the appropriate administrator. Always be sensitive to the fact that sometimes unexpected meetings can serve to defuse a situation better than a planned one. Try to inform families in advance if phone calls at home are acceptable and meetings can take place during "off-hours."

Remember, it is always acceptable to state that it is necessary "to have their child's records and work samples available" as one way to positively communicate a willingness to listen but less so in an unplanned way. Keep such records and work samples readily available if parents/caregivers should drop by school unannounced.

Be aware of professionals who provide other services in the school and community so that references can be made or a family can be given a referral as the situation requires (e.g., "My son ran away from home on Friday and I don't know where he is!").

It is of utmost importance that educators use effective communication skills. Even in situations where it is not advantageous to engage in lengthy discussion or problem solving, it is still important to acknowledge the parent's/caregiver's comments and concerns, indicating an understanding of their thoughts and feelings. Always make sure to avoid making agreements, commitments, or decisions in haste. Whenever there is a time of uncertainty, give additional time to consider the ramifications.

Group Family Meetings

For group family meetings, always be well prepared. Make sure the invitation to such meetings (e.g., open house) are planned well in advance. It is important that families have plenty of time to arrange attending, and it is important not to transmit the message that the meeting is an imposition.

Group meetings can provide an opportunity to give information to larger numbers of people at one time, answer questions, and listen to comments; therefore, they can be more efficient. Typically, attendance for families should be optional, although strong encouragement to attend can also be appropriate. Group meetings should include time and activities to let families get to know one another and make connections among themselves.

Families can also be involved in the school context through attending and participating in school events and activities. To some extent, the previous strategies address these areas. However, families sometimes need more specific strategies to encourage attendance and participation. Families can frequently feel isolated or struggle to join the group. Be sure to note families that are experiencing this challenge and be welcoming. For example, families of students with significant disabilities may know fewer families because their child has few friends or acquaintances and may need assistance meeting and building relationships with other families. It is often appreciated when an offer is made to introduce one family to another family. It could be possible to survey families in advance of special events or occasions to identify areas of interest (e.g., in recreation) so that those who have common interests can be supported in finding each other. It is also beneficial to "match" a new family with a veteran family to be a mentor for the year.

Special events (e.g., art, music events) can be events that capitalize on student interests and deemphasize academic achievement in terms of traditional content areas. Encouraging participation can allow lower achieving students and families to feel more integrated and focus on an area other than areas in which the child has problems in learning.

Finally, the saturation of technology into society can provide new ways of communicating and collaborating with families. Grant (2011) found that "parents, teachers, and children welcomed the idea of using digital technologies to communicate between home and school, hoping that more timely communication could avoid problems at school" (p. 292). Teachers and schools now have "apps" that let families and schools collaborate and connect. Electronic messages provide quick and efficient ways of reaching families in a timely manner. Utilization of video conferences can provide opportunities for families and schools to "see" each other without requiring families to be physically present in the school building.

Keep in mind the following list of possible options as you build collaboration and family involvement throughout the year.

a. If possible, establish a network of mentor families who can provide information and support to families that are newcomers to the neighborhood and school environment.
b. Note any school-wide committees or task forces that need family members and invite membership.
c. Compile a list of volunteering opportunities and make sign-ups available to family members (e.g., fund raising, chaperoning, or assisting in the media center).
d. Identify any special skills or knowledge parents/caregivers may possess and inquire if they would be willing to mentor a student, make a presentation, or provide assistance in some other way (e.g., helping students learn how to track orders and money in a fund raising campaign, coaching an intramural team, or allow a student to job shadow).
e. Devise in-services for parents or informational meetings (e.g., Ohio Job and Family Services representative to share what is available to families through that agency).
f. Encourage and support participation in the school's parent-teacher organization.

Case Study 15.2 provides an opportunity to apply your knowledge from this chapter.

15.2 APPLICATION CASE STUDY

Assume you are a seventh grade teacher in an urban district. Your school traditionally has seen very small numbers of parents and caregivers attend conferences, school day activities, and after-school special events. Knowing how important it is to improve collaborative relationships between school and home, your principal has developed a task force of school representatives throughout your K–8 school and has asked you to be the leader.

Divide your own classroom (college/university classroom) into pairs or small groups and consider and discuss each of the following:

1. What are the possible barriers that are keeping parents and caregivers from attending?
2. How can you address each of those barriers in new and creative ways?
3. What strategies would you utilize to reach out to each family?
4. What resources might you call upon to support your initiatives?

Return to a large group and compare your pair/small group responses. Were different ideas to support the families generated? What different principles, practices, and barriers were identified in different pairs/small groups?

Comprehension Check

1. What are four advantages to using written communication?
2. What are the six written communication strategies presented? How could one use each strategy to promote family involvement?
3. What are three important cautions for educators when using written communication with families?
4. What are considerations for educators in deciding how to address and set limits for unplanned meetings with family members?
5. What are strategies for promoting involvement of families in group family meetings?
6. What are strategies for promoting family involvement in attending and participating in school activities and events?

CHAPTER SUMMARY

A collaborative relationship between the school and the family is essential. The ways in which the school and the family interact can have a direct impact on the student.

✓ One component in building a collaborative relationship with families is through a family conference. Some family conferences may be designed as school-wide events that are able to reach more than one family at a time.

✓ Some families may also be more inclined to participate in a group atmosphere than an individual family meeting.

✓ Family conferences hold four main purposes:

- exchange information about the home and school environments
- allow time to develop rapport and commitment to the student's development
- allow further promotion of the student's development and to discuss progress
- mediation of any concerns or problems that may arise

For a successful conference to take place, appropriate steps should be taken. There are three main steps in developing a successful family conference: preplanning, conducting the conference, and follow-up.

✓ Preplanning for a family conference should also include three steps: notification, preparation, and arrangement.

- Notification involves informing all family members, well in advance, that the meeting is to occur. This is the time educators should also seek to find any barriers that may interfere with the meeting.
- Preparation involves reviewing any relevant information or data needed for the meeting. This could include reviewing achievement levels and progress or organizing examples of the students work.

- Arrangement of the environment can either send positive or negative messages. It is important to ensure that the room is comfortable, affords privacy, and includes ample room and seating.

✓ Conducting the conference has two main components: making introductions and incorporating input.

- Before the conference begins, it is important to introduce each meeting member and make everyone feel as comfortable as possible. In some cultures, just getting down to business can be considered rude.
- Incorporating input happens as the actual meeting begins. At this time it is important for all participating members to feel as if they have had a voice in the meeting. Ask for family members to speak early and often, and always conclude the meeting by asking family members if there is anything that they would like to add.

✓ After the meeting occurs, it is important a follow-up occurs.

- Shortly after the meeting, review the outcomes of the meeting with colleagues and share any information with those who were not able to participate in the meeting but still need to know the outcomes.
- If an intervention or change was made during the meeting, plan and communicate what the steps and procedures are for the intervention.
- Finally, take time to reflect and evaluate how the conference went.

Family conferences are not the only way to build an effective, collaborative relationship with a family. Other approaches such as written strategies or impromptu meetings can occur.

✓ Written strategies have several positive aspects. It is a strategy that does not require technology that the family does not have; written communication is frequently transported by the student who becomes aware that consistent communication between school and home is occurring; written communication is an ongoing record of communication, and it forces the writer to consider carefully the words written and the tone of message.

✓ Written communication can occur in a variety of forms:

- Handbooks
- Handouts
- Newsletters
- Letters, notes, and dialogue
- Report cards, grading, and progress reports
- Occasional "happy grams" or "good news" postcards

✓ Unplanned meetings may occur when a parent calls you at home, drops by school, or in a more unexpected place, such as the grocery store or community event.

✓ It is best, as well as possible, to be "prepared" for these unplanned meetings:

- Talk to other professionals regarding how they handle such situations
- Identify issues that are off-limits, such as issues or ideas for an IEP
- Inform families of acceptable and unacceptable calling hours
- Talk with a school administrator if a difficult situation occurs resulting from an impromptu meeting

APPLICATION ACTIVITIES

1. Have candidates review or create invitations to parents to attend a conference. Including various conferences for varied reasons (such as the four mentioned previously) would be helpful. Analyze the invitation from the viewpoint of a parent/caregiver. Is the invitation nonthreatening? Encouraging? Clear in purpose and meaning? Include who will be in attendance? Address any barriers the family might encounter? Solicit preconference input as needed?
2. Have candidates, individually or in small groups, review, and summarize family involvement opportunities in a local school or district. Candidates should interview classroom teachers to determine their degree of participation in encouraging family involvement. Candidates should compare and contrast how opportunities might vary across grade levels. Candidates should devise ideas on how to increase or improve those opportunities.
3. Have candidates plan for a group family meeting that will actually occur in their field placement school or for a fictitious scenario. Remind candidates to consider the basic elements of notification, preparation, conducting the meeting, and follow-up.

REFERENCES

Boske, C., & Benavente-McEnery, L. (2012). Culturally and linguistically diverse students: Tapping into the Strengths of Families. In A. Honigsfeld & A. Cohan (Eds.), *Breaking the mold of education for culturally and linguistically diverse students* (pp. 75–83). Lanham, MD: Rowman & Littlefield.

Brown, D. F., & Knowles, T. (2014). *What every middle school teacher should know* (3rd ed.). Portsmouth, NH: Heinemann.

Grant, L. (2011). 'I'm a completely different person at home': Using digital technologies to connect learning between home and school. *Journal of Computer Assisted Learning, 27*, 292–302.

LeBel, T.J., Chafouleas, S. M., Britner, P. A., & Simonsen, B. (2012). Use of a daily report card in an intervention package involving home-school communication to reduce disruptive behavior in preschoolers. *Journal of Positive Behavior Interventions, 15*(2), 103–112.

Pugach, M. C., Johnson, L. J., Drame, E. R., & Williamson, P. (2012). *Collaborative practitioners, collaborative schools* (3rd ed.). Denver, CO: Love Publishing.

Staples, K. E., & Diliberto, J. A. (2010). Guidelines for successful parent involvement: Working with parents of students with disabilities. *Teaching Exceptional Children, 42*(6), 58–63.

Turnbull, A., & Turnbull, H. R. (2001). *Families, professionals, and exceptionality: Collaborationg for empowerment.* New York, NY: Prentice Hall.

Turnbull, A., Turnbull, R., Erwin, E. J., Soodak, L. C., & Shogren, K. A. (2015). *Families, professionals, and exceptionality* (7th ed.). Boston, MA: Pearson.

16

COLLABORATING WITH DIVERSE FAMILIES AND LEARNERS

Jackie M. Arnold

Chapter Objectives

Following reading the chapter, students should:

1. Identify diversity in its various forms and the impact on the family and learner
2. Cite barriers to working with diverse families and learners
3. Identify strategies for collaborating with diverse families and learners
4. Understand how professionals need to change
5. Provide ways to promote diversity through collaboration among various stakeholders

BUILDING COLLABORATION

Educators value and embrace the critical importance of collaborating with families. However, it is even more important that educators evaluate with a critical lens what they are doing (or not doing) to reach out to their diverse families. Diverse families may not feel respected and included in the classroom for multiple reasons. Educators must utilize specific strategies to include all families and engage a critical lens on their own practices to reveal any bias and cultural dissonance. This cultural dissonance takes place when "teachers' beliefs and behaviors are incompatible with student/family beliefs and behaviors" (LaRocque, 2013, p. 112). However, research has illustrated that we must collaborate with families if we are to provide a quality education for all students (Olivos, Gallagher, & Aguilar, 2010). In this chapter, we will explore the barriers that diverse families often face, as well as strategies for addressing those barriers and how to embrace our diverse families through collaboration.

Identifying Diversity and the Impacts on the Family and Learner

As previous chapters have discussed, families in today's society are more dynamic and diverse than ever before. Children may be in family contexts that incorporate foster parents, grandparents, aunts, uncles, and older siblings (Olivos, Gallagher, & Aguilar, 2010). It is important that educators use a broader lens of what constitutes a family beyond the traditional "mother, father, and two siblings" stereotype of the past. One family is not inherently better or worse than another. Pugach, Johnson, Drame, and Williamson (2012) clearly support this broader lens by stating, the "notion of the family has to expand to acknowledge the unique structures and consequent pressures of the various types of family units with which teachers come in contact" (p. 253). This understanding and appreciation of diversity in families may be a more recent concern of educators, but it is of utmost importance in building a culture of community and trust.

It is unfortunate that research has clearly illustrated that diverse families from different linguistic and cultural backgrounds often describe their interactions with educators as challenging (Cheatham & Santos, 2011). The first step in changing this dynamic is for educators to remember three important factors when considering cultural differences and diversity in their school families.

First, no culture is inherently better than another. Each culture has its context, traditions, and behaviors that are part of its history and philosophy. As educators, it is important to not critique, judge, or compare one culture against another.

Second, though there may be some culturally based behaviors, these behaviors are always on a spectrum and should not be "assigned" to any given individual. No one falls on any extreme of one end or the other of a given spectrum, and though society often casts anyone from any given culture in a particular light, educators must recognize these stereotypes and set them aside to work with each and every family without prejudice or preconceived notions.

Third, in this same regard, each individual is an individual and may or may not adopt cultural behaviors often assigned to someone from a particular cultural background (Cheatham & Santos, 2011). Other factors in a person's life shape who he or she is beyond just the culture, such as occupation, personality, life experiences, and family income, among others.

In this light, as schools collaborate with families, they need to not limit the work and the lens to that of working with parents but should consider how to broaden their lens of "family" into one that incorporates anyone and everyone who is central to supporting children (Olivos et al., 2010).

Keep in mind that the ways in which families are involved in school collaboration is directly shaped by gender, culture, race, class, and language. However, it is also directly impacted (both positively and negatively) by the school's commitment to diverse families and the power differentials that inherently exist (Auerbach, 2010). A critical component to increasing family involvement is the collaborative nature that exists between the school and the family. This requires that the school commits to developing a relationship that is grounded in honesty, is friendly, and is clear. Families have important information and must be listened to without judgment. They must be cared for and respected.

PRINCIPLES OF INCLUSIVE COLLABORATION

As LaRocque (2013) reminds educators,

> It is important not to assume that lack of participation equals lack of interest in the child or the school. First, educators must broaden the definition of *acceptable forms of participation* to include ways that are more comprehensive, varied, and reflective of how families are able to participate (p. 112).

As families change and adapt to today's culture, many incorporate careers and lifestyles that have all members of the family working full-time jobs and often working multiple jobs at one time. Responsive educators in today's diverse society will need to support families without judgment and think creatively regarding different ways to reach out to them throughout the year. Diverse families need a broader lens for successful collaboration to happen.

Barriers to Working with Diverse Families

The reality for schools today is that many families, in particular our diverse families, have had negative experiences with schools. As a result, they may feel angry or intimidated by the "power" that they perceive the school possesses. In order to overcome those experiences and help build a collaborative relationship, it is first important to identify the potential challenges that may exist between families and the school.

LaRocque (2013) identifies six challenges that create barriers for diverse families in developing collaborative relationships with their school family. These six challenges include work challenges, emotional challenges, language challenges, parent access challenges, cultural dissonance challenges, and self-imposed challenges.

Work challenges can exist for any parent working a full-time or part-time job. If a school only holds school events or parent conferences, for example, during traditional school hours, many families will be unable to participate. Regardless of whether you are a doctor holding traditional office hours or a secretary in an office, opportunities held during traditional school hours only will be a challenge. Frequently schools perceive parents as inflexible or uninvolved when they do not attend these events, and parents often perceive the schools as purposefully planning events during times in which they know they cannot attend (LaRocque, 2013).

Emotional challenges are a second barrier that families and schools often face. Families who have had negative experiences in their own school days may struggle to "come back" to school for any reason. A family's level of education can also be an emotional barrier as they struggle with their perception that they are not "smart" enough. Additionally, a family that is struggling with poverty will have increased stress and anxiety that creates emotional challenges. Finally, a family that is challenged by literacy skills understandably may want to avoid the embarrassment and emotional struggle that this context can cause (LaRocque, 2013).

Language challenges may also exist for many of our diverse families. Nondominant English families often speak different languages and thus may have a limited proficiency in English. Understandably, educational terms, forms, and social contexts can intimidate a family that struggles with the English language. Families that struggle with the English language may thus avoid social situations, deepening their barrier with the school setting. Communication of all kinds, if not translated, will present a challenge and barrier for families speaking diverse languages (LaRocque, 2013).

Parent access challenges typically are categorized in two ways: external or internal. External access challenges include problems such as transportation issues, child-care issues, and other external barriers that may keep a parent from being able to come to the school. For example, a parent may not drive or may not have a car to drive to the school. They may also have young children with no access or financial means to afford child care that keeps them from physically coming to the school. Internal access issues also create barriers for families. A parent may have a very negative attitude toward school and homework that impacts his or her ability to help his or her children. They may also have a limited education that creates a barrier toward any homework assistance (LaRocque, 2013).

Cultural dissonance challenges result from the different ways in which cultures perceive the school and home cultures. There can often be incongruity between the values and norms of the school and family. For example, some cultures would never ask a question or communicate with a teacher, as it would be seen as rude and disrespectful. Other cultures do not see the school as a place they should go unless they receive a personal invitation. If these cultural differences are not considered and appreciated by the school culture, a negative relationship can and potentially will develop with the school's families (LaRocque, 2013).

Finally, families often have self-imposed challenges based upon decisions of the school, sometimes intentional and other times unintentional (LaRocque, 2013). Through these intentional and unintentional actions, educators can create barriers that are hard for families to overcome. For example, teachers may prevent parents from coming into the classroom for fear of being judged. In other instances, educators are reluctant to involve families, as they fear the extra work or burden it might require. They may also assume families have limited understanding or commitment to helping their children at home. Sometimes simple things such as greeting or not greeting parents at the door can send a message of welcome or exclusion. These intentional or unintentional actions may leave families feeling ignored, undervalued, or unappreciated (Olivos et al., 2010).

If these barriers are not recognized and addressed, families will continue to feel intimidated and distrustful (Auerbach, 2010). Those feelings will exacerbate families' perceptions of not being wanted or valued. There is a power imbalance between

families and school personnel, but in particular for culturally diverse families. Culturally diverse families may feel lonely, confused, and isolated (Conroy, 2012). Teachers
should understand and recognize that cultural differences exist and if ignored can
lead to significant and problematic misunderstandings.

Comprehension Check

1. What are the six challenges that can create barriers for diverse families?
2. Identify three outcomes from those barriers for diverse families.
3. Give examples for each of the six challenges that prevent families from feeling
   included in the school setting.

Strategies for Collaborating with Diverse Families

Though there are many and varied ways in which barriers can exist between schools
and families, there are ample ways in which those barriers can be avoided or broken down. It is critical for these potential or existing barriers to be recognized and
addressed if a trusting, collaborative relationship is going to exist between schools and
their families.

The National Association of School Psychologists (NASP) has developed recommendations to enhance collaboration and break down barriers stating that "collaborative partnerships across home, school, and community settings can overcome
important barriers to learning" (Miller, Colebrook, & Ellis, 2014, p. 15). Remember
that in order to build trusting relationships, schools must advocate for time to be
scheduled with families in both informal and formal settings (Conroy, 2012).

First a school must always be attentive for any structural changes that are needed
to support family collaboration. Activities that represent all diversity in the school are
critical, and audits should be taken throughout the year to call attention to any lack
of representation to the cultural, linguistic, and socioeconomic diversity that exists in
the school. School administrators should communicate regularly with their families
to identify and rectify any real or perceived barriers that may exist. Changes should
be made as soon as possible to rectify any structures that are creating discord with
families.

Staff preparation is critical as schools work to build collaborative relationships with
families. All staff members should commit to being culturally literate, meaning that
they are well versed in the values, customs, and traditions of their families. Obtaining
a knowledge base and preparing to know and understand a school's diverse community will build a great deal of respect, trust, and appreciation with the families.

Communication styles are different for each individual and for different cultural
groups. Being knowledgeable in one's own communication style as well as others' is
important. If there is a lack of understanding regarding communication styles, misunderstandings can develop. For example, in the African-American community, it is
appropriate to not make direct eye contact when speaking with someone. In some
cultures, touch is completely expected, while in others it is completely inappropriate.

Understanding and appreciating different communication styles can take time but can also be highly valuable.

Personal identity refers to how one sees oneself within a group of others within one's cultural context. Most minority groups have a collective perspective rather than an individual perspective. For example, group members will often refer to a collective "we" rather than I when in an individual discussion with someone. Recognizing an individual's personal identity as located within his or her cultural context is important for all educators of diverse families.

Trying to ensure there are no surprises will be particularly important for your families that are already feeling apprehensive and uncomfortable in their relationship with schools. Anyone who is distrustful or nervous does not want to get caught off guard or surprised. For example, anyone who comes to a meeting expecting one person and instead finds ten is going to be unpleasantly caught off guard. Rather than surprising a family with such a scenario, clearly communicate as many details as possible ahead of time so the family has time to prepare and understands the context. Anything that can be done to help a family feel valued and appreciated should be considered.

School and family collaboration will benefit from regular and positive communication. It is often the case that families only receive communications from school when there is a problem or a conflict. Meaningful, productive relationships develop when there is clear and systematic communication that emphasizes the positive and only incorporates the negative when necessary. When a negative communication must be sent, some positive components should be incorporated as well. Though teachers often recognize that children need to hear a positive message, they sometimes forget that families need to hear a positive message as well. Meetings held for more negative reasons should nevertheless end on a positive note whenever possible. Research illustrates (Henderson & Mapp, 2002) that families feel more connected and positive about their school relationships when they are the recipients of positive communications.

Conversations that emphasize strengths rather than weaknesses will provide benefits. Always begin and end any interaction with a family with positives and strengths. It is beneficial to incorporate a conversation in which a family has the opportunity to identify and discuss the child's strengths. Additionally, plans to support the child should be grounded in that individual's strengths.

As we collaborate with families, we empower families. Many diverse families have spent an inappropriate amount of time feeling isolated and undervalued. It takes time to build a trusting relationship. Anything that can be done to facilitate that process will be advantageous for all. Remember all of the components in this section when working to empower families. Make sure to build a physical space in any meeting that places everyone at the table. In comparison, it is never empowering to a family to be placed on one side of a table while the school personnel are placed at the other. When talking with families, take time throughout the conversation to ask their thoughts and opinions on the topic. Make sure that any feedback is not entirely negative but always incorporates a positive. Anything and everything that can be done to empower families should be a central focus for educators.

When collaborating with families, remember the four phases of planning as identified by Pugach, Johnson, Drame, and Williamson (2012). First take initiative to meet and get to know the families. Many families, again as part of their culture, will feel it rude to make the first contact. It is critical that educators illustrate their commitment to the family by initiating and beginning a positive relationship. Second, continue to build that foundation throughout the time with the family. Successful collaboration requires commitment and time. Third, consistently make sure to maintain and support family relationships. Remember that communication must be consistently and frequently given. It is of utmost importance that families are not contacted only when there is a problem or a negative situation. Finally, take time to assess, reflect, and grow. What collaborative strategies are working and which ones are not? What families are responding positively and which families are not yet being reached? What can be done to continually develop and enhance the collaborative relationships with each and every family (Pugach et al., 2012)?

In order to build trusting relationship, teachers advocate for time with families both in formal and informal settings (Conroy, 2012). Schools must commit to ensuring families have full access to the school and to the people serving their children's needs. Everyone involved should be part of an ongoing examination to ensure that all members of the collaboration are sharing power equally and that family involvement and authentic decision making is truly supported. Case Study 16.1 offers an illustration of the information included here.

16.1 ILLUSTRATIVE CASE STUDY

As an intervention specialist, Mrs. Kramer knows how important it is to include families in every way possible, but often struggles to make it happen in meaningful ways. In order to improve upon her practice, she asks the teacher education department to partner with her. She contacts their intervention specialist program to see if they will conduct an audit of her program and the ways in which she engages with families. A professor at the university, Dr. Ritchey, specializing in families and collaboration is interested in partnering with Mrs. Kramer to engage in a self-study and see what they can learn together.

Dr. Ritchey visits Mrs. Kramer's classroom and asks her about the families she serves and what cultures are represented in her families. Though Mrs. Kramer knows she has one family that is Spanish, she does not have any other details about her families. Dr. Ritchey gives Mrs. Kramer the first task of investigating the diversity that is represented in their school building and in the families that she serves.

When Dr. Ritchey returns, she has the opportunity to observe Mrs. Kramer conducting a parent-teacher conference with a family. In the room, Dr. Ritchey finds eight individuals and one parent of Turkish descent. Dr. Ritchey notices that everyone is sitting on one side of the table with the exception of the parent. Dr. Ritchey also notices that the parent is not speaking but is nodding almost constantly.

After a few minutes, Dr. Ritchey asks the parent if she understands the conference thus far and if she has any questions. The parent shares that she actually does not speak proficient English and is struggling to understand, especially the educational words. Dr. Ritchey suggests that the conference be postponed until an interpreter can be secured for the next time. Everyone agrees and apologies are made to the mother.

After the conference, Mrs. Kramer and Dr. Ritchey meet to make some goals together. Mrs. Kramer recognizes that she has made assumptions about her families that have not been beneficial for anyone. As a result, Mrs. Kramer makes the following commitments:

- Developing a more open-door policy in which parents can come in at different times just to talk about their child's progress in an informal setting
- Studying different cultures more in depth that are represented in the school to support diversity throughout the year and in particular in one-on-one settings
- Surveying parents (in their native language to learn more about their language and cultural needs) at the beginning of the school year
- Developing an in-service with the help of Dr. Richey for the whole staff to consider ways in which they can be more welcoming and considerate of their diverse families

Professional Change

Teachers have a multitude of experiences and commitments to children and family that can at times become overwhelming. Each person also brings to the classroom their personal experiences, values, and culture. It can therefore be challenging at times to step back and examine how those experiences and personal values may be influencing the collaborative relationships with families. Often an educator must examine belief sets and personal opinions to carefully evaluate where change and growth might benefit all parties involved.

As Olivos et al. (2010) state, culturally and linguistically diverse families are "too frequently viewed by educators as passive in their involvement in their children's education, compliant with authority figures, uniformed about school procedures, and their own rights and duties as parents, and overwhelmed with their life circumstances" (p. 29). Auerbach (2010) adds that "Parents of color and low-income parents are traditionally viewed by educators through a deficit lens, which assumes that they do not care about or support education and which devalues their contribution to student learning" (p. 730).

It is an unfortunate truth that educators often make assumptions about families long before they should be made. The cultural disconnect that can be created will significantly interfere with any collaboration that might possibly happen. It is of critical

Table 16.1 Questions for Educators to Consider

Questions to Support and Further Change and Growth
Are all families consistently contacted?
Do I communicate with all families or just ones I feel most comfortable with?
Do I reach out to families with positive communication or predominately negative communication?
Do I recognize, incorporate, and discuss a variety of family lifestyles in my classroom?
Do I incorporate literature that represents diverse families?
Do I utilize learning materials that portray a diverse representation of family structures?
Do I make sure to vary my availability so that all families have an opportunity to meet and talk with me?
Do I encourage and include family input and information in my educational decisions?
Do I ensure that I am sending positive communications more frequently than negative communications?

importance that these assumptions are addressed and not ignored. The tensions that will result and grow will disadvantage all parties.

Professionals at all times must identify and address any bias or deficit views they may be adapting. It is an ongoing and constant reflection that is critical for professional growth. Educators engaged in this process consider the following questions provided in Table 16.1.

Promote Diversity through Collaboration with Stakeholders

It is always important to step back and recognize that schools are an individual community and yet serve the broader community. In this sense, it is critical to incorporate an intentional collaborative design for all stakeholders to be involved (Harry, 2008). We historically have marginalized and excluded our cultural and diverse families and, consequently, all stakeholders must be involved to reverse these negative tendencies. To build an open-door policy with everyone, consider the following components.

First, try to maintain an open communication policy with families. Everyone involved in supporting the family should try to be available and approachable at all times. Phone calls, emails, written notes, and websites are all ways in which families can be reached and included in day-to-day communication as well as important, time-sensitive communication. Knowing each family and their preferences for means of communicating will also build the collaboration effort. Try to have multilingual staff available if at all possible.

Having an open-door policy in the school building is another essential way to support families. Even if the classroom door cannot be open at all times, providing access to the principal, guidance counselor, special education and general education teachers, and others will help a family feel appreciated and welcome. Nonverbal communication can send a very negative message quickly and make a family feel that the metaphorical door is not open, so be very cognizant of any messages being sent. When the teacher is not available, try to make sure someone in the school community is so the family knows they are valued.

Try to build active parent associations and advisory councils in the school. This often takes an extra commitment on the part of the teachers and other stakeholders but can be so worthwhile for everyone. Building these active parent groups connects families and helps enhance their support systems. Designate a family that is willing to reach out to those not involved, in particular your diverse families that may feel isolated or timid about joining. Come to the meetings to illustrate commitment to the discussions and activities that develop. Try to make sure there is diversity represented in the organizations, striving to recruit as needed.

Be varied and creative about the ways the school involves parent volunteers. Do not ask people to come and then not have a focus or task, as this will devalue their commitment to the school. Be as flexible as possible with the options for different hours that a family could volunteer. Remember that many families have commitments during the school day. Remember to not judge a family if they do not volunteer, as they may be overwhelmed for any number of reasons at that point in time.

Do everything possible to build an inclusive school culture. Diverse families should perceive themselves as represented in every way possible. Make sure your school library incorporates and displays diverse literature. Examine the artwork in the hallways to ensure all families are represented through the images displayed. School celebrations, the curriculum, and cultural activities should be representative of the diverse community in which the students and families live.

Share responsibility for success and failures among all stakeholders. No one person alone creates or destroys a school's collaboration with the community. Invite families to participate in the decision-making structure as this will build relationships and a sense of shared responsible for the school culture. Families are more receptive and positive to changes and improvements when they have been a truly inclusive part of the decision-making process.

Blue-Banning, Summers, Frankland, Nelson, and Beegle (2004) state, "common sense and ordinary human decency are at the heart of positive partnerships between families and professionals serving children" (p. 181). This is truly the heart of what it can mean to be collaborative. As educators it is critical that a focus on serving children and their families is maintained in each and every large and small thing done to support their education and well-being. Case Study 16.2 provides an opportunity to apply your knowledge.

16.2 APPLICATION CASE STUDY

Assume you are an intervention specialist in your urban situated building. Your school serves a significant number of families that are diverse both culturally and socioeconomically. Though you are motivated and committed to supporting your diverse families, you now that your upbringing and previous experiences are somewhat limited and you are nervous about hot to address and meet the needs of your diverse families.

Divide your own classroom (college/university classroom) into pairs or small groups and consider and discuss each of the following:

1. Identify ways you could accidently offend or send a negative message to a diverse family.
2. How can you address each of these in a more positive manner?
3. What strategies would you utilize to support any family of diversity?
4. What resources might you call upon to support your diverse families?

Return to a large group and compare your pair/small group responses. Share together the mistaken ways in which diverse families might be excluded and what you might do to be more inclusive. What resource and strategies were identified that could help build a more inclusive environment?

Comprehension Check

1. What are at least six ways to help families feel a part of the school system?
2. Identify three questions that educators should consistently ask themselves.
3. Describe four ways all stakeholders can reach out to include diverse families.

CHAPTER SUMMARY

It is critically important that educators embrace collaborating and reaching out to diverse families. Many diverse families often do not feel respected or included because of cultural dissonance.

✓ Cultural dissonance takes place when "teachers' beliefs and behaviors are incompatible with student/family beliefs and behaviors" (LaRocque, 2013, p. 13)
✓ Diverse families may include foster parents, grandparents, aunts, uncles, etc.
✓ There are three important factors to consider when examining cultural differences:

  • No culture is better than another—each has its own traditions, behaviors, and contexts. It is important not to judge other cultures differently than our own.
  • All "cultural behaviors" happen on a spectrum. It is important that we do not assign a behavior to a certain person of a culture—or stereotype him or her because of the culture he or she came from and expect certain behaviors or actions.
  • Each individual should be regarded as an individual. He or she may not adopt any cultural customs or behaviors often assigned to a certain culture.

✓ It is important to remember that lack of participation does not mean there is a lack of interest in the child or in school.

✓ Many diverse families have had negative experiences with schools—as a result they may feel intimidated by the power that the school holds. There are six potential barriers that diverse families face when building a collaborative relationship with their child's school.

- Work challenges
- Emotional challenges
- Language challenges
- Parent access challenges
- Cultural dissonance challenges
- Self-imposed challenges

✓ Work challenges can exist for any set of working caregivers. It is important for the school system to hold meetings, events, and conferences during a variety of times so that families with working caregivers will be able to participate.

✓ Emotional challenges can occur when a family has had a negative experience with a school system in the past, when a family feels as if it is not "smart enough" to interact with the staff, or due to emotional issues that poverty or other stressors can have on a family.

✓ Language challenges may occur in many of our diverse families who are from different countries. Families who struggle with English may avoid social situations. This will deepen the barrier between family and school.

✓ Parent access challenges are issues that originate with parents and are categorized in two ways: internal and external.

- External parent access challenges include problems such as transportation, child care, or other external issues.
- Internal parent access challenges include problems such as negative attitudes toward schools, feelings of inequality, or other internal issues.

✓ Cultural dissonance challenges result from the different ways in which cultures and schools perceive the school and home cultures.

✓ Self-imposed challenges can be intentional and unintentional.

- For example, intentional self-imposed challenges would be not allowing families in the classroom for fear of being judged.
- For example, unintentional self-imposed challenges would be not warmly greeting every family during pickup or drop-off times—sending a message of coldness and exclusion.

Just as it is important to identify the potential challenges and barriers to a collaborative relationship, it is just as important to enhance collaboration and break down barriers. There are eight ways to help break down these barriers and develop a more collaborative relationship with families.

✓ School must always be attentive for any structural changes that are needed to support family collaboration.

✓ Staff preparation is critical as schools work to build collaborative relationships with families. All staff members should be culturally literate, or well versed in values, customs, and traditions.

✓ Understand how different cultures communicate and be able to communicate effectively with different cultures and different communication styles.

✓ Understand that personal identity refers to how one sees oneself within a group, within one's culture. Many minority cultural groups' individuals find their personal identity is ingrained in the group rather than themselves.

✓ Ensure that there are no surprises during the collaborative process.

✓ Contact with families should be positive and often. Too often the only time a school contacts a family is when there is an issue.

✓ Emphasize a child's strengths rather their weaknesses during conversation with the family.

✓ Empower the family during the collaborative process.

To foster a strong collaborative relationship with families it is important to have a plan. The four phases discussed in the chapter include:

✓ Take *initiative* to meet and get to know the families
✓ *Continually* build relationships with the families
✓ Consistently make sure you *maintain* and *support* family relationships
✓ Take time to *assess*, *reflect*, and *grow*

Previously we have marginalized and excluded culturally diverse families; because of this, all stakeholders must be involved to remedy these negative tendencies. In order to prevent barriers that may arise with diverse families it is important to:

✓ Maintain an open-door policy with all families
✓ Maintain day-to-day communication, as well as time-sensitive communication
✓ Advocate for an open-door policy for the school building
✓ Build active parent associations and advisory councils in the school
✓ Be varied and creative about the ways the school involves parent volunteers
✓ Build and inclusive school culture
✓ Share responsibility among stakeholders for both successes and failures

APPLICATION ACTIVITIES

1. Have candidates, individually or in small groups, review and summarize family involvement opportunities in a local school or district. Candidates could interview a variety of stakeholders to determine their degree of participation in encouraging family involvement. Candidates should compare and contrast how

opportunities might vary across grade levels. They could also devise ideas on how to increase or improve those opportunities.

2. Ask candidates to develop a school improvement plan for a fictitious school. This could involve devising a calendar, creating before and after-school activities, planning a cultural event, etc. Ask students to incorporate elements of collaboration that might help alleviate ways in which families may have felt isolated or prevented from participating in the school culture. Challenge them to incorporate as many elements as possible.

3. Have students collect and analyze school newsletters and/or websites. In what ways do they see diverse families being included or excluded? In what ways does this happen? Who do they feel is being reached and who do they think might be left out? Have them rewrite one of their choices to be more inclusive of all families.

REFERENCES

Auerbach, S. (2010). Beyond coffee with the principal: Toward leadership for authentic school-family partnerships. *Journal of School Leadership, 20*(6), 728–757.

Blue-Banning, M., Summers, J. A., Frankland, H. C., Nelson, L. L., & Beegle, G. (2004). Dimensions of family and professional partnerships: Constructive guidelines for collaboration. *Exceptional Children, 70*(2), 167–184.

Cheatham, G. A., & Santos, R. M. (2011). Collaborating with families from diverse cultural and linguistic backgrounds. *Young Children, 66*(5), 76–82.

Conroy, P. W. (2012). Collaborating with cultural and linguistically diverse families of students in rural schools who receive special education services. *Rural Special Education Quarterly, 31*(3), 24–28.

Harry, B. (2008). Collaboration with culturally and linguistically diverse families: Ideal versus reality. *Exceptional Children, 74*(3), 372–388.

Henderson, A., & Mapp, K. (2002). A new wave of evidence: The impact of school, family, and community connections on student achievement. Austin: Southwest Educational Development Laboratory.

LaRocque, M. (2013). Addressing cultural and linguistic dissonance between parents and schools. Preventing School Failure: Alternative Education for Children and Youth, 57(2), 111–117.

Miller, G. E., Colebrook, J., & Ellis, B. R. (2014). Advocating for the rights of the child through family-school collaboration. *Journal of Educational and Psychological Consultation, 24*(1), 10–27.

Olivos, E. M., Gallagher, R. J., & Aguilar, J. (2010). Fostering collaboration with culturally and linguistically diverse families of children with moderate to severe disabilities. *Journal of Educational & Psychological Consultation, 20*(1), 28–40.

Pugach, M. C., Johnson, L. J., Drame, E. R., & Williamson, P. (2012). Collaborative practitioners, collaborative schools (3rd ed.). Denver, CO: Love Publishing.

17

STRATEGIES FOR IDENTIFYING COMMUNITY RESOURCES AND WORKING WITH COMMUNITY PARTNERS

Jackie M. Arnold and Stephen B. Richards

Chapter Objectives

Following reading the chapter, students should:

1. Define the features of community collaboration
2. Identify practices for effective interagency collaboration
3. Describe ways in which all involved parties can collaborate

FEATURES AFFECTING COMMUNITY COLLABORATION

As discussed in Chapters Fifteen and Sixteen, families benefit from a collaborative relationship with schools, although the type and intensity of this collaboration varies depending on each family's context. It is critical that educators recognize the ways in which community organizations can collaborate and support all members of the educational process to benefit children. Marzano (2003) identifies three defining features affecting community involvement (including parents/caregivers). They include communication, participation, and governance. Each of these areas should be addressed if an effective and comprehensive collaboration relationship with community partners is to be accomplished.

Communication

Although communication between all parties is ideal, parents/caregivers generally have no legal obligation to communicate with schools (Marzano, 2003). However, schools do have an obligation to keep families and community stakeholders informed. Many states are required to make information known to the public, such as attendance, standardized testing, and graduation rate data. Chapter Fifteen discussed the use of newsletters, webpages, dialogue journals, and other forms by which schools and educators can communicate with families and the community.

It is important to consider forms of communication that provide opportunities for stakeholders to respond and not just inform. Keeping this in mind, educators should consider adapting communications (and the use of questionnaires) to solicit information back from community members (Institute of Education Sciences, 2011 https://nces.ed.gov/programs/slds/pdf/best_practices.pdf).

Equally important is scheduling meetings (again, in-services, information sharing, extracurricular events, special occasions, and organizational meetings such as the PTO) to provide opportunities for community-school interaction. It is important that these strategies not be designed as open invitations to criticize the school, in general, or the personnel in particular. Rather, they should be designed to solicit ways in which the school can enhance and improve community involvement. Because school personnel are more often initiating the communication, they should carefully consider what types of responses they might receive and what meaningful purpose those responses might serve. School personnel should also consider the overall purpose of any meeting and adjust their communications accordingly. For example, an invitation to join others in attending a high school sports event might be quite informal. An invitation to a parent support group might be more formal but still written in a friendly rather than a professional tone. An invitation to an in-service might be written with a more professional tone (Sustaining Reading First, 2009, http://www2.ed.gov/programs/readingfirst/support/stakeholderlores.pdf).

Participation

A second defining feature to involve community collaboration focuses upon participation of community members and school personnel (Marzano, 2003). If collaborative relationships are to be established, meetings should not be strictly for professional or caregiver attendance. While it is appropriate to conduct some meetings with restricted attendance, many collaborative activities should encourage everyone to be involved. Research (Mafora, 2012; Noonan, McCall, Zheng, & Erickson, 2012; LaRocque, 2013) suggests there are benefits and advantages when parents/caregivers and community members participate in schools, particularly in terms of activities related to their child's education. Research has indicated that parent/caregiver involvement in the day-to-day operations of a school tends to strengthen academic performance and lower negative behavioral issues, such as absenteeism and truancy. Involving community members, especially those who are also parents/caregivers, can have other benefits (Engaging Stakeholders, 2009, http://www2.ed.gov/programs/readingfirst/support/stakeholderlores.pdf; NEA Education Policy and Practice Group, 2008, http://www.nea.org/assets/docs/PB11_ParentInvolvement08.pdf).

One benefit of community participation is to call upon the expanded expertise in various subject areas or topics for student learning. Community members can contribute meaningfully to the curriculum and instruction on an ongoing basis (Marzano, 2003). There are many parents/caregivers and other individuals in a community who have knowledge, skills, and/or experiences relevant to the curriculum (Stringer & Hourani, 2013; http://www.nea.org/assets/docs/PB11_ParentInvolvement08.pdf). For example, while one community member may not have formal training in historical studies, she may have actually lived and participated in historical events (e.g., civil rights movement). Particularly in secondary career-technical programs, community member involvement (e.g., business leaders, professionals) are virtually mandatory to building a successful program. Many schools and districts establish advisory councils as teams that provide guidance to school professionals on the needs of the community and how best to address those needs. This is discussed later under the governance section.

A second benefit to involving community members is expanding contacts for school personnel for resources in the community. This is a direct reminder of the old adage that *who* you know is often as important as *what* you know. Knowing who to contact and having an ongoing relationship with that community agency or individual can result in swifter and more successful interventions for a school, student, or family when a need arises. Being connected to the community agencies and individuals who can "get things done" (e.g., emergency housing, food assistance, social security benefits) is a sure way in which school personnel (administrators and faculty) can help meet needs that extend beyond but still affect classroom performance. One example in our experience was consulting with a local ophthalmologist who was able to schedule a quick evaluation of a student's vision so that he could receive appropriate services from a state agency in job and career services. The contact with the ophthalmologist was provided by a parent of another child who had very poor visual acuity.

A third benefit to building collaboration with community members is through the option for direct financial assistance. Community businesses and individuals may provide contributions in money or labor that enhance the overall school climate and performance. In secondary schools, athletic booster clubs, arts organizations, and business leaders are frequently willing to offer their support to programs and students. In elementary schools, parents often contribute to the success of fund drives and projects. Examples from our own experiences include local business people providing funding and venues for school dances and extracurricular events, and providing funding and labor for school beautification projects such as landscaping.

Finally, when relationships exist with collaborative partners, the possible benefit for the donation of equipment expands. Businesses are sometimes able and willing to contribute to or provide equipment for programs. At times, they may provide equipment and materials at a lower cost. Schools may benefit from playground equipment, landscaping or gardening materials, and business training tools such as computer technology, among many other possibilities. Businesses may also allow students to job shadow or provide paid or unpaid internships. In some secondary programs, businesses ally with career-technical-vocational programs to provide actual job placements following graduation. We have witnessed fund-raising activities for purchasing service dogs, assistive technology, and more mundane equipment, such as eye glasses and even clothing for children in poverty. However, business people may not know or consider the ways in which equipment can benefit schools, and thus the need for ongoing, positive collaboration to build such understandings and considerations.

Governance

A final defining feature to community collaboration focuses upon governance. In order to build true collaborative relationships, it is critical that community members be involved in the governance of the school in some way (e.g., parent advisory board) or in a specific program (Marzano, 2003). Some organizations (e.g., PTO, athletic boosters) often are predominately governed by the community participants and less so by school personnel. Stringer & Hourani (2011) indicate that community members are more often interested in governance decisions directly affecting students and school outcomes rather than decisions that affect faculty or administrators.

While community members including families may or may not have the same levels of expertise in areas such as scheduling, curriculum and textbook adoptions, and achievement assessments, the participation of those community members can serve at least three benefits. First, collaboration with community constituents may be helpful in avoiding unnecessary and divisive disagreements. One example of this is the adoption of books for reading that might lead to strong objections among many or at least a significant number of families. A second possible benefit is to gain support for initiatives. One example of a possibly divisive initiative might be "sex education". Some families might opt out their children's involvement but others may see a benefit to such a class. Collaboration is likely to help identify whether such initiatives have any significant support among community members. Another example might be in deciding how funds might be expended. A district or school might enlist community collaboration in deciding whether to make sports a "pay-to-play" activity in order to save funds for academic matters. A third benefit might be in the provision of overall support for the school and district. Many families rate their local school services better than educational services in the country in general. Collaboration with and participation of community members is likely to open doors to a better understanding of how decisions are made, how monies are spent, what successes have been accomplished, and what hurdles remain in providing a quality educational and extracurricular experience for students and families. In Case Study 17.1, we provide an illustration of how collaboration with the community benefits both school and community members.

17.1 ILLUSTRATIVE CASE STUDY

As a new middle school teacher, Ms. Kuebel is struggling to meet the needs of her students in her classroom. In addition to her daily lesson planning, teaching, and data assessment review process, she is frequently receiving requests from parents. The parents and caregivers are frequently looking for not only educational advice but support at home.

For example, one parent wrote this week stating she wanted to come in and meet with Ms. Kuebel but was unable to get a ride and she did not own a car. She added a note to Ms. Kuebel wondering if she knew of any agencies that might be able to help her obtain a car.

Another parent wrote to tell Ms. Kuebel that they would not be able to receive any electronic information, as they did not have a computer nor could the school call, as the family phone had been disconnected and their limited budget did not have room for a cell phone plan. The parent asked if the school had any technology available for check out to provide the electronic and phone call options.

Finally, Ms. Kuebel has been noticing that one of her students comes to school in the morning hungry, voraciously so on Mondays. After some careful questions, Ms. Kuebel determined that there was a very limited amount of food available to eat at home so that the student was only dependably eating breakfast and lunch on school days.

Upon analyzing these numerous needs of her students (and knowing that these may only be a few of many), Ms. Kuebel decides to take action. She asks her leadership team to partner with her in calling a meeting in which partners from multiple community support services are invited. As a team, each collaborative agency identifies the services that they could offer students and their families. A master list is organized for dissemination.

In addition, space is allocated within the building for the different collaborative agencies to utilize so that services and conversations can be facilitated for parents and caregivers within the school context. In this way, the building is off to becoming a full-service school with a shared mission of supporting families and students in all ways possible.

Comprehension Check

1. What are the three defining features of establishing school-community collaborative relationships? What are important considerations in making each of the three features successful?
2. What are three benefits to community member participation to enhance the school? Give examples.

PRACTICES FOR EFFECTIVE INTERAGENCY COLLABORATION

One way in which schools have adapted to an expanded role in school-family-community collaboration is by becoming full-service (or community) schools. Fiedler, Simpson, and Clark (2007) describe full-service schools as schools that become a "one-stop" information and resource entity that provides both educational services and is a conduit to community agency services as well. Full-service schools, through collaboration with community agencies, offer entry to or information about such services as physical health services, mental health services, employment services, child care, parent/caregiver education, case management and referral for services to agencies, recreation, cultural events, and community policing and organizing neighborhood watch programs. A full-service community school can provide a seamless entry into community agency services from the school so the complexity of navigating another system (e.g., Job and Family Services) is greatly reduced (Fiedler et al., 2007).

Fiedler et al. (2007) identifies three collaborative components that can support effective interagency collaboration. They are 1) collaboration among administrators, 2) collaboration among community service providers, and 3) collaboration among members of a participating agency. Building a cohesive fabric across these parties will support a highly functioning, full-service community school while providing for the complex interests of students and their families.

Collaboration among administrators incorporates multiple components to support effective implementation. It is important that shared leadership exists among all parties. Communication is critical as shared goals, resources, and services are utilized to the fullest extent. It is also important that all involved have a shared vision and evaluation of services provided to support constant growth and improvement (Fiedler et al., 2007). Administrators of various community agencies will inevitably have their own agendas and concerns for which they are responsible. To the degree that administrators cooperate and collaborate, understand and support the missions of the various agencies, and identify ways in which funding concerns can be "spread around" equitably, the more likely administrators will be willing to enter into formal or informal collaborative agreements.

Collaboration among community service providers and school professionals can establish a context of reciprocity and generativity (Fiedler et al., 2007). When all involved are sharing and working together, all members benefit. In the same way, when there is mutual trust and support, innovative work can happen. To establish this successful context, everyone involved must be supportive and committed. There exists a unity of purpose and shared commitment for positive results. By working collaboratively and joining resources, there is a heightened sense of efficacy that supports everyone, but students and their families in particular. One example from our experiences involved a young man who was a high school student who exhibited the characteristics of severe mental illness (e.g., auditory and visual hallucinations). His behavior involved seemingly unprovoked and random violence toward others that made it difficult for him to participate in public school classes and activities. The agency that provided home-living services was also having difficulty with the young man and made it clear that it would be impossible for him to remain in their program if he did not have an educational or vocational day program to attend, as their homes were not staffed typically during school hours. During a meeting of various agencies, the representatives agreed that the public school would provide the funding for the young man to attend a daytime educational/psychiatric program. The administrator for that program had actually known the young man since he was six years old, and this administrator was very knowledgeable about the young man's psychiatric and educational history. The agency providing the home-living services agreed he would remain in their care and they would provide additional behavioral/psychological monitoring and services. This agency also stressed that they would attempt to involve the young man's family, although they had been "out of the picture" for some time. The representative from a government agency agreed his agency would provide for additional psychiatric assessment and treatment as recommended by the young man's attending physicians. In the end, everyone shared in the responsibilities and costs so that this young man would have the best possible opportunities to remain in his community and the least restrictive environment.

Finally, interagency collaboration should also include collaborative work among members of a participating agency (Fiedler et al., 2007). Members within a team must work together efficiently and professionally to support families and students. Team goals, participation, and cohesion are critical elements for successful inter-group collaboration. As in the earlier example, the various agency representatives knew each other well and had worked together for several years. They trusted each other to follow through on commitments and to be available if and when new problems might arise. In turn, these collaborative relationships allowed the representatives to focus on problem solving how best to help the young man with psychiatric issues rather than to focus on hidden agenda items, such as how will this affect me or my agency.

Ways in Which All Involved Come Together

Effective interagency collaboration truly takes place when all of these entities are working together successfully. Schools and parents/caregivers work together to identify educational and additional support needs. Collaborative partners with the school system are identified and contacted and matched with the family. All members of the team focus on the main goal of doing everything possible to meet the needs of the student and family.

IDEA, in particular, supports this concept of providing referral and access to community services for families with children with disabilities. In general, for all students, when families are able to reduce the stressors of other family needs (discussed in Chapter Sixteen), children's academic and behavioral performance also tends to be improved. Finally, it is worthwhile to note that while teachers are not directly responsible for such services that extend beyond their typical areas for instruction, a full-service or community school tends to emphasize a holistic view of nurturance, development, and educational performance. Faculty become more aware of the resources available to them and students' families; the faculty may benefit from professional development provided by such agencies, establishing partnerships and relationships with community agency personnel, and, finally, learning more about their roles as advocates for students.

A final area for consideration in school-family-community collaboration is interagency agreements. Whether in specific full-service schools or through broader community collaboration, it is sometimes necessary for schools and community agencies to formalize their working relationships. Interagency agreements are written agreements that commit schools and agencies to work together, determine which is responsible for what services and costs, and how each agency will engage in their collaborative relationships. Such agreements are particularly important in early intervention services (in transition from early intervention to preschool programs) and in transition from school to post-school living for students with disabilities. Each of these transitions is mandated under IDEA, and there are specific guidelines in the law and in state regulations to govern such transitions and that provide guidance for states to assist in the development of interagency agreements (Crane, Gramlich, & Peterson, 2004; Taylor, Smiley, and Richards, 2015). Case Study 17.2 offers an opportunity to apply your knowledge.

17.2 APPLICATION CASE STUDY

Assume you are a brand new teacher getting started in your first year in a community that is also brand new to you. Your school serves a significant number of families that have a multitude of needs, including economic, education, and daily care needs. Though you are motivated and committed to supporting your families, you know that because you are new to teaching and to the community, your knowledge of outside and additional resources is significantly limited. You want to help your families in any and all ways possible, but you are not sure where to start.

With a partner or in small groups, explore what you might do to locate and provide support to your families in need. Consider the following questions as you work:

1. Who are some experienced and knowledgeable individuals in your building who could help you get started?
2. What are some national resources that you have previously heard about or utilized that might also be available in your new community?
3. What are some Internet resources that you might access to help you in your search?

Return to a large group and compare your pair/small group responses. Share the resources that you have found and the resources you have not found.

Comprehension Check

1. What is a full-service or community school? What are some services that might be available in such a school?
2. What is an interagency agreement?
3. What two transitions are mandated by IDEA?

CHAPTER SUMMARY

It is important that educators recognize the importance of a collaborative relationship with family members as well as members of the community. When collaborating with community organizations and community members, it is important to remember *communication, participation,* and *governance* in order to build a successful collaborative relationship.

Communication

✓ Caregivers and community members have no legal obligation to communicate with schools; however, schools do hold the legal obligation to communicate with families and keep stakeholders informed.

✓ Considering the forms of communication dispersed can help build a successful collaborative relationship, educators should allow community members to respond, not just inform.

✓ When scheduling meetings, remember it is important to invite all community members and stakeholders to appropriate meetings.

Participation

✓ It may be appropriate to hold some meetings with a restricted audience, but at least some school meetings should involve more than strictly caregiver or professional attendance.

✓ Outside involvement in the day-to-day operations of a school strengthens academic performance and lowers behavioral issues such as truancy.

✓ Community participation can expand the expertise in various subject areas for student learning.

✓ Expanded community involvement can provide additional resources for school personnel. These resources may be directly financial, allow educators to save time, be informational in nature, or appear as equipment donations.

Governance

✓ To build a truly collaborative relationship in the community, it is crucial that community members be involved in the governance of schools in some way.

✓ Community members are often times more interested in governing decisions that affect students and school outcomes rather than decisions that directly affect faculty or administrators.

✓ Allowing some community governance may be helpful in avoiding unnecessary disagreements.

✓ Allowing some community governance may transfer into increased support for school initiatives.

✓ Allowing some community governance may increase the support overall for schools and districts.

Effective Strategies for Collaboration

✓ Some schools have adapted to an expanded role in the community to increase community involvement. These schools have become "community" or "full-service" schools and are "one-stop" information and resource entities that provide educational resources as well as serves as a conduit to other community resources.

✓ Community schools make effective use among :

- Collaborations among administrators
- Collaborations among community service providers
- Collaborations among members of any participating agencies

✓ Collaborations among schools and community service providers can produce reciprocity and generativity.

✓ When operating a community school, it is important to understand and support the missions of various community agencies and identify ways in which funding concerns can be "spread around" equally.

✓ Interagency agreements may be written so that community agencies and schools can commit to work together. These agreements are particularly important for early intervention services as well as transitions from school to post-school living for children with disabilities—both of which are required under IDEA.

It is important to remember that IDEA supports the idea of community schools in the sense of providing referral and access to community resources. It is also important to note that while teachers are not directly responsible for any services that are outside of their expertise, collaborating with community resources and becoming a conduit for those resources will dramatically increase community support and provide benefits for educators, schools, and districts alike.

APPLICATION ACTIVITIES

1. Have students communicate with a school or district administrator or appropriate personnel, family members, and/or community agencies to identify specific organizations, agencies, or groups that provide services to families. More than one source for identification of specific organizations, agencies, or groups is recommended. This allows for identification of multiple support services that may be unknown to any single source of information about various organizations, agencies, or groups within a school or district community. University students may construct an organizational chart of school and support teams and agencies.

2. Have students arrange face-to-face, telephone or possibly email interviews with relevant sources for services. Students could use multiple technologies or any other appropriate venue for compiling the template information for each organization, agency, or group. Have the students compile their information into a template to be provided to a family in need in hard or soft copy. The arrangement (likely in some type of binder or notebook form in hard copy) should be attractive and professional in appearance. It should include an introduction and tabs/headings that delineate each area of family need and the types of support services (e.g., Employment Services could include Ohio Job and Family Services, Goodwill, and a variety of other possible agencies, organizations, or groups). Also include a brief master list of all service agencies as an appendix if appropriate—alphabetical order or by family need area could both be appropriate options for this master list. The master list should include only the most basic information:

Name of organization, agency, or group
Location, telephone number, website address, email address of contact person
Brief entry for services (e.g., employment, housing, or funding for utilities assistance)

REFERENCES

Crane, K., Gramlich, M., & Peterson, K. (2004, September). Putting interagency agreements into action. *Issue Brief. Examining Current Challenges in Second Education and Transition, 3*(2). Retrieved from www.ncset.org

Fiedler, C. R., Simpson, R. L., & Clark, D. M. (2007). *Parents and families of children with disabilities.* Upper Saddle River, NJ: Merrill.

Institute of Education Sciences. (2011). *SLDS best practices brief.* Washington, DC: National Center for Education Statistics.

LaRocque, M. (2013). Addressing cultural and linguistic dissonance between parents and schools. *Preventing School Failure: Alternative Education for Children and Youth, 57*(2), 111–117.

Mafora, P. (2012). Shared decision making. *The International Journal of Learning, 18*(6) 97–108.

Marzano, R. J. (2003). *What works in schools: Translating research into action.* Alexandria, VA: Association for Supervision & Curriculum Development.

NEA Education Policy and Practice Department. (2008). *Parent, family, community involvement in education.* Washington, DC: National Education Association.

Noonan, P. M., McCall, Z. A., Zheng, C., & Erickson, A.S.G. (2012). An analysis of collaboration in a state-level interagency transition team. *Career Development and Transition for Exceptional Children, 35*(3), 143–154.

Stringer, P., & Hourani, R. B. (2013). Home-school relationships: A school management perspective. *Educational Research Policy Practice, 12*(2), 149–174.

Sustaining Reading First. (2009). *Engaging stakeholders.* Arlington, VA: RMC Research.

Taylor, R. L., Smiley, L. R., & Richards, S. B. (2015). *Exceptional students. Preparing teachers for the 21st century* (2nd ed.). New York, NY: McGraw-Hill Education.

INDEX

Note: figures and tables are denoted with italicized page numbers.